Neuroscience and Connectionist Theory

Developments in Connectionist Theory

David E. Rumelhart, Series Editor

GLUCK/RUMELHART • Neuroscience and
Connectionist Theory

Neuroscience
and
Connectionist Theory

Edited by

Mark A. Gluck
David E. Rumelhart
Stanford University

LEA LAWRENCE ERLBAUM ASSOCIATES, PUBLISHERS
1990 Hillsdale, New Jersey   Hove and London

Lawrence Erlbaum Associates, Inc., Publishers
365 Broadway
Hillsdale, New Jersey 07642

Library of Congress Cataloging in Publication Data

Neuroscience and connectionist theory / edited by Mark A. Gluck, David
E. Rumelhart.
      p.   cm.
    ISBN 0-8058-0504-4. — ISBN 0-8058-0619-9 (pbk.)
    1. Neurobiology—Computer simulation.   2. Connectionism.
I. Gluck, Mark A.   II. Rumelhart, David E.
QP356.N4829   1990
596′.0188—dc20   89-17080
                                                                                                              CIP

Printed in the United States of America
10 9 8 7 6 5 4 3 2 1

Contents

List of Contributors

José Ambros-Ingerson
Center for the Neurobiology
of Learning and Memory
University of California

Mark F. Bear
Center for Neural Science
and Physics Department
Brown University

Costa M. Colbert
Department of Neurological
Surgery and the Neuroscience
Program
University of Virginia
School of Medicine

Leon N. Cooper
Center for Neural Science
and Physics Department
Brown University

Nancy L Desmond
Department of Neurological
Surgery and the Neuroscience
Program

University of Virginia
School of Medicine

Mark A. Gluck
Department of Psychology
Stanford University

Richard Granger
Center for the Neurobiology
of Learning and Memory
University of California

Christof Koch
Division of Biology
California Institute of Technology

William B Levy
Department of Neurological
Surgery and the Neuroscience
Program
University of Virginia
School of Medicine

Gary Lynch
Center for the Neurobiology
of Learning and Memory
University of California

Bimal Mathur
Science Center
Rockwell International

Bruce L. McNaughton
Department of Psychology
University of Colorado

Kenneth D. Miller
Department of Psychology
University of California,
San Francisco and
Stanford University

Lynn Nadel
Cognitive Sciences Program
and Center for the Study
of Complex Systems
University of Arizona

Eric S. Reifsnider
Department of Psychology
Stanford University

Ursula Staubli
Center for the Neurobiology
of Learning and Memory
University of California

Richard F. Thompson
Department of Psychology
University of Southern California

H. Taichi Wang
Science Center
Rockwell Inernational

David Zipser
Institute for Cognitive Science
University of California,
San Diego

Series Foreword

The last several years have witnessed a remarkable growth in interest in the study of brain-style computation. This effort has variously been characterized as the study of neural networks, connectionist architectures, parallel distributed processing systems, neuromorphic computation, artificial neural systems and other names as well. For purposes of the present series we have chosen the phrase *connectionist theory*. The common theme to all of these efforts has been an interest in looking at the brain as a model of a parallel computational device very different from that of a traditional serial computer. The strategy has been to develop simplified mathematical models of brain-like systems, and then to study these models to understand how various computation problems can be solved by such devices. The work has attracted scientists from a number of disciplines. It has attracted neuroscientists who are interested in making models of the neural circuitry found in specific areas of the brains of various animals, physicists who see analogies between the dynamical behavior of brain-like systems and the kinds of non-linear dynamical systems familiar in physics, computer engineers who are interested in fabricating brain-like computers, workers in artificial intelligence who are interested in building machines with the intelligence of biological organisms, psychologists who are interested in the mechanisms of human information processing, mathematicians who are interested in the mathematics of such brain-style systems, philosophers who are interested in how such systems change our view of the nature of mind and its relationship to brain, and many others. The wealth of talent and the breadth of interest have made the area a magnet for bright young students.

In the face of this exponential growth and multidisciplinary set of contributions, it is difficult for workers in the area, let alone those outside of the area interested in current developments, to keep up with the work or to find the important new papers which, as likely as not, have been published in: conference proceedings which are always difficult to obtain, one of the large set of disciplinary journals from the home disciplines of the contributors, or in one of the many new journals in the connectionist field which often still have only small circulation. As a result, it is very difficult to find the best work in the field. Eventually, as the field matures, I expect that this situation will sort itself out and it will be clear where to find the newest and best contributions. In the meantime, I have decided to launch a series aimed at making available to workers in the field and to those who are interested simply in knowing what is happening in the field, the latest and best work as it is published. The book series, entitled simply *Developments in Connectionist Theory,* will take the form of a series of books, each organized around a topic of current interest in the field. I have in mind something like a series of special issues of a journal. My plan is to jointly edit each with an editor with special expertise in the area of focus for that volume. The authors are selected from among those whom we believe are making the most important new contributions to the area and who are able to communicate their findings to the broad interdisciplinary group of readers to whom this series is aimed. The volumes themselves consist of contributions especially written for these volumes and designed both to provide the context so that the reader not familiar with the details of the work will understand the nature and importance of the contributions and to provide the content necessary for those working close to the field to use the volume as a teaching and reference work.

This foreword is being written as the first volume of the series, *Neuroscience and Connectionist Theory,* edited jointly with Mark Gluck, is going to press. Even as this volume is being completed, five other volumes are filling the pipelines. These include volumes tentatively entitled: *Speech and Connectionist Theory, Backpropagation and Connectionist Theory, Language and Connectionist Theory, The Mathematics of Connectionist Theory,* and *Philosophy and Connectionist Theory.* These volumes should appear at roughly 6-month intervals over the next couple of years. Other volumes are planned as future developments warrant them. My goal is to bring together, in one place, the key developments in this rapidly moving field as they occur and put them in a form so they can form a basis for communication among the disparate areas of work in the field.

David E. Rumelhart

Preface

It is appropriate that the first volume in a series on connectionist theory and brain style computation should choose neuroscience as its focus. Neuroscience is at once a major contributor to the theory and a major consumer of the theory. Naturally, neuroscience is a contributor in the sense that the very definition of brain style computation and connectionist theory is, of course, an abstraction and formalization of what we know about how brains process information. It is the hard-won empirical contributions of neuroscientists that form the basis for the development of a connectionist theory in the first place. At the same time, neuroscience is, perhaps, the most natural consumer of connectionist theory. Because they are more tempered by data than some of other areas of connectionist theory, we have seen the applications of connectionist models to neuroscience grow at a much slower pace than, for example, the application to certain engineering problems. Nevertheless, they have been growing and maturing. Although a good deal of modeling has been done on invertebrate neural networks, we have chosen to focus on models of mammalian nervous systems. Moreover, we have focused on those neural applications closest to those areas in which connectionist theory is best developed; namely, the ways networks change their patterns of connectivity and the ways in which networks can solve constraint satisfaction problems. Although these applications are only a small part of the work on neural modeling, they are those parts of the neural modeling enterprise closest to the formal work in connectionist theory.

We begin our volume with a chapter by McNaughton and Nadel. These authors focus on the hippocampus and show how the anatomy and physiology of the hippocampus can be mapped, in a useful way, onto the structure of models developed by David Marr and others. They show that the empirical physiological characteristics of plasticity (synaptic learning) in the hippocampus are generally consistent with the kinds of Hebbian autoassociative models frequently studied in connectionist theory. They point out, however, the important role of the temporal interactions among diverse circuit elements, especially inhibitory interneurons, which are often ignored in more abstract formal models. This is an excellent example of an interaction between the facts of neuroscience and the development of formal theories and models.

The chapters by Bear and Cooper (chapter 2) and by Miller (chapter 7) form an interesting pair. Both focus on plasticity during the early developmental period in the visual cortex. Bear and Cooper have proposed a formal synaptic learning rule to explain a wide body of behavioral and physiological evidence on the role of experience in the development of visual cortex. Their work illustrates how theoretical concerns lead to identifying a candidate set of synaptic rules which, in turn, suggest empirical investigations to evaluate and search for possible molecular bases for synaptic modifications.

Granger, Ambros-Ingerson, Staubli, and Lynch (chapter 3), present a model of piriform (olfactory) cortex and its role as an unsupervised preprocessing stage for incoming olfactory (odor) information. Their approach is more "bottom-up" than that taken by many others in this book. They begin with a great deal of biological detail on the anatomical structure and physiological function of specific brain structures. Using simulations, they have explored the interactions among olfactory structures and their cooperative roles in odor classification and recognition. This work has resulted in an increased awareness of the role of multiple sampling of the environment for stimulus recognition, the need for classification of inputs at various levels of generality, and the importance of distinct learning rules for different brain modules.

In chapter 4, Gluck, Reifsnider, and Thompson focus on the cerebellum and its role in classical (Pavlovian) conditioning of the eye blink reflex. Their work draws heavily on both engineering theories for adaptive signal processing and animal learning theories which have been developed to capture a wide range of behavioral properties of associative learning. Moreover, they show how the kind of error-correction models used in both animal learning and connectionist theories can be mapped onto the architecture of the cerebellum. Drawing heavily on the implications of distributed "course-coded" representations of temporal behaviors, their conditioning model suggests possible reconciliations of both behavioral and physiological data on two behaviors believed to be mediated by the cerebellar circuitry: classical conditioning and adaptation of the vestibulo-occular reflex (VOR).

Levy, Colbert, and Desmond, in chapter 5, take a somewhat different approach to modeling the hippocampus than McNaughton and Nadel. Their major point is to study the details of the rules whereby connections are changed. They offer a general functional account of the hippocampus and empirically document the kinds of situations in which connections are seen to weaken, strengthen, or remain unchanged. Their approach draws heavily on the fundamentals of probability and statistics.

The problem of computing optical flow—labeling points in a visual image with a velocity vector—is a key problem for both natural and artificial vision systems. Wang, Mathur, and Koch show, in chapter 6, how a well-known relaxation minimization algorithm for computing optical flow can be mapped onto the early visual system of primates. Whereas most of the other chapters in this book are concerned with learning and synaptic plasticity, this chapter focuses on another aspect of connectionist theory—namely, real-time constraint satisfaction.

In chapter 7, Miller reviews some of the evidence for correlation-based models of synaptic modification in the neural development of visual cortex. In contrast to the sliding-threshold synaptic rule of Bear and Cooper, Miller proposes that a constraint on the total synaptic strength over a cortical cell will yield the necessary stability.

In the final chapter, Zipser adopts an entirely different methodology than the other authors for understanding the kinds of neurons found in the parietal area of the visual system. Using known inputs for the region, he trains a connectionist network to convert information from retinocentric coordinants to head centered coordinates and shows that the kinds of "hidden units" developed by the model were very similar to those actually found in the parietal region of the brain. Zipser than makes some general methodological points about how this and similar applications can be of use in developing an understanding of the parts of the brain and its function.

In all seven of these chapters we see a crucial interplay between data and theory. As we observe characteristics of neural information processing not well represented in our current connectionist models, we are led to extend the general theory to incorporate these new features. As we better understand the implications of our models we are better able to understand the functionality of what we observe in the brains we study. Inasmuch as models of specific neural systems can be viewed as applications of a general mathematical theory of brain style computation, we can see neuroscience as using general connectionist theory to develop specific neural models.

In addition to the contributing authors, many other people have made important contributions to this volume; we would like to briefly acknowledge, and thank them, here. For their assistance in the preparation of the manuscript of this book, we are grateful for the editorial and administrative assistance of Dan Rosen, Carol Miller, and Marilyn Hershey, and to our editors at Lawrence Erlbaum Associates, Judi Suben Amsel and Julia Hough.

This book would not have been possible without the assistance of the various funding agencies who supported the contributing authors and their research. Deserving of special note is the Office of Naval Research, especially Joel Davis and the Biological Intelligence program, which provided support to the editors of this volume and to many of the contributing authors, making possible much of the interdisciplinary research reported herein. A final word of thanks is due to Jonathan Bachrach for providing the original artwork for the cover and to Noreen Greeno for the cover design.

Mark A. Gluck
David E. Rumelhart

1

Hebb-Marr Networks
and the Neurobiological
Representation
of Action in Space

Bruce L. McNaughton
Department of Psychology, University of Colorado

Lynn Nadel
*Cognitive Sciences Program and Center for the
Study of Complex Systems, University of Arizona*

The human brain is, arguably, the most complex system in the universe. Its several hundred billion elements, organized at various levels of description, permit organisms to interact adaptively with a wide variety of environments. Understanding how this is done is an important goal of cognitive neuroscience. General principles which could underlie complex brain function were suggested some time ago (cf. Hebb, 1949; Marr, 1969, 1971; McCulloch & Pitts, 1943), but the computational power needed to permit simulations of complex behaviors with neurobiologically realistic neural nets has only recently come into existence. This chapter is intended to illustrate how some simple network models are guiding the design and interpretation of neurophysiological research concerned with understanding the neural coding, storage, and transformation of spatial information. It begins with an analysis of spatial cognition, moves on to a discussion of network models in the nervous system, continues with a description of certain aspects of the anatomy, physiology, and dynamics of a particular neural system—the hippocampal formation—known to be critical in spatial cognition, and concludes with the description of a conceptual model of spatial representation and cognition that reflects many of these structural and functional features.

SPATIAL REPRESENTATION AND COGNITION

A "model system" approach that currently holds considerable promise for the understanding of the higher level processes of internal representation is

1

the study of spatial behavior and its neuronal substrates in the rat. Spatial orientation and navigation necessarily involve the integration of complex, polysensory information, associative memory both for complex stimulus configurations and for the conditional consequences of the organism's own movements with respect to the sources of these stimuli. Finally, spatial cognition requires the computation, either from previous experience or from relatively "hardwired" circuitry, of spatially equivalent sequences of movements leading to the generation of novel trajectories between various starting locations and some goal; trajectories never before experienced directly by the organism. The assumption is that such an ability must involve the internal manipulation of spatial representations, and may serve as a general model for the ability to foresee the consequences of particular actions in specific contexts. This, after all, is the essence of higher cognitive function.

Understanding how a system as complex as the brain works would be a hopeless task without some understanding of what it does—what sort of computational operations underlie the behaviors exhibited. Accordingly, we begin with an overview of spatial behaviors in the rat, as well as some discussion of the role in such behavior of a particular region of the brain— the hippocampus—that seems to be essential for the development of representations of space and other aspects of the animal's experience which, although not strictly spatial, appear to involve similar modes of processing.

It may seem obvious that much of behavior is founded on predictions based on the prior manipulation of internal images or representations of the external world. However, in the first half of this century, psychologists dug themselves into a deep conceptual hole in which such internal processing was assumed to be outside the realm of observation and careful study. The field became dominated by the view that adequate and complete laws of behavior could be derived from experimentally observed relations between external stimuli and corresponding motor responses. The recent history of cognitive psychology can largely be seen as an effort to escape from this conceptual "local minimum." This effort has culminated in the rediscovery and blossoming of the notion that mental computation can be understood as a set of orderly and logically interpretable transitions among internal states of the nervous system, transitions dictated primarily by interactions among a large number of rather simple elements whose interconnections exhibit particular patterns and physiological logic.

A striking illustration of the experimental accessibility of such internal processing was provided by Shepard and Metzler (1971; Shepard & Cooper, 1982). Human subjects were briefly shown two images of a complex three-dimensional shape. In some cases the two images differed only in terms of an arbitrary rotation. In others the images differed both in rotation and chirality (handedness). When subjects had to indicate whether the two images were the same or mirror images of one another, a precise linear relation between the number of degrees of rotation between the two objects and decision time was observed. The most plausible inference from this result appears to be that the subjects mentally rotated the images, and that this operation reflected an ordered sequence of internal states, a sequence whose length was proportional to how much rotation was required. In subsequent work, subjects were presented with a perspective view of a three-dimensional object (a parallel projection of a solid cube) undergoing a continuous spatial transformation (Cooper, Gibson, Mowafy, & Tataryn, 1987). Following a complete rotation of the object, a blackout period of variable duration was interpolated, after which the object reappeared. The critical variable was the point in the rotation cycle at which the object reappeared. In half the trials it was correct with respect to the previously observed rotation speed, in the other half it either undershot or overshot the correct point, by 6°, 16°, 26°, or 36°. Although there appears to be a systematic tendency to accept slight undershoots as accurate, the main conclusion is that our perceptual system continues, in the absence of the external object, internally to transform a representation of the object in a way that closely mimics the natural world (cf. Shepard, 1989).

In recent work (Neiworth & Rilling, 1987) this principle has been extended to animals (pigeons), who correctly extrapolated the movement of a clock hand when a part of that movement was invisible. The authors concluded that neither stimulus-response associations nor rule-based strategies could account for the observed ability of the birds to extrapolate accurately to novel locations not used during training. Rather, it must be assumed that, as in humans, these animals were transforming internal representations in a way that closely matched the spatial transformations of the clock hand in the external world. Dramatic confirmation of this assumption has also recently been provided by Georgopoulos and his colleagues (Georgopoulos, Lurito, Petrides, Schwartz, & Massey, 1989; Georgopoulos, Schwartz, & Kettner, 1986). Single unit recordings from the primate motor cortex during a task requiring the monkey to make spatially directed arm movements showed that the direction of arm movement is closely predicted by the vector sum of the activities of a population of broadly tuned directionally selective neurons. The network behaves as though each neuron "votes" for its preferred direction with a weighting proportional to its firing rate. If the target for the movement is co-localized with the visual signal to move the arm, the "population vector" emerges from the background noise pointing directly at the stimulus, some time before the overt movement. If, however, the animal is trained to reach at some angle relative to the stimulus, the first detectable population vector also points toward the stimulus. As the vector lengthens, the angle changes as a linear function of time until it is pointing in the direction of the subsequent movement. As in the mental rotation studies, both the rotation of the population vector in the motor cortex and the reaction time for the movement are linearly related to the angle of rotation. Observations such as these lend credence to the idea that study of the neurobiological and computational mechanisms of cognitive processes in animals will have relevance to understanding more complex forms of human cognition.

Other insights into the nature of spatial representation can be gained from the results of neurological studies of patients with various types of brain damage. For example, in the neurological disorder known as Balint's syndrome there appears to be a decoupling between visual perception of the world and the ability to make directed movements in response to that perception (Hausser, Robert, & Giard, 1980). Both visual perception and the ability to make coordinated movements per se are apparently intact. However, such patients persistently and systematically direct their movements to inappropriate locations when required to manipulate or to interact with the visually perceived world. Thus, there appear to be two different representational systems, one for visual images, and one for movement. These are normally "mapped" to one another. The mapping function, however, is subject to disruption. This is even more convincingly demonstrated in experiments in which subjects have worn glasses containing prisms that shift or invert the visual image. After several days, the subjects report that the world appears normal, and their visually guided movements are correctly mapped to the world. Removal of the prisms results in a period of disorientation and misdirection of movements in the opposite direction.

If we are to learn something of how such representations and mappings are implemented in corresponding states and state trajectories in the human nervous system we must be able to study the physical structure and behavior of the brain. The sort of information required necessitates the use of technologies that are generally not acceptable in human subjects. Furthermore, it is likely that the fundamental characteristics of such operations will be more easily interpreted in simpler organisms, particularly in cases where the neuroanatomical organization can be clearly seen to be homologous, but less differentiated than in the human. In order to make this bridge, however, it is necessary to convince ourselves that the behavior and its underlying computational structure are likewise homologous, but less differentiated. The foregoing makes it clear that at least pigeons possess some of the same internal transformational systems as humans. What follows is a brief and highly selected review of studies of spatial cognition in the rodent, studies which provide both an indication of such homologous computation, and set the stage for an interpretation of neurophysiological studies carried out during the execution of the corresponding behaviors.

Rodents are highly exploratory, and learn things about the relationships among the features of their world independently of any assignment of affective or adaptive significance (i.e., reinforcement, drive reduction, etc.), although such assignment also occurs. Rodents brought into a familiar place notice if there has been some rearrangement or alteration of nearby or remote visual features, as can reasonably be inferred from the resulting increase in exploratory behaviors (e.g., Thinus-Blanc, Bouzouba, Chaix, Chapuis, Durup, & Poucet, 1987; Kurz & Nadel, unpublished observations; Sutherland, 1985). If rats happen to turn in one direction upon first exposure to some "T" junction they will, with probability much greater than chance, turn the other way on the next trial, a phenomenon known as "spontaneous alternation" (Walker, Dember, Earl, & Karoly, 1955). If the "T" is rotated 180°, they will choose the alternate location rather than the alternate body turn. If one releases rats reared in cages into a large space, a characteristic and revealing set of observations can be made. At first the animals make numerous excursions from some central point. After some time the reference point shifts to a new spot within the limit of the first exploration radius. Gradually, this tendency merges into more continuous, linear movement. If observed over several days it can be seen that distributed sites where the experimenter has deposited food have all been visited, and, on the basis of the pattern of fecal droppings and shed hair, that certain locations are occupied with significantly higher probability than others. Whereas the rat first released can be easily recovered, recovery is difficult after several days, because the animals are extremely adept at navigating rapidly between one inaccessible location and another, locations widely dispersed within the environment. Although such observational studies can lead to considerable insight, and clearly suggest the presence of some fairly sophisticated forms of cognitive and mnemonic activity, separation of this activity into its component parts for the purpose of analysis requires carefully designed experiments.

Partly in the course of trying to develop laws governing stimulus–response contingencies, and partly prompted by deeper insight, a number of psychologists in the first half of the century noted that rats not only attend to and learn about spatial relationships, but that this process in fact dominates their behavior to the extent that it becomes a nuisance in simple studies of learning and perceptual discrimination (cf. Munn, 1950). It became known as the problem of the "spatial habit." Before one can teach a rat a visual discrimination problem, for example, many trials may be required to dissuade the rat from its conviction, gained on the first trial, that reinforcement is associated with a particular place. An insightful discussion of these earlier findings can be found in Hebb (1949). The general conclusion, supported by a number of more recent studies, is that acquisition of information about spatial relationships in the environment is extremely high in the rat's list of cognitive priorities, and involves a mode of information processing that differs in rather fundamental ways from the formation of simple conditioned responses, or the association of particular sensory or motor events with reward.

Over time, and depending on the experimental circumstances, either the nature of the spatial representation itself changes, or the relative predominance of particular components of the representation in determining behavior changes (Mackintosh, 1965). If a group of animals is repeatedly rewarded at one end of a "T" maze, about 50% of responses at the junction come to be determined by the sensorimotor attributes of the corresponding body turn. Rotation of the maze leads to "errors." Only about 25% of responses is governed by spatial location. The other 25% is governed by local characteristics of the correct arm of the "T" (presuming there are salient differences), as can be inferred by switching either the arms themselves, or some prominent local distinguishing feature (Barnes, Nadel, & Honig, 1980). Early in training, spatial learning is disrupted by functional interference with particular parts of the brain (notably the hippocampal formation), whereas the same interference may not lead to performance disruption after the response is well established. This may be partly a reflection of a shift in the relative dominance of certain components of the representation (cf. Means & Douglas, 1970), and partly because the structures that are responsible for developing the representation may not be the same ones in which these representations are ultimately incorporated, and from which they are applied to the control of behavior.

Several experimental paradigms have been developed in which the spatial components of learning and behavior are dissociated to some degree from the purely motor components and from the direct association of specific local features with reward. In one case (illustrated in Fig. 1.1) animals were released with a random orientation from an enclosure onto a brightly illuminated circular platform (Barnes, 1979). Rats find bright open spaces distressing, for reasons that are obvious from an evolutionary perspective, and so learned readily to find and enter the one of 18 peripherally located holes that led to a dark tunnel. As the initial orientation was random, and the surface itself was rotated from trial to trial, holding the escape tunnel fixed, the animals must have learned something about the relation between the tunnel and the remote visual cues. In general, several studies have shown that if these cues are restricted to discrete objects within an otherwise featureless enclosure, removal of any subset of the cues does not impair performance (Barnes, Nadel, & Honig, 1980; O'Keefe & Conway, 1980; Pico, Gerbrandt, Pondel, & Ivy, 1985).

From such observations emerge two different, but not necessarily exclusive, notions about the nature of the underlying encoding. One is that the geometrical relations between the features and the target are independently coded, thus providing a redundant solution. The other is that relations among many features of the environment are stored in such a way

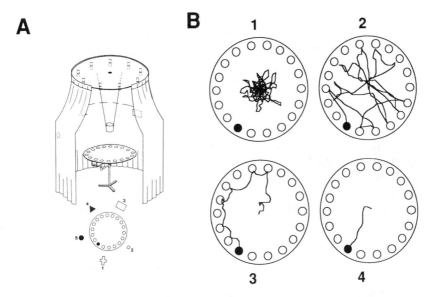

FIG. 1.1.   (A) Illustration of the circular platform apparatus used to assess spatial memory ability in rats (from Barnes, 1979; Barnes, Nadel, & Honig, 1980; McNaughton, Barnes, Rao, Baldwin, & Rasmussen, 1986). The animals are released from a false-bottomed start chamber onto the center of a brightly illuminated white circular platform. Beneath one of 18 peripherally located holes is a dark tunnel into which the naturally photophobic rats are highly motivated to escape. The maze surface is rotated randomly from trial to trial holding the tunnel fixed relative to the distal visual cue array. Following training, any two of the cues can be removed without effect on performance. Removal of all cues causes performance to deteriorate drastically. (B) Schematic illustration of the typical sequence of behavioral patterns observed on successive days of training at one trial per day.

that presentation of some of them will lead to the regeneration of the representation of the complete set.

A conceptually similar task, developed by Morris (1981), requires the animal to escape from a pool of opaque water to a small platform submerged just below the surface at one, constant, location. Rats learn readily to swim from any starting point in the pool directly to this platform. Once trained, they will concentrate most of their search time in the correct location if the platform itself is removed. Interestingly, if rats are first trained on the problem in one room, and then the pool is relocated to another room, they can make use of information gained by placing them directly on the platform to navigate to it when subsequently placed in the water for the first time in the new room (Keith & McVety, 1988). It would appear that they know something of the general rules of how visual scenes are transformed by locomotion, and can compute an approximate trajectory leading to the appropriate inverse transformation, given a current, novel view of the environment from the pool, and a memory of the view from the platform.

Another apparatus that, because of its power and adaptability, is frequently used in studying spatial behavior is known as the "radial-arm maze" (Fig. 1.2). A variable number of arms can be used under different circumstances, and food or water reward is generally located at the ends of one or more arms. This apparatus can be used to assess spatial behavior and the nature of learned spatial representations. Olton and Samuelson (1976) demonstrated that rats have a prodigious spatial memory capacity, being able to remember with considerable accuracy which of up to 17 arms have been recently visited. They are thus able to know from which arms they

FIG. 1.2.   Illustration of one version of the radial eight-arm maze that has been widely used in both behavioral and neurophysiological investigations of rats' spatial abilities. In general, the animal is required to visit one or more arms (depending on the specific application) in order to obtain food reward at the arm ends. The apparatus is easily adapted to several different experimental paradigms, including short- and long-term spatial memory problems, and nonspatial problems in which salient tactile cues are inserted into one or more arms, with positions varied so as to dissociate them from the fixed distal cues. In this photograph, the animal has been prepared for recording the activity of single hippocampal neurons during performance of a spatial problem.

have not yet obtained food (which is not replaced during the trial). The animals do not use odor trails or any other local cues to solve the problem, nor, at least initially, are simple motor sequences adopted. The memory for which arms have already been visited persists for a considerable time (at least several hours), as can be shown by permitting the animal to choose only a subset of arms, imposing a variable delay, and then determining if the animal chooses only those arms not visited prior to the delay.

Several studies have attempted to address the problem of exactly how spatial features (landmarks) are used by the animal in the course of spatial navigation. As a simple example, consider the case in which rats were trained that each day only one of the eight arms of a radial arm maze will contain food reward (McNaughton, Elkins, & Meltzer, unpublished observations). On the first trial of a day, they were simply shown which arm by making it the only one available. On subsequent trials, they were required to choose the correct arm among all eight. The animals learned to do this with considerable accuracy, seldom making errors after the third or fourth trial. After the fourth trial, the maze itself was physically translocated into a partitioned area within the same room, an area that differed markedly with respect to the available spatial cues. The only features in common in the two cases were the experimenter and a single 25-watt lamp pointing into one upper corner of the partition (see Fig.1.3). In the new configuration, however, the relative positions of these features were mirror reversed. The correct solution to this problem for the animals would be to go in the same absolute compass heading from the maze center, or to attend to some local feature of the particular arm designated as correct on that day. The animals failed to learn this problem. Instead, in the majority of cases, they tended to orient relative to the lamp. Moreover, the probability of using the lamp as the principal landmark was the same whether, in the initial training partition, the target was located towards the lamp, away from it, or at some intermediate angle. This leads to the conclusion that the landmark was not used merely as a stimulus to be approached for reward. Rather, it seems that the animals possess the ability to remember headings relative to the landmark, whatever the angle.

This ability to compute headings was studied in greater depth by Collett, Cartwright, and Smith (1986), who examined the ability of rodents to learn the location of a buried food reward relative to several distinct visual landmarks (white cylinders) located in an otherwise visually featureless arena. Of several interesting observations, the most revealing can be illustrated by the consequence of training the animal to find food at a site equidistant from two identical landmarks, and then increasing the distance between them. If the animal had constructed some form of topological representation of the space, then one might have predicted that the search pattern would have focused at the equidistant location. Surprisingly, the

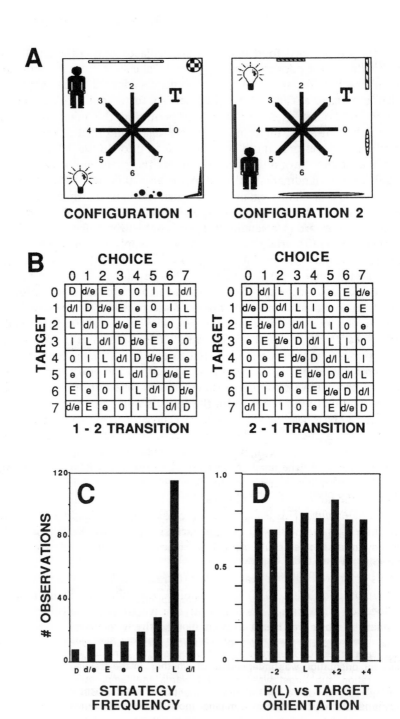

FIG. 1.3

animals tended to divide their search time now between two sites, each at the original distance from one landmark. These and other results led the authors to the conclusion that the animals compute separate vectors to the goal based on each different landmark. If the vectors are each different, then more than one site is searched. If more than one landmark is involved, and if a majority of the resulting vectors agree, then the correct location is searched, in spite of the possibility of other solutions based on the minority of landmarks. Thus, topological distortions of the landmark array do not always lead to the topologically appropriate solution; rather, the animal

FIG. 1.3. Illustration of an experiment in which the radial eight-arm maze was used to assess the manner in which prominent visual landmarks are incorporated into the rat's internal representation of spatial relationships. (A) On each day, a single target arm (T) was selected at random to contain food reward. After a single "information" trial in which only this arm was presented, three additional trials were given at roughly 15-minute intervals in which the animal had to select the correct arm from all eight. Following the third trial, in which well-trained animals made very few errors, the maze was physically moved into a separate enclosure in which the configuration of distal spatial cues was completely different except for the presence of the experimenter (E) and a lamp (L). The relative positions of these two cues, however, were mirror reversed in the two configurations. This permitted an assessment of the extent to which these two visual cues guided the animal's spatial responses. (B) For example, if maze arm 1 was designated as target in configuration 1, and in configuration 2 the animal chose arm 7, then one could infer that its choice was based on orientation relative to the lamp (L). Alternatively, if the animal chose arm 3 then one could infer that the experimenter (E) was the dominant feature, as this arm is located two positions clockwise to the experimenter as was the assigned target in configuration 1. A choice of the correct arm (1) would have indicated that the animal was using either some directional sense (D) or some cue local to the arms themselves. Similarly, other choices could be assigned to composite strategy categories (d/e, e, l, d/l) by virtue of the selected arm being one arm off from an unambiguous category. Strategy category 0 was assigned to the case that the choice was two arms away from both the E and L categories in the direction opposite the correct arm. (C) In the overwhelming majority of trials it was clear that the animal's choice was based on orientation relative to the lamp. Orientation based on the D strategy (direction or local cue) was used least of all. (D) The probability of selecting the lamp as the basis for orientation was independent of whether, in the training configuration, the target was located towards the lamp, away from it, or at some intermediate orientation. Thus, distal landmarks are used by rats in a manner more sophisticated than merely as objects whose distance is to be minimized in order to obtain reward.

appears to compute a set of heading vectors based on the remembered view of the landmarks from the goal and their current appearance. This raises a computational problem because a single point landmark cannot by itself convey information about the correct spot, only about the circle on which the correct spot must lie. There are at least two ways this problem could be solved. One would be to search for the point of intersection in the domain of possible solutions for the set of landmarks; this might be computationally expensive. A simpler solution would be to maintain some internal heading indicator independently of the external input. There is both behavioral evidence for this solution, which is presented here, and neurophysiological evidence, which is discussed in a later section.

The behavioral evidence comes from two sources. Mittlestaedt and Mittelstaedt (1980) carried out a series of experiments showing that rodents were able to use a combination of vestibular input and "efference copy" from their own motor output (plus the associated proprioceptive feedback) to "integrate" a complex search path in such a way that a direct return path could be taken to the origin in complete darkness, and in the absence of other spatial cues. The accuracy of this path integration was not disrupted by rotations of the apparatus at angular velocities sufficient to activate the vestibular system, but slower rotations introduced corresponding heading errors. The importance of the rat's hippocampal formation in this inertial direction sense was shown in experiments by Matthews, Campbell, and Deadwyler (1988), in which rats were trained to follow a particular heading from a start location in order to obtain food. They were then confined to an apparatus in which they could not see the spatial cues, and subjected to various rotations. The design of the apparatus was such that it could be determined whether they had compensated for the rotation in their selection of a heading. It was found that the animals could indeed compensate with reasonable accuracy for up to several complete rotations. Performance did not fall to chance until about 10 revolutions at about 30 rpm. This compensatory ability was severely disrupted by damage to the hippocampal formation.

As a final example of the power of the rat's spatial representation system, consider the following: O'Keefe and Conway (1980) trained rats inside an enclosed circular arena to find food at one arm of a "+" shaped maze when started from any of the other arms selected at random. The enclosure was essentially featureless except for an array of controlled spatial cues (various objects distributed around the enclosure). Both the cue array and the location of reinforcement were rotated from trial to trial, randomly with respect to the cardinal points of the maze. As expected, the animals learned readily to choose the correct arm on the basis of the cue array. If introduced into the apparatus in the absence of the cues, their choices were random. If, however, they were introduced into the enclosure in the presence of the cues, but confined to the start arm while the cues were removed, then, when subsequently allowed access to the other arms they were still able to make the correct choice. This memory was very persistent, showing no decline after half an hour, and also was not disrupted by forcing the animal into other (nonreward) arms prior to allowing it to choose. Thus no simple hypothesis based on the preloading of some motor program (e.g., "turn left") can account for the phenomenon.

There appear to be only three classes of possible solutions to this problem, and these possibilities will form the background for the discussion of the neurophysiological evidence to be discussed subsequently. First, it is possible that the animal does indeed load a motor program when it first sees the cue array, but that it can modify the program to compensate for intervening, unanticipated movements by using the internal direction sense previously alluded to, and/or the ability to compute alternate sets of movements on the basis of their spatially equivalent consequences. It is also possible (O'Keefe & Speakman, 1987) that the animals possess two global topological representations of the spatial features of the task environment. One of these would encompass the features of the rotating, controlled cue array, and the other the features of the uncontrolled fixed reference frame, such as noise sources or any distinctive features of the arena itself. In principle, by rotating these representations relative to each other, in a manner analogous to the human mental rotation studies previously described, it would then be possible to use the fixed cues as a basis for response selection. Finally, it is possible that, in the course of previous experience on the maze, the animals learn the conditional relations between their own motor actions and the corresponding sensory consequences (McNaughton, 1987). In other words, given one local view of the world and a particular motor act, say left turn, the animal comes through experience to develop an internal representation, or expectation of the resulting local view. Even if the usual elements of the visual scene are removed, this remembered view would be sufficient to inform the animal of its location. Such conditional relations between movements and views could be chained together to keep the animal continuously informed of its location relative to the last seen configuration of the principal (controlled) spatial cues, and might also be used in an inverse fashion as a basis for a plan of action.

Regardless of which of these possibilities turns out to provide the best description of the systems involved in spatial computation, the role of the hippocampal formation is going to be integral to any neurally based analysis (Barnes, 1979; Barnes, 1988, McNaughton, Barnes, & O'Keefe, 1983; Morris, Garrud, Rawlins, & O'Keefe, 1982; Nadel, 1980; O'Keefe, 1976; O'Keefe & Nadel, 1978; Olton, Becker, & Handelmann, 1979; Sutherland, Whishaw, & Kolb, 1983). Thus, single-neuron studies have demonstrated a strong relation between an animal's location in space and the activity of the principal output cells in the hippocampus. Furthermore, animals with damage in the hippocampus fail to learn the kinds of spatial tasks described above—the circular platform, the water pool, and the radial-arm maze. These and other considerations have led to the emergence of a number of models of how the hippocampal formation might play a role in spatial cognition (McNaughton, 1989; O'Keefe, 1989); the foregoing analysis of various aspects of spatial cognition thus provides the essential background for understanding the computational purpose of the system whose anatomical and physiological properties are to be discussed below. Before turning to those details, however, we must consider some basic aspects of information storage and transformation in nervous systems.

COMPUTATION IN
THE CENTRAL NERVOUS SYSTEM

In many respects, the essence of computation in the nervous system concerns the ability to establish behaviorally adaptive mappings among its internal states. The archetypical case of this ability is simple associative memory: the process whereby the co-occurrence of two patterns results in what is called a *heteroassociative* mapping, whereby subsequent presentation of one input pattern leads to a system state corresponding to the other. For example, input of the sound or visual pattern of the word *apple* evokes activity, at some level, of those neural elements representing the features red and round that are activated when we see a real apple. Such heteroassociation is a special case of a more general paradigm known as *autoassociative* mapping. The essence of autoassociation is the formation of linkages among all elements that are active in a particular system state. The result of this linkage is the formation of what is known in the language of dynamical systems as a "basin of attraction" in a neural state space of dimension equal to the number of neurons and with parameters corresponding to the output state of each neuron. The latter can be either binary or continuous, depending on how the model is formulated. If the system is subsequently placed in a state within the basin, the state trajectory will be in the direction of the original attractor. This general property is known as "pattern completion."

Although there now exists a rich literature on the mathematical principles of associative mappings between states of dynamical systems (see Cowan & Sharp, 1988, for a concise and informative discussion of much of this work), in this chapter we focus on the essentials of a conceptual framework that we hope will elucidate our current understanding of how these principles are actually implemented biologically, and how they might usefully be applied to an understanding of some of the mechanisms of spatial representation in the nervous system.

It is of historical interest to note that, although not rigorously defined, many of the fundamental mathematical concepts now applied to the study of theoretical "neural" nets were explicitly or implicitly expressed by Hebb

(1949). Indeed, the word *connectionism* appears in several places in Hebb's book. Hebb thought of sensory events and conscious experience as corresponding to specific patterns of neural activation, patterns that are now referred to as vectors in neural *state space*. He coined the term *phase sequence* to refer to the neural state trajectories underlying specific sequences of sensory-motor events. In Hebb's view the pattern of interconnections within the brain enabled the occurrence of what he called "reverberatory activity," which was equivalent to the existence of quasi-periodic attractors in neural state space. He envisioned such periodic activity as forming the basis for one type of short-term memory. Those particular neural elements that were active while the system was in a particular limit cycle were assumed to undergo a strengthening of their interconnections leading to the formation of what Hebb called a "cell assembly." This is conceptually equivalent to a deepening of a basin of attraction. Hebb proposed a fundamental feature of neural connections that he considered would lead to the formation of cell assemblies, a feature which has come to be known as "Hebb's rule": "When an axon of cell A is near enough to excite a cell B and repeatedly or persistently takes part in firing it, some growth process or metabolic change takes place in one or both cells such that A's efficiency, as one of the cells firing B, is increased." (Hebb, 1949) Almost without exception, mathematical models of associative mapping in the nervous system or in abstract "neurally inspired" systems, have relied on some variant of Hebb's rule. The search for its implementation in the nervous system has been subject to a considerable experimental effort by neurophysiologists, an effort that now appears to have been rewarded.

In the decades subsequent to the publication of Hebb's book, a number of people developed explicit formulations of these ideas, either as strictly abstract models, as electrical circuit analogs, or as models intended to capture the essential features of some particular neural circuitry (e.g., Kohonen, 1972; Marr, 1969, 1970, 1971; Milner, 1957; Rochester, Holland, Haibt, & Duda, 1956; Steinbuch, 1961; Willshaw, Buneman, & Longuet-Higgins, 1969). Most of the ideas in what follows are derived from these works, and represent an attempt to present the essence of these abstract concepts in their simplest form. We then consider possible neuronal implementations of these principles that have proven extremely useful in interpreting the structure and physiology of the hippocampal formation.

A simple conceptual scheme for associative memory involving storage of a paired associate and subsequent recall of one element given the other is shown in Fig.1.4a. Storage of an association can be thought of as the formation of the outer product matrix (often called either an association or correlation matrix) of two binary representation vectors $(\mathbf{X}, \mathbf{Y})$. Recall of one vector of a paired associate results from the formation of the inner product of the association matrix and the other vector of the pair, followed

		Y INPUTS
A		1 0 0 1 1 0 Y3
		0 0 1 0 1 1 Y2
		1 1 0 1 0 0 Y1
X	0 1 0	0 0 1 0 1 1
I	0 0 0	0 0 0 0 0 0
N	1 1 0	1 0 1 1 1 1
P	0 0 1	1 1 0 1 0 0
U	1 1 1	1 1 1 1 1 1
T	1 0 1	1 1 0 1 1 0
S	X3 X2 X1	

		Y INPUTS
B		1 1 0 0 0 1 Y4
		1 0 0 1 1 0 Y3
		0 0 1 0 1 1 Y2
		1 1 0 1 0 0 Y1
X	0 0 1 0	0 0 1 0 1 1
I	1 0 0 0	1 1 0 0 0 1
N	1 1 1 0	1 1 1 1 1 1
P	1 0 0 1	1 1 0 1 0 1
U	0 0 1 1	1 1 1 1 1 1
T	0 1 0 1	1 1 0 1 1 0
S	X4 X3 X2 X1	

C	
	0 0 1 0 1 1 Y2
	1 0 1 1 0 0 Y1
0 1	1 0 1 1 0 0
0 0	0 0 0 0 0 0
1 1	1 0 1 1 1 1
0 1	1 0 1 1 0 0
1 0	0 0 1 0 1 1
1 0	0 0 1 0 1 1
X2 X1	

HETEROASSOCIATION   AUTOASSOCIATION

CORRECT RECALL
001011 = X3
X3 • C = 322332
$$\frac{322332 = 100110}{3} = Y3$$

PATTERN COMPLETION
001001 ⊂ X3
001001 • C = 211221
$$\frac{211221 = 100110}{2} = Y3$$

SATURATION
011100 ⊂ X4
X4 • C = 331213
$$\frac{331213 = 110001}{3} = Y4$$

BUT
001011 = X3
X3 • C = 332332
$$\frac{332332 = 110110}{3} \neq Y3$$

PATTERN COMPLETION
001001 ⊂ X2
001001 • C = 102122
$$\frac{102122 = 001011}{2} = X2$$

ERROR CORRECTION
000111 is a corrupted X2
000111 • C = 103122
$$\frac{103122 = 000000}{3} \neq X2$$
BUT $\dfrac{103122 = 001011}{2} = X2$

FIG. 1.4. The fundamental principles of distributed associative memory are most simply illustrated using a formalism that is generally known as a correlation matrix (e.g., Kohonen, 1972, Steinbuch, 1961; Willshaw et al., 1969). In this example, pairs of six element binary vectors (e.g., X1:Y1) are presented to the system for storage. The "learning" mechanism is an analog of Hebb's rule, namely that if corresponding vector elements are "on" (i.e., both have a value of one), then their intersection in the square matrix is set permanently to one. Recall of one element given its corresponding paired associate is achieved by matrix-vector multiplication. For example, pattern Y3 in A is correctly extracted from the matrix by multiplying the matrix rows by corresponding elements of vector X3, summing the columns, and then performing an integer division (i.e., truncating any remainder to zero) on the result. The divisor corresponds to the number of bits in the input vector that are "on." Provided not too many patterns have been stored, any unique subset of an X vector will recall the correct Y vector if the divisor is reduced according to the size of the subset. This is generally known as pattern completion. Attempts to store too much information (saturation) lead to errors in recall (B). There are several ways of alleviating this problem, in particular, keeping the number of input vector elements that are "on" in any particular input to a minimum, and keeping the patterns to be stored as different from one another as possible. This may require some preprocessing. Paired associate learning or "heteroassociation" (A,B) is just a special case of a more general paradigm known as autoassociation (C). This is best illustrated by imagining that the matrix in C is partitioned into four 3 by 3 matrices. The diagonal partitions are autoassociative in that the X and Y inputs are identical. The off-diagonal partitions are heteroassociative, having different X

by a normalization operation involving integer division of the result by the squared length of the input vector (i.e., the sum of its binary components). The latter operation is responsible for the existence of a basin of attraction in the system which, in the case of a single stored pattern, includes all subsets of the input vector. In other words, turning on any bit or combination of bits in the input vector that was on during the association operation recalls the complete paired associate vector. If the original **X** and **Y** vectors happened to be identical, as in autoassociation (Fig. 1.4c), this basin of attraction endows the system with the property of pattern completion. A complete stored representation can be recalled by presentation of a few of its elements.

Within certain limits, the outer product association matrices from a number of event pairs can be combined in a single matrix of the same dimensionality, from which the individual paired associates can still be extracted reliably using the recall procedure just defined. The combination is carried out by performing successive inclusive "or" operations on the corresponding outer product matrix elements. A rigorous mathematical treatment of the properties and limitations of such systems and their continuous counterparts can be found in Kohonen (1978, 1988).

A strong case can be made that the implementation of something like these operations has been a driving force in the evolution of nervous systems. The first clear proposals, based on actual anatomical data, as to how this might occur were presented by Marr in his early studies. The model neural circuits presented in Fig. 1.5 are largely abstracted from this work. Accordingly, we propose that such networks might appropriately be referred to as *Hebb–Marr* nets.

Minimal Hebb–Marr nets consist of three or four classes of neurons coupled in specific ways by at least three classes of connection, each with rather fundamentally different properties. In Fig.1.5a, for example, which is an implementation of heteroassociative memory (cf. Marr 1969), there is a population of "principal cells" whose output state is to convey the desired representation vector. The principal cells receive and "integrate" three types of input from other neurons. The desired representation vector is conveyed via one input (**Y** in Fig. 1.5) that is connected in a one-to-one fashion with the principal cells via powerful synaptic contacts ("detonator synapses"). The strength of these connections is sufficient to ensure that the input

---

and Y inputs. From this emerges the notion that the essential property of association is the completion of stored patterns from fragmentary input. Such a system is also capable of some degree of error correction. In the example shown, a novel input is presented that is more similar (in terms of having the least number of bits that differ) to X2 than it is to X1. By relaxing the recall criterion (i.e., dividing by two instead of by three) the most similar pattern emerges.

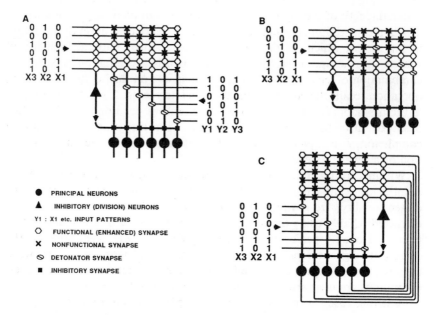

FIG. 1.5. Several variants of Hebb–Marr networks illustrating how the simple correlation matrix formalism for association might be implemented in neural circuitry. The heteroassociative network in (A) is equivalent in information content to the matrix of Fig. 1.4a. (B) and (C) are two versions of autoassociative networks. The essential functional components of these networks are: a set of powerful, point-to-point inputs (detonators) that impose on the network the pattern to be stored, a set of extensively connected inputs with modifiable synapses that (to use Marr's description) encode the contexts in which particular cells learn to fire, and a set of inhibitory interneurons whose role is to set the criterion for output on the principal cells. The latter criterion is that if all n of n active inputs on a particular cell have been modified then the cell should respond. Otherwise it should remain silent. In order to make this assessment, the principal cell in question must receive an independent signal reflecting the total activity on the modifiable input path. In spite of the obvious oversimplifications of these theoretical networks, the overall conceptual framework they provide goes a remarkably long way towards accounting for the structure, physiology, and information processing characteristics of the mammalian hippocampal formation. See text for further details. From "Hippocampal Synaptic Enhancement and Information Storage within a Distributed Memory System" by B. L. McNaughton and R. G. M. Morris, 1987, *Trends in Neuroscience*, 10. Copyright. 1987. Reprinted with permission.

18

vector is mapped exactly onto the output of the principal cells. A second input (**X** in Fig. 1.5) is connected exhaustively with the principal cells via Hebb synapses that are initially nonfunctional, but can be modified or "enhanced" to some fixed strength according to the simplest variant of Hebb's rule; that is, if and only if the presynaptic and postsynaptic elements are simultaneously in a 'one' state, the connection undergoes an irreversible transition from its ineffective to its effective form. The synaptic "weights" (0 or 1) of active inputs of the **X** type summate linearly on the principal cell to determine its "activation state." The third input comes from a so-called inhibitory interneuron, whose connection has the property that it *divides* the activation parameter of each principal neuron by a term equal to the number of elements of the modifiable input pathway that were coactive during an "event" (i.e., the sum of the activations in the **X** path, which in Fig. 1.5, is three in each event). The latter term is obtained from the fact that the inhibitory interneuron has connections of fixed strength from all components of the modifiable pathway. There are several physiologically plausible ways that the influence of the inhibitory cell on the principal cells can be made proportional to the activation of the former. Because the output threshold of the principal cells is one, an element of the output vector will be set to one if the result of the division operation is one or greater, and zero otherwise. Thus, inhibition implements the integer division in the conceptual scheme for recall illustrated in Fig. 1.4. In fact, the networks illustrated in Fig. 1.4a and 1.5a are equivalent except for the lack of symmetry in the latter with respect to the recall of paired associates. In a formal sense, the division operation informs each principal cell whether or not its current **X** input belongs to the class of events which it has previously experienced in conjunction with some **Y** input. If the result of the division is less than one, then the current **X** event must be unfamiliar, and hence the cell should not respond (unless of course there is also a **Y** input, in which case new learning should take place). A crucial point that we shall return to, however, concerns the timing of this postulated division operation. In the usual discrete-time formulation of such models, the postulated recall operation will fail because, whereas the excitation of a particular input pattern reaches the principal cells after one synaptic delay, the corresponding inhibition requires two such delays and hence arrives too late to perform the appropriate normalization function. Thus, for simplicity, let us assume that the delay for the principal cells to generate output is substantially greater than that required for the inhibitory cells. As becomes evident below, this appears to be the solution actually adopted in biological circuitry.

The network of Fig. 1.5a can implement autoassociation if the representation vectors on the detonator and modifiable pathways are made identical. Conceptually the elements of the detonator path could be branches of the elements of the modifiable path. This is formally equivalent to the situation of Fig. 1.5b where there is a single input pathway that makes two kinds of synapse, one a detonator and the rest Hebb.

There is a second formal way to implement autoassociation in such networks that leads to a number of additional interesting functional possibilities (Fig. 1.5c). One could make the modifiable input pathway from collateral branches of the output axons of the principal cells themselves. In this system, if a representation vector on the input (detonator) path is held constant long enough for the output to feed back onto the principal cells, then the output vector is associated with the input vector. In the language of dynamics, an attractor is formed whose basin includes any unique subset of the input vector. In other words, any part of the original stored input drives the system to the state corresponding to the complete input. The attractor is stable, or self-maintaining, because the feedback continuously reactivates the original state unless the network is explicitly turned off by some extrinsic influence (e.g., increasing inhibition). Note that this behavior is exactly the sort that Hebb called "reverberation" and suggested might underlie a form of short-term memory. In more modern terminology, this might correspond to what some have called "working" memory, because of its property of persisting in an active state until it is no longer required, or until other inputs are directed to the network.

There are several other features of this sort of recurrent network that are of computational interest and also, as we discuss presently, have clear analogies in the anatomy and physiology of the hippocampus. First, to enable accurate recall, this network must be explicitly set to zero prior to presentation of an incomplete representation vector, otherwise interference will occur. An interesting use can be made of this "interference" if, during storage, the input representations are changed from cycle to cycle. In this case, the system associates the input on cycle n with the output of cycle $n-1$. As a result, sequences of states are stored. Again, this is a rather direct illustration of Hebb's notion of a "phase sequence." Of course, in this simple system, sequences with common events will lead to indeterminate results. One approach to a solution of this problem is to introduce some temporal dispersion into the input pattern using, for example, various delay lines. Another approach is to make use of certain additional static inputs that can be thought of as representing the differing contexts in which similar sequences occur (see Kohonen, 1988 for discussion).

A second interesting feature of recurrent nets has to do with the idea of *error correction*. Up to this point in the discussion the basins of attraction of stored representation vectors have been restricted to their unique subsets. In other words, the system completes patterns that are correct but incomplete. If, however, noise can occur in the input vector, for example, a random state reversal of a few elements, patterns may appear that contain approximately the correct number of active elements, some of which are inappropriate. The system described so far will fail to recall the correct pattern (i.e., the stored pattern that most closely resembles the current input). If the input is removed after one cycle, all activity will tend to cease because none of the units have sufficient support in the input to overcome the inhibitory division. Suppose, however, that as a result of this failure to find an appropriate attractor (i.e., if the output is insufficient), the inhibitory strength is reduced by one unit and the input reinstated. Provided not too many patterns have been stored, there will usually come a point in this process when the attractor with the nearest Hamming distance to the input (i.e., the one that differs by the least number of elements) will emerge. This effect was illustrated in the rightmost column of Fig. 1.4c, in which a corrupted version of pattern Y2 containing the correct number (i.e., three) of active elements was presented to the matrix. Division of the matrix-vector inner product by three resulted in a spurious output with only a single active element. Reduction of the divisor to two resulted in recall of the desired pattern (X2).

Error correction can also be implemented in large recurrent systems with sparse rather than exhaustive connectivity in the modifiable pathway, an assumption that is, of course, much more biologically plausible. The general idea, which is currently under study by Recce and Gardner-Medwin (M. Recce, pers. commun., 1987), is that the test pattern is presented once at the input and then extinguished. If the input resembles a stored pattern, the output will normally be an even closer approximation. By successively feeding the output back to the input of the system the target will generally emerge after several cycles. Both of these mechanisms may be employed concurrently.

The preceding assertions about association and recall all depend on the operation of the system within certain limits on the number of stored patterns. In general, as the number of stored patterns increases, a point will be reached where performance begins to deteriorate. This was illustrated in Fig. 1.4b in which an attempt to store a fourth pair of input vectors resulted in degradation of the ability of pattern X3 to elicit output of its paired associate, Y3. It is interesting to note that recent calculations (Baum, Moody, & Wilczek, 1988) demonstrate that the general Hebb–Marr formalism has a substantially larger information-storage capacity for a given error tolerance than, for example, the dynamical system formulations of Hopfield (1982) and others. There are several stock procedures for minimizing the problem of "saturation" with its concomitant increase in error probability. The first obvious one involves the concept of efficient coding, that is, keeping the "event size" (i.e., the length of the representation vector) as small as possible given the constraint of preserving sufficient detail. A clear example of this is seen in the visual system of mammals in which considerable circuitry appears to be devoted to recoding a visual image into information about lines and edges. Also, familiar elements can be assigned tokens as, for example, in language. Another related solution is the generation of orthogonal representations for similar input features that occur frequently in different contexts. This might be accomplished through appropriate weight adjustments at some prestorage level, or, more generally, by expanding the storage matrix. In other words, if two representations are projected from a small population of neurons to a larger one, in such a way that the total number of active elements per representation is the same in the two populations, the connections can be arranged so that the proportion of shared elements is smaller in the second population. Marr (1969, 1971) referred to this process as "codon" formation. A possible way in which the hippocampal formation might implement such an orthogonalization process is illustrated in Fig. 1.7.

The foregoing overview represents what we think is the simplest possible implementation of the distributed associative memory paradigm. Given our limited understanding of the nervous system itself, in spite of the myriad and bewildering details of brain anatomy and physiology, it is perhaps wise to keep our conceptual models as simple as possible. Nonetheless, in spite of the simplicity of the foregoing conceptual framework, it does carry a number of implications concerning brain organization. A surprising proportion of these is consistent with experimental data on the hippocampal formation. Some of these implications are listed here. This list serves as a reference point for much of the experimental neurophysiological data to be presented in the following sections.

The first set of implications concerns the logic of the rules governing synaptic modification in a system whose function is to store single events in such a way that their uniqueness is preserved. This stands in contrast to systems, examples of which are discussed elsewhere, in which the object appears to be the development of optimum (orthogonal) feature detectors, or in which there is some correct output that may not be known a priori (e.g., Sutton & Barto, 1981).

1. Adaptive modification (enhancement) of synapses should occur only when there is intense postsynaptic depolarization. In order logically to fulfill Hebb's rule the mechanism of control must involve some registration of the co-occurrence of activities on two or more units. The most biologically expedient way of ensuring this is by postsynaptic integration, in which the degree of depolarization is related to the sum of the synaptic weights of the active inputs.

2. Synaptic enhancement should have both pre- and postsynaptic specificity. That is, the mechanism that alters a synapse must not affect other synapses either on the sending axon or on the receiving cell unless the conditions for Hebb's rule are fulfilled there as well.

3. The principal cells of a system should receive mostly weak synapses, but also a small proportion of much stronger ones. The "detonator" concept need not be taken too seriously as summation of a small set of inputs will

likely lead to the same result so long as the weights are still relatively strong. The connectivity of the detonator pathway will be very limited, whereas that of modifiable pathways is likely to be highly diffuse. There will probably be some compromise between exhaustiveness of connectivity (faster recall) and sparse connectivity (requiring progressive recall but also enabling error correction). Note: If synaptic enhancement actually involves the formation of *new* connections, then the matrix is potentially exhaustively connected within the anatomical domain of the axonal plexus of individual fibers in the modifiable pathway.

4. Synaptic enhancement will tend to be an all-or-none phenomenon, going from very weak (or zero strength) synapses to some fixed moderate strength. This is not an absolute requirement, as other, continuous formulations of associative memories are possible. However, most of these suffer from the constraint of requiring many trials for learning.

5. The population of modifiable connections will be susceptible (in principle) to saturation. This will cause retrograde corruption of existing stored information and anterograde impairment of acquisition.

6. Specific blockade of the enhancement process should cause anterograde memory impairment only.

7. Under conditions of normal use, synaptic enhancement will be very difficult to observe in population responses in any system that has a large, long-term information-storage capacity, as only a small proportion of synaptic space can be allocated for each event. Systems with spontaneous decay are more likely to exhibit changes of detectable magnitude. However, there may be a steady-state condition where the rate of loss of information equals the rate of addition of new information.

8. If there is deterministic decay of enhanced synaptic strength, then the mechanism controlling decay should reset each time the conditions for enhancement are met at a synapse, regardless of whether the synapse is already enhanced, in order to maintain a "last in-last out" organization.

Some of the clearest predictions of the Hebb–Marr formulation concern the characteristics of the physiology of the inhibitory mechanisms within the system. These are radically different from the negative weights used in most current neural net models.

9. The inhibitory mechanism must implement a division operation on the excitation that reaches the principal cell integration zone, usually located at the neuronal cell body. Under certain conditions this effect can be accomplished by varying the electrical conductance of the cell membrane at that point.

10. Inhibitory cells can be much fewer in number than principal cells, but they must have extensive connectivity.

11. Inhibitory cells must be driven by excitatory afferents if these are modifiable, and by the excitatory feedback pathway in recurrent systems.

12. Inhibitory cells must respond to a synchronous input at lower threshold and at shorter latency than principal cells. The latter property is necessary to ensure that the appropriate division operation is already set up at the somata of the principal cells by the time the excitation from the same input arrives there via the principal cell dendrites.

13. In unfamiliar situations (i.e., when current input elicits no recall) extrinsic modulation of inhibitory neurons might lower output threshold, successively probing for a complete pattern. This might also serve as a gate enabling the activation of the synaptic modification process.

Finally, several inferences can be drawn from these sorts of networks concerning the behavioral or information processing correlates of single units in the system as well as certain general characteristics of the dynamics of the system as a whole.

14. The principal cells of the network will each participate in multiple representations; that is, the representation is encoded in the population state vector, not in the activity of any particular cell.

15. On the other hand, the activity level of a particular principal cell (i.e., the number of events in which it participates) must be kept as low as possible to avoid saturation. This constraint does not hold for systems that represent, but do not store information. In this case, the same number of patterns can be represented using fewer cells with a higher activity level.

16. Inhibitory neurons will not be particular about *which* afferents are active at a given time, only about *how many* are active. Thus they will not appear to convey any information in the principal cells' response domain.

17. In general, the responsiveness of a principal cell to an unfamiliar input configuration will appear "hard-wired" in that it will be present on the first exposure. There will be no apparent learning period for the response.

18. Principal cells will perform "pattern completion" in a familiar environment. It will be very difficult to identify a particular feature of the input constellation that activates them, and it will be very hard to disrupt firing patterns by systematic cue deletion.

19. During periods when inputs are changing rapidly, recurrent autoassociative networks will periodically and globally shut down toavoid interference between the current pattern and recall of the target pattern. New information will be presented to a silent network.

In the ensuing discussion we refer back to these conjectures by number (e.g., §19 refers to implication 19).

ANATOMICAL ORGANIZATION
OF THE HIPPOCAMPAL FORMATION

Based on the pattern of projections it receives from the neocortex, there is now general agreement that the hippocampal formation, although phylogenetically an old system, represents the *highest level of association cortex* in the mammalian nervous system, in the sense that it receives refined information from virtually all sensory modalities, both exteroceptive and interoceptive. Indeed, the elaboration and differentiation of neocortical areas can (only partly facetiously) be thought of as the development of an increasingly sophisticated "user interface" for a fundamental processing structure whose general organization has remained relatively stable throughout evolution, and without which the neocortex is seriously disabled. Primary sensory systems project to essentially unimodal cortical fields (e.g., visual, auditory, somatosensory, etc). Each of these projects to its so-called association areas, which receive input from primary areas, sometimes from several different modalities. Within the polymodal association areas, there is usually some loss of the point-to-point topological mapping that is a characteristic feature of almost all primary sensory regions. This topological dispersion is reflected, for example, in larger visual receptive fields. In general, association areas do not receive primary sensory input from the thalamus, which is a major relay structure for most sensory modalities. It is these polymodal association areas that converge directly or indirectly on one particular cortical field, the "entorhinal" cortex, which in turn forms the principle source of afferent information to the hippocampus. Within the hippocampus extensive lateral interactions insure the virtually complete loss of any topological mapping from the sensory receptor arrays onto hippocampal coordinates.

The fundamental organizational principle in cortical systems is that information from specific sources undergoes progressive stages of convergence and convolution until, by the time it has been processed by the diffuse elements of the hippocampal circuitry, it is "supramodal" (Swanson, Kohler, & Bjorklund, 1987) in character. The activity projected back toward the association cortex by individual hippocampal neurons can be shown to represent the conjunctions of a broad range of specific sensory features. In general, the return projections from the hippocampus can be thought of as providing cells in unimodal cortex with a condensed "summary sketch" of the broader, polymodal sensory context in which the specific unimodal sensory experiences to which they are tuned have occurred.

The hippocampus proper consists of three separate anatomical subfields (see Fig. 1.6), each with its own distinct structural organization, afferent, efferent, and internal connections. Each area consists of a large number of

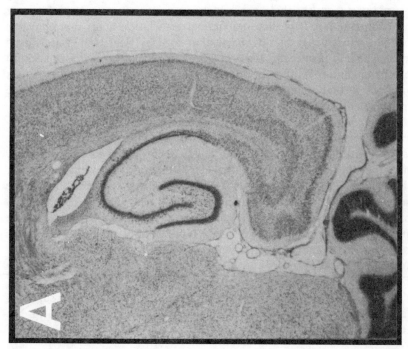

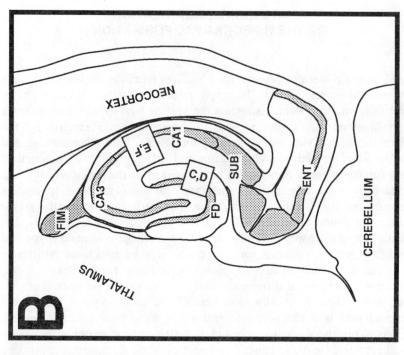

FIG. 1.6.

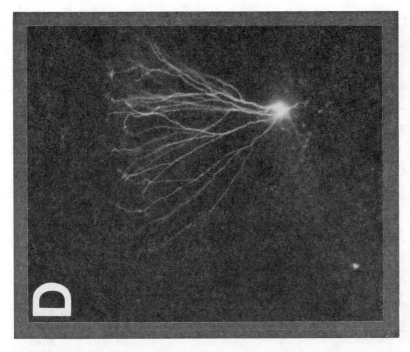

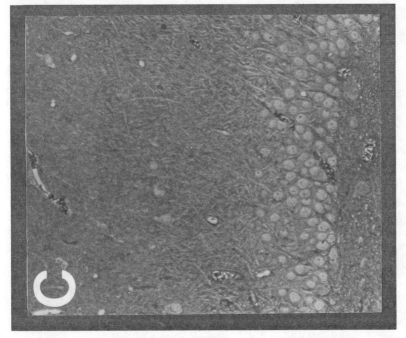

FIG. 1.6. (continued)

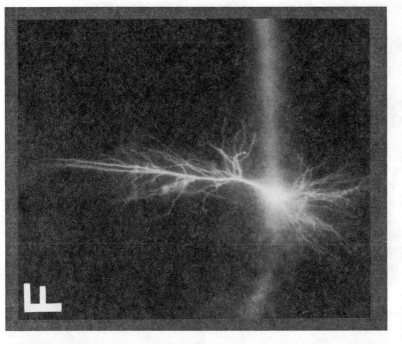

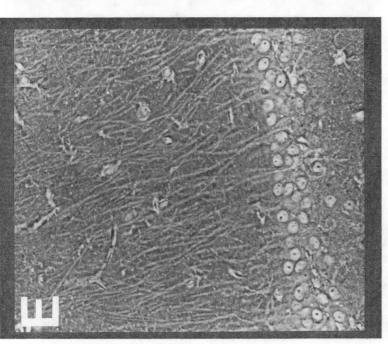

FIG. 1.6. The principal subfields of the mammalian hippocampal formation are illustrated in a micrograph (A) of a histological section cut in the horizontal plane through the rat brain and in the corresponding diagram (B). The rectangles in B labelled C,D and E,F show the approximate regions enlarged in the corresponding parts of this figure. Parts C,D and E,F show high power photomicrographs of granule cells of the fascia dentata and pyramidal cells of CA1 respectively, each prepared using two different methods. The left figures were prepared using phase-contrast microscopy of 2μm thick sections of epoxy embedded tissue, and illustrate the close packing of neuronal cell bodies, and the dense meshwork of dendrites in the neuropil (the regions where most excitatory synapses occur). The right figures illustrate single cells stained in their entirety by ejecting a fluorescent dye from a micropipette inserted into the cell body during intracellular recording experiments. Abbreviations in (B): ENT-entorhinal cortex; SUB-subiculum; FD-fascia dentata; FIM-fimbria.

what are considered "principal" neurons of a single class, and a very much smaller number of "interneurons" of several classes. The principal neuron of the region known as the fascia dentata (FD) or, alternatively, dentate gyrus (DG) is the granule cell, whereas in fields CA3 and CA1, it is the pyramidal cell. The abbreviation CA refers to "Cornu Ammonis" after the Egyptian god Ammon, who had the head of a ram. This term was applied by early anatomists because of the resemblance of the human hippocampus to a ram's horn. There is a small transitional CA2 field. In the rat, there are about 10^6 FD granule cells, 1.8×10^5 CA3 pyramidal cells, and 2×10^5 CA1 pyramidal cells per hemisphere. In all subfields, there is a relatively much smaller number of interneurons that function to inhibit the principal cells. Although these cells are much fewer in number, they are essential to the normal physiology of the system, with epileptic seizures resulting from their inactivation (e.g., Sloviter, 1987). As is discussed later, these inhibitory interneurons probably play a fundamental computational role in the implementation of distributed associative memory in hippocampal neural circuitry.

An earlier conceptualization of the hippocampal circuitry led to the coining of the term *trisynaptic loop* (Andersen, Bliss, & Skrede, 1971), based on the notion that cortical information was projected through a set of parallel modular pathways, first to FD and from there through CA3 to CA1 before leaving the hippocampus via the subiculum. Although this concept still provides a useful framework for discussion, a number of recent findings make the scheme untenable (e.g., Witter & Groenewegen, 1988). It is now well established that all three principal subfields receive direct projections from the entorhinal cortex, and that there are extensive lateral interactions among the principal cells, at least within FD and CA3. In the former area, the interactions are indirect, being mediated by a relatively small number of large excitatory interneurons located in the so-called *hilar* region just below the granular layer. CA3 pyramidal cells engage extensively in direct excitatory interactions, a feature that is of major computational significance. This lateral interaction system exhibits a clear but complex topology, the significance of which is not yet understood (Amaral, personal communication 1988). The trisynaptic loop concept is correct to the extent that, between areas, the information flow is strictly from FD to CA3 to CA1 to subiculum. There is virtually no skipping over, say from FD to CA1 or from CA3 to subiculum, and there are no direct reverse projections. There is, however, extensive indirect feedback within this network, because the output of subiculum, besides returning information to other association cortices, projects directly back to the entorhinal cortex. Entorhinal cortex is also a major pathway for return of information to association cortex after its transformation in the hippocampus. Thus, the hippocampus can be thought of as a directed recurrent circuit containing several recurrent subcircuits. Information is received from the rest of the cortex, processed through one or more cycles within this circuitry, and fed back into the cortical networks from which it arose.

The "unit circuits" of each subfield share a common feature. The extrinsic input to the principal cells is excitatory in character, and these same excitatory afferent fibers also excite the inhibitory interneurons (cf. Figs. 1.5 and 1.9). The latter configuration is known as "feedforward" inhibition, in contrast to "feedback inhibition," which involves excitation of the interneurons by the principal cell, followed by inhibition of the principal cell by the interneuron. It appears that all inhibitory interneurons engage in feedforward inhibition, whereas only a subset of them engage in feedback inhibition. Although there may be several subvarieties of inhibitory inter-neurons, the best characterized (and probably most prevalent) is the "basket" cell, so called because its connections onto the principal cells have the form of a "basket" of contacts around the principal cell body. As discussed earlier, this configuration is also of considerable computational significance, and we discuss its physiological characteristics presently.

A few numerical data serve to illustrate the complexity and vast range of combinatorial possibilities inherent in the system. From the projection cells of entorhinal cortex to FD, there is a roughly tenfold expansion of principal cell numbers, suggesting a possible implementation of an orthogonalizing function (cf. Marr's codon formation). How this may work is suggested in Fig. 1.7. Within FD, each granule cell receives about 6,000 weak excitatory contacts from the entorhinal cortex of which 5% to 10% must cooperate to induce the receiving cell to fire. There appears also to be a much smaller subset of inputs whose relative synaptic efficacy is about tenfold greater (§3; McNaughton, Barnes, & Andersen, 1981). The existence of multiple contacts from single entorhinal cells is probably rare. Each granule cell communicates with as few as 15 pyramidal cells (§3) in CA3 (Claiborne, Amaral, & Cowan, 1986), via contacts that are relatively powerful and have a unique morphology. Each CA3 pyramidal cell receives as many as 16,000 other modifiable excitatory contacts (§3), about a third of which come from the entorhinal cortex, the remainder arising from other CA3 pyramidal cells (Squire, Shimamura, & Amaral, in press).

The foregoing discussion has concerned the primary circuitry of the hippocampal formation encompassing most of its neuronal elements and connections. By far the greatest proportion of synaptic contacts originate either from the neocortex, or from within the hippocampus itself. In addition, however, there exist several "subcortical" inputs that, although arising from relatively few neurons compared to the cortical input, can exert powerful effects on the information-processing mode of the primary circuitry. Interestingly, many of these inputs appear to exert their principal effects by tuning up or down the excitability of the inhibitory interneurons, particularly in FD (Mizumori, McNaughton, & Barnes, 1989) and CA3. The details of these connections can be found in Swanson and colleagues (1987). In general, these systems are thought of as "modulatory" in the sense that they tend to affect the response of hippocampal neurons to other inputs, rather than conveying detailed information.

In summary, the hippocampus: (a) receives its main inputs from polymodal cortical association fields, and returns the result of whatever computations it performs to the same areas from which the inputs arose; (b) numerically expands the input vector by a factor of about 10 and then contracts it again in such a way that the outputs may overlap less than the inputs; (c) contains principal neurons — granule and pyramidal cells — and far fewer inhibitory neurons, both types receiving excitatory inputs from modifiable pathways; (d) is organized in recurrent circuitry with multiple recurrent subcircuits; and finally (e), there is some evidence for an organization consisting of a sparse set of strong (detonator) connections and a more diffuse set of modifiable ones, as called for by the Hebb–Marr formalism.

PROPERTIES OF SYNAPTIC WEIGHT CHANGES
IN HIPPOCAMPUS

Since the formulation of Hebb's ideas on association in neural circuits and their extension by other theorists, the Holy Grail of much neurophysiological research has been the discovery of properties of neuronal connections in the mammalian brain corresponding to the logic of the Hebb synapse in some form. The past 15 years has seen the accumulation of a substantial body of evidence indicating that at least one version of the Hebb synapse has been found, and possibly others. This phenomenon was first observed in hippocampal connections (Bliss & Lomo, 1973; Bliss & Gardner-Medwin, 1973), and has been most thoroughly studied there. It involves a long-lasting increase in the average magnitude of synaptic potentials (EPSPs) recorded from groups of connections. The increase results from electrical activation of the presynaptic elements (input fibers) at frequencies within the high end of the range of physiological activity. This phenomenon is referred to either as long-term potentiation (LTP) or, to emphasize its distinction from various short-lasting and nonassociative weight changes that also occur at the same synapses, as long-term enhancement (LTE). As several reviews of the historical details and empirical characterization of LTE are available (McNaughton, 1983; McNaughton & Morris, 1987; Landfield & Deadwyler, 1987; Swanson, Teyler, & Thompson, 1982), we proceed directly to current knowledge about its mechanism, from which its logical properties, and Hebbian character should become clear. The reader

A

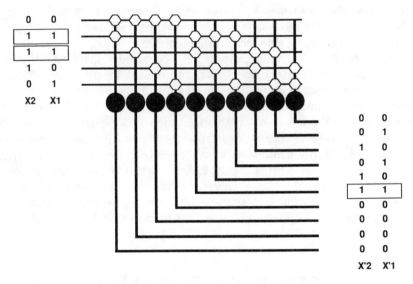

B

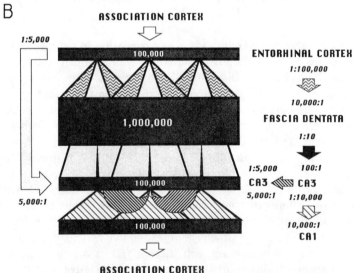

FIG. 1.7. The principal underlying orthogonalization of representation vectors using Marr's "codon" expansion is shown in (A). In this simple example, two input patterns that overlap considerably are projected onto a larger system, each of whose elements respond to subsets of size 2 of the input. The resulting output patterns overlap less than the inputs (i.e., they are more ortho-

should refer to the review articles for detailed citations of the original research reports.

In the hippocampus, and most parts of the cortex, the main inputs to the principal cells, as well as most of their excitatory interconnections (e.g., the recurrent association pathway in region CA3) utilize as their neurotransmitter an ionized amino acid called glutamate. In pathways exhibiting LTE, each synapse contains two types of postsynaptic receptor molecule, each of which binds glutamate with high affinity, and each of which is associated with a different type of cation-selective channel. The type 1 receptor (usually designated the "Quis" receptor because of its relatively high affinity for a glutamate analog called quisqualate) is associated with a channel that, in the presence of glutamate bound to the receptor, is permeable to sodium and potassium ions (Na^+ and K^+). When opened during normal synaptic transmission, this conductance channel thus shifts the membrane equilibrium point, causing the membrane potential to be driven from its rest state near -70 mV towards a new equilibrium potential near 0 mV. Of course, whereas a shift of only about 10–20 mV (depending on which type of principal cell one is dealing with) is all that is needed to cross the threshold for an action potential, most individual synapses make a rather small contribution on their own, on the order of 100 to 300 μV. The

---

gonal). There is a drawback to this simple solution because, to preserve this orthogonality, the higher dimension of the expanded representation vector must be maintained in subsequent processing. This may become biologically expensive. A solution to this is suggested in (B). In B, an attempt is made to illustrate the approximate numerical convergence and divergence relations of the main hippocampal circuitry, as well as the anatomical topography of these interconnections. Of major interest is the large expansion and divergence that occurs from entorhinal cortex to the fascia dentata, suggesting the codon expansion of A, and the correspondingly dramatic compression that occurs from fascia dentata to CA3. To illustrate how this may result in an orthogonalized representation of *the same dimensionality* as the original entorhinal input, consider two representations in entorhinal cortex that involve activity of highly overlapping populations of cells restricted to a small region near the middle. In the expanded representation in fascia dentata, the representations would not only share fewer elements in common, but would also overlap less anatomically. This anatomical dispersion would be maintained during the recompression of the representation onto CA3, by virtue of the highly restricted divergence and parallel geometry of this projection. Thus, the well-known "lamellar" organization of the granule cell projection to CA3 may reflect a mechanism for increasing the difference between the representations of two initially similar events, without changing the final size of the neuronal population used to code these events.

type 2 (usually called NMDA) receptor-channel complex has the rather interesting property of being sensitive not only to the binding of glutamate, but also to the membrane potential itself. In fact, the membrane potential acts as a gate which prevents the channel from opening at potentials more negative than about -40 mV, in spite of the presence of bound glutamate at the receptor. When the channel does open, it is permeable primarily to calcium ion (Ca^{++}). The entry of Ca^{++} into the postsynaptic dendritic spine (a high surface-to-volume ratio compartment) sets in motion a chain of metabolic events that leads rapidly to a persistent increase in the synaptic weight. This mechanism thus provides the basis for fulfillment of the first two of the inferences drawn from the Hebb–Marr formalism already discussed. Consistent with this mechanism, LTE occurs on a given postsynaptic cell only when convergent input has resulted in intense postsynaptic depolarization (§1, §2), and only at those connections emanating from a given presynaptic cell that converge with other inputs coactive in the same representational event (§2). The precise mechanism of expression of the enhanced weight is unknown. In particular, the proposition of a binary state change (§4) awaits experimental confirmation. Repeated activation does lead both to saturation of the enhancement process (§5), and to a stabilization of the enhanced state (§8). Nevertheless, there does appear to be an inevitable, slow reversion to the "ground" state over weeks or months (§7), at least at some of the hippocampal synapses at which the phenomenon has been studied. Repeated bilateral electrical stimulation of the perforant path (the axon bundle conveying information from entorhinal cortex), which leads to saturation of LTE, results in impairment of the ability to acquire new spatial associations (anterograde amnesia), and the disruption of spatial associations recently acquired by the animal (§5)(temporally limited retrograde amnesia). Pharmacological blockade of the NMDA receptor with a selective competitive antagonist called APV, while apparently not affecting normal information transmission in the hippocampus, prevents the acquisition of new spatial information (§6). Finally, conjecture §3 calls for the existence of a small population of relatively powerful synapses to provide the "detonator" or "teaching" input to the network. Evidence for such a bimodal distribution of synaptic strengths has been obtained using intracellular recording from granule cells of the fascia dentata in vitro (McNaughton, Barnes, & Andersen 1981). A second candidate would be the projection of the dentate granule cells to the CA3 pyramidal cells, which as we have seen, is of a highly restricted, point-to-point nature. These synapses are also relatively strong, only a small number of active ones being required to drive a pyramidal cell. Further evidence for a relatively hardwired teaching input to the system is considered later.

Although LTE appears to satisfy most of the demands of the Hebb–Marr formalism in terms of its underlying logic and persistence, and the indirect case for its involvement in associative memory is rather substantial, there is as yet no demonstration that the phenomenon actually occurs in the normal brain as a result of neural activity related to the storage of information. The technical difficulties in making such a demonstration are formidable. Nevertheless, recent studies have revealed changes in the responsiveness of populations of hippocampal synapses that result from behavioral situations in which it can reasonably be inferred that the hippocampus is particularly activated, and in which new information is acquired. These changes have some but not all of the characteristics of electrically induced LTE. Whether or not they reflect the same biological mechanism, they are of interest in their own right as possible reflections of actual information storage within hippocampal circuitry.

Before describing these changes, a brief discussion is needed about the methods available for studying synaptic phenomena and cellular interactions in the alert behaving animal. All of these techniques involve the measurement and interpretation of extracellular electrical fields in the brain. A uniform change in the conductance over the surface of a spherical cell would generate a change in transmembrane voltage as the membrane sought its new equilibrium. However, there would be no observable electrical field in the vicinity, because the current flow is entirely absorbed by the membrane capacitance. This is not the case if a spatially inhomogeneous cell is subject to a *local* conductance change. In this case, a local, membrane-generated voltage drop is inserted in series with a resistive pathway that includes the long axis of the dendrite, the cell membrane, and the resistive medium surrounding the cell, returning in a loop to the outside of the membrane site of origin. The resulting current flow can be detected as an extracellular electric field relative to a remote reference point. Because the extracellular space is of much lower resistivity than the cell membrane, these fields are much smaller typically by a factor of about 10^{-3} than transmembrane voltage changes. Moreover, although they fall off steeply with distance, these fields are not precisely localized to their cells of origin, and superimposed fields from many cells may be detected from a single electrode. Nevertheless, by positioning a microelectrode near the soma of a single cell, or under situations where many regularly arrayed cells can be activated in synchrony, as in the hippocampus, then extracellular fields provide the physiologist with a window on cellular and system dynamics that are otherwise inaccessible in behaving animals. Although subject to certain problems of interpretation, particularly when population activity is monitored, most of what is known about neural information processing and the long-term dynamics of synaptic transmission has come from the use of such techniques (e.g., Figs. 1.8, 1.9, and 1.17 show recordings of various physiological events measured as temporal fluctuations in extracellular electric fields).

We describe here two different types of experience-dependent change in

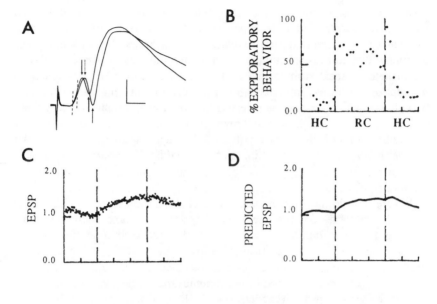

$$d(EPSP)/dt = - K1(EPSP - 1) + K2(B)$$

FIG. 1.8.   Exploration dependent modulation of synaptic efficacy in the fascia dentata of the hippocampus: (A) Examples of population synaptic potentials recorded in the fascia dentata of the hippocampus in response to application of electrical stimuli to the perforant path, the main source of cortical input to the hippocampus. The responses consist of two components. The first, a slow, positive going field potential (EPSP), reflects the flow of currents due to the activation of afferent synapses. Measurements taken on the rising phase of this component (dashed lines) can, with certain important caveats, be taken as an indication of the average synaptic weight of the population of inputs activated by the electrical stimulus. Linearly superimposed on the synaptic component is a fast, negative going wave whose onset and peak are designated by arrows in the figure. This "population spike" reflects the discharge of the granule cells in the fascia dentata that are driven to threshold by the synaptic input. To a first approximation, the size of this component is a relative measure of how many of these granule cells reach threshold during a synchronous input event. Numerous studies have shown that, provided the electrical stimuli are delivered at a rate of not more than once every 5 to 10 seconds, the stimuli themselves have no detectable effect on the system beyond the evoked response. Electrical activation at higher frequencies, of course, leads to a variety of presistent and transient changes in responsiveness. In the present study the stimulus frequency was 0.1 Hz.

(B) The basic experiment consisted of three phases during which both evoked responses and the animal's behavior were

functional connectivity of hippocampal circuits that have been observed with the technique of delivering single electrical stimuli (at no more than 1/10 Hz) to the main source of cortical input to the hippocampus (the perforant path) and recording the resulting population field potentials in the fascia dentata. Numerous studies have shown that such low-rate stimulation has no lasting effect on the magnitude of the resulting response potentials. These potentials consist of two main components, one reflecting

---

recorded every 10 seconds. Behaviors were classified as either exploratory or nonexploratory. In the first phase, the animal was briefly picked up, the chronically implanted recording and stimulating electrodes were attached to the recording apparatus, and the animal was replaced in the home cage (HC). In the second phase, the animal was placed in a plastic recording chamber (RC) to which the animal had been exposed on previous days, but not on the current day. After 15 minutes the animal was returned to its home cage. Exploratory activity increased abruptly at each transition. In the home cage this increase subsided over 5 to 10 minutes. In the relatively novel chamber it persisted. (Time marks indicate 5-minute intervals)

(C) The synaptic component of the response (EPSP) underwent a series of changes related to the three phases of the experiment. There was a slow rise followed by a return to baseline in phase 1 (HC). In phase 2 (RC) it increased slowly to a constant elevated plateau. In phase 3 (HC) it slowly subsided towards the original baseline.

(D) The change in the synaptic response was clearly not related to the *instantaneous* behavior of the animal. Rather, it was related to the *time integral* of exploratory behavior over the previous 5 to 10 minutes. The variance in the synaptic weight measure (EPSP) was quite well characterized by numerically integrating a simple expression for the change in EPSP size as a function of time and exploratory behavior: $d(EPSP)/dt = -K_1(EPSP - 1) + K_2B$, where EPSP is the magnitude of the synaptic response, normalized to a baseline of 1, B is the behavioral measure of the amount of exploration (1 or 0), and K_1 and K_2 are positive constants regulating the decay and increase, respectively, of the synaptic response. Thus, the synaptic weight function has the characteristics of a "leaky integrator," with a decay time constant of about 5 to 10 minutes. Whether or not this effect reflects the temporary storage of information acquired during exploratory episodes remains to be determined. Data in (a) from *Exploration Dependent Modulation of Synaptic Responses in Fascia Denta II. Dissociation of Motor and Sensory Factors, and Evidence for a Synaptic conductance change* by E. J. Green et al., 1988. (b), (c), (d) from "Exploration Dependent Modulation of Evoked Responses in Fascia Dentata: Fundamental Observations and Time Course" by P. E. Sharp, B. L. McNaughton, and C. A. Barnes, *Psychobiology*, in press.

the flow of synaptic currents into the granule cell dendrites (EPSP), and one reflecting the output discharges of those granule cells that reach threshold during this semisynchronous input event (population spike).

In the first series of experiments (Sharp, McNaughton, & Barnes, 1985; Sharp, Barnes, & McNaughton, 1987), such evoked synaptic and postsynaptic responses were monitored daily in rats, both before and after the animals were released from their spatially restricted colony cages into a 12' by 18' room filled with a variety of junk objects. As previously described in the section on spatial behavior, over the course of 2 or 3 days the animals appeared to develop an effective representation of this space. During this time there also developed a 40% to 50% increase in the number of hippocampal granule cells that discharged as a result of the electrical stimulus. This increased responsiveness persisted, with gradual decay, for 2 to 3 weeks following return of the animals to the spatially restricted colony cages. This is about the duration over which electrically induced enhancement of synaptic and postsynaptic responses (LTE) persists in this system. Surprisingly, there was little or no substantial change in the component of the extracellular fields reflecting the flow of synaptic current. This does not necessarily mean, however, that there was no change in synaptic strength. One possibilty is that of a substantial redistribution of synaptic weights among cells in the system with the population sum remaining constant (see Levy, Colbert, & Desmond, chap. 5 in this volume). This could easily have resulted in the observed changes. There remain several alternative explanations, however, such as a global modulation of inhibition in the system, or a combination of increased synaptic conductance and a tonic depolarization of the granule cells, which would have a masking effect on the extracellular assessment of a synaptic weight increase. Further study is required to sort out these alternatives. Nevertheless, we can conclude that extensive spatial exploration is accompanied by a substantial and persistent change in either the hippocampal circuitry itself or in systems projecting into this circuitry.

In the study just described, the physiological recordings were carried out separately from the actual exploratory behavior which, presumably, resulted in the persistent network alteration. A second series of experiments (Sharp, 1987; Sharp, McNaughton, & Barnes, in press; Green, McNaughton, Keith, & Barnes, 1988) has addressed the question of whether any direct effect of spatial exploration can be observed. It was already known from the work of Winson and Abzug (1977, 1978a, 1978b) that the behavioral state of the animal has a *moment-to-moment* influence on the transmission of electrically induced activation through the fascia dentata to the rest of the hippocampal circuitry. The purpose of this study was to address the possibility that information acquired while an animal moves about its immediate environment, or shifts its attention from place to place, may leave some form of *lasting trace* that can be measured in the extracellular field potentials evoked by constant, low-rate stimulation of the perforant path.

When a rat is picked up momentarily, and then replaced either in its original location or in some other one, a period of "exploratory" behavior generally ensues. This behavior includes head movements accompanied by sniffing, rearing up on its hind legs and looking around, and translocation. If the location is relatively familiar, this exploration is short-lived. If the location is relatively unfamiliar, the period of increased activity is more protracted. In this study, the behavior was carefully monitored and classified each 10 seconds according to whether or not it was exploratory. What was observed was that in addition to a moment-to-moment fluctuation in the field potential that appeared to be related to the current level of motor activation, there was also a gradual increase in the size of the synaptic component of the evoked potential during exploration (Fig. 1.8). This increase persisted beyond the bout of exploration and decayed back to baseline with a time constant of 5 to 15 minutes. The overall effect could be well described by assuming that each short episode of exploration resulted in a small increment in the response over a fixed baseline, and that the accumulated increment was subject to slow exponential decay. As a consequence, a step increase in exploration resulted in a slow rise of the response to some steady state, whereas a step decrease in exploration resulted in a slow return to baseline. Obviously, considerably more work will be needed to determine whether this change might represent the temporary storage of traces of recent sensory input into the system. A first step in this direction, however, is the finding that forced locomotion in a motorized treadmill did not lead to the increase in synaptic response (Green, McNaughton, Keith, & Barnes, 1989). Thus it is not the motor component of the exploratory activity that generates the change.

In the context of the Hebb–Marr framework one other observation made in these studies is of interest. Whenever something unexpected happened to the animals, such as transfer to a new location, switching on the motorized treadmill, or even extinguishing the room lights, there was a substantial but transient elevation in the postsynaptic discharge component of the evoked response (i.e., the population spike), as though the level of inhibition in the system had been suddenly reduced. This effect is consistent with the conjecture (§13) that inputs that are unable to generate completed output patterns (i.e., unexpected inputs) might result in a search procedure involving a lowering of the strength of inhibition.

In summary, a change in the efficacy of synaptic transmission (LTE/LTP) that is consistent in many respects with the Hebb–Marr formalism can be induced in hippocampal synapses by electrical activation of certain pathways. Although it cannot yet be assured that this phenomenon actually underlies associative storage in hippocampal circuits, there is good evidence that these circuits do change as a result of exploratory activity during which information about the animal's immediate and extended environment is being acquired.

INHIBITORY MECHANISMS

One of the greatest strengths of the application of the Hebb–Marr network concept to the hippocampal formation is the way in which it accounts for many of the properties of inhibitory cells in this system. We have already discussed the agreement between the observed anatomy and the prediction concerning the low relative numbers of inhibitory cells compared to principal cells, and the existence of the necessary direct excitatory connections onto the inhibitory cells. That the action of at least one major class of inhibitory synapses in the hippocampus is in fact equivalent to a division operation, as also required (§9), can be illustrated in two ways. The first has to do with the observation, now confirmed in a number of studies, that the equilibrium potential for the chloride conducting, $GABA_1$ mediated, inhibitory synapses is very nearly the same as the cell resting potential for most hippocampal neurons recorded under in vitro conditions. Thus, the action of these synapses is primarily to short circuit, or "shunt" the membrane of the cell (which, without inhibitory input, has very low conductivity) at its spike trigger zone. Reference to Ohm's law, $V = I / G$ (using conductance rather than its reciprocal, resistance) indicates why any excitatory synaptic current crossing this membrane will generate a voltage change that is roughly inversely proportional to the strength of the inhibitory input (G).

The same conclusion has also been drawn on the basis of the study of extracellular fields in the intact hippocampus in vivo (McNaughton, 1989). Antidromic activation of the granule cells (i.e., stimulating their axons so that the impulse travels backwards towards the cell body) results in massive activation of the inhibitory neurons, via the recurrent collateral of the granule cell axon. This causes a complete inhibition of the evoked discharge of the granule cells when the perforant path is stimulated some tens of milliseconds later. There is no effect, however, on the size of the synaptic field potential, which there should be if the inhibition were generating opposing currents (i.e., acting in a subtractive manner). Thus, the inhibition in this system does appear to perform the necessary division.

The next question is whether this division is proportional to the density of activity on the modifiable input pathway. There are several factors that probably contribute to the necessary proportionality, and at the same time fulfill the other requirement of having the inhibitory division from a synchronous input event implemented on the principal cells before they reach their discharge threshold (§12). That inhibitory cells in the pyramidal layers of the hippocampus respond sooner than the principal cells to afferent activation, and at lower threshold, has been demonstrated both by Fox and Ranck (1981) and by Ashwood, Lancaster, and Wheal (1984). The same phenomena have been demonstrated for interneurons in the fascia dentata by Mizumori, McNaughton, and Barnes (1989). In this study, individual inhibitory cells were identified in intact animals using the following electrophysiological criterion (see Figs. 1.9 and 1.10): the perforant pathway was stimulated twice in rapid succession while recording from a single neuron in the dentate gyrus. Under these conditions, it is well known that the evoked spike discharge of the granule cells can be completely inhibited on the second response, as a result of activation of both feed-forward and feed-back inhibition. It follows that any single neurons that respond on the second stimulus are not granule cells. By default, they are most likely interneurons. It was found that these cells responded to perforant path activation not only at much lower threshold than the granule cells, but also at considerably shorter latency. Moreover, the discharge probability increased monotonically with the number of perforant path fibers activated, over a broad range of input levels. Conversely, granule cells tended to have a sharp activation threshold, near the high end of the input range. Thus, the number of inhibitory cells that respond during a given event is roughly proportional to the input strength. Moreover, because the latency to onset of the inhibitory conductance in the granule cells is roughly inversely proportional to the input level, the effectiveness of the inhibition from a single inhibitory cell at the critical time that the granule cells should be reaching threshold is likewise proportional to the input density.

There is also a clear prediction made by the Hebb–Marr hypothesis concerning how inhibitory cells should behave with respect to ongoing information processing (§16). This is considered below in the context of our discussion of the dynamics of hippocampal cellular activity in relation to spatially directed behavior.

ACTION IN SPACE
AND THE NEURONAL EXPRESSION
OF SPATIAL RELATIONSHIPS

A substantial body of results from studies of motor behavior in humans, lower primates, and other animals indicates clearly that virtually all of the initial components of voluntary spatially directed movements of the body, eyes, or limbs occur under so-called "open loop" conditions (Evarts, Shinoda, & Wise, 1984). That is, a trajectory of some sort has been

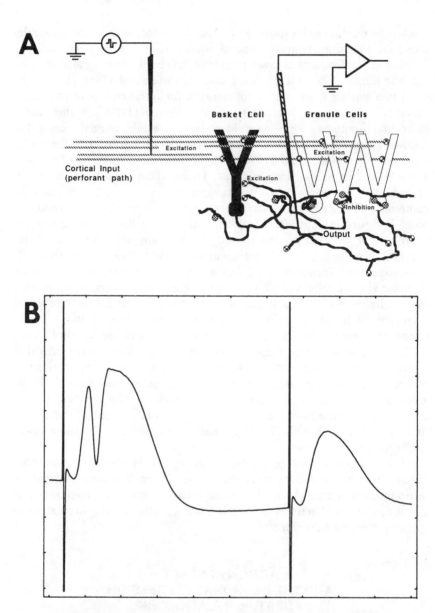

FIG. 1.9 (A) The main cell layer of the fascia dentata consists of two major cell types: the granule cells (about 10^6 per hemisphere in the rat), which are the principal output cells, and the basket cells (about 10^4 per hemisphere), which are inhibitory interneurons. These two cell types can be distinguished in physiological recordings on the basis of their response to double stimuli delivered to the perforant path afferent fibers at short intervals (about 25 msec). During this interval, inhibition, initiated

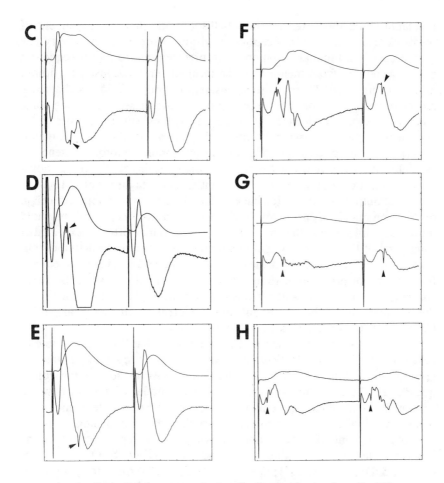

by the first stimulus, prevents the discharge of granule cells. This is illustrated in B, which represents the population field potentials recorded in response to a pair of stimuli delivered at a 25 msec interval. On the first response, there is a sharp negative component reflecting the postsynaptic discharge of the granule cells. This "population spike" is abolished on the second response, which reflects the flow of synaptic currents that fail to discharge the granule cells because of the presence of inhibition set up by the first stimulus.

In order to record the activities of single cells in the granular layer during perforant path stimulation, the signal must be filtered with a narrow frequency band-pass, and weaker stimulation (near population spike threshold) must be used. In C-H, the upper traces show the unfiltered record, whereas the lower traces show the filtered records at higher gain. The arrows indicate spike discharges of single units resolvable in the filtered record. In

(*continued*)

preplanned and then executed in a ballistic mode that is independent of feedback from either proprioception or vision. Moreover, with a very few spatial cues in a familiar situation, such preprogrammed motor sequences can be generated from memory of the local spatial relationships, without direct sensory input. There is also a considerable body of evidence that these motor programs can be held in preparation ("motor set"), awaiting some conditional signal. If one closely watches a Japanese sushi chef (as we did, for scientific purposes, several times during the preparation of this manuscript) one would observe that an entire complex motor sequence is carefully internally rehearsed before the blade begins its lightning movement. In most cases, part of the signal sent from the higher control levels to the spinal output neurons is fed back directly into the site of apparent origin of the command. Considerable evidence from studies of subthreshold muscle activity suggests that such motor programs may often be executed at some level of the nervous system under conditions where the actual output is gated off. One suspects that the brain is, in some way, using the feedback from the motor program, without actually executing the movements. These concepts of "motor set" and "efference copy" have played a major role in the development of thought about motor control (cf. Evarts et al., 1984; Gallistel, 1980; von Holst & Mittelstaedt, 1950).

These sorts of observations lead to the notion that the brain is able to develop stored models of spatial relationships, to compute plans for appropriate actions in relation to them, and possibly to test the consequences of these actions against the internal model of the local world without actually executing the plan. In this section we consider some of the neurophysiological processes underlying such internal modelling.

From the point of view of understanding spatial representation in the brain, a major breakthrough occurred with the discovery by O'Keefe (1976; O'Keefe & Dostrovsky, 1971; O'Keefe & Nadel, 1978) that most, if not all, of the pyramidal neurons of the hippocampus exhibit a systematic and reliable bias in terms of the location within any particular apparatus in which they discharge action potentials. During any directed action in space,

---

three examples (C-E), the single units fire in response to the first stimulus, during the small population spike seen in the unfiltered record, but do not respond to the second stimulus. In the other three cases (F-H), the cells fire before the population spike following the first stimulus, and again following the second stimulus, during the period in which the granule cells are inhibited. On the basis of this behavior, the cells of C-E were classified as granule cells, whereas those of F-H were classified as basket inhibitory cells. Further analysis of the different properties of these two cell types is presented in Fig. 1.10. (Unpublished data from Chen, McNaughton, & Mizumori, 1988).

these neurons are virtually silent except within their own preferred "place field" (§15), which typically encompasses a few percent of the accessible space (although there can be considerable variation). In most circumstances, the firing depends not only on where the animal is, but on the direction in which it is facing (McNaughton, Barnes, & O'Keefe, 1983). It turns out that any given cell will have such a preferred activity location in a given environment with about 70% probability. Thus, a given "local view" of an environment is represented in the hippocampus as the group activity of a rather small subset of the total population (§16). Interestingly, these place fields are usually expressed during the animal's first exposure to the field (Hill, 1978), suggesting the possible presence of something like "detonator" circuitry (§18).

These modes of activity are exactly in accordance with the conceptual framework for the principal cells of the associative memory system developed above. In recent years, it has been possible to identify reliably, on the basis of electrophysiological criteria, the activity of individual inhibitory interneurons in the hippocampus as well, under the same behavioral conditions in which the pyramidal "place " cells have been studied. The predictions of the Hebb–Marr conceptual framework concerning these cells (§11, §12, §13) are that they should respond in a graded fashion to variations in the instantaneous number of active input fibers, and that their response should be earlier than that of the principal cells by an amount that enables them to affect the output of the principal cells (i.e., division). As described earlier, these properties have been unambiguously verified in hippocampal inhibitory cells using variable electrical activation of groups of axons in the modifiable synaptic pathways. An additional major prediction is that these cells should convey little or no information in the response domain of the principal cells (§16). Their main firing correlate should be not *which* inputs are active, but *how many* of them are active. Figure 1.11 illustrates some examples of the spatial distributions of electrical discharge activity for these two classes of cell. Whereas pyramidal cell discharge is spatially restricted, the inhibitory cells are active wherever the animal moves in the apparatus. Moreover, they are most active during active movement through space, as opposed, for example, to motion associated with eating, grooming, and so forth. Because of the property of accommodation and possibly other effects, it is during *changes* in spatial location that the inputs are most active. Thus, under normal behavioral conditions, there is some proportionality between the number of active inputs and the output of the inhibitory cells (§12). The Hebb–Marr framework also appears to account for the fact that it is primarily the inhibitory interneurons that are modulated by a variety of subcortical inputs from systems whose main function appears to be an involvement in the mediation of "attention" and "arousal."

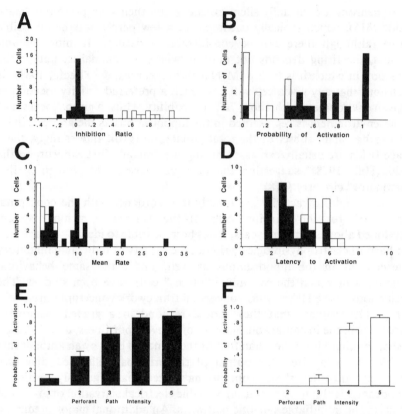

FIG. 1.10. (A) In experiments such as those described in Fig. 1.9, an "inhibition ratio" for the degree of suppression of unit discharge in response to the second synchronous input event was calculated as $(p_2-p_1)/(p_2+p_1)$, where p_1 and p_2 refer to the probabilities of cell discharge in response to the first and second stimuli. Two separate populations are revealed. One (open bars) is strongly inhibited during the second input, and thus corresponds to granule cells, the principal neurons of the network. The other population is virtually unaffected and thus cannot be granule cells. By default they are most likely the basket inhibitory cells.

(B,C,D) The cells classified as inhibitory interneurons according to the criterion of A exhibit a higher probability of activation for a given stimulus event, a higher mean spontaneous rate, and a considerably shorter latency to activation upon stimulation of the input pathway. All of these properties are consistent with the Hebb–Marr network hypothesis, and property D is required by it.

(E,F) Also as required by the Hebb–Marr hypothesis, the number of inhibitory cells (E) that respond to an input event is smoothly graded with the magnitude of the event (i.e., the number of activated fibers). The principle (granule) cells, on the other hand

The most critical requirement of the conceptual scheme is that the principal cells of the network exhibit the property of *pattern completion* (§18). As previously indicated, spatial behavior appears to be characterized by a property that might lead one to suspect that such pattern completion was being effected. These behaviors all appear to be very resistant to disruption by removal of subsets of the dominant spatial cues. It turns out that, in familiar situations, the firing characteristics of hippocampal place cells are likewise insensitive to removal of any particular subset of the distal visual cues that determine their firing fields. This has been most dramatically demonstrated by O'Keefe and Speakman (1987). They studied place cell activity in the same controlled spatial environment as described earlier for the spatial memory studies of O'Keefe and Conway; a "+" shaped maze within a curtained circular partition in which was distributed a set of controlled spatial cues. On each trial, the whole set of spatial cues was rotated at random relative to the laboratory, and the animal was required to locate one goal arm (fixed in relation to the controlled cues), having been started from one of the other three. In "memory" trials, once the animals were exposed to the current cue orientation, the cues were removed and the animals required to make their choice on the basis of memory for the last seen configuration. The animals had little difficulty, and made few errors. O'Keefe and Speakman showed that under these conditions, the hippocampal place fields were intact so long as the animals made correct choices. Moreover, when errors were made, the place fields tended to shift according to where the animal *thought* it was in relation to the cue array, as inferred from its choice.

A similar demonstration of this phenomenon was carried out using a radial arm maze of the sort already described (Jones Leonard, McNaughton, & Barnes, 1985). Several hippocampal cells were recorded simultaneously from the same animal over the course of about 2 weeks. Each cell had a clearly defined locational and directional firing bias that was stable over consecutive days. On one day, the animal was introduced into the maze with the room in total darkness, with steps being taken to ensure that it did not know its starting orientation. Rats, which are naturally

---

have a relatively sharp activation threshold during electrical stimulation of the input pathway (F). Such stimulation is equivalent to the random selection of input vectors of different sizes. As none of these vectors are likely to have been stored, the principle cells essentially do not respond except when the system is driven well above its normal operating level. Data from "A Comparison of Supramamillary and Medial Septal Influences on Hippocampal Field Potentials and Single Unit Activity" by S.J.Y. Mizumori, B.L. McNaughton, and C.A. Barnes, 1989, *Journal of Neurophysiology*, 61.

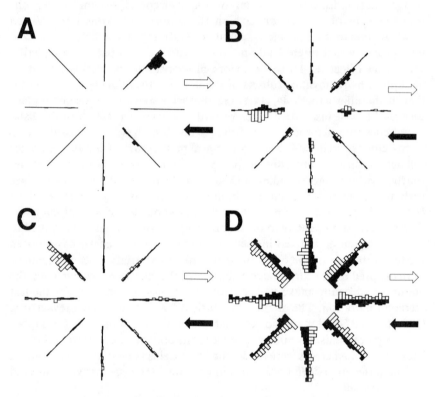

FIG. 1.11. In the pyramidal layers of the hippocampus, it is possible to distinguish the principal (pyramidal) cells from the inhibitory cells on the basis of physiological criteria (including those described in Fig. 1.9) during recordings made while the animal is freely moving on the radial eight-arm maze. Such recordings support the conjecture (§16) that, in a network that implements something like the Hebb–Marr algorithm, the principal cells should be quite selective on some information dimension (in this case spatial location), whereas the inhibitory cells should be nonselective on this dimension. Inhibitory cells should respond to *how many* rather than to *which* of the inputs are active.

A,B,C) Spatial firing plots for three different hippocampal pyramidal cells recorded during execution of a radial maze spatial task. Each radial histogram corresponds to a maze arm, and the location specific firing rates are computed separately for radially inward (filled bars) and radially outward (open bars) orientations of the rat.

D) Same as in A, B, and C except that data are from an inhibitory interneuron.

nocturnal, have no difficulty traversing the radial maze in darkness, making use of local tactile cues to identify their location with respect to the radial coordinate, in spite of their uncertainty about their angular coordinate (i.e., which arm they were on). Under these conditions, the hippocampal cells' firing biases were disrupted. One cell stopped firing altogether, another fired in the correct location and direction with respect to the radial coordinate, but on all of the arms. Yet another cell fired in the correct radial position but on the wrong arm. When the lights were turned on, all cells reverted to their normal firing fields. The room lights were then turned off again, and the animal was again allowed to traverse the maze. The only difference between these and the initial dark trials was that in this case the animals knew their initial orientation. Under these conditions, both the angular and radial coordinates of the firing specificity were maintained. These sorts of observations strongly suggest that the hippocampus and its ancillary circuitry are able to complete representations of local views of the environment given partial input. In addition, in familiar environments, they appear in some way to be able to update these representations on the basis of the animal's movements alone, and to plan appropriate motor trajectories in the complete absence of the sensory landmarks on which the spatial representation is based. How does the nervous system accomplish this remarkable feat?

Some important clues come from recordings from neurons outside of the hippocampus itself, in regions that send information to it. One of these, the presubiculum, is a major site of direct input to the entorhinal cortex. We also discuss the parietal association cortex, a polysensory/motor area that sends afferents indirectly to the presubiculum. The presubiculum contains a significant population of units called "head direction cells" (Taube, Muller, & Ranck, 1987). These cells are virtually silent except for a sharply tuned peak of activity whenever the animal's head is pointing in a particular direction, irrespective of its spatial location. Different cells have different direction vectors. These vectors are maintained even if the visual landmarks are removed in the animal's presence or the lights are extinguished, but they do rotate in the presence of the landmark array, if the latter itself is rotated relative to the geomagnetic compass (Barnes & McNaughton, unpublished observations). Clearly, such cells could form the basis of an inertial direction sense that computes head orientation, possibly in much the same way as eye position appears to be computed from vestibular inputs (e.g., Cannon, Robinson, & Shamma, 1983). As discussed earlier, such a sense could form the basis for computing a novel trajectory to a hidden goal on the basis of knowledge of its relation to a single distal landmark. Although we have very little idea about how this inertial direction system works, recordings carried out in the rat parietal cortex (McNaughton, Green, &

Mizumori, 1986; Chen & McNaughton, 1988) suggest at least part of the answer.

These recordings were made from neurons of the posterior parietal cortical area of rats while they traversed the radial maze. A few of these cells had a kind of location specificity that, unlike hippocampal place cells, required the presence of specific visual landmarks. More interesting in the present context, however, is the approximately 40% of cells in this region that generated discriminative responses according to whether the animal was turning left, turning right, or moving forward. An illustration of this activity is shown in Fig. 1.12. A few of these cells were even more striking in that they required both rotation of the head axis in one direction, and the presence of either some visual landmark or some feature local to the maze itself, thus indicating the presence of units representing specific conjunctions of movements and locations (Figs. 1.13 and 1.14). By passively moving the animal, it could be inferred that a number of these cells receive input from the vestibular system. Others appeared to receive their turn-direction information either from the somatosensory receptors in the animal's neck and trunk or from the direction of movement of the visual field. Still others appeared to have motor components, responding only to active turns by the animal (efference copy?). Many cells responded to various combinations of these inputs. In summary, the rat's parietal cortex appears to provide a robust and redundant representation of the mode of movement of the animal through its world.

There are two ways in which such movement representations might contribute to the sophisticated spatial capacities revealed by the behavioral studies discussed. Clearly, the presubicular head-direction cells must integrate information about angular movement in order to update their population direction vector and hence maintain the inertial direction sense. The necessary angular velocity information might be provided by the parietal cortex. It is also possible, however, that the parietal cortex movement cells play an important role in their own right in the generation of global spatial representations. Figure 1.15 illustrates one way this might work in abstract terms.

Suppose that, during exploration, the animals are able to make use of a kind of heteroassociation to learn the conditional relations between their current local view of the world and the preceding movements that brought them to it. Such a scheme can be thought of as a transition matrix in which stored representations of local views of the world are linked together by representations of the elementary movements that connect them. If, for example, the animal has learned that a left turn executed from position A results in position B, then, some time later, the neural state corresponding to the sensory inputs at position B could be recalled from the combination of the A state information and information from the motion representation of a left turn. The actual sensory input corresponding to B would, in

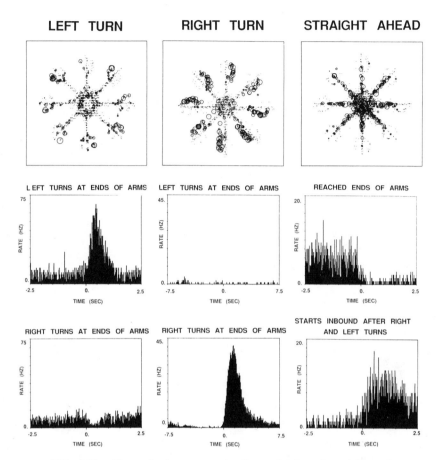

FIG. 1.12. Many single neurons in the parietal cortex of the rat appear to provide a robust representation of the animal's specific state of motion. Cells were recorded while the animals ran the radial eight-arm maze task. In the figure, each column illustrates data from a single cell. The uppermost portion of each column is a two-dimensional firing rate plot in which the locally computed firing rate is represented by the diameter of the corresponding circle. For the left and middle columns, the histograms reflect the average neural activity in the perievent interval for the onsets of left and right turns at the arm ends. For the right column, the histogram origins correspond to the cessation of forward motion as the animal moved outward, and the onset of inwardly directed forward motion following about turns at the arm-ends. Roughly 40% of cells recorded from a wide region of the parietal cortical area could reasonably be classified as selective for one of the three general modes of motion categorized as left-turns, right turns, or forward motion. Data from "Representation of Body-Motion Trajectory by Rat Sensory-Motor Cortex Neurons" by B.L. McNaughton, E. Green, and S.J.Y. Mizumori, 1986, *Society for Neuroscience Abstracts,* 12.

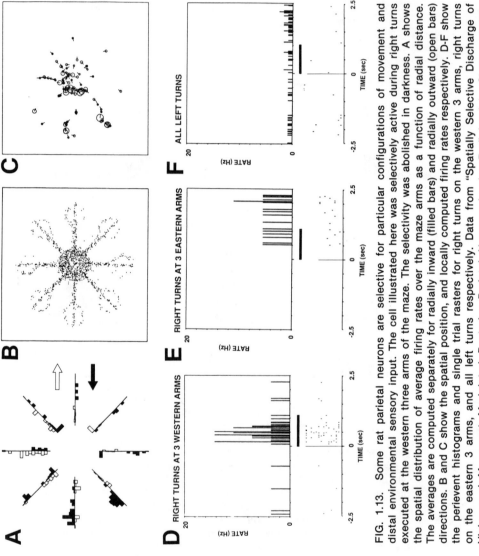

FIG. 1.13. Some rat parietal neurons are selective for particular configurations of movement and distal environmental sensory input. The cell illustrated here was selectively active during right turns executed at the western three arms of the maze. The selectivity was abolished in darkness. A shows the spatial distribution of average firing rates over the maze arms as a function of radial distance. The averages are computed separately for radially inward (filled bars) and radially outward (open bars) directions. B and C show the spatial position, and locally computed firing rates respectively. D-F show the perievent histograms and single trial rasters for right turns on the western 3 arms, right turns on the eastern 3 arms, and all left turns respectively. Data from "Spatially Selective Discharge of Vision and Movement Modulated Posterier Parietal Neurons in the Rat" by L.L. Chen and B.L.

52

principle, be unnecessary for the recall of the B state. Having updated the current spatial representation vector, subsequent movements could be used to recall images of other locations. This chaining of local view representations and movements could proceed in complete darkness or following the removal of the spatial cues as in O'Keefe and Speakman's experiments. Moreover, completely novel chains could be successfully executed, so long as the elemental conditional place-movement associations had been formed separately on prior occasions. All that is required is information about the starting position and orientation. With a little imagination, one can see how, in this general way, the consequences of possible motor sequences might be tested without actually executing them, and hence trajectories might be preplanned. With the addition of certain simple information about which movement sequences have spatially equivalent consequences, one can begin to see how apparently novel spatial trajectories and other insightful behaviors might be generated. For example, we have serendipitously observed one parietal cell that responded equally to 90° left and 270° right turns (McNaughton, 1989).

Recent observations (Fig. 1.16) support the importance of movement information in the representation of spatial relationships (Foster, Castro, & McNaughton, 1988). Using food reward, a group of rats was trained to tolerate complete body restraint implemented by wrapping the animal

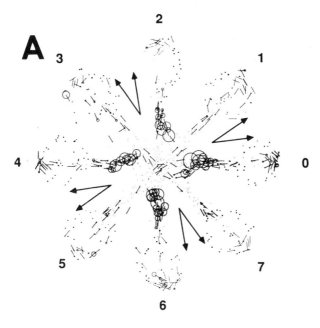

FIG. 1.14   (continued)

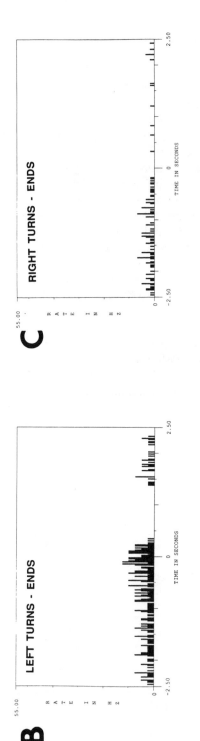

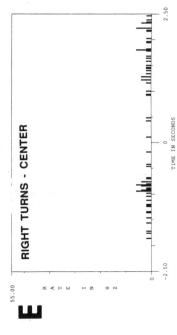

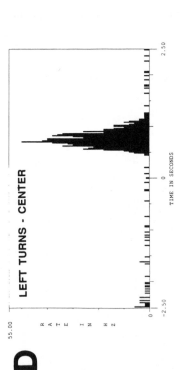

FIG. 1.14. Some rat parietal neurons are selective for particular configurations of movement and local environmental sensory input. The cell illustrated here was selectively active during the latter part of acute left turns executed in the maze center, but was not activated by left turns executed at the arm-ends. To illustrate this property, the animal was allowed access to only two adjacent arms at a time (indicated by pairs of arrows in the spatial rate plot in A), and rewarded for simply running repeatedly from the end of one arm to the end of the other. Thus, left turns were made into odd numbered arms and right turns were made into even numbered ones. The spatial firing rate plots (A) and the perievent histograms (B-D) illustrate that the fact activity was restricted to left turns in the center of the maze. (Unpublished data from Leonard, Barnes, & McNaughton)

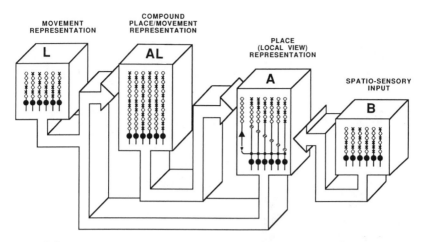

FIG. 1.15 Illustration of one working hypothesis concerning the way in which information about spatial location and orientation (as defined by unique constellations of distal and proximal sensory cues) might be combined with information about specific movements (e.g., left turn, right turn, or forward motion) to generate an associative representation of spatial relationships. In this hypothesis, an heteroassociative matrix is used whose forcing input, and corresponding output represent spatial locations such as can be observed in hippocampal pyramidal cells. The output of this system is combined with a simple motion representation, such as can be observed in many parietal neurons, to form representations of specific configurations of movements and locations (e.g., position **A** plus a left turn produces the specific configuration **AL**). Such configural representations can also be observed in parietal neurons. By projecting these place-motion configurations back to the matrix via modifiable synapses, these become associated with the spatial result of the most recently executed movement. In the present example, a left turn at location **A** is associated with a representation of location **B**. In principle, in a well-explored environment, all that is required is information about the starting location. Subsequent movements will elicit associative recall of the corresponding location representations, even in the absence of the spatial sensory information. A model such as this is sufficient to account for the fact that hippocampal spatial selectivity persists following removal of the spatial cues, provided that the animal is first shown its starting position relative to the cues. From "Neuronal Mechanisms for Spatial Computation and Information Storage" by B.L. McNaughton. In L. Nadel, L.A. Cooper, P. Culicover, and R.M. Harnish (Eds.), *Neural Connections and Mental Computation,* Cambridge: MIT Press/Bradford Books. Copyright 1989 by MIT Press/Bradford Books. Reprinted by permission.

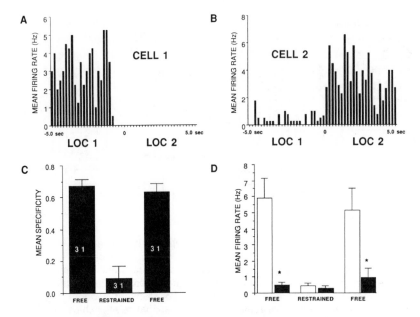

FIG. 1.16 Spatially selective activity of hippocampal neurons depends crucially on the state of the animal's motor system (i.e., "motor set"). The data illustrated here are from studies in which rats were trained to tolerate complete body restraint, implemented by wrapping the animal snugly in a hand towel fastened tightly with towel clips. The limbs were completely restrained, although head movements and myostatial sniffing were still possible. The animals learned to sit quietly without struggling under these conditions for periods of about 20 minutes, during which they could be picked up and moved from location to location. During the recording sessions, the unrestrained animals were first allowed to move freely about a table until a "place field" for the neuron under study was identified. The animals were then moved by hand repeatedly between the center of the place field and some neutral location, while unit activity was recorded. During this phase of the recording session, although the animals were free to move, there was little or no voluntary locomotion. Examples of data from two simultaneously recorded hippocampal neurons are shown in A and B. The "place field" for one cell served as the neutral location for the other and visa versa (**LOC1** and **LOC2**). The origins of the histograms represent the transition times from one location to the other. From such data, in-field and out-of-field firing rates were computed (open and closed bars in D), and a spatial specificity index was computed by dividing the difference of these measures by their sum (C).

Following assessment of specificity in the unrestrained condition, the animals were restrained and the procedure was repeated, with care being taken to orient the animals in the two locations

56

snugly in a hand-towel. This allowed slight head movements and sniffing, but completely restricted limb or body movement. The animals learned that struggling was useless and were rewarded for sitting still. Place cells were recorded, first while the animal was free to move about a platform, and subsequently under restraint, while the experimenter passively moved it through the same locations. Under the condition of suppressed motor activity, virtually all location selective cellular activity in the hippocampus was abolished. The normal selectivity returned as soon as the animals were once again free to move themselves through the space, even if they were not actually moving. These observations suggest that the existence of some-motor set or program is a fundamental determinant of the spatial representation generated by hippocampal circuitry.

CONCLUDING COMMENTS

For many years it has been known that the rodent hippocampus exhibits a periodic oscillation between activity and quiescence whenever the animal engages in behaviors, such as walking or other forms of exploration or sensory scanning. This oscillation, known as the theta rhythm, has a fundamental frequency of about 6-8 Hz, and can be recorded as a global fluctuation in the electric field of the hippocampus (i.e., the EEG). Hippocampal inhibitory interneurons are also known as theta cells because their activity fluctuates in phase with this rhythm. When the animal is in the appropriate location, place cells also fire with the same phase relationship. This characteristic of hippocampal system dynamics can be interpreted in terms of the overall Hebb–Marr framework. Conjecture §19 expressed the general idea that, during the process of active associative recall, a recurrent network such as the hippocampal formation might benefit from some mechanism that periodically shut down the network globally. This would

---

in exactly the same manner as in the unrestrained condition. The animals were then released from restraint, and the procedure was repeated a third time to assess recovery.

Restraint almost completely suppressed in-field firing, as shown by the spatial specificity measures in C and the mean firing rate measures in D (open and filled bars represent in-field and out-of-field rates respectively).

These data indicate that, in spite of the fact that specific movements appear not to be represented by hippocampal cells, there appears to be a very strong relation between hippocampal spatial information processing and the state of the motor system. Data from "Influence of Motor Set on Hippocampal Complex Spike Cell Activity" by T.C. Foster, C.A. Castro, and B.L. McNaughton, 1988, *Society for Neuroscience Abstracts, 14.*

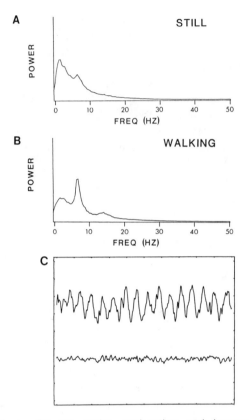

FIG. 1.17. In the rat, active exploration and locomotion are accompanied by a rhythmical oscillation of the gross electrical activity (EEG) of the hippocampal formation. This oscillation, known as the theta rhythm, is reflected in a sharp peak in the power spectrum of the EEG at about 7 Hz during walking (B) as compared to when the animal is sitting quietly (A). Normally, the activities of both principal neurons and inhibitory cells throughout the hippocampal formation are phase locked to this rhythm. Thus the rhythm reflects the periodic global silencing of the network during the time that important environmental information is arriving. The Hebb–Marr formalism for recurrent autoassociation (Fig. 1.5c) provides a possible explanation for this phenomenon, because it requires that incoming information be presented to a silent network in order for efficient recall to occur.

Recent studies by Mizumori and colleagues (1988) have shown that the theta rhythm can be totally but reversibly abolished by applying microinjections (0.5 μl) of a local anaesthetic (lidocaine) to the medial septal nucleus, a major source of subcortical modulatory input to the hippocampus. The upper and lower traces in C illustrate the EEG during walking in the normal animal and under lidocaine block respectively. During the period of blockade

terminate the reverberatory activity from the previous recall operation, and prepare the system for the arrival of the next input. Without this, the various states would interfere, making pattern completion difficult. Recently it has been found that the theta rhythm can be temporarily abolished (Fig. 1.17) by injecting submicroliter volumes of a local anaesthetic similar to novacaine into one of the subcortical sources of modulatory afferents to the hippocampus (the medial septal nucleus). During the 15 to 20 minutes that the theta rhythm is abolished, the animal's memory capacity is severely impaired. Nevertheless, the spatial selectivity of the hippocampal pyramidal cells, in the presence of the usual visual landmarks, is virtually unaffected (Mizumori, McNaughton, Barnes, & Fox, 1987). Thus, the periodic excitability change associated with the theta rhythm appears not to be required for principal cells to respond to their proper inputs, but is necessary for the expression of the system's memory function.

In this chapter we have discussed aspects of spatial cognition and how these might be implemented in the nervous system. Current research on "neural" networks has provided a wealth of sophisticated formal models for understanding associative memory and computation in the nervous system. Even the simplest of these models, for example the Hebb–Marr formulation, appears to provide a remarkably encompassing framework for the interpretation of neurobiological data. The success of this approach in accounting for a wealth of neurobiological phenomena, including many that were unknown at the time the models were generated, stands as a lasting tribute to the extraordinary prescience of these early pioneers.

ACKNOWLEDGMENTS

Preparation of this manuscript and some of the experimental work described were supported by grants from the National Science Foundation (BNS8617464), the National Institute for Communicative Disorders and Stroke (R01-NS20331) and the Sloan Foundation. We also thank G. Rao for assistance with figure preparation.

REFERENCES

Andersen, P. Bliss, T. V. P., & Skrede, K. (1971). Lamellar organization of hippocampal excitatory pathways. *Experimental Brain Research, 13,* 222–238.

---

of the theta rhythm, which lasts for 15 to 20 minutes, the ability of the animal to perform a spatial memory task on the eight-arm maze is very severely disrupted. Performance recovers in parallel with the recovery of the theta rhythm. (unpublished data in A from Green et al., 1989, and in C from Mizumori et al., 1987).

Ashwood, T. J., Lancaster, B., & Wheal, H. V. (1984). In vivo and in vitro studies on putative interneurons in the rat hippocampus: Possible mediators of feed-forward inhibition. *Brain Research, 293,* 279–291.

Barnes, C. A. (1979). Memory deficits associated with senescence: A neurophysiological and behavioral study in the rat. *Journal of Comparative and Physiological Psychology, 93,* 74–104.

Barnes, C. A. (1988). Spatial learning and memory processes: the search for their neurobiological mechanisms in the rat. *Trends in Neurosciences, 11,* 163–169.

Barnes, C. A., Nadel, L., & Honig, W. K. (1980). Spatial memory deficit in senescent rats. *Canadian Journal of Psychology, 34,* 29–39.

Baum, E. B., Moody, J., & Wilczek, F. (1988). Internal representations for associative memory. *Biological Cybernetics, 59,* 217–228.

Bliss, T. V. P., & Gardner-Medwin, A. R. (1973). Long-lasting potentiation of synaptic transmission in the dentate area of the unanaesthetised rabbit following stimulation of the perforant path. *Journal of Physiology, 232,* 357–374.

Bliss, T. V. P., & Lomo, T. (1973). Long-lasting potentiation of synaptic transmission in the dentate area of the anaesthetised rabbit following stimulation of the perforant path. *Journal of Physiology, 232,* 331–356.

Cannon, S. C., Robinson, D. A., & Shamma, S. (1983). A proposed neural network for the integrator of the oculomotor system. *Biological Cybernetics, 49,* 127–136.

Chen, L. L., & McNaughton, B. L. (1988). Spatially selective discharge of vision and movement modulated posterior parietal neurons in the rat. *Society for Neuroscience Abstracts, 14,* 818.

Claiborne, B. J., Amaral, D. G., & Cowan, W. M. (1986). A light and electron microscopic analysis of the mossy fibers of the rat dentate gyrus. *The Journal of Comparative Neurology, 246,* 435–458.

Collett, T. S., Cartwright, B. A., & Smith, B. A. (1986). Landmark learning and visuo-spatial memories in gerbils. *Journal of Comparative Physiology A, 158,* 835–851.

Cooper, L. A., Gibson, B. S., Mowafy, L., & Tataryn, D. J. (1987). *Mental extrapolation of perceptually-driven spatial transformations.* Paper presented to the Psychonomic Society, Seattle.

Cowan, J. D., & Sharp, D. H. (1988). Neural nets. *Quarterly Review of Biophysics,* 365–427.

Evarts, E. V., Shinoda, Y., & Wise, S. P. (1984). *Neurophysiological approaches to higher brain functions.* New York: Wiley.

Foster, T. C., Castro, C. A., & McNaughton, B. L. (1988). Influence of motor set on hippocampal complex spike activity. *Society for Neuroscience Abstracts, 14,* 396.

Fox, S. E., & Ranck, J. B., Jr. (1981). Electrophysiological characteristics of hippocampal complex-spike cells in dorsal hippocampal formation of rats. *Experimental Neurology, 49,* 299–313.

Gallistel, C. R. (1980). *The organization of action: a new synthesis.* Hillsdale, NJ: Lawrence Erlbaum Associates.

Georgopoulos, A. P., Schwartz, A. B., & Kettner, R. E. (1986). Neuronal population coding of movement direction. *Science, 233,* 1416–1419.

Georgopoulos, A. P., Lurito, J. T., Petrides, M., Schwartz, A. B., & Massey, J. T. (1989). Mental rotation of the neuronal population vector. *Science, 243,* 234–236.

Green, E. J., McNaughton, B. L., Keith, J. R., & Barnes, C. A. (1989). Exploration dependent modulation of synaptic responses in fascia dentata. II. Dissociation of motor and sensory factors, and evidence for a synaptic conductance change. Manuscript submitted for publication.

Hausser, C. O., Robert, F., & Giard, N. (1980). Balint's syndrome. *Canadian Journal of Neurological Science, 7,* 157–161.

Hebb, D. O. (1949). *The organization of behavior.* New York: Wiley.

Hill, A. J. (1978). First occurrence of hippocampal spatial firing in a new environment. *Experimental Neurology, 62,* 282–297.

Holst, E. von, & Mittelstaedt, H. (1950). Das Reafferenzprinzip. Wechselwirkung zwischen Zentralnervensystem und Peripherie. *Naturwissenschaften, 37,* 464–476. (Translated in *The behavioral physiology of animals and man: Selected papers of E. von Holst.* Vol. 1. Coral Gables, FL: University of Miami Press, 1973).

Hopfield, J. J. (1982). Neural networks and physical systems with emergent collective computational abilities. *Proceedings of the National Academy of Sciences, 79,* 2554–2558.

Jones Leonard, B., McNaughton, B. L., & Barnes, C. A. (1985). Long-term studies of place field interrelationships in dentate gyrus neurons. *Society for Neuroscience Abstracts, 11,* 1108.

Keith, J. R., & McVety, K. M. (1988). Latent place learning in a novel environment and the influences of prior training in rats. *Psychobiology, 16,* 146–151.

Kohonen, T. (1972). Correlation matrix memories. *IEEE Transactions on Computers,* C-21, 353–359.

Kohonen, T. (1978). *Associative memory: A system-theoretic approach.* New York: Springer-Verlag.

Kohonen, T. (1988). *Self-Organization and Associative memory.* New York: Springer-Verlag.

Landfield, P. W., & Deadwyler, S. A. (Eds.). (1987). *Long-term potentiation: From biophysics to behavior.* New York: A. R. Liss.

Mackintosh, N. J. (1965). Overtraining, transfer to proprioceptive control, and position reversal. *Quarterly Journal of Experimental Psychology, 17,* 26–36.

Marr, D. (1969). A theory of cerebellar cortex. *Journal of Physiology, 202,* 437–470.

Marr, D. (1970). A theory for cerebral neocortex. *Proceedings of the Royal Society (Lond.) B, 176,* 161–234.

Marr, D. (1971). Simple memory: A theory for archicortex. *Philosophical Transactions of the Royal Society (Lond.) B, 262,* 23–81.

Matthews, B. L., Campbell, K. A., & Deadwyler, S. A. (1988). Rotational stimulation disrupts spatial learning in fornix-lesioned rats. *Behavioral Neuroscience, 102,* 35–42.

McCulloch, W. S., & Pitts, W. (1943). A logical calculus of the ideas immanent in nervous activity. *Bulletin of Mathematical Biophysics, 5,* 115–133.

McNaughton, B. L. (1983). Activity dependent modulation of hippocampal synaptic efficacy: Some implications for memory processes. In W. Seifert (Ed.), *Neurobiology of the hippocampus.* New York: Academic Press.

McNaughton, B. L. (1987). Neural association of movement and space: preliminary steps toward a non-cartographic theory of spatial representation and learning. *Neuroscience Letters* Suppl., *29,* S143–S144.

McNaughton, B. L. (1989). Neuronal mechanisms for spatial computation and information storage. In L. Nadel, L. A. Cooper, P. Culicover, & R. M. Harnish (Eds.), *Neural connections and mental computation.* Cambridge, MA: MIT Press/Bradford Books.

McNaughton, B. L., Barnes, C. A., & Andersen, P. (1981). Synaptic efficacy and EPSP summation in granule cells of rat fascia dentata studied *in vitro. Journal of Neurophysiology, 46,* 952–966.

McNaughton, B. L., Barnes, C. A., & O'Keefe, J. (1983). The contribution of position, direction and velocity to single unit activity in the hippocampus of freely-moving rats. *Experimental Brain Research, 52,* 41–49.

McNaughton, B. L., Barnes, C. A., Rao, G., Baldwin, J., & Rasmussen, M. (1986). Long-term enhancement of hippocampal synaptic transmission and the acquisition of spatial information. *Journal of Neuroscience, 6,* 563–571.

McNaughton, B. L., Green, E., & Mizumori, S. J. Y. (1986). Representation of body-motion trajectory by rat sensory-motor cortex neurons. *Society for Neuroscience Abstracts, 12,* 260.

McNaughton, B. L., & Morris, R. G. M. (1987). Hippocampal synaptic enhancement and information storage within a distributed memory system. *Trends in Neurosciences, 10,* 408–415.

Means, L. W., & Douglas, R. J. (1970). Effects of hippocampal lesions on cue utilization in spatial discrimination in rats. *Journal of Comparative and Physiological Psychology, 73,* 254–260.

Milner, P. M. (1957). The cell assembly: Mark II. *Psychological Review, 64,* 242–252.

Mittelstaedt, M. L., & Mittelstaedt, H. (1980). Homing by path integration in a mammal. *Naturwissenschaften, 67S,* 566.

Mizumori, S. J. Y., McNaughton, B. L., & Barnes, C. A. (1989). A comparison of supramammillary and medial septal influences on hippocampal field potentials and single unit activity. *Journal of Neurophysiology, 61,* 1–17.

Mizumori, S. J. Y., McNaughton, B. L., Barnes, C. A., & Fox, K. B. (1987). Reversible inactivation of hippocampal afferents selectively reduces the spontaneous discharge rate of dentate units. *Society for Neuroscience Abstracts, 13,* 1102.

Morris, R. G. M. (1981). Spatial localization does not require the presence of local cues. *Learning and Motivation, 12,* 239–261.

Morris, R. G. M., Garrud, P., Rawlins, J. N. P., & O'Keefe, J. (1982). Place navigation impaired in rats with hippocampal lesions. *Nature, 297,* 681–683.

Munn, N. L. (1950). *Handbook of psychological research on the rat.* Cambridge: Riverside Press.

Neiworth, J. J., & Rilling, M. E. (1987). A method for studying imagery in animals. *Journal of Experimental Psychology: Animal Behavior Processes, 13,* 203–214.

O'Keefe, J. (1976). Place units in the hippocampus of the freely moving rat. *Experimental Neurology, 51,* 78–109.

O'Keefe, J. (1989). Computations the hippocampus might perform. In L. Nadel, L. A. Cooper, P. Culicover, & R. M. Harnish (Eds.), *Neural connections and mental computation.* Cambridge, MA: MIT Press/Bradford Books.

O'Keefe, J., & Conway, D. H. (1980). On the trail of the hippocampal engram. *Physiological Psychology, 8,* 229–238.

O'Keefe, J., & Dostrovsky, J. (1971). The hippocampus as a spatial map. Preliminary evidence from unit activity in the freely-moving rat. *Brain Research, 34,* 171–175.

O'Keefe, J., & Nadel, L. (1978). *The hippocampus as a cognitive map.* Oxford: Oxford University Press.

O'Keefe, J., & Speakman, A. (1987). Single unit activity in the rat hippocampus during a spatial memory task. *Experimental Brain Research, 68,* 1–27.

Olton, D. S., Becker, J. T., & Handelmann, G. E. (1979). Hippocampus, space and memory. *The Behavioral and Brain Sciences, 2,* 313–365.

Olton, D. S., & Samuelson, R. J. (1976). Remembrance of places passed: spatial memory in rats. *Journal of Experimental Psychology: Animal Behavior Processes, 2,* 97–116.

Pico, R. M., Gerbrandt, L. K., Pondel, M., & Ivy, G. (1985). During stepwise cue deletion, rat place behaviors correlate with place unit responses. *Brain Research, 330,* 369–372.

Rochester, N., Holland, J. H., Haibt, L. H., & Duda, W. L. (1956). Tests on a cell assembly theory of the action of the brain, using a large digital computer. *IRE Transactions on Information Theory, IT-2,* 80–93.

Sharp, P. E. (1987). *Effects of environmental manipulations on perforant path-evoked dentate granule cell population responses in the rat.* Unpublished doctoral dissertation, department of psychology, University of Colorado.

Sharp, P. E., Barnes, C. A., & McNaughton, B. L. (1987). Effects of aging on environmental modulation of hippocampal evoked responses. *Behavioral Neuroscience, 101,* 170–178.

Sharp, P. E., McNaughton, B. L., & Barnes, C. A. (1985). Enhancement of hippocampal field potentials in rats exposed to a novel, complex environment. *Brain Research, 339,* 361–365.

Sharp, P. E., McNaughton, B. L., & Barnes, C. A. (in press). Exploration dependent modulation of evoked responses in fascia dentata: fundamental observations and time course. *Psychobiology*.

Shepard, R. N. (1989). Internal representation of universal regularities: A challenge for connectionism. In L. Nadel, L. A. Cooper, P. Culicover, & R. M. Harnish (Eds.), *Neural connections and mental computation*. Cambridge, MA: MIT Press/Bradford Books.

Shepard, R. N., & Cooper, L. A. (1982). *Mental images and their transformations*. Cambridge, MA: MIT Press/Bradford Books.

Shepard, R. N., & Metzler, J. (1971). Mental rotation of three-dimensional objects. *Science, 171*, 701–703.

Sloviter, R. S. (1987). Decreased hippocampal inhibition and a selective loss of interneurons in experimental epilepsy. *Science, 235*, 73–76.

Squire, L. R., Shimamura, A. P., & Amaral, D. G. (in press). Memory and hippocampus. In J. Byrne & W. Berry (Eds.), *Neural models of plasticity*. New York: Academic Press.

Steinbuch, K. (1961). Die Lernmatrix. *Kybernetik, 1*, 36–45.

Sutherland, R. J. (1985). The navigating hippocampus: An individual medley of space, memory, and movement. In G. Buzsaki & C. Vanderwolf (Eds.), *Electrical activity of the archicortex*. Budapest: Hungarian Academy of Sciences Press.

Sutherland, R. J., Whishaw, I. Q., & Kolb, B. (1983). A behavioral analysis of spatial localization following electrolytic, kainate- or colchicine-induced damage to the hippocampal formation in the rat. *Behavioral Brain Research, 7*, 133–153.

Sutton, R. S., & Barto, A. G. (1981). Toward a modern theory of adaptive networks: Expectation and prediction. *Psychological Review, 88*, 135–170.

Swanson, L. W., Kohler, C., & Bjorklund, A. (1987). The limbic region. I. The septohippocampal system. In A. Bjorklund, T. Hokfelt, & L. W. Swanson (Eds.), *Handbook of chemical neuroanatomy. Vol. 5: Integrated systems of the CNS, Part 1*. New York: Elsevier.

Swanson, L. W., Teyler, T. J., & Thompson, R. F. (1982). Hippocampal long-term potentiation: Mechanisms and implications for memory. *Neurosciences Research Program Bulletin, 20*, 613–765.

Taube, J. S., Muller, R. U., & Ranck, J. B., Jr. (1987). A quantitative analysis of head-direction cells in the postsubiculum. *Society for Neuroscience Abstracts, 13*, 1332.

Thinus-Blanc, C., Bouzouba, L., Chaix, K., Chapuis, N., Durup, M., & Poucet, B. (1987). A study of spatial parameters encoded during exploration in hamsters. *Journal of Experimental Psychology: Animal Behavior Processes, 13*, 418–427.

Walker, E. L., Dember, W. N., Earl, R. W., & Karoly, A. J. (1955). Choice alternation: I. Stimulus vs. place vs. response. *Journal of Comparative and Physiological Psychology, 48*, 19–23.

Willshaw, D. J., Buneman, O. P., & Longuet-Higgins, H. C. (1969). Nonholographic associative memory. *Nature, 222*, 960–962.

Winson, J., & Abzug, C. (1977). Gating of neuronal transmission in the hippocampus: efficacy of transmission varies with behavioral state. *Science, 196*, 1222–1225.

Winson, J., & Abzug, C. (1978a). Neuronal transmission through the hippocampal pathways dependent upon behavior. *Journal of Neurophysiology, 41*, 716–732.

Winson, J., & Abzug, C. (1978b). Dependence upon behavior of neuronal transmission from perforant pathway through entorhinal cortex. *Brain Research, 147*, 422–427.

Witter, M. P., & Groenewegen, H. J. (1988). *A new look at the hippocampal connectional network*. Paper presented to the European Neuroscience Association, Zürich.

2

Molecular Mechanisms for Synaptic Modification in the Visual Cortex: Interaction Between Theory and Experiment

Mark F. Bear and Leon N. Cooper
Center for Neural Science and Physics Department
Brown University

INTRODUCTION

As this volume attests, in the last several years we have witnessed an explosion of interest in computational neural network models of learning and memory. In each of these models information is stored in the "synaptic" coupling between vast arrays of converging inputs. Such distributed memories can be shown to display many properties of human memory: recognition, association, generalization, and resistance to the partial destruction of elements within the network. An interesting feature of these models is that the performance is constrained by the patterns of connectivity within the network. This reinforces the view, long held by neurobiologists, that an understanding of neural circuitry holds a key to elucidating brain function. Hence, modern neural network models attempt to incorporate the salient architectural features of the brain regions of interest. However, another crucial aspect of network function concerns the way that the synaptic junctions are modified to change their strength of coupling. Most models have assumed a form of modification based on Hebb's (1949) proposal that synaptic coupling increases when the activity of converging elements is coincident. Variations on this venerable "learning rule" have been enormously successful in simulations of various forms of animal learning. However, this work has also shown that just as network behavior depends on connectivity, the capabilities of the network vary profoundly with different modification rules. What forms of synaptic modification are most appropriate? Again, we must look to the brain for the answer.

Concurrent with the recent developments in neural network theories of

65

learning and memory has been the experimental demonstration of experience-dependent synaptic plasticity at the highest level of the mammalian nervous system, the cerebral neocortex. A neurobiological problem of extraordinary interest is to identify the molecular mechanisms that underlie this process of cortical modification. For the complex forms of plasticity evoked in neocortex by changes in the sensory environment, an essential first step in sorting out the various possibilities is to derive a set of rules that can adequately account for the observed modifications. These rules serve as a guide toward identifying candidate mechanisms that can then be tested experimentally. Hence, it can be seen that two lines of inquiry — one concerning neural network theory, the other concerning molecular mechanisms of synapse modification — converge at the level of the modification rule.

We have proposed such a modification rule to explain the rich body of experimental evidence available on the experience-dependent plasticity of the feline visual cortex during early postnatal development. This theoretical form of modification is able to account for the results of a wide variety of visual deprivation experiments, and has led to a number of predictions that appear to have been confirmed by more recent experiments. In this chapter we illustrate how this theory has interacted with experiment to suggest a possible molecular basis for synapse modification in the visual cortex.

ANALYSIS OF VISUAL CORTICAL PLASTICITY

The central visual pathway arises at the two retinae with the axonal projections of retinal ganglion cells into the optic nerves (Fig.2.1). The first central synaptic relay occurs in the lateral geniculate nucleus (LGN) of the dorsal thalamus. The lateral geniculate projects via the optic radiation to the primary visual cortex, otherwise known as striate cortex or area 17.

Neurons in the striate cortex of normal adult cats respond selectively to the visual presentation of oriented bars of light and most are activated by stimulation of either eye (Hubel & Wiesel, 1962). Both of these properties — orientation selectivity and binocularity — can be modified by visual experience during a critical period of early postnatal development that, in the cat, extends from approximately 3 weeks to 3 months of age (Frégnac & Imbert, 1984; Sherman & Spear, 1982). The problem of visual cortical plasticity can be divided into three parts. First, what controls the onset and duration of the critical period? The answer to this question is unknown at present, but some interesting possibilities include specific patterns of gene expression (Neve & Bear, 1988; Sur, Frost, & Hockfield, 1988) which may be under hormonal control (Daw, Sato, & Fox, 1988). Second, within the plastic period, what factors enable synaptic modification to proceed? This ques-

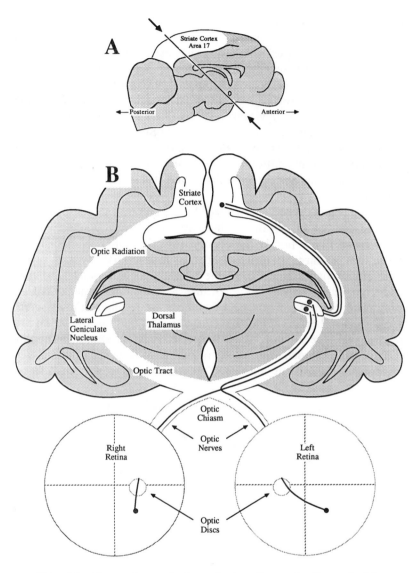

FIG. 2.1. The retino-geniculo-cortical pathway in the cat. (a) Mid-sagittal view of a cat brain. The primary visual cortex, also called striate cortex or area 17, lies on the medial wall of the postlateral gyrus. If the brain were cut in the plane indicated by the two arrows, the resulting cross-section would reveal the major components of the primary visual pathway, as illustrated in (b). Visual information arising at homotypic points in the two retinae (points viewing the same region of visual space) remains segregated in the lateral geniculate nucleus. Cortical neurons are responsive to stimulation of either eye due to the convergence of geniculocortical projections.

tion is prompted by the observation that experience-dependent modifications of visual cortex seem to require that animals attend to visual stimuli and use vision to guide behavior (Singer, 1979). The best candidates for "enabling factors" are the neuromodulators acetylcholine and norepinephrine that are released in visual cortex by fibers arising from neurons in the basal forebrain and brain stem (Bear & Singer, 1986). Third, when modifications are allowed to occur during the critical period, what controls their direction and magnitude? This is where the interaction between theory and experiment has been most fruitful, and this is the question we address in this chapter.

Kitten striate cortex, illustrated in Fig.2.2, is a well-differentiated structure with six layers and an intricate intracortical connectivity whose details remain only poorly understood (Martin, 1987). Nonetheless, it is known that the large majority of neurons in layers III, IV and VI receive direct monosynaptic input from the lateral geniculate nucleus (Ferster & Lindstrom, 1983; Martin, 1987; Toyama, Matsunami, Ohmo, & Tokashiki, 1974). The receptive fields of LGN neurons resemble those of retinal ganglion cells: they are monocular (i.e., they respond to stimulation of only one eye) and, for the most part, lack selectivity for stimulus orientation. Hence, cortical binocularity results from the convergence of lateral geniculate inputs onto cortical neurons. This convergence is not equal for every

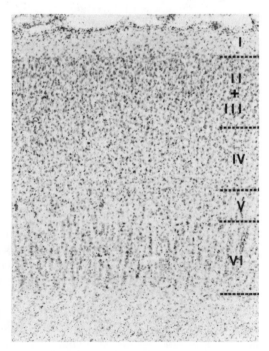

FIG. 2.2. Photomicrograph of a cross section of kitten area 17. This section was stained with Cresyl violet, which reveals the distribution of neuronal cell bodies. The six cortical layers are indicated. Magnification = 50x.

neuron and the term *ocular dominance* is used to describe the relative contribution of the two eyes to the cell's response. Although intracortical inhibition is acknowledged to play an important role in the refinement of orientation selectivity (Ramoa, Paradiso, & Freeman, 1988; Sillito et al., 1980), there is evidence that this property is also generated by the pattern of convergence of LGN inputs onto cortical neurons (Ferster, 1986; Hubel & Wiesel, 1962). Thus, in the first stage of the theoretical analysis, there is some justification for stripping away much of the complexity of the striate cortex, and considering a single cortical neuron receiving converging inputs from the two eyes via the LGN (Fig.2.1).

Cortical binocularity can be disrupted by a number of manipulations of visual experience during the critical period. For example, if the eyes are misaligned by severing one of the extraocular muscles, then cortical neurons lose their binocularity and become responsive only to one eye or the other (Blakemore & van Sluyters, 1974). Likewise, if one eye is deprived of patterned visual input (usually by suturing the eyelid closed), the ocular dominance of cortical neurons shifts such that most cells become responsive exclusively to stimulation of the open eye (Wiesel & Hubel, 1965). These changes in cortical binocularity can occur quite rapidly and are presumed to reflect the modification of the synaptic effectiveness of the converging inputs from the two eyes.

The consequences of binocular deprivation on visual cortex stand in striking contrast to those observed after monocular lid closure. First, binocular deprivation leads to a loss of orientation selectivity, an effect never seen after monocular deprivation. Second, although a week of monocular deprivation during the second postnatal month leaves few neurons in striate cortex responsive to stimulation of the deprived eye, most cells remain responsive to visual stimulation through either eye after a comparable period of binocular deprivation (Wiesel & Hubel, 1965). Thus, it is not merely the absence of patterned activity in the deprived geniculo-cortical projection that causes the decrease in synaptic efficacy after monocular deprivation.

Gunther Stent (1973) pointed out that one difference between monocular and binocular deprivation is that only in the former instance are cortical neurons active. This consideration led him to hypothesize that evoked postsynaptic activity is a necessary condition for synaptic modification in the striate cortex, and the sign of the change (+ or −) depends on the concurrent level of presynaptic input activity. Synaptic disconnection of afferent inputs deprived of patterned activity occurs only after monocular deprivation because only under these conditions are cortical neurons still driven by visual stimulation (through the open eye). Subsequent work suggested, however, that the generation of action potentials in a cortical neuron does not ensure that ocular dominance modifications will occur after monocular deprivation (Bear & Singer, 1986; Kasamatsu & Pettigrew, 1979; Singer, 1982). To reconcile these data with the Stent model, Wolf Singer (1979) introduced the idea that there is a critical level of postsynaptic activation that must be reached before experience-dependent modifications will occur, and that this threshold is higher than the depolarization required for somatic sodium-spikes. A similar type of modification rule has been proposed for the activity-dependent synaptic changes in the dentate gyrus (Levy, Colbert & Desmond, chap. 5 in this volume). According to this hypothesis, the "enabling factors" mentioned could be any inputs that render cortical neurons more excitable and hence more likely to exceed this "plasticity threshold" (Bear & Singer, 1986; Greuel, Luhman, & Singer, 1987).

This hypothesis is challenged by the finding that the effects of monocular deprivation can be rapidly reversed by opening the deprived eye and suturing closed the other eye. Such a "reverse suture" leads to a robust ocular dominance shift back to the newly opened eye, even though visually evoked postsynaptic activity is low or absent at the time of the reversal (because the only source of patterned visual input to cortical neurons is the functionally disconnected afferents from the unsutured eye). The effects of reducing cortical inhibition on ocular dominance modification are also difficult to explain by this hypothesis. Intracortical infusion of bicuculline, an antagonist of the inhibitory neurotransmitter γ-aminobutyric acid (GABA) that decreases orientation selectivity and generally increases cortical responsiveness, retards rather than facilitates the functional disconnection of the deprived eye after monocular deprivation (Ramoa et al., 1988).

Reiter and Stryker (1988) recently performed a direct test of the hypothesis that postsynaptic activation is simply permissive to the process of synaptic modification. They continuously infused muscimol into striate cortex as kittens were monocularly deprived for 7 days. Muscimol is a GABA receptor agonist that prohibits cortical neurons from firing, presumably by clamping the membrane near the chloride equilibrium potential. With the muscimol still present in cortex, they mapped the cortex to determine the extent of activity blockade. They found that all cortical cell responses were eliminated within several millimeters of the infusion cannula, even though LGN fiber activity was readily demonstrated. When the muscimol wore off, they measured the ocular dominance of neurons in the zone of cortex whose activity had been blocked. They observed an unexpected ocular dominance shift toward the deprived eye; that is, most neurons were no longer responsive to stimulation of the retina that had been more active during the period of monocular deprivation.

Although all experiments involving chronic intracortical drug infusion must be interpreted with extreme caution, these muscimol results seem to indicate that ocular dominance modifications can occur in the absence of evoked action potentials. Furthermore, the data suggest that patterned presynaptic activity can lead to either an increase or a decrease in synaptic strength, depending on whether or not the target neurons are allowed to respond.

An alternative theoretical solution to the problem of visual cortical plasticity, proposed by Cooper, Liberman, and Oja (1979), is able to account for these varied results. According to this theory, the synaptic efficacy of active inputs increases when the postsynaptic target is concurrently depolarized beyond a "modification threshold", θ_M. However, when the level of postsynaptic activity falls below θ_M, then the strength of active synapses decreases.

An important additional feature was added to this theory in 1982 by Bienenstock, Cooper, and Munro (BCM). They proposed that the value of the modification threshold is not fixed, but instead varies as a nonlinear function of the average output of the postsynaptic neuron. This feature provides the stability properties of the model, and is necessary to explain, for example, why the low level of postsynaptic activity caused by binocular deprivation does not drive the strengths of all cortical synapses to zero.

This form of synaptic modification can be written:

$$dm_j / dt = \phi (c, \bar{c}) d_j$$

where m_j is the efficacy of the jth LGN synapse onto a cortical neuron, d_j is the level of presynaptic activity of the jth LGN afferent, c is the level of activation of the postsynaptic neuron,[1] and $\bar{c}$ is the time average of postsynaptic neuronal activity (d_j and c are viewed as averages over about half a second; $\bar{c}$ is the average over a period that could be several hours). The crucial function, ϕ, is shown in Fig.2.3.

One significant feature of this model is the change of sign of ϕ at the modification threshold, θ_M. When the jth synapse is active ($d_j > 0$) and the level of postsynaptic activation exceeds the modification threshold ($c > \theta_M$), then the sign of the modification is positive and the strength of the synapse increases. However, when the jth synapse is active and the level of postsynaptic activation slips below the modification threshold ($c < \theta_M$), then the sign of the modification is negative and the strength of the synapse decreases. Thus, effective synapses are strengthened and ineffective synapses are weakened, where synaptic effectiveness is determined by whether or not the presynaptic pattern of activity is accompanied by the simulta-

---

[1]In a linear approximation, $c = \mathbf{m}^l \cdot \mathbf{d}^l + \mathbf{m}^r \cdot \mathbf{d}^r$, where $\mathbf{d}$ and $\mathbf{m}$ are vectors representing the total input activity and synaptic weight of the array of fibers carrying information from the left or right eyes.

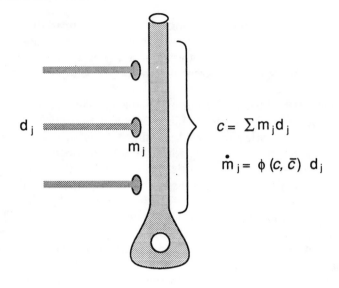

$$c = \sum m_j d_j$$

$$\dot{m}_j = \phi(c, \bar{c})\, d_j$$

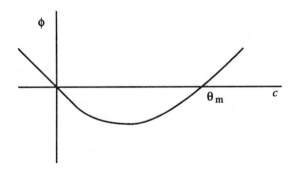

FIG. 2.3.   TOP: Cartoon of a cortical neuron receiving LGN input
to illustrate the BCM theoretical notation. BOTTOM: The BCM
modification function.

neous depolarization of the target dendrite beyond the modification
threshold.

   According to this model, synaptic weakening requires that the postsynaptic membrane potential falls below the modification threshold. Thus,
during monocular deprivation, the deprived-eye synapses will decrease in
strength each time the open-eye input activity does not strongly depolarize
the cortical neuron. This occurs when the input patterns conveyed by the
open-eye afferents fail to match the stimulus selectivity of the neuron.

Therefore, the theory predicts a relationship between the ocular dominance shift after monocular deprivation and the degree of orientation tuning of cortical neurons.

The application of bicuculline to cortex, by reducing the stimulus selectivity of cortical neurons, increases the probability that the unstructured activity from the deprived eye correlates with cortical activation at or beyond the modification threshold. Therefore, in agreement with experimental results (Ramoa, Paradiso, & Freeman, 1988), the theory predicts that no synaptic disconnection of deprived-eye afferents would occur when cortex is disinhibited. On the other hand, muscimol treatment would suppress the postsynaptic response well below the modification threshold regardless of the afferent input. In accordance with experimental observations of Reiter and Stryker (1988) the theory would predict an ocular dominance bias toward the less active eye.

Another significant feature of this theory is that the value of the modification threshold (θ_M) is not fixed, but instead varies as a nonlinear function of the average output of the cell ($\bar{c}$). In a simple situation:

$$\theta_M = (\bar{c})^2$$

This feature allows neuronal responses to evolve to selective and stable "fixed points" (Bienenstock, Cooper, & Munro, 1982). However, more importantly in the context of the present discussion, it is this feature of the theory that accounts for the differences between monocular and binocular deprivation. Deprivation of patterned input leads to synaptic disconnection after monocular deprivation because open-eye input activity continues to drive cortical neurons sufficiently to maintain θ_M at a high value. However, because average cortical activity falls during binocular deprivation, the value of θ_M approaches zero (Fig.2.4). In this case, the unstructured input activity causes synaptic strengths to perform a "random walk" (Bienenstock et al., 1982). Consequently, the theory also predicts the loss of orientation selectivity that has been observed after binocular deprivation.

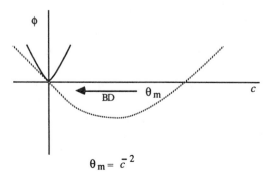

FIG. 2.4. A period of binocular deprivation (BD) decreases the value of the modification threshold, and therefore changes the shape of ϕ.

The sliding modification threshold also permits a theoretical explanation for the effects of reverse suture. The output of a cortical neuron in area 17 approaches zero just after the reversal because its only source of patterned input is through the eye whose synapses had been weakened as a consequence of the prior monocular deprivation. However as $\bar{c}$ diminishes, so does the value of θ_M. Eventually, the modification threshold attains a value below the small output that is evoked by stimulation of the unsutured eye, allowing these active synapses to increase in strength. If θ_M does not adjust to the new average firing rate too rapidly, the cell's response to the previously open eye will diminish before its response to the newly opened eye increases.

Analysis and computer simulations using this theoretical form of synaptic modification are able to reproduce the classical results of manipulating visual experience during the critical period (Bienenstock et al., 1982; Clothiaux, Bear, & Cooper, 1988). The theory can account for the acquisition of orientation selectivity with normal visual experience as well as the effects of monocular deprivation, binocular deprivation, and reverse suture. In addition, as we have seen, this form of modification offers a solution to the seemingly paradoxical effects of pharmacologically manipulating cortical activity during monocular deprivation. It is worthwhile to note that there need not be any modification of inhibitory circuitry to account for the experience-dependent modifications in striate cortex using this theory (Cooper & Scofield, 1988). This is reassuring because experimental efforts to uncover modifications of inhibitory circuits in visual cortex have consistently yielded negative results (Bear, Schmechel, & Ebner, 1985; Mower, White, & Rustad, 1987; Singer, 1977).

The success of this theory encourages us to ask whether this form of synaptic modification has a plausible neurobiological basis. The remainder of this chapter summarizes the progress we have made in answering this question (as of October 1988).

A Molecular Mechanism
for Increasing Synaptic Strength in Visual Cortex

According to the theory, synaptic strength increases when presynaptic inputs are active ($d > 0$) and the target dendrite is depolarized beyond the modification threshold ($c > \theta_M$). The relevant measure of input activity is likely to be the rate of transmitter release at the geniculocortical synapses. Although the exact identity of this transmitter substance is still not known with certainty, available evidence indicates strongly that it acts via excitatory amino acid receptors (Tsumoto, Masui, & Sato, 1986). This leads to the following question: When excitatory amino acid receptors are activated, what distinguishes the response at depolarized membrane potentials ($c > \theta_M$) from the response at the resting potential ($c < \theta_M$)?

As elsewhere, cortical excitatory amino acid receptors fall into two broad categories: NMDA and non-NMDA. Both types of excitatory amino acid receptor are thought to coexist subsynaptically (Fig.2.5). The ionic conductances activated by non-NMDA receptors at any instant depend only on the input activity, and are independent of the postsynaptic membrane potential. However, the ionic channels linked to NMDA receptors are blocked with Mg^{++} at the resting potential, and become effective only upon membrane depolarization (Mayer & Westbrook, 1987; Nowak et al., 1984). Another distinctive feature of the NMDA receptor channel is that it will conduct calcium ions (Dingledine, 1984; MacDermott et al., 1986). Hence, the

POSTSYNAPTIC RESPONSE TO GLUTAMATE

(1) AT RESTING MEMBRANE POTENTIAL

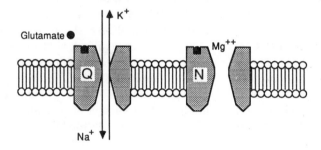

(2) AT DEPOLARIZED MEMBRANE POTENTIALS

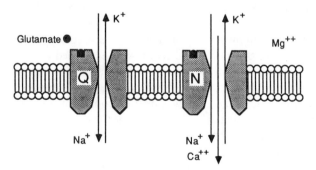

FIG. 2.5.   Cartoon to illustrate the two types of excitatory amino acid (EAA) receptor and the ionic conductances they activate. Glutamate acts at all subtypes of EAA receptor and is likely to be the neurotransmitter at geniculocortical synapses. Note that the binding of glutamate to the NMDA (N) receptor activates a calcium conductance, but only when the Mg^{++} block is lifted at depolarized membrane potentials. Q is meant to represent the quisqualate subtype of EAA receptor.

passage of Ca^{++} through the NMDA channel could specifically signal when pre- and postsynaptic elements are concurrently active. These considerations have led us to propose that θ_M relates to the dendritic membrane depolarization at which presynaptic activity leads to a critical postsynaptic Ca^{++} flux, and that the Ca^{++}, acting as a second messenger, leads to an enhancement of synaptic strength (Bear, Cooper, & Ebner, 1987).

Data from *in vitro* brain slice experiments lend strong support to this hypothesis. Long-term potentiation (LTP) of synaptic effectiveness that normally results from tetanic afferent stimulation cannot be induced in either the CA1 subfield of the hippocampus (Collingridge, Kehl, & McLennan, 1983; Harris, Ganong, & Cotman, 1984) or the visual cortex of rats (Artola & Singer, 1987; Kimura, Tsumoto, Nishigori, & Shirokawa, 1988) and kittens (Connors & Bear, 1988) when NMDA receptors are blocked (see also Granger, Ambrose-Ingerson, Staubli, & Lynch, Chap. 3 in this volume). On the other hand, the application of N-methyl-D-aspartate (the selective agonist that gives the NMDA receptor its name) to hippocampal slices can induce a form of synaptic potentiation that can last for 30 minutes (Kauer, Malenka, & Nicoll, 1988) or longer (Thibault et al., 1988). The idea that elevations in postsynaptic Ca^{++} trigger the increase in synaptic strength is supported by the finding that intracellular injection of the Ca^{++} chelator EGTA, which essentially removes ionic calcium, blocks the induction LTP in CA1 pyramidal cells (Lynch et al., 1983). Furthermore, the intracellular release of Ca^{++} from the photolabile calcium chelator nitr-5 produces a long-lasting potentiation of synaptic transmission that resembles LTP (Malenka, Kauer, & Nicoll, 1988). Taken together, these data indicate that the calcium conductance mediated by the NMDA receptor plays a special role in strengthening synaptic relationships in the cortex.

The possible involvement of NMDA receptors in the experience-dependent modification of visual cortex was examined in a recent series of experiments carried out in Wolf Singer's laboratory (Kleinschmidt, Bear, & Singer, 1987). The selective NMDA receptor antagonist 2-amino-5-phosphonovaleric acid (APV) was infused continuously into striate cortex as kittens were monocularly deprived (Fig.2.6). After 7 days the APV treatment was stopped and the cortex 3-6 mm away from the infusion cannula was assayed electrophysiologically for changes in ocular dominance and orientation selectivity. The APV treatment was found to produce a concentration-dependent increase in the percentage of neurons with binocular, unoriented receptive fields (Fig.2.7). Qualitatively, the results resembled those expected in visual cortex after binocular deprivation. Yet, electrophysiological recordings during the week of APV infusion revealed that NMDA receptor blockade did not eliminate visual responsiveness in striate cortex.

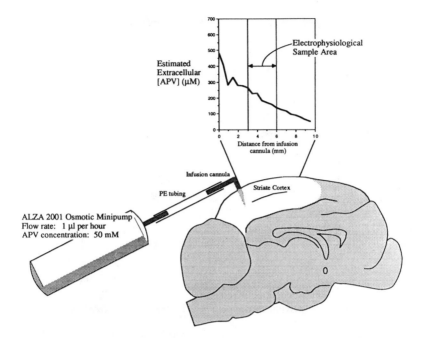

FIG. 2.6. Method used by Kleinschmidt, Bear, and Singer (1987) to block cortical NMDA receptors *in vivo.* Osmotic minipumps were implanted that could deliver the NMDA receptor antagonist APV to the visual cortex at a rate of 50 nmol per hour for 7 days. As indicated, the extracellular APV concentration in the cortex varies as a function of distance from the infusion cannula. As a rule, sites were studied electrophysiologically between 3 and 6 mm from the infusion cannula where APV concentrations were approximately 200 μM.

According to the "NMDA hypothesis" (Bear et al., 1987) APV infusion should, in effect, raise the value of θ_M. If cortical neurons remain moderately responsive to visual stimulation, but are unable to achieve θ_M, then a theoretical consequence will be a modified "random walk".[2] This will result in a loss of orientation selectivity and a slow loss of synaptic efficacy—a result similar to that of binocular deprivation.

However, if the postsynaptic response is low, the predicted effect of NMDA receptor blockade during monocular deprivation is a loss of

---

[2]This effect requires that **d** have positive and negative components. According to Bienenstock, Cooper, and Munro (1982), when input fibers are spontaneously active, **d** = 0; when they carry noise (an effect of lid suture or dark rearing), **d** averages to zero. In a patterned input environment, **d** has positive and negative components, but the average is likely to be greater than zero.

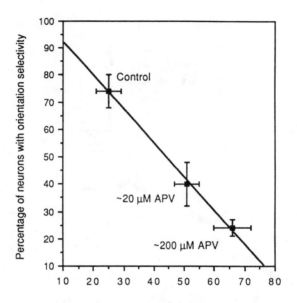

FIG. 2.7. The effects of NMDA receptor blockade on the response of visual cortex to monocular deprivation. Increasing extracellular concentrations of APV (estimated concentrations are indicated) increases the percentage of neurons with binocular, unoriented receptive fields. Data from "Blockade of 'NMDA' Receptors Disrupts Experience-Dependent Modifications of Kitten Striate Cortex" by A. Kleinschmidt, M. F. Bear, and W. Singer, 1987, *Science, 238*. Reprinted with permission.

synaptic strength at a rate proportional to the level of presynaptic activity. This could explain the observations of Reiter and Stryker (1988), assuming that the hyperpolarization produced by muscimol treatment renders cortical NMDA receptors ineffective. In a recent study, APV infusion was also found to have this effect (Bear et al., 1989). In this experiment, the cortex was studied at various distances from the infusion cannula after 2 days of monocular deprivation and APV treatment. The ocular dominance of units studied within 3 mm of the cannula, where APV concentrations are highest (Fig.2.6), was found to be strongly biased toward the deprived eye (Fig.2.8). Most neurons were binocular at sites ≥ 4 mm from the cannula.

To summarize, available experimental evidence supports the hypothesis that the consolidation or strengthening of at least some geniculocortical synapses depends on the activation of NMDA receptors. This molecular mechanism is consistent with the BCM theory assuming that NMDA receptors become sufficiently active to increase synaptic strength only

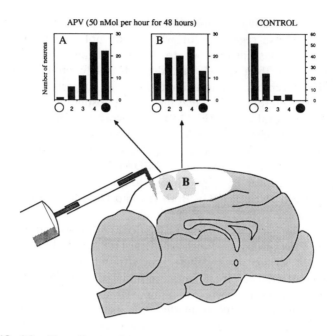

FIG. 2.8. The effects of high (APV) on the cortical response to monocular deprivation. At the top of this figure are ocular dominance histograms; bar height indicates the number of neurons in each ocular dominance category. Filled and open circles indicate the ocular dominance categories containing neurons responsive only to deprived-eye or open-eye stimulation, respectively. Neurons in category 3 were equally responsive to stimulation of either eye; neurons in categories 2 and 4 were binocularly activated, but showed a preference for stimulation of the open or deprived eyes, respectively. Note that within 3 mm of the infusion cannula (A), most neurons responded preferentially to stimulation of the eye that had been deprived of normal patterned vision.

when the postsynaptic target is depolarized beyond the modification threshold, θ_M.

A Molecular Mechanism
for Decreasing Synaptic Strength in Visual Cortex

The theory states that when the postsynaptic depolarization falls below the modification threshold then synaptic strengths decrease at a rate proportional to input activity. What signals input activity when the membrane is hyperpolarized and the NMDA channel is fully blocked with Mg^{++}?

Certainly the activity of non-NMDA receptors reflects the amount of transmitter release regardless of whether or not NMDA receptors are effective. This has inspired us to search for an intracellular second messenger other than Ca^{++} that depends solely on the activation of non-NMDA receptors. One possibility has been suggested by recent investigations of excitatory amino acid mediated phosphoinositide (PIns) turnover in the cerebral cortex (Fig.2.9). This work has shown that during a finite period of postnatal development, stimulation of rat hippocampus (Nicoletti et al., 1986) or neocortex (Dudek, Bowen, & Bear, 1988) with glutamate or ibotenate (but not NMDA) leads to the hydrolysis of phosphatidyl inositol-4,5 biphosphate to produce inositol triphosphate (IP_3) and diacyl glycerol (DG). Both IP_3 and DG function as intracellular second messengers (Berridge, 1984).

Of particular interest is the age-dependence of the excitatory amino acid stimulated PIns turnover. Dudek and Bear (1989) found very recently that in the kitten striate cortex, there is a striking correlation between the developmental changes in ibotenate-stimulated PIns hydrolysis and the susceptibility of visual cortex to monocular deprivation (Fig.2.10). It is difficult to resist the suggestion that this mechanism is likely to play a central role in the modification of cortical synapses during the critical period.

At present there is not a shred of evidence to indicate the nature of this role. However, the theory suggests one interesting possibility. Namely, that the stimulation of PIns hydrolysis by non-NMDA receptor activation leads to a decrease in synaptic strength. According to this hypothesis, changes in synaptic efficacy would result from changes in a balance between NMDA receptor mediated Ca^{++} entry and non-NMDA receptor mediated PIns turnover (Bear, 1988). Synaptic strength would increase when the NMDA

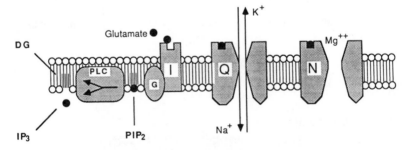

FIG. 2.9. Recently characterized EAA receptor site (I) that is linked to PIns turnover. The receptor is linked via a G protein to the enzyme phospholipase C (PLC) which hydrolyzes phosphatidyl inositol-4,5 biphosphate (PIP_2) to produce inositol triphosphate (IP_3) and diacyl glycerol (DG). Both IP_3 and DG function as intracellular second messengers.

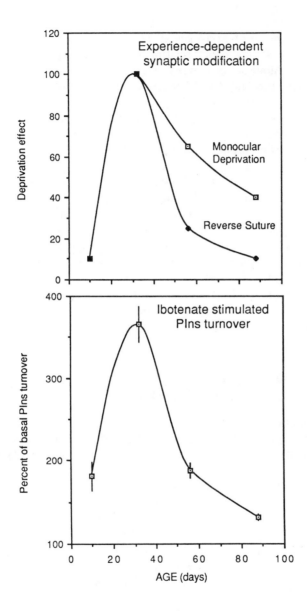

FIG. 2.10. TOP: Visual cortical plasticity as a function of age, estimated by Blakemore and van Sluyters (1974) using reverse suture and Olson and Freeman (1980) using monocular deprivation. BOTTOM: Postnatal changes in ibotenate stimulated PIns turnover in kitten striate cortex (from Dudek & Bear, submitted for publication).

signal exceeds the non-NMDA signal. This occurs when the input activity is coincident with strong depolarization $(c > \theta_M)$. Synaptic strength would decrease when input activity consistently correlates with insufficient membrane depolarization $(c < \theta_M)$ because the non-NMDA signal exceeds the NMDA signal.

Although this hypothesis was formulated purely on theoretical grounds (Bear, 1988), some recent work in Carl Cotman's laboratory supports the idea that the second messenger systems linked to NMDA and non-NMDA receptors might be antagonistic (Palmer et al., 1988). They find in the neonatal hippocampus that NMDA inhibits excitatory amino acid stimulated PIns turnover in a Ca^{++} dependent fashion.

To summarize, the theory states that synaptic strength decreases when input activity fails to coincide with postsynaptic depolarization beyond the modification threshold. In the previous section, we argued that this occurs when NMDA receptor activation falls below a critical level. Recent experimental evidence suggests that input activity in the absence of NMDA receptor activation is a favorable condition for the hydrolysis of membrane inositol phospholipids. These considerations lead us to suggest that phosphoinositide hydrolysis might provide the biochemical trigger for decreases in synaptic efficacy.

A Molecular Mechanism
for the Sliding Modification Threshold

A critical feature of this theory of synapse modification is that θ_M, the level of dendritic depolarization at which the sign of the synaptic modification changes, floats as a nonlinear function of average cell activity $(\bar{c})$. θ_M is "quasi-local," in the sense that it has the same value at all synapses on a given neuron (Bear, et al., 1987; Bienenstock et al., 1982). Thus, we search for a molecular mechanism that would provide a signal that is (a) uniformly available throughout the dendritic tree and (b) is regulated by average neuronal activity.

One mechanism that fits this description is the activity-dependent expression of specific neuronal genes (Black et al., 1987). Indeed, Neve and Bear (1988) recently demonstrated that visual experience can regulate gene expression in the kitten striate cortex. For example, the mRNA transcript for the neuronal growth associated protein GAP43 (Benowitz & Routtenberg, 1987) was found to be increased by rearing kittens in complete darkness. Moreover, this increase in GAP43 gene expression was reversed by only 12 hours of light exposure (Fig.2.11).

According to the molecular model developed so far, adjustments of the modification threshold conceivably could occur by changing the balance between the synaptic reward and punishment signals generated by the

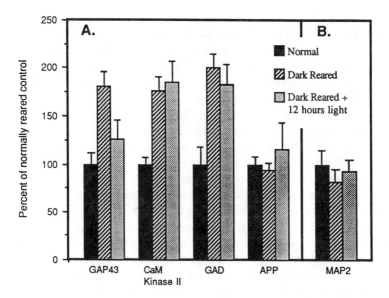

FIG. 2.11. Expression of growth associated protein GAP43, calcium calmodulin dependent protein kinase II (CaM kinase II), glutamic acid decarboxylase (GAD) and Alzheimer amyloid precursor protein (APP) genes in striate cortex of dark-reared and age-matched normal kittens (postnatal day 40–50). In order to reduce the variance, all individual values in (A) are normalized against those for the MAP2 gene, which did not change significantly under the conditions tested (B). Data from "Visual Experience Regulates Gene Expression in the Developing Striate Cortex" by R. L. Neve and M. F. Bear, 1988. *Proc Nat Acad Sci USA.*

NMDA and non-NMDA receptors, respectively. Therefore, we have focused our search on the products of activity-dependent gene expression that could potentially affect this balance. Calcium-calmodulin dependent protein kinase II (CaM kinase II) is one such molecule. CaM kinase II is a major constituent of the postsynaptic density, and is a critical link in the biochemical cascade of events that is triggered by Ca^{++} entry. It is not difficult to imagine how changes in the level of CaM kinase might alter the effectiveness of NMDA receptor mediated Ca^{++} signals. Indeed, in the striate cortex of dark-reared kittens, Neve and Bear (1988) found that the CaM kinase transcript is elevated over control levels. Similarly, Hendry and Kennedy (1988) found in primate visual cortex that immunoreactive CaM kinase II is increased in columns deprived of normal input after monocular deprivation.

Another way to change the balance between NMDA and non-NMDA receptors is to alter the effectiveness of the receptors in generating second messengers. For the NMDA receptor this could be accomplished in several ways, including changes in the properties of the ion channel (MacDonald, Salter, & Mody, 1988) or of the binding sites (Lodge, Aram, & Fletcher, 1988). Due to this abundance of potential regulatory mechanisms, we decided to address this issue using a functional assay of receptor effectiveness: NMDA-stimulated uptake of ^{45}Ca into slices of kitten visual cortex maintained *in vitro* (Sherin, Feldman, & Bear, 1988).

We predicted that under conditions where the modification threshold had a low value, slices of visual cortex should show heightened sensitivity to applied NMDA. One such condition is binocular deprivation. In Fig.2.12, the NMDA stimulated calcium uptake of slices from normal kittens is compared with that measured in slices from animals binocularly deprived for 4 days. There is a significant decrease in the maximum Ca^{++} uptake evoked by saturating concentrations of NMDA in slices from binocularly deprived kittens (Fig.2.12a). One simple explanation for this result is a decrease in the total number of NMDA receptors in binocularly deprived striate cortex, perhaps reflecting a global loss of synaptic strength. However, if this is the case, then uptake in slices from binocularly deprived animals should be lower at all concentrations of NMDA. Yet, at low concentrations (12.5-25 μM) the measured uptake is the same for normal and binocularly deprived cortex. Thus, it is possible that the NMDA receptors that remain in BD cortex might be relatively more effective in generating a calcium signal. This is illustrated in Fig.2.12b, where uptake from control and BD kittens is expressed as a percentage of maximal uptake. It is clearly premature to draw any firm conclusions from these data because calcium uptake depends on a complex interaction between NMDA and voltage-gated calcium entry, as well as on calcium extrusion and sequestration. Nonetheless, this work indicates that this question is worth exploring in more detail, perhaps now with receptor binding techniques.

Although still in its infancy, this work has already been able to show that the changes in average cortical activity produced by visual deprivation lead to alterations in gene expression and NMDA stimulated calcium uptake. Thus, the biological precedent for a sliding threshold mechanism in striate cortex is now established. Future work will be aimed at teasing out which changes are relevant for experience-dependent synaptic modification.

A molecular model that captures the essence of the BCM theory is presented in Fig.2.13. According to this model, the efficacy of an active synapse increases when the postsynaptic signal generated by NMDA receptor activation ("N," probably Ca^{++}) exceeds the signal produced by the activation of non-NMDA receptors ("Q," possibly a product of PIns turnover). This occurs when the summed postsynaptic depolarization ($\Sigma m_j d_j$) is greater than the modification threshold (θ_M). When the level of postsynaptic depolarization falls below the modification threshold, N < Q and the synapse weakens. Considered in this way, the modification

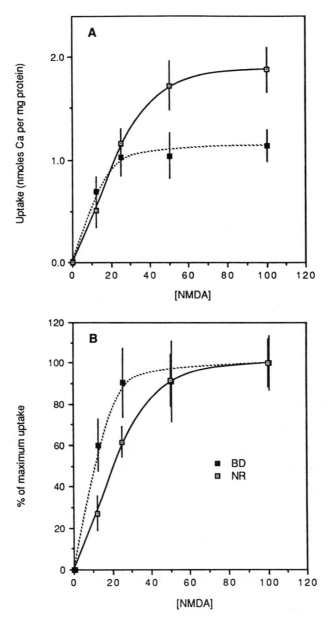

FIG. 2.12. Slices of visual cortex were prepared and maintained *in vitro,* and uptake of ^{45}Ca was monitored as different concentrations of NMDA were applied for 2 minutes. Shown here is NMDA stimulated ^{45}Ca uptake by slices of striate cortex from normally reared 4- to 6-week-old kittens and age-matched kittens that had been binocularly deprived for 4 days prior to sacrifice. In A uptake is expressed in nmoles per mg protein; in B uptake is expressed as the percentage of maximum uptake. Data from "NMDA-evoked Calcium Uptake by Slices of Visual Cortex Maintained In Vitro" by J. E. Sherin, D. Feldman, and M. F. Bear, 1988, *Neuroscience Abstracts,* 14.

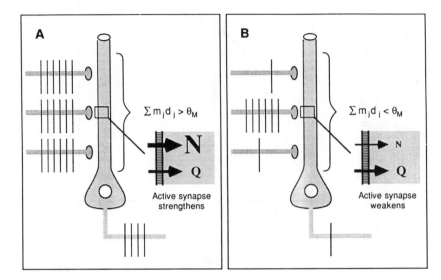

FIG. 2.13. A molecular model for synapse modification in the striate cortex. According to this model, changes in the efficacy of an active synapse depend on the balance between postsynaptic signals linked to activation of NMDA ("N") and non-NMDA ("Q") receptors. See text for further explanation.

threshold becomes the critical level of postsynaptic depolarization at which the NMDA receptor dependent Ca^{++} flux is sufficient to balance the synaptic "punishment" produced by activation of non-NMDA receptors. We imagine that whether or not a given Ca^{++} flux is sufficient possibly depends on the availability of postsynaptic Ca^{++}-activated enzymes that, in turn, depends on the regulation of gene expression by average neuronal activity (Bear, 1988).

Generalization to a Many-neuron System

The BCM theory of synaptic modification deals with a single cortical neuron receiving input from the lateral geniculate nucleus only. The second stage of the theoretical analysis requires that relevant intracortical connections be incorporated into the model. Consider the simple network illustrated in Fig.2.14a in which cortical neurons (both excitatory and inhibitory) receive input from the LGN and from each other. The integrated output of the ith neuron (in the linear region) may be written

$$c_i = m_i^1 \cdot d^1 + m_i^r \cdot d^r + \Sigma L_{ij} c_j \qquad (3)$$

where the term $\Sigma L_{ij} c_j$ is the sum of the output from other cells in the network multiplied by the strength of their synapses on the ith cell. It is assumed that the intracortical synapses do not modify, or modify only slowly, and that the net influence of the intracortical connections is inhibitory.

Analysis of geniculocortical modification in this network leads to a very complex set of coupled nonlinear stochastic equations (Scofield & Cooper, 1985). However a mean-field approximation permits dramatic simplification of these equations (Cooper & Scofield, 1988). In a manner similar to the theory of magnetism, the individual effects of other cortical neurons are replaced by their average effect. The integrated output of the ith cortical neuron now becomes

$$c_i = (\mathbf{m}_i^1 - \alpha^1) \cdot \mathbf{d}^1 + (\mathbf{m}_i^r - \alpha^r) \cdot \mathbf{d}^r \tag{4}$$

$$= (m_i - \alpha)d \tag{5}$$

where $-\alpha$ represents the average inhibitory influence of the intracortical connections (Fig.2.14b).

There is an interesting theoretical consequence of assuming that each cortical neuron is under the influence of an inhibitory mean field. According to the BCM theory, monocular deprivation leads to convergence of geniculocortical synapses to a state where stimulation of the deprived eye input results in an output that equals zero ($c = 0$). However, with average network inhibition, the evolution of the cell to this state does not require that the efficacy of deprived-eye synapses be driven completely to zero. Instead, these excitatory synapses will evolve to a state where their influence is exactly offset by intracortical inhibition. Thus, the removal of intracortical inhibition in this network would reveal responses from otherwise ineffective inputs. This result is in accordance with the experimental observation of "unmasking" of synapses when the inhibitory effects of GABA are antagonized with bicuculline (Duffy, Snodgrass, Burchfiel, & Conway, 1976).

No revisions in the molecular model (Fig.2.13) are required to incorporate the mean field theory, although it is clear that the balance between NMDA and non-NMDA receptor activation will vary depending on network inhibition. α depends on the average connection strengths of intracortical synpases (L_o), which are assumed to not be modified, and the spatial average of the geniculocortical synapses "viewing" the same point in visual space, which changes only slowly (in comparison with the modification of m_j). Hence, in simulations of the evolution of the cortical network, α remains relatively constant from iteration to iteration.

However, it is interesting to note that if the value of α were to vary as a

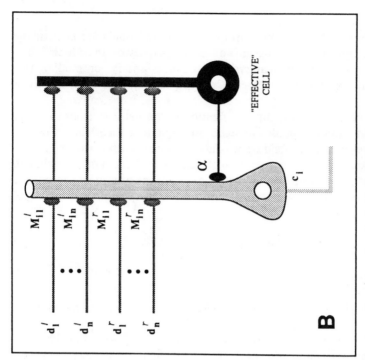

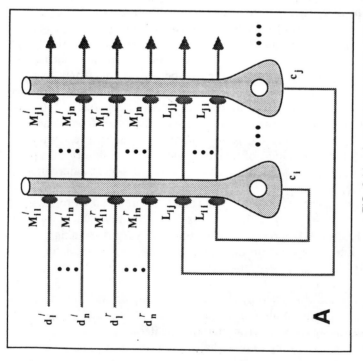

FIG. 2.14. A neural network in which every neuron receives inputs from the LGN and from each other. In B, using a mean field approximation, all other cortical neurons are replaced by an "effective cell," and the individual effects of the intracortical connections are replaced by their average effect (α), assumed to be inhibitory.

function of the timing of coherent inputs, the model could account for the changes in hippocampal synapses induced by patterned electrical stimulation (see Granger, Ambros-Ingerson, Staubli & Lynch, chap. 3 in this volume). Input activity coincident with $\alpha = 0$ (which, according to Larson and Lynch [1986], occurs when hippocampal inputs are stimulated at theta frequency) would be more likely to depolarize the neuron beyond θ_M and consequently would increase synaptic strength (Fig.2.15a). Conversely, input activity patterned in such a way as to coincide with strong inhibition ($\alpha > > 0$) should yield a depression of synaptic strength (Fig.2.15b). Such an effect has been reported very recently by Stanton and Sejnowski (1988) in hippocampus.

CONCLUDING REMARKS

We have presented a theoretical model for synaptic modification that can explain the results of normal rearing and various deprivation experiments in visual cortex. Further, we have shown that crucial concepts of the theory have a plausible molecular basis. Although some of this work is in a preliminary state, it provides an excellent illustration of the benefit of the interaction of theory with experiment.

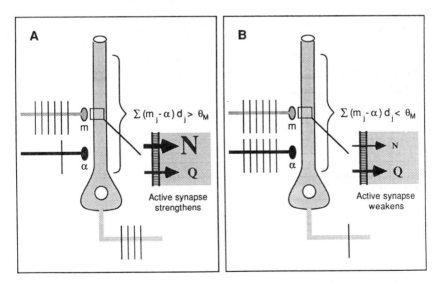

FIG. 2.15.   Incorporation of inhibition into the model of Fig. 2.13. When input activity is coincident with strong inhibition (B), the balance of postsynaptic second messenger signals favors the non-NMDA receptors, and the active geniculocortical synapses weaken.

Theory enables us to follow a long chain of arguments and to connect, in a fairly precise way, various hypotheses with their consequences. It forces us to refine our language so that questions can be formulated with clarity and precision. Experiment focuses our attention on what is real; it separates what might be from what is; it tells us what must be explained and what is possible among explanations.

The theoretician who develops his arguments with close attention to the experimental results may thereby create a concrete structure of sufficient clarity so that new questions, of great interest and amenable to experimental verification, become apparent. The sliding threshold provides an excellent example. The concept of the modification threshold was introduced to account for such classical results as the development of neuron selectivity in normal visual environments and the various deprivation experiments. This led to unexpected theoretical consequences such as the correlation between ocular dominance and selectivity (now supported experimentally) and is sufficient to explain the results of the various pharmacological experiments.

Once convinced of the utility of this concept, the question of its physical basis became of great interest. This led us to the efforts concerning NMDA receptors, phosphoinositide turnover and regulation of gene expression in visual cortex (on a grander scale, Gregor Mendel's concept of the gene, introduced to explain the color of the sweet peas in his garden, was sufficiently attractive to provoke the activity that finally resulted in our present understanding of gene structure). And, as is almost always the case for an idea of richness, when the physical basis of the abstract concept is finally delineated, it contains a wealth of detail, subtlety, and possibility for manipulation that would have been not only impossible but ludicrous as part of the original proposal.

ACKNOWLEDGMENTS

The work on which this article is based was supported in part by the Office of Naval Research, the National Eye Institute, and the Alfred P. Sloan Foundation

REFERENCES

Artola, A., & Singer, W. (1987). Long-term potentiation and NMDA receptors in rat visual cortex. *Nature, 330,* 649–652.

Bear, M. F. (1988) Involvement of excitatory amino acid receptors in the experience-dependent development of visual cortex. In E. A. Cavalheiro, J. Lehman, & L. Turski (Eds.), *Recent advances in excitatory amino acid research.* New York: Alan R. Liss.

Bear, M. F., Cooper, L. N., & Ebner, F. F. (1987). A physiological basis for a theory of synapse modification. *Science, 237,* 42–48.

Bear, M. F., Kleinschmidt, A., Gu, Q., & Singer, W. (1989). Disruption of experience-dependent synaptic modifications in striate cortex by infusion of an NMDA receptor antagonist. Manuscript submitted for publication.

Bear, M. F., Schmechel, D. E., & Ebner, F. F. (1985). Glutamic acid decarboxylase in the striate cortex of normal and monocularly deprived kittens. *Journal of Neuroscience, 5,* 1262-1275.

Bear, M. F., & Singer, W. (1986). Modulation of visual cortical plasticity by acetylcholine and noradrenaline. *Nature, 320,* 172-176.

Benowitz, L. I., & Routtenberg, A. (1987). A membrane phosphoprotein associated with neural development, axonal regeneration, phospholipid metabolism, and synaptic plasticity. *Trends in Neuroscience 10,* 527-532.

Berridge, M. J. (1984). Inositol trisphosphate and diacylglycerol as second messengers. *Biochemical Journal, 220,* 345-360.

Bienenstock, E. L., Cooper, L. N., & Munro, P. W., (1982). Theory for the development of neuron selectivity: Orientation specificity and binocular interaction in visual cortex. *Journal of Neuroscience, 2,* 32-48.

Black, I. B., Adler, J. E., Dreyfus, C. F., Friedman, W. F., LaGamma, E. F., & Roach, A. H. (1987) Biochemistry of information storage in the nervous system. *Science, 236,* 1263-1268.

Blakemore, C., & van Sluyters, R. C. (1974). Experimental analysis of amblyopia and strabismus. *British Journal of Ophthalmology, 58;*176-182.

Clothiaux, E., Bear, M. F., & Cooper, L. N (1988). Experience-dependent synaptic modifications in the visual cortex studied using a neural network model. *Neuroscience Abstracts 14,* 81.13.

Collingridge, G. L., Kehl, S. L., & McLennan, H. (1983). Excitatory amino acids in synaptic transmission in the Schaffer collateral-commisural pathway of the rat hippocampus. *Journal of Physiology, 334,*33-46.

Connors, B. W., & Bear, M. F. (1988). Pharmacological modulation of long term potentiation in slices of visual cortex. *Neuroscience Abstracts, 14,* 298.8.

Cooper L. N, Lieberman, F., & Oja, E. (1979). A theory for the acquisition and loss of neuron specificity in visual cortex. *Biological Cybernetics, 33,* 9-28.

Cooper L. N., & Scofield, C. L. (1988). Mean-field theory of a neural network. *Proceedings of the National Academy of Sciences, USA, 85,* 1973-1977.

Daw, N. W., Sato, H., & Fox, K. (1988). Effect of cortisol on plasticity in the cat visual cortex. *Neuroscience Abstracts, 14,* 81.11.

Dingledine, R. (1983). N-methylaspartate activates voltage-dependent calcium conductance in rat hippocampal pyramidal cells. *Journal of Physiology 343,* 385-405.

Dudek, S. M. & Bear, M. F. (1989). Ibotenate-stimulated phosphoinositide turnover: A biochemical correlate of the critical period for synaptic modification in visual cortex. Manuscript submitted for publication.

Dudek, S. M., Bowen, W. D., & Bear, M. F. (1988). Postnatal changes in glutamate stimulated PI turnover in rat neocortical synaptoneurosomes. *Developmental Brain Research, 47,* 123-128.

Duffy, F. H., Snodgrass, S. R., Burchfiel, J. L., & Conway, J. L. (1976). Bicuculline reversal of deprivation amblyopia in the cat. *Nature, 260,* 256-257.

Ferster, D. (1986). Orientation selectivity of synaptic potentials in neurons of cat primary visual cortex. *Journal of Neuroscience, 6,* 1284-1301.

Ferster, D., & Lindström, S. (1983). An intracellular analysis of geniculo-cortical connectivity in area 17 of the cat. *Journal of Physiology, 342,* 181-215.

Frégnac, Y., & Imbert, M. (1984). Development of neuronal selectivity in the primary visual cortex of the cat. *Physiological Review, 64,* 325-434.

Greuel, J. M., Luhman, H. J., & Singer, W. (1987). Evidence for a threshold in experience-dependent long-term changes of kitten visual cortex. *Developmental Brain Research, 34,* 141–149.

Harris, E. W., Ganong, A. H., & Cotman, C. W. (1984). Long-term potentiation involves activation of N-methyl D-aspartate receptors. *Brain Research, 323,* 132–137.

Hebb, D. O. (1949). *The organization of behavior.* New York: Wiley.

Hendry, S. H., & Kennedy, M. B. (1986). Immunoreactivity for a calmodulin-dependent protein kinase is selectively increased in macaque striate cortex after monocular deprivation. *Proceedings of the National Academy of Sciences USA, 83,* 1536–1541.

Hubel, D. H., & Wiesel, T. N. (1962). Receptive fields, binocular interactions and functional architecture in the cat's visual cortex. *Journal of Physiology (Lon.), 160,* 106–154.

Hubel, D. H., & Wiesel, T. N. (1970). The period of susceptibility to the physiological effects of unilateral eye closure in kittens. *Journal of Physiology (Lon.) 206;* 419–436.

Kasamatsu, T., & Pettigrew, J. D. (1979). Preservation of binocularity after monocular deprivation in the striate cortex of kittens treated with 6-hydroxydopamine. *Journal of Comparative Neurology 185,* 139–162.

Kauer, J. A., Malenka, R. C., & Nicoll, R. A. (1988). NMDA application potentiates synaptic transmission in the hippocampus. *Nature, 334,* 250–252.

Kimura, F., Tsumoto, T., Nishigori, A., & Shirokawa, T. (1988). Long-term synaptic potentiation and NMDA receptors in the rat pup visual cortex. *Neuroscience Abstracts 14,* 81.10.

Kleinschmidt, A., Bear, M. F., & Singer, W. (1987). Blockade of "NMDA" receptors disrupts experience-dependent modifications of kitten striate cortex. *Science, 238,* 355–358.

Larson, J., & Lynch, G. (1986). Synaptic potentiation in hippocampus by patterned stimulation involves two events. *Science 232,* 985–988.

Lodge D., Aram J. A., & Fletcher, E. J. (1988). Modulation of N-methylaspartate receptor-channel complexes: An overview. In E. A. Cavalheiro, J. Lehman, & L. Turski (Eds.), *Recent advances in excitatory amino acid research.* New York: Alan R. Liss.

Lynch, G., Larson, J., Kelso, S., Barrionuevo S., & Schottler, F. (1983). Intracellular injections of EGTA block induction of hippocampal long-term potentiation. *Nature, 305,* 719–721.

MacDermott, A. B., Mayer, M. L., Westbrook, G. L., Smith, S. J., & Barker, J. L. (1986). NMDA receptor activation increases cytoplasmic calcium concentration in cultured spinal cord neurones. *Nature, 321,* 519–522.

MacDonald, J. F., Salter , M. W., & Mody, I. (1988). Intracellular regulation of the NMDA receptor. In E. A. Cavalheiro, J. Lehman, & L. Turski (Eds.), *Recent advances in excitatory amino acid research.* New York: Alan R. Liss.

Malenka, R. C., Kauer, J. A., & Nicoll, R. A. (1988). Postsynaptic calcium is sufficient for potentiation of hippocampal synaptic transmission. *Science, 242,* 81–84

Martin, K. A. C. (1987). Neuronal circuits in cat striate cortex. In E. G. Jones & A. Peters (Eds,), *The cerebral cortex.* New York: Plenum Press.

Mayer, M. L., & Westbrook, G. L. (1987). The physiology of excitatory amino acids in the vertebrate central nervous system. *Prog. Neurobiol, 28,* 197–276.

Mower, G. D., White, W. F., & Rustad, R. (1986). [^{3}H] Muscimol binding of GABA receptors in the visual cortex of normal and monocularly deprived cats. *Brain Research, 380,* 253–260.

Neve, R. L., & Bear, M. F. (in press). Visual experience regulates gene expression in the developing striate cortex. *Proceedings of the National Academy of Sciences USA.*

Nicoletti, F., Iadarola, M. J., Wroblewski, J. T., & Costa, E. (1986). Excitatory amino acid recognition sites coupled with inositol phospholipid metabolism: Developmental changes and interaction with α1-adrenoreceptors. *Proceedings of the National Academy of Sciences USA, 83,* 1931–1935.

Nowak, L., Bregostovski, P., Ascher, P., Herbert, A., & Prochiantz, A. (1984). Magnesium gates glutamate-activated channels in mouse central neurones. *Nature, 307,* 462–465.

Olson, C. R., & Freeman, R. D. (1980). Profile of the sensitive period for monocular deprivation in kittens. *Experimental Brain Research, 39,* 17–21.

Palmer, E., Monaghan, D. T., Kahle, J., & Cotman, C. W. (1988). Bidirectional regulation of phosphoinositide metabolism by glutamate receptors: Stimulation by two classes of QA receptors and inhibition by NMDA receptors. *Neuroscience Abstracts, 14,* 37.16.

Ramoa, A. S., Paradiso, M. A., & Freeman, R. D. (1988). Blockade of intracortical inhibition in kitten striate cortex: Effects on receptive field properties and associated loss of ocular dominance plasticity. *Experimental Brain Research, 73,* 285–296.

Reiter, H. O., & Stryker, M. P. (1988). Neural plasticity without action potentials: Less active inputs become dominant when kitten visual cortical cells are pharmacologically inhibited. *Proceedings of the National Academy of Sciences USA, 85,* 3623–3627.

Scofield, C. L., & Cooper, L. N. (1985). Development and properties of neural networks. *Contemporary Physics 26,* 125–145.

Sherin, J. E., Feldman, D., & Bear, M. F. (1988). NMDA-evoked calcium uptake by slices of visual cortex maintained in vitro. *Neuroscience Abstracts, 14,* 298.7.

Sherman, S. M., & Spear, P. D. (1982). Organization in visual pathways in normal and visually deprived cats. *Physiological Review, 62,* 738–855.

Sillito, A. M., Kemp, J. A., Milson, J. A., & Berardi, N. (1980). A re-evaluation of the mechanisms underlying simple cell orientation selectivity. *Brain Research, 194,* 517–520.

Singer, W. (1977). Effects of monocular deprivation on excitatory and inhibitory pathways in cat striate cortex. *Experimental Brain Research, 134,* 508–518.

Singer, W. (1979). Central core control of visual cortex functions. In F. O. Schmitt & F. G. Worden (Eds.), *The Neurosciences Fourth Study Program* (pp. 1093–1109). Cambridge, MA: MIT Press.

Singer, W. (1982). Central core control of developmental plasticity in the kitten visual cortex: I. Diencephalic lesions. *Experimental Brain Research, 47,* 209–222.

Stanton, P. K., & Sejnowski, J. J. (in press). Associative long-term depression in the hippocampus: Induction of synaptic plasticity by Hebbion Covariance. *Nature.*

Stent, G. S. (1973). A physiological mechanism for Hebb's postulate of learning. *Proceedings of the National Academy of Sciences USA, 70,* 997–1001.

Sur, M., Frost, D. O., & Hockfield, S. (1988). Expression of a surface-associated antigen on Y-cells in the cat lateral geniculate nucleus is regulated by visual experience. *Journal of Neuroscience, 8,* 874–882.

Thibault, O., Joly, M., Müller, D., Schottler, F., Dudek, S., & Lynch, G. (1989). Long-lasting physiological effects of bath applied N-methyl-D-aspartate. *Brain Research, 476,* 170–173.

Toyama, K. K., Matsunami, Ohno, T., & Tokashiki, S. (1974). An intracellular study of neuronal organization in the visual cortex. *Experimental Brain Research, 21,* 45–66.

Tsumoto, T., Masui, H., & Sato, H. (1986). Excitatory amino acid neurotransmitters in neuronal circuits of the cat visual cortex. *Journal of Neurophysiology, 55,* 469–483.

Wiesel, T. N., & Hubel, D. H. (1965). Comparison of the effects of unilateral and bilateral eye closure on cortical unit responses in kittens. *Journal of Neurophysiology, 28,* 1029–1040.

3

Memorial Operation of Multiple, Interacting Simulated Brain Structures

Richard Granger, José Ambros-Ingerson,
Ursula Staubli, and Gary Lynch
*Center for the Neurobiology of Learning
and Memory*
University of California

INTRODUCTION

The brain uses repetitive sampling to analyze the complex stimuli with which it is confronted. "Taking a second look" is an understandable phrase because it describes a common and essential perceptual phenomenon. Although collecting successive samples of stimuli and extracting different information from them may be a routine operation, the machinery involved must be complex indeed, involving interaction and synchronization of activities in sensory and motor systems. Neurobiological studies of perception have treated sensory systems as passive entities responding to but not acting on input signals; computer models of brain systems have (with some notable exceptions) also used networks that process a relatively invariant signal, in an all-or-none fashion. Thus little is known about the roles played by physiological and anatomical characteristics of sensory systems in the analysis of sequentially sampled stimuli.

Repetitive sampling is a readily observed, characteristic behavior in olfaction: Animals sniff at odors often in a highly stereotyped pattern. Experiments using rats have shown that the EEG waves in the chain of structures leading from the nasal receptors to higher brain regions are synchronized with these sniffs. Furthermore, cells in at least one of these areas (hippocampus) discharge in short bursts occurring in phase with sniffing, at a 5 Hz rhythm termed the theta rhythm, with a delay commensurate with the synaptic transmission time from the periphery (Macrides, Eishenbaum, & Forbes, 1982). These observations suggest that the pace at which cues are sampled is directly reflected in the timing operations of brain networks involved in analyzing those cues. This mode of operation imposes constraints on the functionality of the networks involved. At both the cellular and behavioral levels, neurobiological and computational studies have recently provided some insight into how the alignment of behavioral and cellular time produce interesting functional effects. Neurobiological studies have shown that the rhythm of behavioral sniffing (the theta rhythm) is the biophysically optimal rhythm of stimulation of synapses for the induction of long-term potentiation (LTP) in those synapses. LTP, like at least some forms of behavioral learning, is rapidly induced and extremely long-lasting, and is widely thought to be responsible for at least some forms of memory encoding. Thus the possibility is raised that successive sampling at the theta rhythm may cause learning via direct induction of LTP. Even this can be only part of the story, because it must be the case that successive samples are also used in perceptual performance (e.g., recognition) as well as perceptual learning.

To study these issues, we constructed simulations of the superficial layers of olfactory cortex that received inputs at the theta frequency. Our primary findings have been that repeated sampling of stimuli has two major effects: first, multiple samples greatly increase the information capacity of a network compared to that for a single sample, and second, the breaking of the response into distinct samples imposes an organization on the memories thus read out. It was found that repetitive sampling allows the network to form and read out a sequence of different representations of a stimulus, denoting information ranging from the membership of that stimulus in a group of similar stimuli, to specific information unique to the stimulus itself. This led us to the hypothesis that the combination of particular cellular physiological features, anatomical designs, and repetitive sampling performance, allows cortical networks to construct perceptual hierarchies (Lynch & Granger, 1989). Those initial simulation experiments did not address what is presumably an essential feature of repetitive sampling: namely, the interaction between the cortex and its inputs. This chapter reviews both our isolated cortical simulations and our first efforts to explore the issue of interaction between cortex and peripheral structures.

Biological Background:
A Substrate for Long-term Learning

Although we have the capability to acquire lifelong memories within moments, neuroscience for decades identified no candidate neural substrate that could be changed so rapidly and, once changed, persist for the required months or years. Recent results in a number of subfields of neurobiology have introduced and supported the notion that long-term potentiation (LTP) of synaptic connections between neurons may have the requisite properties of a neural substrate for rapidly acquired long-term memory: it is rapidly induced (Bliss & Lomo, 1973), specific to the activated synapses (Dunwiddie & Lynch, 1978), lasts undecremented for as long as can be measured (Staubli & Lynch, 1987), selectively blocked by treatments that block behavioral learning (Morris, Anderson, Lynch, & Baudry, 1986; Staubli, Baudry, & Lynch, 1984; Staubli, Baudry, & Lynch, 1985a), and induced by physiological inputs that give rise to learning in behaving animals (Larson & Lynch, 1986; Roman Staubli, & Lynch, 1987; Staubli, Roman, & Lynch, 1985b).

Although this mechanism may be able to account for the rapidity and longevity of long-term memory, it nonetheless does not address other crucial properties such as organization of memories (by physical similarity and temporal contiguity), and retrieval of memories on demand (as opposed to encoding). Not only must a substrate be rapidly changed and persistent, but it must be part of a system in which such changes can nondestructively incorporate new information into an organized and retrievable set of memories; even if all were known about the mechanisms of LTP, an understanding of its role in behavioral learning and memory would require an integrated model of its functioning in the context of brain structures as they are used during behavior.

Our research program has been based on the construction of simulations of brain structures, using detailed data on the physiology of synaptic LTP, embedded in the anatomical architecture of specific brain structures known to support LTP. We have used olfactory (piriform) cortex to base our simulations on, due to its cortical nature, its relative simplicity (compared to neocortex), its peripheral placement (avoiding excessive preprocessing by other brain structures), its direct relation to known behavioral characteristics in olfactory learning and memory, and experiments that have identified a behaviorally relevant physiological input to the structure. Figures 3.1 and 3.2 illustrate the relative locations, size, and connectivity of olfactory cortex to other key brain structures.

Ninety percent of human brain is telencephalic (forebrain, most of which is neocortex); neocortical structures are widely assumed to play the major role in human cognition. Much research aimed at understanding how brain function gives rise to mental activity has focused on the structures underlying visual processing, in large part because vision plays such a central role in our everyday experience. Yet the study of the cortical processing of visual information is complicated by brain structures intervening between peripheral visual receptors and visual neocortex, most notably nuclei in the thalamus, which are unlikely to be simply way stations that pass signals on unchanged to cortex. Neocortex itself is structurally complex, composed of multiple distinct layers, each receiving inputs from different sources and sending outputs to different targets, and yet interacting vertically across

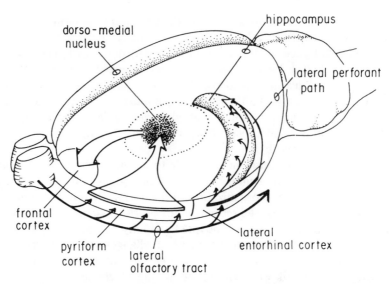

FIG. 3.1. Relative anatomical placement of olfactory bulbs (far left), piriform cortex, dorso-medial nucleus of thalamus (DMN), frontal cortex, and hippocampus, in rat brain. Output axons from olfactory bulbs form the lateral olfactory tract, which directly (monosynaptically) contacts the piriform cortex. Cortex in turn contacts a number of structures, including the DMN (via cortical layer 4), hippocampus (via lateral entorhinal cortex), and frontal cortex.

layers. We have chosen to study a simpler cortical structure, olfactory (piriform) cortex, suspected to be an evolutionary precursor of neocortical designs (cf. Lynch, 1986). Whereas visual cortex consists of six layers, and receives its inputs from retina via thalamic nuclei, olfactory cortex consists of only four layers, and receives input much more directly from the periphery: primary olfactory receptors in the nose are chemically stimulated by olfactants in the air; the receptors in turn directly stimulate the olfactory bulb (a structure in many ways analogous to retina; cf. Shepherd, 1970, 1972), and the bulb then directly (monosynaptically) innervates the olfactory cortex. This direct line of input has enabled the study of the behavior of these structures in freely moving animals actively engaged in learning olfactory cues; in fact, a series of behavioral experiments has bypassed the nose and olfactory bulb, substituting instead direct electrical stimulation of olfactory cortex, with two striking results: long-term potentiation of the synapses in the cortex, accompanied by behavioral learning of these "electrical odors" (Otto, Staubli, & Lynch, 1988; Roman et al., 1987; Staubli et al., 1985b;). This approach thereby avoids a key problem with behavioral studies of olfaction: the fact that difficulties arise in punctate and carefully

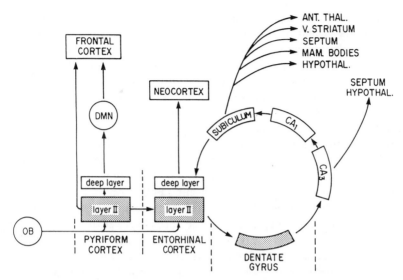

FIG. 3.2. Connections of olfactory structures and other brain structures. The olfactory bulbs (OB) directly contact piriform cortex layer 2, which in turn contacts frontal cortex, dorso-medial nucleus of thalamus (DMN) via piriform cortex layer 4, and the hippocampal formation (consisting of the dentate gyrus, fields CA_3 and CA_1 and subiculum) via entorhinal cortex.

timed and metered presentation of olfactory stimuli. More significantly, use of this paradigm has enabled identification of (at least one of) the behaviorally relevant physiological inputs to this cortical structure: information not otherwise known for any sensory modalities or cortical regions. We hope by this program of research eventually to uncover some of the fundamental operating principles of cortical networks, and to identify basic computational operations that they give rise to: We would hypothesize that such operations would be the building blocks for primary mental activity arising from cortex.

Psychological Background: Rapid Everyday Learning

Experimental paradigms for animal research tend to involve tasks that are slowly learned and not necessarily long remembered by the subject; classical conditioning experiments often involve training an animal on relatively few stimuli, for dozens to hundreds of trials over weeks, without tests of long-term retention weeks or months later (see, e.g., Gluck, Reifsnider, & Thompson chap. 4 in this volume). In contrast, much of human everyday memory is characterized by rapid acquisition (1-2 trials), large capacity, and long retention: Walking into a novel room at the university, we may rapidly recognize its similarities to other such rooms and yet note its differences; moreover, we are capable (at least in principle, and certainly in many instances) of remembering many of its details for a lifetime, even though we may have been exposed to the room for only seconds or minutes. We have studied an olfactory learning task in which rats learn hundreds of different odors, each in very few (> 5) trials, and retain the memories for as long as they have been tested (months) (Staubli et al., 1987). In this task, rats are presented with a novel pair of odors each day, ejected from different spatial locations in a six-arm maze on each of 10-20 trials. Each odor pair consists of an odor with a positive valence (leading to a water reward) and a negative odor (leading to a mildly aversive flashing light). Animals take dozens of trials to learn the valences of the first two or three pairs of odors, but by the third or fourth novel pair, they learn the odors in fewer than five trials, and maintain this pace for as many odors as they have been tested on (130 in the longest such experiment to date). Although the valence of the odors provides a supervised portion of the learning task (i.e., the animals must learn which of two categories, positive and negative, a given odor belongs to), they are also learning to recognize the odors, as evidenced by the rapidity of response to familiar (previously presented) odors relative to novel odors. We have hypothesized that this type of learning is distinct from other forms, such as active and passive avoidance learning: tasks in which an animal is trained to either move or not move in response to a stimulus. It has been shown pharmacologically that these two types of tasks can be doubly dissociated: Drugs that block the olfactory learning have no effect on an avoidance learning task, and vice versa (Staubli et al., 1985a).

The form of learning exhibited in these olfactory tasks is linked in two key ways with synaptic long-term potentiation. First, those drugs that block olfactory learning are those that also block LTP; the other drugs have no effect on LTP. Second, as referred to earlier, a series of experiments has been performed in which stimulating electrodes are inserted that bypass the nose and olfactory bulb, and directly stimulate the olfactory cortex, using precisely those input patterns that are known to induce LTP in in vitro brain slices (Larson & Lynch, 1986), with the result that LTP is selectively induced in just those synapses that are activated by the electrical signal in the olfactory cortex of these animals, and the animals behaviorally learn the task as though there were an actual odor present (Roman et al., 1987; Staubli et al., 1985b). Moreover, the animals are able to distinguish between different electrical odors (i.e., different stimulating electrodes), and between electrical odors and real odors. The electrical odors are learned over the same number of trials and for the same duration as are actual odors (Otto et al., 1988). Thus we may assume that this form of electrical stimulation is a behaviorally relevant stimulus to the animal, and it is possible that the induction of synaptic LTP may be directly driving the behavioral learning of the electrical odors. These behavioral studies thus provide a valuable context within which to study the relationship between synaptic change and behavioral learning and memory. Our initial computer simulations have modeled cortical processing of inputs akin to those in the electrical odor experiments: repeated stimulation at a fixed frequency.

Computational Background:
Unsupervised Learning of Representations

Research on neurally inspired networks has shown, using hypothesized and analytically tractable learning and performance rules, how such networks can learn and store information (see, e.g., Rumelhart & McClelland, 1986, for reviews). At least two fundamentally distinct approaches have been taken with such networks: those that take *input pairs* (e.g., {Paris,France}; {Rome,Italy} . . .) and learn associations between the pair members, and those that take *individual* (unpaired) *inputs* and learn similarity relations among them. The former (variously termed *pattern association* or *associative learning* or a form of *supervised* learning) has been a topic of much interest in the burgeoning field of neural networks, and a number of mechanisms have been invented to deal with paired inputs (e.g., Parker, 1985; Rumelhart, Hinton, & Williams, 1986; Werbos, 1974; Widrow & Hoff, 1959). Similarly, the latter area (*regularity detection* or *unsupervised learning*) has also yielded a number of interesting results (Grossberg, 1976; Linsker, 1988; von der Malsburg, 1973; Rumelhart & Zipser, 1986). Supervised learning algorithms have been successfully related to behavioral tasks in which associations are learned, such as classical conditioning in animals (Granger & Schlimmer, 1986; Sutton & Barto, 1981) and category learning in humans (Gluck & Bower, 1988) as well as to brain structures that may be involved in associative learning in the hippocampus (McNaughton & Nadel, chap. 1 in this volume); and the cerebellum: (Gluck, Reifsnider, & Thompson, chap. 4 in this volume). Certain unsupervised learning algorithms have thus far been linked to developmental processes and possible underlying brain mechanisms (e.g., Linsker, 1986; von der Malsburg, 1973), as well as to adult learning and its neurobiology (Lynch & Granger, 1989; Granger, Ambros-Ingerson, & Lynch, 1989). We have hypothesized that adult unsupervised learning may be the behavior generated by synaptic long-term potentiation in olfactory cortex.

BIOLOGICAL SIMULATION
OF PIRIFORM CORTEX

Our simulated cortical mechanism departs from other unsupervised learning networks in a number of ways. The learning and performance rules in our simulation are based on physiological rules for LTP and the performance of these networks as identified by studies in awake, freely moving animals with implanted electrodes measuring the activity of individual cortical cells. In particular, the LTP learning rules are related to a correlational (or Hebb) rule (in which the connections between cells that are coactive are increased, while those between cells that are not coactive are decreased), but differ in a number of ways, including:

- connection strengths can only increase, not decrease (evidence for long-term depression, an apparent inverse of LTP, is being gathered, but is not yet understood systematically);
- strengths are "clipped," i.e., can only increase up to a fixed maximum strength (as in other related models, such as that of Linsker, 1986).
- there are distinct learning and performance thresholds, yielding distinct learning versus performance modes of operation of the network: unlike a typical correlational or Hebb rule, cells may repeatedly and persistently be coactive without any synaptic change.

Each of these differences gives rise to differences in the resulting aggregate properties of the network and alters the learning power of the net (see Granger, Ambros-Ingerson, Henry, & Lynch, 1987; Granger et al., 1989). Moreover, the performance rules of the network involve both repetitive sampling of an input stimulus, as in repetitive sniffing of olfactory cues in rats (Macrides et al., 1982), and a refractory period for activated cells: once activated sufficiently, a cell cannot be reactivated for many performance cycles. Taken together, these rules cause the network to generate a sequence of distinct spatial cell-firing responses to a single cue. Our analysis of these responses has shown that initial responses are coarse, that is, are identical across a range of different inputs, whereas later responses are increasingly finer-grained, successively approximating a unique identifier for the input.

Figure 3.3 contains a sketch of the essential rules underlying learning and performance in the simulated network, synthesizing the characteristics already described. Learning mode in the simulation is characterized by its receiving short burst inputs at the theta rhythm; in performance mode the network receives single pulse inputs at 40 Hz, and frequency facilitation occurs as these pulses repeat. The figure describes the essential input and output characteristics of cells depending on their priming and frequency-facilitation state, in learning and performance modes, as described earlier. Initially, cells are unprimed, quiescent, not refractory, and have zero frequency facilitation. In the top-left quadrant of Fig. 3.3, unprimed cells (cells that did not fire 200 ms ago) that win their winner-take-all patch in

Learning mode

−primed	primed
winners: S ∧ P	winners: B ∧ P ∧ λ ∧ R
else: Q ∧ P̄	else: Q ∧ P̄

Performance mode

ff ≤ φ	ff > φ
winners: S ∧ ff incr	winners: B ∧ R ∧ ff incr
else: Q ∧ ff decr	else: Q ∧ ff decr

S: spike; B: burst
P: primed; P̄: not primed
λ: synaptic increment (learning)
R: refractory period; Q: quiescent
ff: frequency facilitation
φ: ff threshold for cell becoming refractory

FIG. 3.3. Simplified schematic of network learning and performance rules.

learning mode will both spike (S) and become primed (P); other cells are quiescent (Q) and remain unprimed (P̄). In the top-right quadrant of the table, primed cells in learning mode burst (B), remain primed (P), increment the synaptic strengths of their active synapses (λ) and become refractory(R): refractory cells remain so for 1,000 ms simulated time, which would correspond to five bursts at the theta rhythm in learning mode. The bottom-left quadrant of the figure shows that cells in performance mode whose responses have not yet frequency facilitated up to their bursting threshold (φ) will spike (S) and increment their frequency facilitation (ff incr) if they are patch winners, and are quiescent and decrease their ff (down to a 'floor' limit) otherwise. Once frequency facilitation causes a cell to reach its bursting threshold (lower right), it will burst (B) and become refractory (R). The frequency facilitation threshold for bursting and becoming refractory is typically set at a single firing instance in the simulation, for convenience: Thus, each separate input stimulation in performance mode causes cells to become refractory, and thus different cells fire in response to each input. In reality, this effect would correspond to a situation in which multiple (identical) input stimulations (e.g., electrical odors) would elicit approximately the same spatial firing pattern (probabilistically) for a number of responses, until the frequency facilitation built up to the point that these responding cells became refractory, and then new cells would be recruited. Throughout the discussion in this chapter, we refer for convenience to the responses to the first sniff, second sniff, and so forth; this then corresponds to responses to the first series of sniffs, second series of sniffs, and so forth.

Unsupervised learning implies that a set of codes is being learned corresponding to the learned inputs; to the extent that the codes are unique for different inputs, then each training instance (in learning mode) sets up a fixed category, which can subsequently be used in performance mode to identify which member of the training set is closest to the current input. If such a mechanism is trained on a desired set of categories, then during performance it can determine which of a (presumably larger) set of inputs belongs to which of the predetermined categories: that is, in performance mode, each input vector is interpreted by the algorithm as a degraded version of the training set member closest to it (see, e.g., Anderson & Mozer, 1981). However, further training on any of these novel vectors will cause the network to define new categories, distinguished from the previously learned ones. A generalization of this notion is one in which an unsupervised learning mechanism produces outputs that are not unique for its inputs. Then the learning has essentially partitioned the training set into categories, and the previous example is a special case in which each training instance is put into its own category. Such learning can be interpreted as the learning of representations of the input population; these representations may then become input to subsequent mechanisms (e.g., those that learn associations among cues). The value of such representation learning includes the properties that similar cues are encoded similarly, and different cues encoded differently (canonicity), and that novel cues can be interpreted either as degraded versions of learned cues (generalization) or as members of learned categories (categorization). The problems of generalization and graceful degradation in response to unpredicted inputs are well-known among researchers in advanced software engineering and artificial intelligence who attempt to design systems to interpret and react to loosely specified inputs. (Indeed, it has been accepted wisdom in both fields for decades that identification of the appropriate representation for a particular problem is among the largest single steps towards solving it.)

This problem of identifying the appropriate representation for a set of cues in an input environment gives rise to one of the key tensions in theories of perception and cognition: generalization versus specificity; too few categories (or too much generalization) versus too many categories (or too little generalization). Distinguishing among every possible model of car is a wasteful representation if the task at hand requires only choosing a vehicle for transportation in a particular medium (ground, water, air); yet such distinctions are crucial for, for example, assigning insurance rates. Presumably an animal sometimes needs to distinguish carefully among different types of mushrooms, if, for example, specific mushrooms are used as learned spatial landmarks for following a path through a forest; but the mushrooms need only be differentiated as edible versus poisonous when the animal is hungry.

The emergent performance mechanism from the cortical model generates multiple responses on successive cycles for any given input; these distinct responses have been shown to correspond to different levels of encoding of the input, ranging from categorical to individual responses. Thus we propose that this cortical mechanism may learn multiple representations of its inputs, and uses time, via sequential cycles, to read out the different levels. Figure 3.4 illustrates the results of the sequential cycling behavior of the network. After being trained on 10 cues that all share 75% of their input lines, the piriform cortical cell firing response is shown on the first and fourth cycles (sniffs) to each of the cues, for a 1,000-cell network. The cortical responses to each cue are superimposed, and the size of each box corresponds to the number of cues to which that cell responded (cells that responded to 9 or 10 cues having the largest boxes and 1 to 2 cues the smallest). The first sniff responses superimpose very closely after learning, that is, any cell that responded to any of the cues responded to all of them, meaning that the spatial patterns in response to each of the ten cues are nearly identical. In contrast, by the fourth sniff, there is almost no overlap among the 10 spatial response patterns to the 10 cues; each of the cues gives rise to a unique spatial pattern. What has been learned is a sequence of encodings of each of the 10 cues, such that the first encoding, which is identical for all 10 cues, denotes the similarity-based category of which they are all members, whereas the later encodings correspond to successive approximations of unique encodings of each individual cue.

BEYOND ISOLATED CORTICAL PROCESSING: INTERACTING STRUCTURES

A dog presented with a novel scent can learn it rapidly and then detect, recognize, and track it even in the presence of many other strong odors; rats can recognize and follow the trace remnants of a familiar odor from a previous experiment even in a well-cleaned olfactory maze; in general, we may hypothesize that mammals are capable of rapidly learning large numbers of distinct olfactory stimuli, as well as identifying familiar odors, even when these cues occur in masking environments consisting of many other, stronger odors, both familiar and unfamiliar. Though this is apparently a primary olfactory behavior, our cortical model does not provide an account of it. We have expanded our original cortical model with a simple simulation of the more peripheral structure that provides input to the olfactory cortex: the olfactory bulb, and its primary input, the olfactory nerve. Using simplifications of the known physiology and anatomy, we have illustrated how the coherent operation of the olfactory nerve,

First and Fourth Sniff Responses (10 cues)

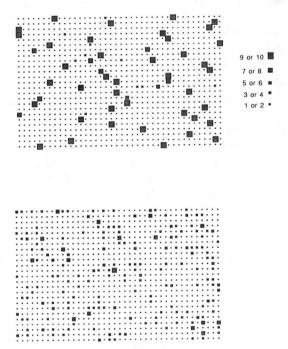

FIG. 3.4. First-sniff and fourth-sniff responses of piriform cortical simulation to ten similar learned cues. The ten cues overlap with each other by 70%, i.e., the vectors are roughly at angles of 45° (.79 radians) angles to each other. First- and fourth-sniff responses to each of the ten cues in a 1000-cell piriform simulation are overlaid: the size of the box on a given cell indicates the number of cues (out of the ten total) that that cell responded to, on sniff 1 (top) and on sniff 4 (bottom). The first sniff responses overlay almost entirely onto each other; that is, each cell tended to respond either to all ten cues or to none of the cues. This means that these first-sniff responses to each of the ten cues were almost identical; i.e., the response simply denotes the fact that one of the ten members of this category was present, but not which one. In contrast, the fourth sniff responses were all quite distinct; few cells responded to more than one or two of the cues. This means that each cue elicited a unique fourth-sniff response from the network

bulb, and cortex can yield a mechanism to learn and remember cues, and to identify them in masking environments (the hidden odor problem).

Figure 3.5 schematically illustrates the key anatomical and physiological relationships among the structures modeled. In rat, roughly 50 million epithelial receptors, differentially sensitive to distinct chemical odors,

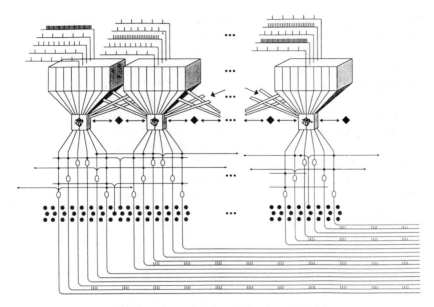

FIG. 3.5. Simulation of olfactory bulb. Output of the olfactory receptors (not shown) constitute the olfactory nerve (top of diagram), which converges onto the glomerular layer of bulb, and there makes axo-dendritic synaptic contacts with the dendrites of mitral and tufted cells (white ovals) and periglomerular cells (black diamonds). Mitral and tufted cells are also contacted by granule cells (black circles), via dendrodendritic synapses (see text). In rat, 50 million receptor cell axons make contact with mitral and tufted cell dendrites in the glomeruli; each of the approximately 1,900 glomeruli contains the dendrites of roughly 25 mitral cells; there are approximately 50,000 mitral cells and approximately ten times as many granule cells.

project onto approximately 50,000 mitral and tufted cells via dendritic glomeruli in the olfactory bulb; the mitral/tufted axons in turn form the primary innervation of the 500,000 layer 2 cells of olfactory (piriform) cortex (Mori, 1987, for a review). This enormously convergent and then divergent anatomical organization suggests a severe loss of information from the numerous receptor cells. Moreover, although topography from the epithelial receptors is roughly preserved in the glomeruli (modulo the three orders of magnitude convergence), and the glomerular topography is preserved in the mitral/tufted layers of olfactory bulb, the mitral/tufted axonal projections shed their topography in their connectivity with the olfactory cortex, which is very sparsely and semirandomly connected to bulb.

Among the identified aspects of the epithelial receptor encoding of odors are the facts that spatial coding of odors is apparently constant across the receptor sheet, even across different animals (MacKay-Sim, Shaman, &

Moulton, 1982); and each receptor cell firing rate is at least in part a monotonic function of the concentration of the chemical it is sensitive to: that is, chemical olfactants present at higher concentrations tend to generate higher frequency firing (Kauer, 1987). We distinguish between two possible encoding mechanisms: the use of different frequencies to encode information (e.g., the concentration of intensity of an odor) versus nonfrequency-coded cells, that is, those that make no use of differential frequency information, but use only spatial coding to encode information.

The extent to which the former mechanism, frequency coding, occurs in bulb and piriform cortex is not well understood. The receptor sheet is an unusually simple structure, lacking interneurons and extensive interconnections among neurons or feedback from central structures; thus it seems reasonable to assume that the intensity-to-frequency relationships observed in experiments with anesthetized animals are likely to obtain during behavior. The same cannot be said for bulb and cortical cells, which are targets of a variety of brain systems and are embedded in complex networks that are almost certainly influenced by events occurring in many brain regions (as illustrated in Figs. 3.1 and 3.2). Chronic recording studies of bulb and cortex in animals engaged in naturalistic behaviors are extremely rare. Preliminary results collected in piriform cortex strongly suggest that most neurons in layer 2, the region that is directly innervated by the bulb mitral cells, fire in short bursts possibly synchronized with global EEG rhythms (Macrides et al., 1982; McCollum, Larson, Otto, & Lynch, 1988). Cells firing in synchrony cannot be exploiting frequency coding; for purposes of discussion we assume that frequency coding is lost at the mitral cell stage in the chain connecting receptors to brain strctures. Though this would seem to involve a loss in principle of information-storage capacity, it will be seen that the capacity remains high due to mechanisms of multiple sampling.

As previously mentioned, a series of experiments bypassing the nose and bulb and directly electrically stimulating the mitral cell axon bundle (the lateral olfactory tract or LOT) at a fixed frequency, elicits both stable strengthening of LOT-piriform synapses via long-term potentiation (LTP) and behavioral learning of the electric odor; distinct electrodes in the LOT generate stimuli that are learned and recognized by the animal, and can be distinguished from each other and from real odors in a way that resembles their learning of real odors (Roman et al., 1987; Staubli et al., 1985b). This demonstrates that spatial patterns of LOT activity at fixed firing frequencies can encode behaviorally relevant olfactory stimuli (see also Mouly, Vigouroux, & Holley, 1987). Both natural odor and electric odor learning results suggest a loss of frequency information that is available at the input periphery, and demonstrate that the fixed-frequency input stimulation used in the electric odor experiments can be assumed to be at least one of the behaviorally relevant input codes to the cortex, providing a powerful tool for simulation and analysis not yet available for any sensory modalities or cortical regions.

Finally, long-term potentiation (LTP) of synapses has been shown recently in both the LOT and association fiber system in piriform cortex in slices (Jung et al., unpublished data); experiments in field CA1 of hippocampus (in which LTP occurs) have suggested that different synapticmodification rules may hold during early development than in adulthood (Oliver et al., unpublished data). The possible existence of distinct developmental and adult learning rules raises the question of the effect of the former on the performance of the latter. (Indeed, this question is also raised by other studies of learning rules occurring during development, as in the rules proposed and studied by Bear & Cooper, chap. 2 in this volume).

In the following sections we outline the interaction of periphery and cortex that can give rise to analysis of complex odors and detection of odors at a wide range of intensities, even when masked by other confounding stimuli.

Step 1. Receptors to Bulb:
Frequency Coding to Cyclic Sampling

As mentioned, the 50 million nasal receptors (in rat) project to 50,000 mitral cells in olfactory bulb, via the fewer than 2,000 bulb glomeruli (see Fig. 3.5), thus losing at least three to four orders of magnitude of information. The encoding capacity of these structures, in terms of number of bits of information that can be represented in principle, is related to the number of frequencies raised to the power of the number of cells (because for any particular input stimulus, each cell can fire with any one frequency). For cells that can fire at frequencies ranging from about 1 Hz to about 200 Hz, we may assume that this range of available frequencies can be roughly broken into order 10 distinguishable subranges; then we may estimate that a measure of the encoding capacity of the receptor sheet is about $10^{50,000,000}$, whereas the encoding capacity of the (nonfrequency-coded) mitral cells can be estimated based on no more than three states for these cells (quiescence, pulsing, and bursting): $3^{50,000} \approx 10^{25,000}$. Note that these numbers are extremely large, and are not intended to directly represent the number of, say, olfactory cues that can be represented. Rather, these figures indicate the number of bits of information in principle that can be encoded by structures using frequency versus multiply-sampled, nonfrequency encoding strategies; any given cue stimulus may require many orders of magnitude of such bits of information to store a single cue. Hence, the figures may be used for purposes of comparing the relative capacities of different size structures using different encoding strategies, but not for direct measurement of the number of items of information that can be stored.

One element of the apparent puzzle of so much lost information can be addressed by noting that the feedback from cortex to bulb (see Fig. 3.5) enables cyclic activity in bulb, such that the bulb glomerular patches can selectively sample the epithelial receptor firing (for a fixed short-time interval), and may then pass on the resulting spatially coded information to cortex, which in turn may selectively inhibit the most strongly responding bulb regions, masking them, at which point resampling of the receptors will give a quite distinct spatial pattern of activity in the glomeruli; repeated cycling in this fashion enables a sequence of successively more faint receptor patterns to be encoded in the bulb, until the feedback inhibition has masked out so much that the bulb becomes quiescent, after repeated cycling. Via this performance rule, much more of the spatial information in the receptors can be captured than either with a single sample or with continuous sampling. The mechanism of time-locked cyclic activity thus greatly increases the capacity of the networks involved. For a given number of cells (n), assuming 10 distinguishable subranges of frequency coding for each cell yields 10^n bits of coding capacity; reducing those cells to three-state cells with repeated sampling gives a capacity of 3^{ns}, where s is the number of cycles or repeated samples. Thus just two cycles of these nonfrequency-coded cells roughly equals the capacity of the frequency-coded versions (because $3^2 \approx 10$); more importantly, increasing the number of sampling cycles to just four or five would be equivalent to having 100 distinguishable subranges of frequencies for the same number of frequency-coded cells, which, even assuming minimal noise, would be impracticable in a biological system. Thus the capacity of the 50,000 three-state mitral cells, with no frequency coding but with four sampling cycles, is $3^{200,000}$, which is approximately comparable to that of 100,000 frequency-coded cells each with 10 distinguishable subranges. Moreover, the sampling regimen may be capable of less noisy encoding than frequency coding, and this use of fixed-frequency time invites the encoding of specific types of distinct information at distinct samples. This notion of using the same cells and transmission lines to transmit time-locked sequences of information is one that has been fruitful in our studies of the cortical processing that results; this is discussed later in this chapter. In general, this mode of processing, in which time-locked cyclic feedback repeatedly samples an input pattern in order to generate distinct successive responses to the input, is a performance rule that recurs throughout the structures we have investigated in the olfactory system, and, we hypothesize, in other telencephalic brain structures as well. Much of our analysis of the capabilities of these structures rests on this processing mechanism (cf. Granger et al., 1989; Lynch & Granger, 1989).

Step 2. Within-bulb Processing:
Frequency to Spatial Transform

The electric odor experiments described earlier (Roman et al., 1987; Staubli et al., 1985b) demonstrate that although there is frequency coding at the periphery, that fixed-frequency spatial coding is a behaviorally relevant cue provided to the cortex by the bulb mitral cells, via the lateral olfactory tract (LOT). We have hypothesized that the olfactory bulb serves in part to perform a transformation from frequency to spatial coding, of a particular type.

Figure 3.5 schematically illustrates the gross anatomy of bulb: receptor axons (comprising the olfactory nerve) converge onto glomerular regions and contact both periglomerular cells and mitral and tufted cell dendrites, which in turn are densely contacted via dendro-dendritic synapses with granule cells; mitral and tufted cell axons form the LOT input to piriform cortex, which feeds back to the granule and periglomerular cells via the anterior olfactory nucleus (AON). Spatial and frequency-coded inputs corresponding respectively to the chemical constituents of an odor and their concentrations, are assumed to be transmitted to the mitral/tufted cells at the glomeruli. The mitral cell possesses a long thin central dendrite originating from the cell body (in the mitral cell layer) that runs through the external plexiform layer (EPL) and then ramifies extensively in the glomerulus. Each glomerulus receives the terminal arbor of several ($\approx$ 25; cf. Mori, 1987) mitral cell dendrites. The mitral cell also emits several lateral dendritic processes (secondary dendrites) that course for considerable distances through the EPL, perpendicular to the vertically oriented primary mitral dendrites. The granule cells are densely packed in a layer beneath the mitral cells (i.e., deeper in the bulb), and send dendritic branches that ramify in the EPL but do not enter the glomerulus. These dendrites form two-way dendro-dendritic synapses with the secondary mitral cell dendrites; that is, the granule cell dendrites directly contact the mitral cell dendrites, and can directly inhibit them in a graded (continuous) fashion, in contrast to the discretized activation (either excitatory or inhibitory) afforded by more typical axo-dendritic synapses, in which the axon must be activated in an all-or-none way before it can transmit quanta of information to the dendrite it contacts. The mitral-to-granule synapses are excitatory (depolarizing) whereas the granule to mitral synapses are inhibitory (hyperpolarizing). Thus excitation of the mitral cell by the olfactory nerve will lead to a spread of depolarization down the central dendrite and into the secondary dendrites and branches; these latter processes will then excite a series of granule cell dendrites all along their extensive trajectory across bulb. The granule cells then presumably produce inhibitory potentials on the active mitral cell as well as any other mitral cells they contact. In this way, a field of lateral inhibition can be set up surrounding any site in bulb containing mitral cells stimulated by the olfactory nerve; there is some experimental support for this idea (see Kauer, 1987, for a discussion). Note that the intensity of this inhibitory field will be dependent on the number of depolarized mitral cells in a particular locus, as well as the degree to which they are depolarized.

The mitral-granule system seems well-suited to normalize the total activity of the bulb, that is, to produce approximately a constant number of active mitral cells for any given stimulus: Activation of one region should suppress physiological activity in other regions, whereas multiple foci will tend to suppress each other, and profoundly depress intervening regions. The story, however, becomes more complex. The mitral cell axons form axo-dendritic contacts with granule cell basal dendrites. This projection can cause the granule cells to discharge, thereby presumably sending additional depolarization out their dendrites and thereby trigger greater inhibition. This could be more focal in nature than the inhibition triggered by the lateral secondary mitral dendrites, because the axons do not appear to distribute as widely as the dendrites (Mori, 1987). We assume that the axo-dendritic system provides a conventional negative feedback loop by which intensely firing mitral cells generate local inhibition that terminates their activity (cf. Shepherd, 1970). Two layers of inhibitory activity are thus postulated: a broadly distributed effect set up by the branches of the depolarized mitral cells that emanates away from the active focus, and a feedback effect, which comes into play when cells in the focus are beginning to emit action potentials, and that is directed primarily at the focus itself.

Further complexity is added by the fact that inhibitory systems in the bulb are massively innervated by projections originating in the brain. The anterior olfactory nucleus terminates densely on the granule cells and receives input from a variety of central structures, the most notable of which is the piriform cortex (extensive afferents also arise in the hippo-campal formations). The anterior olfactory nucleus (AON) is also the recipient of a very dense collateral input from the mitral and tufted cells. The output of bulb thus directly contacts inhibitory granule cells (via collateral fibers in the bulb) and indirectly affects these cells via the AON. Moreover, the piriform cortical target cells of the mitral neurons, if driven to discharging, have a feedback route to the granule cell inhibitory network through their extensive connections in the AON.

In addition to afferents from the AON, the inhibitory networks in bulb also receive direct input from a variety of brain areas, the most prominent of which is the diagonal bands (DBB). Neurons in the DBB send a very large cholinergic projection to the granule cells and the periglomerular region, probably to the periglomerular interneurons (Mori, 1987). Shipley (personal communication, 1988) found that stimulation of the DBB at the 4–7 Hz theta frequency suppresses mitral cell discharges; this is a particularly interesting finding because as noted earlier, this is the frequency at which rats sniff. It is not unreasonable to assume then that the flow of information through the bulb is paced by the same basal forebrain regions that pace physiological activity in the central areas that receive bulbar output (e.g., piriform cortex and disynaptically the hippocampus). This could be of great importance in translating relatively long-lasting events in the nasal receptors at the periphery into punctate but repetitive patterns that are synchronized in diverse areas. It may be that inhalation-exhalation cycles present and then remove odorants from the epithelium with insufficient temporal precision to allow for the timing operations needed by the various stations in the chain of circuitry leading away from the bulb into higher levels of brain; cholinergic (and other) inputs, we assume, impose the needed temporal tuning.

Discussion of the multiple influences acting on inhibitory networks in bulb brings us back to the issue of how the excitatory inputs, the olfactory nerve fibers, drive the mitral neurons. Of considerable interest in this regard is the observation that the target cells of the nerve are differentially sensitive to it. Four classes of neurons have dendrites that make contacts in the glomerulus: external-, middle-, and deep-tufted cells and the mitral neurons. These groups of neurons have cell bodies located in progressively deeper layers of the bulb and require different amounts of olfactory nerve stimulation to discharge (Scott, 1987). Although anatomical studies have not yet satisfactorily resolved the different projection patterns of the four groups, it appears that the superficial- (external-) tufted cells project within the bulb whereas the deep-tufted and mitral cells have axons that reach all parts of olfactory cortex; the middle-tufted cell axons also leave the bulb but reach only the AON and the rostral parts of cortex.

If tufted cells and mitral cells have different thresholds and if, by extension, the mitral neurons vary in this regard amongst themselves, then the numbers of cells contacting a particular glomerulus that responds to an olfactory nerve input will vary according to the properties of that input. Critically important would be the frequency at which inputs fire, a variable that should reflect stimulus intensity. To the extent that different thresholds are the rule in a glomerular region, the system should work to convert a frequency encoding of intensity into a spatial coding. This means that for a relatively low concentration of the stimulus, a relatively fixed pool of (mostly tufted) cells will preferentially respond; for higher concentrations, those same cells will be activated, and, in addition, the less readily activated deep-tufted and mitral cells will be recruited. Thus, the spatial pattern of activation on the bulb (and hence in the bulb output, which is the input to the piriform cortex) should be relatively deterministic for particular concentrations of given odors, ensuring that the spatial pattern input to the cortex can be thought of as topographically encoding both quality and concentration of the odor, via choice of glomerular patches and numbers of mitral and tufted cells recruited within the patches, respectively.

Step 3. Mitral Cells to Cortex:
Learning of Odor Representations

The anatomically preserved topography from receptors to bulb mitral cells is discarded in the connectivity from bulb to piriform cortex, via the lateral olfactory tract in piriform layer Ia, becoming instead a combinatorial random matrix of connections (Haberly, 1985; Haberly & Price, 1977). This may be seen as being of value when viewed as enabling the assignation of cortical cells to fire preferentially to denote the coöccurrence of multiple distinct chemicals comprising a single coherent olfactory stimulus. That is, topography maintains the integrity of components, but combinatorics introduces encodings that represent whole odors, which happen to be comprised of these constituents. In the olfactory modality, there is no (known) inherent topography in the input, so there is no reason for the spatical arrangement of the receptor inputs to be maintained in cortex. However, in inherently topographic modalities such as vision and audition, the neighbor relations at the periphery contain information about the stimulus, and must not be discarded. Yet even in these modalities, it is presumably equally advantageous to create encodings of unitary stimuli, and again the existence of nontopographic as well as topographic mappings to cortex is of use. Indeed, in both the visual and auditory modalities, there are distinct thalamic nuclear regions, each of which receives the same or similar peripheral sensory input, and yet one of which projects topographically to layer 4 of its sensory cortical area, whereas the other projects nontopographically to the superficial layers (layers 1 and 2). This repeated organization suggests that there are functions for both topographic and nontopographic organizations in cortex, and that perhaps the phylogenetically old olfactory cortex exhibited only the nontopographic version, whereas the subsequent sensory cortices added topographically mapped deeper layers to integrate these functions.

Figure 3.6 illustrates the major structural components of the superficial layers of piriform cortex: the LOT input axons very sparsely contact layer 2 cell apical dendrites; each layer 2 cell sends out its own collateral axons, which contact the basal dendrites of neighboring layer 2 cells within a relatively short radius around the cell, and that then rise up to layer Ib and travel predominantly from the front (rostral) end of the cortex toward the posterior (caudal) end (Price 1985; Schwob & Price, 1978), synapsing more proximally (closer to the cell body) than the LOT axons on other layer 2 cell dendrites. Layer 1 inhibitory interneurons are predominantly feedforward, whereas inhibitory interneurons within layer 2 are activated both feedfor-

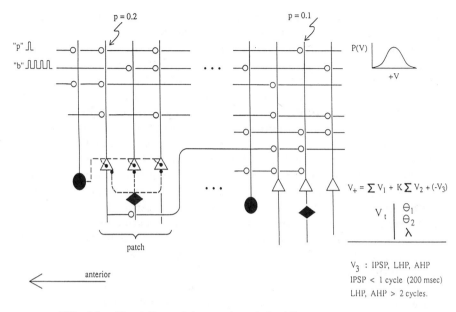

FIG. 3.6. Simulation of layers 1 and 2 piriform cortex. Lateral olfactory tract axons (LOT) from bulb arrive at the anterior portion of cortex (upper left) and synapse sparsely in layer 1a (top portion of diagram), becoming increasingly sparse posteriorly (right-hand side). Axon collaterals from cortical layer 2 cells (white triangles) flow predominantly from rostral (anterior) to caudal (posterior), left to right in the diagram (Schwob & Price, 1978). Inhibitory cells (black diamonds) organize layer 2 into patches with dense local connectivity; three types of inhibition are present: IPSPs, long hyperpolarization or LHP, and cell-specific afterhyperpolarization (AHP); see text for description. Synaptic transmission is probabilistic; there are distinct voltage thresholds for performance (spiking) and learning (NMDA receptor threshold).

ward and feedback by layer 2 cell collaterals. These latter inhibitory interneurons have relatively short axonal radius, forming local patches of excitatory cells that are dominated by a single inhibitory cell. We have hypothesized that the timing of feedforward and feedback activation of these inhibitory cells preferentially allows firing of layer 2 cells that are most strongly activated by a given input within a patch, and then inhibits all other cells within the patch, thereby forming rough winner-take-all local circuits, one per inhibitory cell. The collateral axons of the layer 2 cells also feed back to bulb via the anterior olfactory nucleus (AON): these feedback connections contact inhibitory granule and periglomerular cells in bulb.

The electric odor experiments described previously (Roman et al., 1987; Staubli et al., 1985b) have shown that time-locked burst inputs to the structure can both strengthen synapses and generate behavioral learning of these electrical olfactory cues in the intact animal; in vitro studies have confirmed that long-term potentiation (LTP) of the LOT-piriform synapses is induced by fixed-frequency stimulation (Jung, Larson et al., unpublished results). Simulated spatially coded time-locked firing produced by a model of bulb activity initiates a sequence of events synchronized to the fixed frequency of mitral/tufted activation. The first cycle of bulb activation activates cells in piriform according to the sparse LOT-piriform connectivity. Feedback from piriform to bulb then selectively inhibits the most strongly firing bulb mitral/tufted cells, via a process described in the next section. The dendrodendritic granule-mitral interaction renormalizes the now partially inhibited bulb response, allowing more weakly activated glomeruli to activate more mitral cells in those glomerular patches. This in turn sends a new spatial pattern to piriform (the next cycle), which feeds back inhibiting the now-strongest bulb responses, and so on, until the piriform feedback inhibits the bulb to quiescence, typically after four to five cycles in our simulations.

Using the LTP-based learning rule previously described (Fig. 3.1), we have simulated the effect of learning on cortical responses, finding that, after learning, the previously described sequence of responses generated to any individual input consists of a relatively coarse-grained response followed by increasingly finer-grained responses, such that the initial, coarse response is identical across a range of similar inputs, whereas the subsequent responses are increasingly distinct even for very similar inputs. The distinct responses are due to a combination of the refractory periods of the cells, and the winner-take-all organization of the patches of cells in the cortex. Each input activates cells according to their connectivity and synaptic strengths, and only the most strongly activated cell in each patch can fire (the winner in a winner-take-all patch, as described earlier). The firing cells then become refractory: they cannot respond again for four to five cycles (or sniffs). The sequence of responses thus provides a category response, followed by successive approximations of a unique encoding of the individual input stimulus: The resulting hierarchy corresponds to multiple learned encodings of each individual stimulus, each conveying a different level of information about the stimulus. The reason that the sequence of responses first denotes coarse-grained categories and then successively finer-grained encodings is essentially that the most specific encoding of the input corresponds to those cortical cells whose synaptic contacts best match the input activity in the input lines; however, synaptic strengthening over many instances of similar cues strengthens the contacts of those overlapping portions of these similar cues, thus activating just these less-specific cells first (those that have been strengthened in response to the many members of a similarity-based category), and only subsequently activating the cells that are specific to a given input cue. (For a more detailed description and derivation of these effects, see Granger et al., 1989; Lynch & Granger, 1989).

Development Effect on Adult Category Encodings: Interaction of Two Learning Rules

The model so far described performs unsupervised learning of representations of inputs, that is, learning that is not mediated by externally provided information about category membership. This is in contrast with supervised learning, in which each input is explicitly learned as being a member of some specified category, such as, for example, "odors that lead to water" versus those that do not. Rather than learning to assign inputs to specified categories, unsupervised learning form categories based solely on the similarities among the learned stimuli in the environment. Measurement of the utility of the categories thus formed can be done with respect to some task, for example, the usefulness of those categories for predicting aspects of novel stimuli that are identified as sufficiently similar to some familiar set of stimuli, and thus a member of their category. (For instance, it is likely that a novel object that smells like cheese will behave like cheese, that is, will be a food.)

However, different olfactory environments imply different optimal categorizations of the stimuli in that environment, depending on the overall homogeneity or heterogeneity of the odors in the environment. For example, in an environment with many extremely disparate odors (a very heterogeneous environment), even slight similarity among odors may be salient and worth representing, whereas in a very homogeneous environment (consisting of many very similar odors), even slightly different odors may be worth placing in different categories. As extreme examples, a rat living in a cheese factory may wish to distinguish among even slight variants of cheeses; one living in a household kitchen may wish instead to simply recognize all cheeses as being members of a single category; and one living in an extremely sparse food environment may represent the odors of all dairy products as a single category. Similarly, most numerical clustering algorithms are typically optimized for their clustering performance via parameter adjustment based on being given some information about the distribution characteristics of the cue environment or input space (see Duda & Hart, 1973, for excellent reviews of many of the standard numerical clustering methods).

Development time in an animal provides a potentially valuable period for sampling the environment and possibly setting biological parameters that may affect the eventual categorization performance of the adult. In the current simulations, we have experimented with learning algorithms distinct from the adult LTP learning rule already described, which we hypothesize may occur at development time. These development-time algorithms, rather than learning information or encodings of specific stimuli, instead sample a range of stimuli and set global parameters (corresponding to particular biological parameters) according to characteristics of the sampled stimuli, with the result that the simulation's categorization behavior is altered. In particular, we have shown both empirically (in the simulations) and analytically that global increase of the naive strengths of synapses in the model at simulated development time, that is, before any learning of cues, will decrease the breadth of categories subsequently learned by the adult model thus produced, and vice versa: Global decrease of naive synaptic weights increases the breadth of learned categories in the adult (Granger et al., 1989). In the simulation, the developmental algorithm proceeds by sampling cues and allowing these inputs to drive cortical cells, which in turn raise their synaptic weights globally, proportionately to the average firing strength of the most strongly active cells in each patch. This hypothesized global synaptic change may be tied to the activation by strongly firing cells of the cortical cells, via collaterals. (This developmental learning algorithm is related to that proposed by Cooper and his colleagues and described by Bear & Cooper, chap. 2 in this volume).

Recalling that LTP consists of stepwise increments of synaptic strength up to a fixed ceiling, we may give an intuitive understanding of these results: If naive weights are low, then the distance between naive and maximally strengthened synapses is relatively large, so that two different inputs that both activate even a few of these strengthened synapses will tend to both fire the cell, because these synapses will so far outweigh naive synapses. Conversely, if naive weights are high, so that the distance between naive and strengthened contacts is small, then it will take a larger amount of shared input lines (and thus shared strengthened synapses) between two inputs to ensure that both inputs will activate the same target cells and thus will generate the same (category cell) responses.

Piriform-bulb Feedback: Developmental Learning of Topography

The loss of topographic information from bulb to piriform indicates that piriform-to-bulb feedback cannot itself be topographic; there is no pre-served information about which bulb cells may have activated a given piriform cell. However, it is possible to recapture and encode the lost topography in the piriform-bulb feedback connections, via learning. We have incorporated into our simulation model a correlational (Hebbian) learning algorithm that occurs during simulated development time; that is, before any learning of cues, in contrast to its adult learning mechanism based on synaptic LTP, as described. The model is presented with a series of random simulated odors at the receptors, which give rise to a set of responses in bulb and piriform, simply by the performance rules and random connectivity of the network as described. Direct feedback from piriform to bulb in the model (not faithful to the piriform-AON-bulb feedback connectivity in the real olfactory system) lands on periglomerular and granule bulb cells. The feedback synapses landing on bulb cells co-activated by both olfactory nerve input and piriform feedback are strengthened; noncoincident cells are weakened, according to a simple correlational rule. Over trials, this strengthens feedback contacts from any given piriform cell to those bulb cells that were involved in activating it. In this way, the lost topography between bulb and piriform is recaptured; this mechanism is related to the similar Hebbian algorithm proposed by Linsker (1986).

There are potentially interesting interactions that arise between this developmental Hebbian learning and adult learning and performance in the model. The learned feedback topography enables cortical feedback to selectively mask out bulb responses, in that the most strongly active bulb patches will tend to give rise to the most piriform cell firing response, and those piriform cells will have been trained during development to preferentially feed back inhibition to those bulb patches. This brings the mechanism one step closer to the ability to mask out strong odors in order to detect weak ones, as in the task that has been one of our foci of study (the hidden odor task of detecting and recognizing weak familiar stimuli in the presence of other much stronger stimuli). However, this feedback masking effect will not quite have the entire desired effect in a hidden odor situation, unless the odors to be detected and recognized have been learned by the animal, that is, the odors give a learned cortical response. This can be seen by imagining that a strong odor is composed of two constituents, A and B, in the ratio of two As for every B; then the presentation of that strong odor (A_2B) will generate a novel (and weak, because unlearned) piriform response. This response will have been mostly generated by the strongest components of the input: in this case, component A. Developmental learning will have selectively strengthened the feedback connections from these cortical cells to those bulb regions corresponding to the spatial code for component A; thus that bulb region will be preferentially inhibited by the cortical feedback. What this will leave behind is the weak component(s) of the odor, in this case, component B.

ILLUSTRATION
OF INTERACTION AMONG STRUCTURES
AND LEARNING MECHANISMS:
THE HIDDEN ODOR TASK SOLVED

We have constructed a simulation consisting of extremely simplified models of the olfactory nerve and olfactory bulb, and a more elaborate model of layers I and II piriform cortex, all of which function according to our hypotheses of the coherent behavior of these structures described up to this point in this chapter. The laminar organization of the model corresponds to four functional layers in bulb: a glomerular input from the olfactory nerve, a granule layer that serves to normalize the size of bulb mitral activity, a feedback inhibition layer intended to model a combination of periglomerular and granule cells, and a layer of mitral/tufted cells. The olfactory nerve provides inputs to 40 simulated glomeruli, with each input axon bundle consisting of simulated frequency-coded receptor activity. These inputs activate simulated mitral/tufted, periglomerular, and granule layers. The number of mitral cells activated by excitatory input to a glomerulus is a monotonic function of the frequency of the input; granule cell activity serves to normalize the overall size of the mitral response over the surface of the simulated bulb. Feedback from piriform (discussed in the next section), goes to a simulated inhibitory layer (intended to model a combination of periglomerular and granule cells); this feedback inhibition selectively prevents firing in mitral patches.

The following script describes the response sequence of the integrated bulb/piriform model to a simulated version of the hidden odor problem described earlier in the chapter, in which a familiar weak odor is presented masked by a much stronger odor. Two versions are shown, illustrating the effect of learning on the behavior: if the weak odor has not been previously learned by itself in isolation, then it cannot be detected; but if it has been learned by itself prior to the task, then the simulation successfully performs the detection.

In the case of a compound consisting of two unlearned stimuli, the sequence is as follows:

1. The simulation is presented with a mixture of two odors, neither of which it has previously experienced, with one (W) weakly present and the other (S) strongly present.
2. The mixture thus presented at the receptors (W + S) generates a mixed pattern of activation in the bulb, normalized by mitral-granule interaction, as described earlier, so that the stronger odor is more represented in the spatial pattern of mitral cell responses than the weak odor.

3. This spatial pattern is a novel one, and generates a response pattern in piriform based solely on the mitral-piriform connectivity, because no prior learning of the odors or their combination has occurred.
4. The resulting feedback from piriform is weak, and masks out some parts of odor W and some parts of odor S.
5. Again mitral-granule dendrodendritic interaction re-normalizes the (now partially inhibited) bulb response.
6. Piriform response is again determined solely by connectivity, in the absence of prior learning, and the sequence continues, until the bulb response is entirely inhibited by successive piriform feedback.

In the second case, both odors (W and S) have been previously presented to the simulation, separately, and they have each been learned as individual odors.

1. The simulation is presented with W and S as before.
2. The mixture generates the same mixed spatial pattern in bulb as before, so that the stronger odor is more represented in the spatial pattern of mitral cell responses than the weak odor. In spite of the fact that the two components are familiar, the combined spatial pattern is, as before, a novel one (if these two odors have never been presented in this combined fashion before), because of the normalization process in the bulb.
3. The novel bulb pattern is nonetheless similar enough to the strong odor to yield a degraded version of the piriform category response for that odor (S).
4. The resulting piriform-bulb inhibitory feedback preferentially masks out the recognized odor (S).
5. Renormalization in bulb activates the remaining odor (W), together with the few remaining remnants of odor S.
6. Piriform response is a degraded version of the learned category response to the individual odor W.
7. Feedback masks out most of the remaining response; the cycle continues until bulb quiescence.

Table 3.1 provides a brief summary of these results.

Figure 3.7 and Figure 3.8 show the responses of the simulation to a mixture of two simulated odors A and C, both of which have been previously learned individually by the simulation. In Fig. 3.7, the spatial pattern of receptor cell activation for A and C is superimposed on the left-hand side of the figure, with the concentration of A (black squares) twice that of C (white squares); the relative sizes of the squares correspond

TABLE 3.1
Sequential Cortical Responses to Learned and Unlearned Odor Mixtures.

	Odor mixture	Response 1	Response 2
Before learning of odors S or W	S + W	part S, part W	remainder S, W
After learning of odors S and W, individually	S + W	S	W

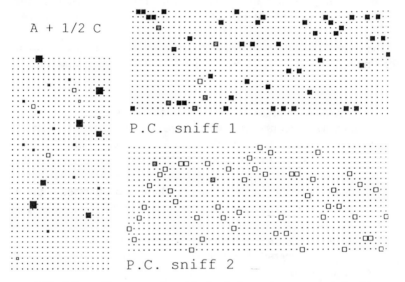

A + 1/2 C

P.C. sniff 1

P.C. sniff 2

FIG. 3.7.   The operation of simulation when presented with mixture of familiar odors. The input pattern in the olfactory nerve (leftmost side) is coded to show the presence of a strong simulated odor A (black) mixed with a weaker odor C (white); the size of the boxes shows frequency of firing of these axons, indicating simulated concentration of the odor. At right, piriform cortex responses are coded to show the extent to which the firing cells correspond to those that encode odor A (black) versus odor C (white), or neither (grey). Sniff 1 response (top) of the simulation when presented with this mixture corresponds to the learned cortical response for odor A; i.e., this response is what would have occurred if odor A had been presented alone. Sniff 2 (below) corresponds to the learned response for the hidden odor, C.

to the firing frequency of each cell. This simulated receptor response is followed by the simulated piriform cortex response, on two successive cycles or sniffs. For each sniff, the cortical cells that respond are labeled black, white, or grey, according to whether they are part of the learned cortical response to odor A presented alone (black), C presented alone

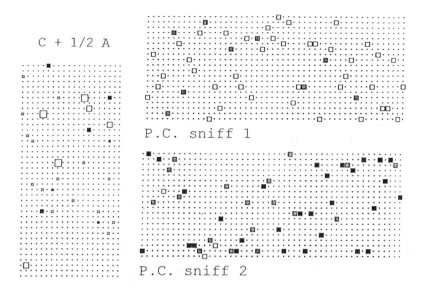

C + 1/2 A

P.C. sniff 1

P.C. sniff 2

FIG. 3.8. The operation of simulation when presented with mixture of familiar odors; compare with previous figure. The input pattern in the olfactory nerve (leftmost side) is now reversed relative to the previous figure: the previously weak simulated odor (C; white) is now strongly present, with the previously strong odor (A; black) now weakly present. As before, the size of the boxes shows frequency of firing of these axons, indicating simulated concentration of the odor. At right, piriform cortex responses are coded to show the extent to which the firing cells correspond to those that encode odor A (black) versus odor C (white), or neither (grey). Sniff 1 response (top) of the simulation to the mixture now is to odor C (white), because it is the strong odor; whereas sniff 2 corresponds to the now-weak odor, A (black).

(white), or neither (grey). It will be seen that the first sniff cortical response corresponds almost exclusively (90%) to the high-concentration odor (which is A in this example); only 4 cells out of 50 correspond to the cortical responses of neither odors A nor C, and only 1 cell corresponds to the response for C. The second sniff cortical response, however, corresponds almost exclusively (96%) to odor C: only two cells out of 50 correspond to neither odor A nor C, and no cells whatsoever correspond to the response for the high-concentration odor, A. Correspondingly, Figure 3.10 displays the simulated receptor response to the same two odors but in the opposite concentration ratio: twice as much C as A. The first-sniff cortical response again corresponds strongly to the high-concentration odor, which this time is odor C; none of the firing cells are part of the representation of odor A, and 9 cells correspond to neither odor. The second-sniff response contains only 3 cells out of 50 that correspond to the high-concentration odor, and the majority of the cells correspond to the weak odor (although this response is noisy: 18 cells correspond to neither odor). This example illustrates the ability of the simulation to analyze the composition of environmental odors.

DISCUSSION

In our previous work on the piriform cortex, we incorporated a great deal of biological detail into simulations, including physiological properties that are common to many brain systems as well as details that are specific to the piriform: the model uses different forms of inhibition with different durations, LTP-based learning rules, asymmetric distributions of input and associational fiber systems, different voltage thresholds for different physiological events, and so forth. (Lynch & Granger, 1989). The simulation of olfactory bulb is, in contrast, an extreme simplification of a very complex structure, and does not include anything like the detail used in the piriform simulation. Nonetheless, it has been useful in developing ideas about the interactions between repetitive sampling and feedback from brain at the first control stage of olfactory processing. Moreover, these preliminary models uncovered ways in which learning during simulated development and adulthood facilitates perceptual and memorial operations.

It may be useful to review the stages of bulb operation as they are summarized in the present model:

1. A simulated sniff cycle brings odorant to the epithelial receptors and also sets in motion inputs from the diagonal bands of Broca (DBB) that have been implicated in driving inhibitory cells rhythmically; these latter projections limit the cycles by setting a time window, the end of which is masked by intense inhibition.

2. The activated receptors send excitatory inputs to one or more glomeruli using frequency of firing to encode intensity of the stimulus.

3. The frequency of firing of the stimulated input lines to a particular glomerulus determines the number of mitral/tufted cells with dendrites in that glomerulus that will be strongly depolarized.

4. The depolarized dendrites set in motion a broad inhibitory surround via contacts with granule cells made by lateral dendrites; this serves to normalize activity throughout the bulb. Depolarization on a mitral cell is thus a balance of how intense its inputs are and the degree of inhibition it receives from neighboring zones.

5. Cells that are sufficiently depolarized emit spikes that activate inhibitory feedback (via both dendrodendritic connections with

granule cells and collateral mitral axons contacting granule cells) that terminates their activity.

6. Projections to the piriform cortex stimulate layer 2 cells in that structure to discharge. This activates a further, profound and long-lasting inhibition in the bulb via piriform-AON-bulb connections.

7. This feedback will exert its greatest effect on the granule cells associated with bulbar regions that are active, because of learning (using the correlational or Hebb rule) that occurred during simulated development. That is, collections of cells in piriform that respond to the activation of a particular bulb area will have their strongest effects in those same bulbar regions.

8. On a successive sample, the previously dominant bulbar regions will be maximally suppressed, allowing less intensely activated areas to become dominant.

9. Adult (LTP-based) learning in cortex interacts with these events: familiar inputs produce cortical responses that respond primarily to the learned components; the presence of extra components that were not part of the training (i.e., noise) will affect cortical response only minimally.

In summary, interaction among these simulated olfactory structures yields a relatively rich range of behaviors, including recognition learning of olfactory cues, learning of multiple levels of cue information ranging from categories to individual encodings, detection of wide ranges of concentrations of a given odor, and detection of a weak hidden odor masked by a stronger one. It seems noteworthy that any particular feature of the simulation (rhythmic firing, three distinct learning rules, feedback and feedforward connectivity) is not there specifically to perform any one of the range of tasks that the simulation carries out; rather, the combined action of these mechanisms and properties carries out different tasks depending on the inputs to the structures. We take this as one indication of the power of the approach: although it would be possible to design a number of separate mechanisms, each optimized to perform one of these tasks, the integrated mechanism may well turn out to be more parsimonious in its design, given that it must carry out all of these tasks (and quite likely more that we have not yet investigated). Different simulations optimized for any one of these many functions might well perform better (or at least equivalently well) at its specialized task, but would undoubtedly not perform well at the others; it is the richness of behaviors that makes the combined tasks difficult to untangle.

Novel aspects of the work include multiple interacting networks consisting of quite-distinct architectures, performance rules, and learning rules.

In addition to having constructed a novel network design that performs these potentially useful encoding and detection functions, we may be a step closer to an understanding of how particular brain circuits act and interact coherently to yield behavior. The performance rules using sequential sampling of inputs has the dual effect of enlarging the encoding capacity of the networks involved, and imposing an organization on the memories thus encoded.

Epithelium and bulb may be relatively specialized structures in brain (indeed, Shepherd [1970, 1979] pointed out many similarities between bulb and another specialized peripheral structure, retina, both in terms of architecture and function), but layer 2 piriform cortex resembles layer 2 neocortex; thus we may hope that our initial findings in this structure may transfer to the study of neocortical operation.

Our philosophy has been to attempt to construct bottom-up simulations, that is, simulations motivated solely by our knowledge of the anatomical structure and physiological function of specific brain structures, receiving inputs that are behaviorally relevant to a learning, behaving animal. It was not expected initially that this approach would lead rapidly to network models that gave rise to coherent behaviors, carrying out useful computations; yet these results have indeed emerged. Our approach is related to efforts such as those in this volume of McNaughton and Nadel, and Bear and Cooper; yet those efforts have the Marr flavor of beginning with specific problems to be solved (i.e., computations to be accomplished by the mechanism), as well as proposed tools to be used, based on known neuronal structure and function. This approach is laudable, where the computations are known and mechanisms have previously been worked out. However, we began with the assumption that we may not yet know all of the computations to be performed by the structures we are investigating; rather, we empirically tested our simulations on these tasks to see what types of operations might be carried out under these circumstances. Surprisingly, this approach has led to a number of results that have some computational use, such as the operating rule that multiply samples its inputs, yielding a sequence of distinct responses, rather than a unitary response; the interaction among multiple distinct learning rules applied at distinct times (adult verses developmental learning stages); and the interaction of multiple brain modules, each with its own structural design, cell types, operating rules, inputs, and learning rules. Much work in neural networks, artificial intelligence, and cognitive psychology has provided many useful hypotheses about computations that animals perform, and has developed top-down mechanisms by which they may perform them; however, we suggest that few of the many computations and behaviors generated by brain have yet been investigated systematically, and that therefore it is still useful to supplement this largely top-down work by bottom-up empirical discovery of as-yet-unexpected behaviors and computations that may be embedded in the workings of actual brain structures and interactions among them. We have begun by studying a simple cortical structure and its connections with the periphery, in part because we could then have some assurance of knowing the nature of the behaviorally relevant inputs to that structure. Now that we have developed some initial understanding of the outputs of these systems, we intend to move inward to more central brain structures, whose inputs are provided by the outputs of the structures described here. Because we have been faithful to the bottom-up biological characteristics of these networks, we anticipate that we will be able to build directly on this work when we simulate additional brain structures, and that these new simulations will elide smoothly with the present simulations.

ACKNOWLEDGMENTS

This research was supported in part by the Office of Naval Research under grants N00014-84-K-0391 and N00014-87-K-0838, the National Science Foundation under grant IST-85-12419, and by a grant from the J. Howard Pew Trust.

This work has benefitted greatly from experimental results and theoretical work by Phil Antón, Jim Whitson, and John Larson; we owe them many thanks; we also appreciate the efforts of those who read and commented on this chapter, especially the editors, Mark Gluck and David Rumelhart.

REFERENCES

Anderson, J. A. & Mozer, M. (1981). Categorization and selective neurons. In G. Hinton & J. A. Anderson (Eds.), *Parallel models of associative memory.* Hillsdale, NJ: Lawrence Erlbaum Associates.

Bliss, T. V. P., & Lømo, T. (1973). Long-lasting potentiation of synaptic transmission in the dentate area of the anesthetized rabbit following stimulation of the perforant path. *Journal of Physiology, London, 232,* 357–374.

Duda, R. O., & Hart, P. E. (1973). *Pattern classification and scene analysis.* New York: Wiley.

Dunwiddie, T. V., & Lynch, G. (1978). Long-term potentiation and depression of synaptic responses in the rat hippocampus: Localization and frequency dependency. *Journal of Physiology, London, 276,* 353–367.

Gluck, M. A., & Bower, G. H. (1988). From conditioning to category learning: An adaptive network model. *Journal of Experimental Psychology, 117,* 227–247.

Granger, R., Ambros-Ingerson, J., Henry, H., & Lynch, G. (1987). Partitioning of sensory data by a cortical network. *Proceedings of the IEEE Conference on Neural Information Processing Systems,* American Institute of Physics Publications.

Granger, R., Ambros-Ingerson, J., & Lynch, G. (1989). Derivation of encoding characteristics of layer II cerebral cortex. *Journal of Cognitive Neuroscience, 1,* 61–87.

Granger, R., & Schlimmer, J. C. (1986). The computation of contingency in classical conditioning. *Psychology of Learning and Motivation, 20,* 137–192.

Grossberg, S. (1976). Adaptive pattern classification and universal recoding: Part I. *Biological Cybernetics, 23,* 121–134.

Haberly, L. B., & Price, J. L. (1977). The axonal projection of the mitral and tufted cells of the olfactory bulb in the rat. *Brain Research, 129,* 152–157.

Haberly, L. B. (1985). Neuronal circuitry in olfactory cortex: Anatomy and functional implications. *Chemical Senses, 10,* 219–238.

Kauer, J. S. (1987). Coding in the olfactory system. In T. E. Finger (Ed.) *Neurobiology of taste and smell* (pp. 205–231.) New York: Wiley.

Larson, J., & Lynch, G. (1986). Synaptic potentiation in hippocampus by patterned stimulation involves two events. *Science, 232,* 985–988.

Linsker, R. (1986). From basic network principles to neural architecture. *Proceedings of the National Academy of Sciences, 83,* 7508–7512, 8390–8394, 8779–8783.

Linsker, R. (1988). Self-Organization in a perceptual network. *IEEE Computer, 21,* 105–117.

Lynch, G. (1986). *Synapses, circuits and the beginnings of memory.* Cambridge, MA: MIT Press.

Lynch, G., & Granger, R. (1989). Simulation and analysis of a cortical network. *The psychology of learning and motivation,* Vol. 23.

MacKay-Sim, A., Shaman, P., & Moulton, D. G. (1982). Topographic coding of olfactory quality: Odorant-specific patterns of epithelial responsivity in the salamander. *Journal of Neuropsychology, 48,* 584–596.

Macrides, F., Eichenbaum, H. B., & Forbes, W. B. (1982). Temporal relationship between sniffing and the limbic (theta) rhythm during odor discrimination reversal learning. *Journal of Neuroscience, 2,* 1705–1717.

McCollum, J., Larson, J., Otto, T., & Lynch, G. (1988). Single unit activity in pyriform cortex of rats during olfactory discrimination learning. *Neuroscience Abstracts,* 160.11.

Mori, K. (1987). Membrane and synaptic properties of identified neurons in the olfactory bulb. *Progress in Neurobiology, 29,* 275–320.

Morris, R. G. M., Anderson, E., Lynch, G., & Baudry, M. (1986). Selective impairment of learning and blockade of long-term potentiation by an N-methyl-D-aspartate receptor antagonist, AP-5. *Nature, 319,* 774–776.

Mouly, A. M., Vigouroux, M., & Holley, A. (1987). On the ability of rats to discriminate between microstimulations of the olfactory bulb in different locations. *Behavioral Brain Research, 17,* 45–58.

Otto, T., Staubli, U., & Lynch, G. (1988). Theta stimulation of the lateral olfactory tract serves as a use in a successive-cue olfactory discrimination task. *Neuroscience Abstracts,* 226.8.

Parker, D. B. (1985). *Learning-logic.* TR-47, Cambridge, MA.: MIT Center for research in computational economics and management science.

Price, J. L. (1985). Beyond the primary olfactory cortex: Olfactory-related areas in the neocortex, thalamus and hypothalamus. *Chemical Senses, 10,* 239–258.

Roman, F, Staubli, U., & Lynch, G. (1987). Evidence for synaptic potentiation in a cortical network during learning. *Brain Research, 418,* 221–226.

Rumelhart, D., Hinton, G., & Williams, R. (1986). Learning Internal Representations by Error Propagation. In D. Rumelhart & J. McClelland (Eds.), *Parallel distributed processing.* Cambridge, MA: MIT Press.

Rumelhart, D., & McClelland, J. (Eds.). (1986). Parallel distributed processing. Cambridge, MA: MIT Press.

Rumelhart, D., & Zipser, D. (1986). Competitive Learning. In D. Rumelhart & J. McClelland (Eds.), *Parallel distributed processing.* Cambridge, MA: MIT Press.

Schwob, J. E., & Price, J. L. (1978). The cortical projection of the olfactory bulb: Development in fetal and neonatal rats correlated with quantitative variation in adult rats. *Brain Research, 151,* 369–374.

Scott, J. W. (1987). Organization of olfactory bulb output cells and their local circuits. *Annals of the New York Academy of Science,* 44–48.

Shepherd, G. (1970). The olfactory bulb as a simple cortical system: experimental analysis and functional implications. In F. O. Schmitt (Ed.), *The neurosciences: Second study program,* (pp. 539–552). NY: Rockefeller.

Shepherd, G. (1972). Synaptic organization of the mammalian olfactory bulb. *Physiological Review, 52,* 864–917.

Shepherd, G. (1979). *The synaptic organization of the brain.* Oxford: Oxford University Press.

Staubli, U., Baudry, M., & Lynch, G. (1984). Leupeptin, a thiol-proteinase inhibitor, causes a selective impairment of spatial maze performance in rats. *Behavioral Neural Biology, 40,* 58–69.

Staubli, U., Baudry, M., & Lynch, G. (1985a). Olfactory discrimination learning is blocked by leupeptin, a thiol-proteinase inhibitor. *Brain Research, 337,* 333–336.

Staubli, U., Roman, F., & Lynch, G. (1985b). Selective changes in synaptic responses elicited in a cortical network by behaviorally relevant electrical stimulation. *Neurosci. Abstract, 837.*

Staubli, U., Fraser, D., Faraday, R., & Lynch, G. (1987). Olfaction and the "data" memory system in rats. *Behavioral Neuroscience, 101,* 757–765.

Staubli, U., & Lynch, G. (1987). Stable hippocampal long-term potentiation elicited by "theta" pattern stimulation. *Brain Research, 435,* 227–234.

Sutton, R. S., & Barto, A. G. (1981). Toward a modern theory of adaptive networks: Expectation and prediction. *Psychological Review, 38,* 135–171.

von der Malsburg, C. (1973). Self-organizing of orientation sensitive cells in the striate cortex. *Kybernetik, 14,* 85–100.

Werbos, P. (1974). *Beyond regression: New tools for prediction and analysis in the behavioral sciences.* Unpublished doctoral dissertation, Harvard University.

Widrow, B., & Hoff, M. E. (1959). Adaptive switching circuits. *Institute of radio engineers, Western Electronic Convention Record, Part 4,* pp. 96–104.

4

Adaptive Signal Processing and the Cerebellum: Models of Classical Conditioning and VOR Adaptation

Mark A. Gluck
Eric S. Reifsnider
Department of Psychology, Stanford University

Richard F. Thompson
Department of Psychology,
University of Southern California

INTRODUCTION

Our long-term goal is to analyze how the mammalian brain codes, stores, and retrieves memories. The neural system that forms the core of our research is the cerebellar and brain stem circuits essential for the development and expression of one category of classical conditioning, the most basic form of associative learning. In attempting to identify and characterize the neural substrates of this elementary form of learning, we have found it useful to integrate neurobiological analyses with computational modeling. The resulting computational neural-network models are constrained by both the neurobiological properties of the brain substrates and by the emergent behavioral phenomena exhibited in animals, including humans.

We describe here a neural circuit model proposed by Thompson and colleagues for a basic form of associative learning (see, e.g., Thompson, 1987; Thompson et al., 1988). The model describes the critical brain structures and circuits for the stimulus input, reinforcement, and response generation pathways. Our long-term goal in these computational modeling efforts is to extend this basic circuit model of acquisition to account for the wider range of behavioral phenomena exhibited in classical conditioning. Our strategy for doing this involves drawing heavily on formal behavioral models that account for these behavioral phenomena. An additional constraint on developing neural models of classical conditioning comes from quite a different experimental paradigm: Adaptation of the vestibulo-ocular reflex (VOR). Masao Ito and colleagues presented strong evidence that this adaptation is also mediated by the cerebellum (Ito, 1974, 1982, 1984, 1989). We expect that behavioral and neural models of VOR and classical conditioning should incorporate similar computational components because adaption in both appears to be mediated by common brain substrates.

This chapter is divided into two parts. The first part provides some background in three relevant areas. We summarize the basic behavioral paradigm of classical (Pavlovian) conditioning. We review the work of Thompson and colleages on identifying the neuronal substrates for the acquisition of the conditioned eyeblink response. And finally, we summarize the relevant formal models of conditioning behavior.

The second part describes our recent progress in developing and integrating behavioral and neural models of conditioning; it is also divided into three sections. We describe how Rescorla and Wagner's (1972) model of classical conditioning can be extended to account for the temporal specificity (topography) of the conditioned response. By drawing on engineering theories of adaptive signal processing and adaptive filters (Widrow & Stearns, 1985), this adaptive filter model of conditioning illustrates how the Rescorla–Wagner model of classical conditioning can be extended to account for the temporal specificity of the initial form of the conditioned response (CR) for optimal ISIs; this real-time extension of the Rescorla–Wagner model can capture the **predictive** aspects of conditioned response topography but not the **adaptive** nature of the response. In addition, we note that this model of conditioned response topography bears a strong formal correspondence to Fujita's (1982b) cerebellar model of VOR adaptation. This is important because, as previously noted, neurobiological analyses of both classical conditioning and VOR adaptation have converged quite remarkably toward a common cerebellar substrate. Moreover, we demonstrate that when the temporal sensitivity of the learning algorithm at the synapses is coarse (broadly tuned) rather than precisely tuned, the model exhibits improved noise tolerance. The advantages of coarse coding in distributed representation systems is well-known, especially in models of sensory detection (Baldi & Heiligenberg, 1988; Heiligenberg, 1987; Hinton et al., 1986; Lehky & Sejnowski, 1987, 1988; Sejnowksi, 1988). Ito (1987) reported that the temporal parameters necessary for plasticity at the critical cerebellar sites are broad and coarse, that is, plasticity occurs over a wide range of temporal relationships. Our simulations suggest how these unit-level physiological results might be reconciled with the precise temporal properties and parameters of the behavioral conditioned response.

CLASSICAL CONDITIONING

On a behavioral level, our research focuses on the acquisition of discrete behavioral responses to aversive events, for example, classical conditioning

TABLE 4.1
Classical Conditioning Terminology

Abbreviation	Name	Examples	
		Pavlov	Eye-lid Conditioning
Stimuli			
CS	Conditioned Stimulus	bell	tone
US	Unconditional Stimulus	food	air-puff
Responses			
UR	Unconditional Response	salivating	blinking
CR	Conditioned Response	salivating	blinking

of the eyeblink in rabbits. Classical conditioning is the best understood form of associative learning. Its study dates back to Ivan Pavlov in Russia at the turn of the century. In a series of well-known experiments, Pavlov taught dogs to salivate in response to various cues, such as tones and lights. In general, dogs will not salivate upon hearing a tone. However, after several presentations of a tone followed by food (which does cause salivation), a dog will salivate when presented with the tone alone.

In Pavlov's terminology (see Table 4.1), the tone is a **Conditioned Stimulus** (the CS) and the food an **Unconditional Stimulus**[1] (a US). Salivation, the **Unconditional Response** (UR), is the dog's natural or unconditional response to the food. When the tone (CS) has been repeatedly paired with food (US), the animal comes to generate a **Conditioned Response** (CR) to the tone; in this case, salivation.

Pavlovian (or classical) conditioning is most generally defined as a procedure by which an experimenter presents subjects with stimuli that occur in some prearranged relationship and measures changes in response to one of them. Typically, the experimenter arranges for one of the stimuli, the conditioned stimulus (CS), to be relatively neutral, and for a second stimulus, the unconditional stimulus (US), to reliably elicit a readily measured response. Changes over the course of training in subjects' behavioral response to the conditioned stimulus are said to reflect associative learning when it can be shown that the change is due only to the relationship between the CS and US. Associatively produced changes in subjects' behavior are said to reflect subjects' learning about the causal nature of their environment. When the CS and US are arranged to occur such that the onset of the conditioned stimulus shortly precedes the onset of the unconditional stimulus the conditioned stimulus comes to elicit conditioned responses (CRs) that, in many instances, mimic the unconditional response (UR) to the US (see Donegan & Wagner, 1987; Mackintosh, 1983).

---

[1]The US is often also referred to as an "Unconditioned Response." This is based on an early mistranslation of Pavlov's use of the Russian word for unconditional, *byesyslovny*.

For example, when the CS is a tone and the US is food in the mouth, the CS comes to elicit salivation (Pavlov, 1927); when the US is an air-puff to the eye, the CS comes to elicit eyelid closure (Gormezano, 1972). Within the Pavlovian conditioning literature, much of the research has been designed to determine the ways in which temporal, logical, and qualitative relationships between stimuli influence conditioning (Gormezano, Kehoe, & Marshal, 1983; Rescorla, 1988; Thompson et al., 1988).

Pavlov saw the study of the conditioned reflex as a potential tool for elucidating the neural mechanisms underlying learning. However, the technology necessary to analyze neuronal substrates of classical conditioning was not available in Pavlov's day. In the last 20 years there has been a considerable resurgence of interest in Pavlovian conditioning due to several features of the procedure that make it a very powerful tool for neurobiological analyses. In particular, the occurrence of both the CS and US are determined by the experimenter, not by the subjects' behavior. This has important consequences for the study of the problem of stimulus selection, as subjects' histories of experience with the CS and US can be precisely manipulated. As Lashley (1916) noted, "[In classical conditioning] conditions may be so arranged that only two stimuli, and presumably, one reaction are involved . . . , but its greatest usefulness should be for studies of the temporal relation between the primary and associated stimulus necessary for the formation of the association" (pp. 459–460).

From a neurobiological perspective, the "temporal relation" between the CS and the US is of particular importance because the conditioned response (CR) is time-locked to the conditioned stimulus. Neural events can thereby be analyzed relative to known temporal referents. This feature is a great advantage when trying to detect correlations between changes in neural events, such as electrophysiological recordings, and changes in behavior.

The most productive research strategy for identifying and analyzing neuronal substrates of behavior has been the model system approach: selecting a behavioral paradigm and an organism exhibiting the behavioral phenomena at issue where sufficient experimental control can be exerted and where the essential neuronal circuits can, to some degree, be identified and analyzed. Classical conditioning has proven to be the most powerful model behavioral paradigm for neurobiological analyses of brain substrates of learning and memory, in both invertebrate and vertebrate preparations (see Kandel, 1976; Thompson, 1986; Thompson et al., 1976). Considerable progress has been made in the empirical identification of brain structures and pathways essential for several forms of classical conditioning in the mammalian brain. This chapter focuses on the cerebellar-brain stem circuitry shown by Thompson (1986, 1988) and associates to be essential for classical conditioning of discrete motor responses such as eyeblink and limb flexion conditioning.

Rabbit Eye-blink Conditioning

The rabbit eye-blink preparation was developed and extensively analyzed at the behavioral level by I. Gormezano and colleagues, who sought a suitable animal preparation for the study of physiological, behavioral, and theoretical aspects of conditioning (see Gormezano et al, 1983, for a review). As shown in Fig.4.1, rabbits are restrained in a plexiglass box and movement of their nictitating membrane (an index of eyelid closure) is monitored by a displacement transducer. As summarized in Table 4.1, retraction of the nictitating membrane constitutes both the conditioned response (CR) and the unconditional response (UR). In a typical study, a tone CS is followed 250 ms later by a puff of air (the US) delivered to one eye. Over many blocks of CS-US presentations, the acquisition of the eyeblink proceeds with smooth orderly changes in response frequency, latency, and amplitude, as illustrated in Fig.4.2 (Gormezano et al., 1983). A critically important aspect of this preparation is the fact that the animals do not show nonassociative changes such as sensitization at the behavioral level. In classical condi-

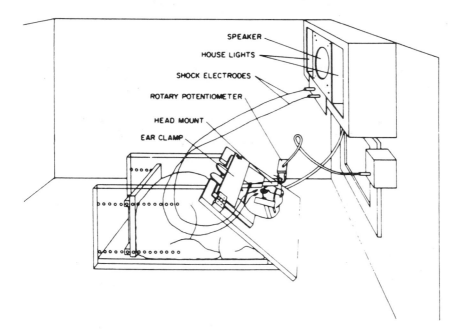

FIG. 4.1. A rabbit in the restraining box with a headset for recording of the nictitating membrane response (NMR). From "Twenty Years of Classical Conditioning Research with the Rabbit" by I. Gormezano, E. K. Kehoe, and B. S. Marshal, 1983, *Progress in Psychobiology and Physiological Psychology,* 10, Fig. 1. Copyright 1983 by Academic Press. Reprinted by permission.

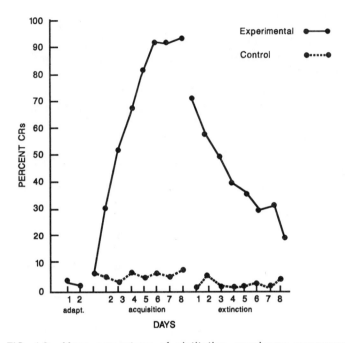

FIG. 4.2. Mean percentage of nictitating membrane responses plotted in 70 trial blocks in acquisition and extinction. Experimental animals received CS-US pairings with an ISI of 500 ms; Control animals received random presentations of the conditioned stimulus alone, and trials of the unconditional stimulus alone. From "Nictitating Membrane: Classical Conditioning and Extinction in the Albino Rabbit" by I. Gormezano, N. Schneiderman, E. Deaux, and I. Fuentes, 1962, Science, 138, Fig. 2. Copyright 1962 by Science. Reprinted with permission.

tioning it is essential to show that learning is truly associative, resulting from the contingent and temporally predictive relationship between the particular CS and the US, rather than due to a generalized increase in responsiveness due to the mere presentation of the stimuli (sensitization). In the rabbit eyelid preparation, the response to the CS does not increase significantly when animals are given unpaired presentations of the CS or the US (see Fig.4.2). Also, the spontaneous level of responding is low, so there is a large signal to noise ratio.[2]

---

[2]In addition to the rabbit eyeblink preparation, two other model systems involving classical conditioning in the mammal have been most productive for analyzing neuronal substrates: learning of cardiovascular responses and learning of "fear." In the cardiovascular conditioning paradigm, an auditory or visual conditioned stimulus of several seconds duration ends with an electric shock to some portion of the body or head. The essential efferent pathway includes

IDENTIFYING MEMORY TRACES
AND MEMORY TRACE CIRCUITS

The problem of localizing the memory trace, first explored in depth by Lashley (1929) and later by Hebb (1949) has been the greatest barrier to progress in identifying the neuronal substrates of learning and memory; it remains fundamental to all work on the biological basis of learning and memory. Mechanisms of memory storage cannot be analyzed until the storage sites have been localized. It is useful to distinguish between the neural circuitry essential (necessary and sufficient) for the development and expression of a particular form of learning—the "essential memory trace circuit"—and the subset of neural elements in this circuit that exhibit the training—induced plasticity necessary for the development of such behavior—the "memory trace" itself. The premise that memory traces are localized does not necessarily imply that a particular trace has a single anatomical location. Rather, the memory trace circuit might involve a number of loci, parallel circuits, and feedback loops. It is important, however, not to confuse the circuitry leading to the memory trace with the circuitry of the trace itself.

To date, the focus of research on mammalian brain substrates of classical conditioning has been on the necessary first step: identification of the essential memory trace circuits (see Thompson et al., 1988). Having done this, the next step is to localize the sites of synaptic plasticity—the memory traces. A powerful tool for localizing sites of memory storage is electrophysiological recording of patterns of neural activity in each synaptic structure in the memory trace circuit. Within a given brain structure it is important to determine whether or not a learning-induced change in activity develops there, or is simply relayed from elsewhere. To evaluate this, one can compare activity of the target structure with activity in sites afferent (earlier in the circuit pathway) to the target structure. Specifically, the activity of output neurons within a nucleus can be compared with the activity of nuclei providing afferent projections to the target nucleus. If the output of the

---

portions of the amygdala, hypothalamus, and descending pathways to the brainstem and spinal cord (Cohen 1980, Kapp et al., 1982; Schneiderman, 1972). Although it is yet not known where the memory traces are located, the amygdala is a possibility—it appears to be more generally involved in conditioned emotional responses such as fear. The acoustic startle response in the rat has been used by Davis and others (Davis et al., 1982) as a model of conditioned emotional state or "fear." Recently, it was discovered that when a light has been paired with a shock, the subsequent potentiating effect of the light on the startle response appears to act on the startle circuit at a brainstem auditory nucleus (the ventral nucleus of the lateral leminiscus, Tischler & Davis, 1983). Essential components of the potentiation circuit involve the geniculo-cortical visual system and the amygdala. The actual sites of memory trace formation for this conditioned fear process have not yet been determined.

target nucleus shows changes over the course of training, but the activity of afferent nuclei does not, then one has evidence of training-induced neural plasticity within the target regions.

When this electrophysiological analysis has been completed for each major synaptic relay in the essential memory trace circuit, the functional neuroanatomy of the conditioned response circuit will have been characterized and the sites of plasticity localized. The cellular-synaptic mechanisms of memory trace formation can then be analyzed. Once this reductionistic odyssey has been completed, it is necessary to show that the identified essential memory trace circuit and the embedded mechanisms of synaptic plasticity can, in fact, generate all the emergent behavioral phenomena of learning and memory, in this case the phenomena of classical conditioning. This is most easily done by developing realistic mathematical-computational models of the identified circuits. At this point it is not merely interesting to develop computational models of the empirically identified neural memory, it is necessary to do so if we wish to understand the functioning of the system; a verbal or qualitative analysis of the behavior of complex neural circuits is rarely possible, even in the simplest of neural systems (Gluck & Thompson, 1987).

Neural Circuits for Conditioning
of Discrete Behavioral Responses

Researchers studying the mammalian brain have been able to identify and characterize much of the learning and memory circuitry that underlies conditioning of discrete behavioral responses. The evidence argues strongly that the cerebellum and its associated brain stem circuitry is essential — both necessary and sufficient — for classical conditioning of eyelid closure, limb flexion, and other discrete responses that are learned in order to deal with aversive stimuli (Thompson, 1986, 1988).

The cerebellum (Latin for "little brain") is a phylogenetically old structure, already well developed in lower animals (see Fig.4.3). The cerebellum has continued to evolve apace with the forebrain (cerebral cortex). Indeed, although it is much smaller in volume, the deeply enfolded cerebellar cortex has a surface area almost as large as the area of the cerebral cortex in mammals, including humans. All areas of the cerebellum share the same cytoarchitectural organization (properties of the layers of the cortex); this contrasts markedly to the cerebral cortex, which has many cytoarchitecturally differing areas (e.g., visual cortex, motor cortex, association cortex). Indeed, this uniformity of cerebellar cortex has fascinated theoretical modelers — computational models of how the cerebellum could function as a system to store motor programs and motor memories have been driven by the simple and uniform elegance of its cellular organization

MOTOR CONTROL SYSTEMS

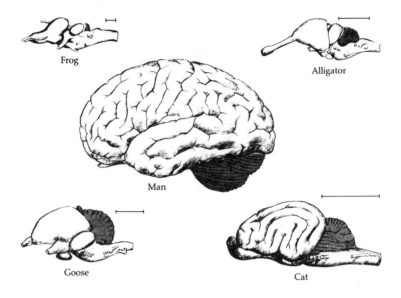

FIG. 4.3A. The location and size of the cerebellum in several species. (After R. R. Llinas, *Scientific American, 232*(1): 56–71, 1975.)

(Albus, 1971; Brindley, 1964; Eccles, 1977; Fujita, 1982a; Grossberg, 1969; Ito, 1974; Marr, 1969; Pellionisz & Llinas, 1979).

The basic organization of the cerebellum is indicated in Fig.4.4. The two principal inputs to the cerebellum are climbing and mossy fibers. Climbing fibers come entirely from the neurons of a structure in the brain stem termed the inferior olive. The climbing fibers send collaterals (branches) to the deep nuclei and project to the cerebellar cortex, where a given Purkinje cell receives a powerful excitatory synaptic input from one, and only one, climbing fiber. The inferior olive, in turn, receives its primary sensory input from the somatic sensory systems (skin, joints, pain, etc.) but it is also connected to other sensory circuits.

The mossy fibers originate predominantly from neurons in the pontine nuclei of the brain stem, but from other sources as well, for example, direct somatic sensory input. They project to the cerebellar cortex, where they synapse on granule cells. Mossy fibers also send collaterals to the deep nuclei. The granule cells in turn project to the Purkinje cells as parallel fibers. A given parallel fiber, in turn, contacts hundreds of Purkinje cells with *en passant* excitatory synapses. The pontine nuclei, in turn, receive projections from many places in the brain, including heavy projections from the cerebral cortex.

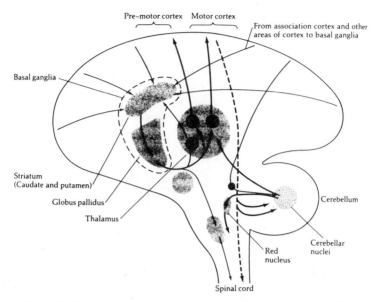

FIG. 4.3B. The major brain systems involved in "voluntary" skilled movements. (Modified from E. V. Evarts, "Brain mechanisms of movement." In *The Brain*, San Francisco: W. H. Freeman & Co., 1979).

The responses of a Purkinje cell to mossy-parallel fiber activation and climbing fiber activation are quite different. Thus, activation by parallel fibers yields single action potentials, termed *simple spikes*. The spontaneous rate of activation of Purkinje cells by granule cells (parallel fibers) in the awake animal is quite variable and can range as high as 50/s or more. Activation of a Purkinje cell by a climbing fiber yields a very brief, high-frequency action potential train (several hundred per second) that lasts for only a few spikes, later spikes in the train showing reduced amplitudes. This Purkinje cell response to activation by a climbing fiber is termed a *complex spike*. The simple spike response to parallel fiber activation and the complex spike response to climbing fiber activation are easily distinguished in extracellular single unit recordings from a Purkinje cell.

There are several types of inhibitory interneurons in cerebellar cortex — Golgi cells, stellate cells, and basket cells. Indeed the only excitatory neurons in cerebellar cortex are the granule cells giving rise to the parallel fibers. All other neurons in cerebellar cortex are inhibitory and are thought to use GABA (gamma amino butyric acid) as their inhibitory neurotransmitter. As can be seen in Fig.4.4, the Golgi neurons are activated primarily by parallel fibers that then make inhibitory synapses on granule cells, thereby constituting an inhibitory feedback loop. The stellate and basket

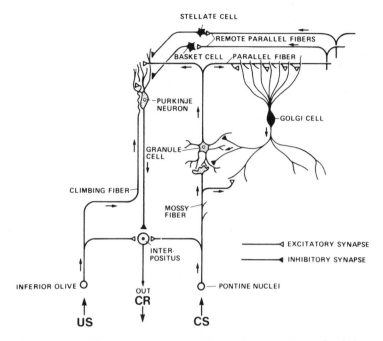

FIG. 4.4. Schematic of the cerebellar brain-stem circuit. Depicts the afferents assumed to carry information about CS and US occurrence, the connectivity of the cerebellar cortex and deep nuclei, and the efferents from the cerebellum involved in the generation of the conditioned eyeblink response (CR). Information about the occurrence of the conditioned stimulus comes from mossy fiber projections to the cerebellum via the pontine nuclei. The reinforcement pathway, which carries information about the unconditional stimulus (US), is taken to be the climbing fibers from the inferior olive. The efferent pathway for the conditioned response (CR) consists of projections from the interpositus nucleus which act ultimately upon motor neurons.

cells are activated by the parallel fibers and exert inhibition on the Purkinje cells (feed forward inhibition).

In terms of input to the cerebellar cortex, the climbing and mossy-parallel fiber systems are thus quite differently organized. The climbing fibers have very localized and powerfully excitatory actions on Purkinje cells and the mossy-parallel fibers have a much more distributed and less strongly excitatory action on Purkinje cells. The organization led theorists to the notions that the localized climbing fiber input is the "teaching" input and the distributed mossy-parallel fiber input is the "learning" input (e.g., Albus, 1971; Marr, 1969).

In terms of its connection with the rest of the brain, the only output from the cerebellum comes from the cerebellar deep nuclei (e.g., dentate n., interpositus n., fastigial n., and vestibular n.), which project both (dentate) to higher brain structure and (interpositus) to lower brain structures. Purkinje cells are the only neurons that project information out from the cerebellar cortex and they project only to the deep nuclei. Furthermore, their synaptic actions are thought to be entirely inhibitory.

A final point concerns the organization of somatic sensory input to the cerebellum. Like the cerebral cortex, there are several different regions of cerebellar cortex that contain representations or maps of the body surface; information about events of the skin and body are represented in multiple redundance. But unlike those in the cerebral cortex, these maps do not have topological "coherence." In cerebral cortex there is a literal, but distorted, representation of the body surface over the region of cortex for each map (distorted in that more sensitive regions, e.g., fingers in primates, have much larger relative representations). However, in cerebellar cortex, the representation of various regions of the body appear to be chaotic (eyelid region next to finger region). This incoherent mapping has been termed *fractured somatotopy* (Kassel, Shambes, & Welker, 1984).

Evidence to date regarding the essential circuitry for classical conditioning of eyeblink and other discrete behavioral responses (Thompson, 1986, 1988) is strikingly consistent with the spirit of computational models of how the cerebellum might function as a motor learning machine (Albus, 1971; Eccles, 1977; Ito, 1984, 1989; Marr, 1969). Information about the tone CS appears to project via mossy fibers to both the cerebellar cortex and the deep nuclei: this is termed the *CS pathway* (see Fig.4.4). The interpositus nucleus sends projections down through the red nucleus, which ultimately drive the conditioned eyeblink response: this is termed the *CR pathway*. Information about the airpuff US has two effects. First, it drives motor neurons that generate an eyeblink UR: This is the *US-UR pathway* in the brainstem and is not shown in Fig.4.4. Information about the airpuff US also projects to a portion of the inferior olive that, in turn, projects via climbing fibers to the cerebellar cortex and deep nuclei: This appears to be the "teaching" or *reinforcement pathway*. Evidence to date argues that the memory traces are stored in the cerebellum; a more detailed description of the empirical support for this circuit model of conditioned response learning and memory is presented in the next section.

Empirical Support for Circuit Model

We (RFT and associates) have shown that a very localized region of the cerebellar interpositus nucleus ipsilateral (same side) to the trained eye is critical in eyelid conditioning. Small lesions of this region completely and permanently abolish the ipsilateral eyelid CR, have no effect on the reflex eyelid closure to the corneal airpuff US and do not impair learning by the contralateral (other side) eye. If the lesion is made before training, the ipsilateral eye is unable to learn (Lincoln, McCormick, & Thompson, 1982; McCormick et al., 1981; McCormick & Thompson, 1984a). Chemical lesions of the interpositus nucleus, which destroy only cell bodies (i.e., spare fibers of passage) abolish the conditioned response with no accompanying degeneration in the inferior olive (Lavond, Hembree, & Thompson, 1985). Although most of our work has used the conditioned eyelid response, our evidence indicates that the cerebellar interpositus nucleus is necessary for the learning of a wide range of discrete behavioral responses and may, in fact, be necessary for all such responses.

Thus, the region of the interpositus nucleus essential for conditioning of the hind limb flexion reflex is medial to the region essential for the learned eyelid response (Donegan, Lowry, & Thompson, 1983; Thompson, 1986). It appears that a complete set of motor programs are present and hardwired from interpositus to motor nuclei and are represented in a somatotopic organization consistent with the patterns of projection of somatic sensory information to the nucleus. Over the course of learning, the region of the interpositus appropriate for the particular unconditional stimulus used (e.g., corneal airpuff, paw shock) becomes activated by the conditioned stimulus. In the next few paragraphs we review the specific empirical evidence for each of the major assumptions of our circuit model.

Role of Purkinje Cells

Thompson and associates (Donegan, Foy, & Thompson, 1985; Foy & Thompson, 1986) found that prior to eyelid conditioning, a great majority of the Purkinje cells that respond to tones in the lobus simplex (an area of cerebellar cortex) show variable increases in simple spike discharge frequency (parallel fiber evoked responses); whereas after training, the majority show a learning-induced decrease in simple spike frequency to the tone conditioned stimulus that precedes and models the conditioned eyeblink response (see Fig.4.5a). Furthermore, the frequency of climbing fiber responses evoked by the corneal airpuff unconditional stimulus decreased markedly as a result of training, consistent with the hypothesized error signal role of climbing fibers.

CR Pathway

The essential efferent (outgoing) CR pathway consists of fibers that exit the interpositus nucleus ipsilateral to the trained side of the body, cross to relay in a contralateral division of the red nucleus, and then cross back to descend in the rubral pathway to act ultimately on motor neurons (see Fig.4.4). We do not know whether other efferent systems are involved in controlling the CR, although descending systems originating rostral to the

PURKINJE CELL

EYEBLINK CR

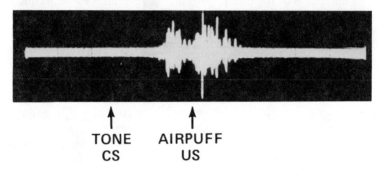

↑ TONE CS

↑ AIRPUFF US

FIG. 4.5. (a)   A Purkinje cell from a well-trained animal showing a decrease in simple spike firing that precedes and models the conditioned eyeblink response. (Unpublished data from Foy & Thompson, 1986.) (b) Histograms of unit recordings obtained from a chronic electrode implanted at the lateral border of the interpositus nucleus. The animal was first given random unpaired presentations of the tone and airpuff (104 of each) and then trained with 2 days of paired training (117 trials/day). Each histogram is an average over the entire day of training indicated. The upper trace represents movement of the nictitating membrane (NM). The first vertical line represents the onset of the tone CS, while the second line represents the onset of the corneal airpuff US. Each histogram bar is 9 ms in duration. Notice that these neurons develop a model of the conditioned but not unconditioned response during learning, and that this neuronal model precedes the learned behavioral response substantially in time. (From McCormick & Thompson, 1984b.)

midbrain are not required for learning or retention of the CR (Mauk & Thompson, 1987; Norman, Buchwald, & Villablanca, 1977).

US Reinforcement Pathway

Recent research using lesion and microstimulation indicates that the essential reinforcement pathway for the US travels from the trigeminal nucleus to the dorsal accessory olive (DAO) portion of the inferior olive,

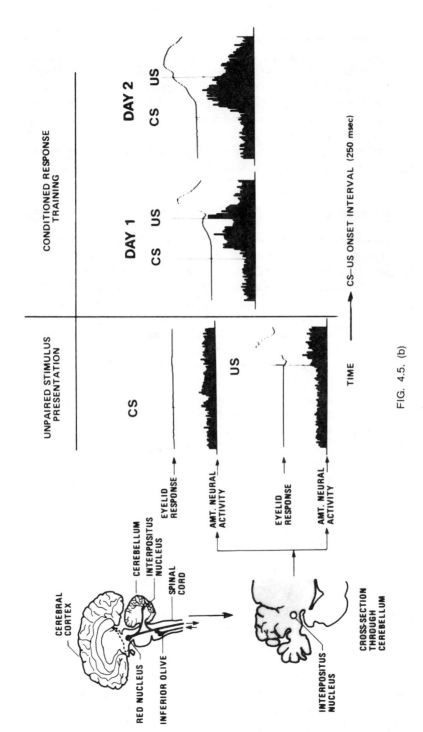

FIG. 4.5. (b)

145

from where climbing fibers arise and project through the inferior cerebellar peduncle to the cerebellum (see Fig.4.4). Thus, lesions of the appropriate region of the DAO prevent acquisition and result in normal extinction of the behavioral CR with continued paired training in animals that already have been trained (McCormick, Steinmetz, & Thompson, 1985). Electrical microstimulation of this same region produces behavioral responses and functions as an effective US for normal learning of behavioral CRs; the precise behavioral response produced by DAO stimulation is learned as a normal conditioned response (CR) to a tone or light CS (Mauk, Steinmetz, & Thompson, 1986).

CS Pathway

Preliminary evidence from our laboratory suggests that the auditory CS pathway projects from the cochlear nuclei to the contralateral lateral pontine nuclear region and from there to the cerebellum via mossy fibers in the middle cerebellar peduncle (Fig.4.4). Thus, lesions of the middle cerebellar peduncle prevent acquisition and immediately abolish retention of the eyelid CR to all CS modalities (Solomon, Lewis, LoTurco, Steinmetz, & Thompson, 1986). However, discrete lesions in the pontine nuclear region can selectively abolish the eyelid conditioned response (CR) to an acoustic conditioned stimulus (CS) with no impairment of responding to a light CS (Steinmetz, Logan, Rosen, J. Thompson, Lavond, & Thompson, 1987). If animals are trained with left pontine nuclear stimulation as the conditioned stimulus and subsequently tested for transfer to right pontine stimulation, transfer takes place immediately (in one trial) if the two electrodes have similar locations on the two sides. This suggests that under these conditions the traces are not formed in the pontine nuclei but instead are formed beyond the mossy fiber terminals in the cerebellum, that is, the pontine nuclei are afferent to the memory trace (Steinmetz, Rosen, Woodruff-Pak, Lavond, & Thompson, 1986).

Role of Interpositus Nucleus

The interpositus nucleus formed an initial focus for electrophysiological analysis in classical conditioning of discrete behavioral responses, particularly conditioned eyelid closure. We have identified a region of the interpositus that, when destroyed, completely prevents learning and memory of the eyelid response. Unit recordings from this region show the development of a pattern of increased frequency of unit discharges that models the amplitude-time course of the learned response (the conditioned eyelid closure) but precedes it in time by as much as 60 ms or more within trials. This activity pattern develops in close association with the development of the eyelid CR and does not model or relate to the reflex eyelid closure UR (see Fig.4.5b; McCormick & Thompson, 1984a, 1984b). This learning-induced unit response in the interpositus is completely predictive of the learned behavioral response both within trials and over the trials of training; it is isomorphic and temporally predictive. Coupled with the interpositus lesion abolition of the CR, this argues strongly that the memory trace must be in the interpositus or in structures afferent to the interpositus. This hypothesis is strongly supported by other evidence as well (Chapman, Steinmetz, Thompson, 1988; Thompson, 1986; Yeo et al., 1985a, 1985b).

Taken together, the interpositus, cochlear nucleus, and pontine recordings argue that the memory trace must be in the cerebellum. Indeed, recordings from identified Purkinje cells in cerebellar cortex do show dramatic, learning related changes in simple spike discharges (responses to mossy-parallel fiber activation). Prior to training the great majority of Purkinje cells that are influenced by the tone CS (in H VI, Crus I, Crus II) show variable increases in simple spike discharge frequency (parallel fiber-evoked responses). After training, the majority show tone CS evoked decreases in frequency of discharge that precede and predict the occurrence of the behavioral CR within trials (Donegan et al., 1985; Foy & Thompson, 1986). Purkinje cells inhibit interpositus cells, and as a result decreased Purkinje cell activity would increase interpositus cell activity. The onset of decreased Purkinje cell activity can precede the onset of the behavioral CR by as much as 85 ms within a trial. Thus, learning-induced changes in Purkinje cell activity and interpositus neuron activity are the shortest onset latency neuronal responses within trials in the memory trace circuit that show learning-induced changes. They are also the first loci in the circuit from conditioned stimulus to conditioned response where learning-induced changes are seen.

How relevant is this animal model of memory storage to human memory? A recent article in the *Journal of Physiology* (London) replicates our rabbit cerebellar lesion studies in a human patient (Lye et al., 1988). In brief, the patient suffered a right cerebellar hemisphere infraction; brain scans verified that damage was limited to the right hemisphere. In essence, the patient's right eye was unable to learn the conditioned eyeblink response with repeated training sessions. The left eye learned rapidly and robustly. Reflex responses of both eyes and sensory sensitivity to both the US and CS were normal. It is very gratifying to see that results of research on an animal model of basic associative learning and memory apply exactly to the human condition. We can now feel reasonable confidence that the basic mechanisms of memory storage we elucidate in the rabbit eyelid preparation will apply in detail to the human brain.

Summary

Our results to date are strikingly consistent with the classical theoretical and computational models of the role of the cerebellum in motor learning

(Albus, 1971; Eccles, 1977; Ito, 1974; Marr, 1969), all of which characterize the mossy-parallel fibers as the learning system and the climbing fibers as the teaching system.

FORMAL BEHAVIORAL MODELS
OF CONDITIONING

Models of Classical Conditioning can be divided into three classes depending on the extent to which they are sensitive to the temporal properties of the paradigm (see Table 4.2).

Trial-level models describe the net effects of a training trial on the strengths of CS-US associations. By definition, trial-level models do not address many important real-time aspects of conditioning such as the intra-trial temporal relationship between the conditioned stimulus (CS) and the unconditional stimulus (US) and the temporal properties of response generation. A notable example is the Rescorla-Wagner (1972) model.

Temporal models capture the animals' sensitivity to the temporal relationships among the stimulus inputs, that is, between CSs and USs. Temporal models account for inter-stimulus interval (ISI) effects on the rate and asymptote of conditioning as well as sequential phenomena such as second order conditioning. Like trial-level models that describe the effects of the net input on the net output, temporal models make predictions only about the net magnitude of the output response. That is, they treat the output of the system, the CR, as a single scalar value. Examples of such models include SOP (Donegan & Wagner, 1987; Mazur & Wagner, 1982; Wagner, 1981), Sutton and Barto's adaptive element model (Sutton & Barto, 1981, 1987), and Klopf's "differential-Hebbian" model (Gluck, Parker, & Reifsnider, 1988, 1989; Klopf, 1988).

Real-time models attempt to capture the animals' sensitivity to temporal relationships on the input as well as the output; these models try to predict the precise form and timing of the conditioned response (see, e.g., Desmond & Moore, 1988; Moore & Blazis, 1989). When an animal is trained in the conditioned eye-blink paradigm it learns more than just an association, it learns to generate a temporally precise motor movement. If the airpuff

TABLE 4.2
Typology of Classical Conditioning Models

	Temporal Sensitivity	
	Stimuli	*Response*
Trial Level	No	No
Temporal	Yes	No
Real Time	Yes	Yes

comes 200 ms after the tone, the animal learns to blink 200 ms after the tone; if the airpuff comes 400 ms after the tone, the animal learns to wait 400 ms. Thus, real-time models should capture the animal's ability to learn to predict and anticipate the precise temporal characteristics of an aversive event.

Later in this chapter we present a first approximation towards a real-time model of conditioned response topography. The model is a natural generalization of Rescorla and Wagner's trial-level model. It is not intended to account for all of the relevant phenomena of response topography. Rather, the primary goal of the model is to see how far we can go in capturing response topography by modifying only the stimulus-representation assumptions of the Rescorla–Wagner model.

The Rescorla-Wagner Model

The Rescorla–Wagner model is of particular interest because of its similarity to learning algorithms influential in adaptive network theories of cognition and adaptive systems. We begin by describing the Rescorla-Wagner model and, as noted by Sutton and Barto (1981), show how it is formally equivalent to the Least-Mean-Squares (LMS) algorithm of Widrow and Hoff (1960).

To review again the terminology of classical Pavlovian conditioning (see Table 4.1): a previously neutral stimulus, the conditioned stimulus (CS), such as a bell, comes to be associated with a biologically significant stimulus, the unconditional stimulus (US), such as food or an air-puff. Early learning theories assumed that the simple temporal contiguity or joint occurrence of a CS and US was sufficient for associative learning (e.g., Hull, 1943; Spence, 1956). Later experiments made clear, however, that simple contiguity was not sufficient. The ability of a CS to become conditioned to a US depended on its imparting reliable and nonredundant information about the occurrence of the US (Kamin, 1969; Rescorla, 1968; Wagner, 1969).

As described later, the Rescorla–Wagner model was designed to account for a variety of phenomena of associative learning observed in classical conditioning, especially phenomena of stimulus selection and conditioned inhibition (see also Donegan, Gluck, & Thompson, 1989). The model computes the effects of a training *trial* — pairings of conditioned stimuli (CSs) with an unconditional stimulus (US) — on the strengths of CS associations. The Rescorla–Wagner model can be viewed as a rule that specifies how the variables of CS and US intensity along with the animal's expectancy for the US on a trial combine to determine the changes in associative strengths produced by the trial.

The Rescorla–Wagner model proposes that phenomena of stimulus selection can be explained by assuming that the effectiveness of a US for producing associative learning depends on the relationship between the US and the expected outcome (Kamin, 1969; Rescorla, 1968; Wagner, 1969). In a critical experiment illustrating this principle, Kamin (1969) began by training animals with a light, the CS, which was paired with a shock US (see Table 4.3).

In the second phase of training a compound stimulus consisting of a light and a tone was paired with the shock. Surprisingly, subjects learned very little about the *tone→shock* relationship as compared to control subjects who had received identical numbers of *tone+light→shock* trials, but no pretraining to the light. Kamin described this as a blocking effect because prior training of the *light→shock* association blocked learning of the *tone→shock* association during the second stage of training.

To account for blocking and related phenomena, the Rescorla–Wagner model assumes that changes in the strength of an association between a particular CS and its outcome is proportional to the degree to which the outcome is unexpected (or unpredicted) given all the stimulus elements present on that trial. To formally describe this assumption, Rescorla and Wagner used V_i to denote the strength of association between stimulus element CS_i and the US. If CS_i is followed by an unconditional stimulus, then the change in association strength between CS_i and the US, ΔV_i, can be described by:

$$\Delta V_i = \alpha_i \beta_1 (\lambda_1 - \sum_{s \in S} V_s), \tag{1}$$

where α_i is a learning rate parameter indexing the salience of CS_i (often ommitted from general usage of the model), β_1 is a learning rate parameter that reflects the salience of the US, λ_1 is equated with the maximum possible level of association strength supported by the US intensity and $\sum_{s \in S} V_s$ is the *sum of the associative strengths* between all the stimulus elements present on that trial — including CS_i — and the US. If CS_i is presented and not reinforced, then the association between CS_i and the US decreases analogously by:

TABLE 4.3
Kamin's Blocking Paradigm

Phase	1 Element Training	2 Compound Training	3 Test
Group I	Light → US	Light+Tone → US	Tone
Group II	—	Light+Tone → US	Tone

Note. Results: Less conditioning to the tone in Phase 2 for Group I than Group II. Prior training on light in Group I "blocks" conditioning to tone.

$$\Delta V_i = \alpha_i \beta_2 (\lambda_2 - \sum_{s \in S} V_s), \tag{2}$$

where λ_2 is generally taken to be 0, β_2 is a parameter which reflects the rate of learning on trials without US presentations, and the other parameters are as in equation 1.

The model accounts for the blocking effect as follows: In Phase 1, CS_1 is paired with the US and V_1 approaches the maximum associative value (e.g., $\lambda_1 = 1$). In Phase 2, CS_1 is presented in compound with a neutral CS_2 (i.e., V_2, begins at zero) and the compound is followed by the US. In a comparison group, CS_1 and CS_2 enter the compound phase with no prior training (i.e., $V_1 = V_2 = 0$). By equation 1, increments in associative strength accruing to the novel stimulus, CS_2, should be less in the blocking (Group I) than in the comparison (Group II) condition.

By a similar logic, the model also accounts for such phenomena as multitrial overshadowing (Wagner, 1969), and conditioned inhibition (Wagner & Rescorla, 1972), and sensitivity to the CS-US contingency (Rescorla, 1968). Despite some limitations of the model in dealing with phenomena such as learned irrelevance and the extinction of conditioned inhibitors (see Zimmer-Hart & Rescorla, 1974), the Rescorla–Wagner model continues to be the most influential trial-level model of the associative changes occurring during classical conditioning.

Relationship to Widrow-Hoff/LMS Rule

Following Sutton and Barto (1981), we note that in equations 1 and 2 of the Rescorla-Wagner model, the summation is taken over only those CSs that are present on a trial. With the introduction of a new variable, a_i, which equals 1 if CS_i is present on a trial and O if CS_i is absent, and assuming that all stimuli are equally salient (i.e., the CS dependent learning rates, $\alpha_i = 1$ for all CS_i), and that $\beta_n = \beta_1 = \beta_2$,[3] we can represent equations 1 and 2 as:

$$\Delta w_i = \beta a_i (\lambda - \sum_{j=1} w_j a_j), \tag{3}$$

where the summation is now over all possible CSs, and w_i, the weight from CS-node i to the US, is equivalent to V_i in the Rescorla–Wagner formulation.

The model now describes the associative changes prescribed for all CSs (present or absent). When the US is present $\lambda > 0$, otherwise $\lambda = 0$. Note that for CSs that are not present (i.e., when $a_i = 0$) no changes in associative strength are predicted. This index of CS presence, a_i, should not be

---

[3]The conditioning phenomena that we address do not require differences in β values or α values. However, for some phenomena, such as conditioning with partial reinforcement or pseudodiscrimination training, it is necessary to assume that $\beta_1 < \beta_2$ (see, e.g., Wagner, Logan, Haberlandt, & Price, 1968).

confused with the CS-dependent learning rate, α_i, which does not enter into the calculation of the US expectation, $\sum_{j=1}^{n} w_j a_j$.

As noted by Sutton and Barto (1981) this is the well-known Least-Means-Squares (LMS) algorithm of adaptive network theory (Widrow & Hoff, 1960) also sometimes referred to as the "delta rule." This rule is called "error-correcting" because associative changes are driven by a discrepancy (error) between what the system expects and what actually occurs.

In its most familiar application, the LMS rule is used with an adaptive linear combiner (ALC) as shown in Fig.4.6. The output of an adaptive linear combiner is a weighted linear combination of the input signals. This output is compared with a special input signal called the "desired response," and the difference is the error signal. To minimize the expected error signal, the weighting coefficients are adjusted according to the Widrow–Hoff LMS rule. For a given task, these rules can be shown to find, asymptotically, the set of association weights that minimize the magnitude of the expected (squared) error. When used in this manner, the adaptive linear combiner is analogous to the trial-level Rescorla–Wagner model. In its original application the LMS algorithm was developed to train an adaptive linear combiner with a threshold output; this was called the "Adaline."

Integrating Animal Learning and Connectionist Theory

It is quite remarkable that the same learning rule emerged from such markedly disparate disciplines, each evolving independently, unaware of

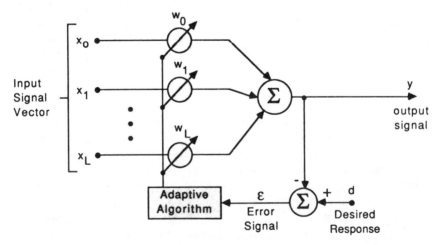

FIG. 4.6. An Adaptive Linear Combiner (ALC). From "Nueral Nets for Adaptive Filtering and Adaptive Pattern Recognition" by B. Widrow and R. Winter, 1988, *Computer*, March, Fig. 1. Copyright 1988. Reprinted with permission.

similar developments in the other field. Animal learning theorists adopted the Rescorla–Wagner/LMS rule because of its elegance and power in predicting a wide range of behavioral phenomena; adaptive network—or connectionist—theorists adopted the rule because of its computational power, convergence properties, and generalizability to multilayered networks (e.g., Parker, 1986; Rumelhart, Hinton, & Williams, 1986; Werbos, 1984). The convergence of animal learning theory and adaptive-network theories realized in the Rescorla–Wagner/LMS rule forms a central focus of our research agenda for three reasons:

1. *Neurobiological Implications.* In searching for biological substrates of conditioning we are greatly facilitated by the theoretical and mathematical studies of the LMS rule and its properties (Kohonen, 1977; Parker, 1986). It is our intent to draw on these theoretical insights in analyzing the capabilities of putative neural circuits for implementing the Rescorla–Wagner/LMS rule (discussed later). Furthermore, there exist temporal extensions of the Rescorla–Wagner/LMS rule whose computational properties are also well understood (e.g., Klopf, 1988; Sutton & Barto, 1987). These models suggest research directions for extending our circuit analyses to capture temporal patterns of behavior evident in mammalian conditioning.

2. *Psychological Implications.* Recent studies by Gluck & Bower (1988a,1988b) have shown that the Rescorla–Wagner/LMS rule may be an important component of human learning and decision making. This suggests that classical conditioning—as characterized by the Rescorla–Wagner/LMS rule—may form a component, or "algorithmic building block," for associative learning. The possibility of deriving processes of complex learning from configurations of the elementary associative processes observed in lower animals, suggests a way by which elucidating the biological substrates of conditioning may apply to higher cognitive processes.

3. *Engineering Implications.* Identification and characterization of the neural substrates of conditioning can be the first step towards building physically realizable devices for pattern recognition and intelligence based on the LMS algorithm and its extensions. The backpropagation rule for training multilayer networks (Parker, 1985, 1986; Rumelhart et al., 1986; Werbos, 1974) is a generalization of the simpler Rescorla–Wagner/LMS rule. Moreover, Parker (1986) showed how backpropagation-LMS can be implemented using more elementary Rescorla–Wagner/LMS components. Thus, a circuit that mediates classical conditioning (and hence implements the Rescorla–Wagner/LMS rule) is a sufficiently powerful building block for implementing backpropagation.

CEREBELLAR MODELS OF MOTOR LEARNING

Adaptive Signal Processing and Response Topography

Conditioned Response Topography

An important aspect of the classically conditioned eyeblink response is that it is both temporally predictive and adaptive. The animal learns more than just an association, it learns to generate a temporally precise motor movement that anticipates and mitigates the aversive characteristics of the airpuff US. If the airpuff comes 200 ms after the tone, then the animal learns to blink with maximum effect 200 ms after the tone. This is the predictive component of the response. Furthermore, over the course of training the animal learns to initiate this blink earlier in the trial so that it is fully prepared with a defensive behavior (the blink) before the onset of the aversive stimulus (the airpuff). This is the adaptive, or defensive, component of the response.

Among the many phenomena associated with the temporal form or topography of the conditioned response, we can identify five (hereinafter referred to as item 1, 2, etc.) features of the conditioned response topography that appear to be most fundamental:

1. *CR peak amplitude occurs at US onset.* Regardless of the ISI duration, the peak amplitude of the CR occurs at the onset of the US. (Millenson, Kehoe, & Gormezano, 1977). This effect is consistent across conditioning procedures and subject types. The location of the peak CR amplitude does not depend on the location of the conditioned stimulus, but on the location of the US with respect to the CS onset.

2. *Discrete CR shift with ISI change.* Procedures involving initial training at one ISI followed by training at other ISIs result in a shift in CR peak location so as to maintain the correlation between CR peak and US onset. This shift does not occur through a smooth interpolative change in which the CR latency gradually increases or decreases. Rather, the response probability and amplitude at the first ISI decreases while, simultaneously, there is an increase in the response probability and amplitude at the second ISI. The direction and speed of the shift have no effect on the ultimate location of the CR peak, which inevitably comes to occur at the US onset (Coleman & Gormezano, 1971, p. 451).

3. *Double-peaked CR with mixed ISI training.* In procedures involving a mixture of different ISIs, multiple peaked CRs occur.

When a randomly ordered, but strictly proportioned mixture of a short and a long ISI are used, a double-peaked response results; it is almost as if each ISI received a separate association despite the use of identical stimuli (Millenson et al., 1977).

4. *Dependence of CR acquisition on ISI.* CR acquisition varies dramatically depending on the ISI employed. Both the rate of CR acquisition and the asymptotic probability of responding depend critically on the ISI employed. The optimal ISI is inherent, and different, for each preparation (Gormezano, Kehoe, & Marshall, 1983, p. 213). For most preparations, however, the optimal ISIs range over a very limited range, for example, zero to several seconds (with taste-aversion conditioning being a notable exception). Procedures employing an optimal ISI yield the fastest acquisition and the highest asymptotic probability of responding. With ISIs at or near zero, no acquisition occurs. Both quantities rise toward a maximum as ISI lengths grow; for the rabbit eyeblink preparation, the optimal ISI is approximately 400 ms. Procedures employing ISIs longer than that experience a gradual decline in both the rate of acquisition and the asymptotic levels of responding.

5. *Decrease in CR onset latency during training.* One of the most interesting, and important, aspects of conditioned response topography is the onset of the conditioned response. In fixed ISI training procedures, the CR has been observed to occur initially at the same temporal location as the UR. However, as training continues, the onset moves gradually away from the US onset, towards a point nearer the onset of the conditioned stimulus (CS). Such a motion, which results in a CR that anticipates the US, would seem to be an attempt by the animal to use the conditioned stimulus to lower the effectiveness of an aversive stimulus (or increase the effects of an appetitive stimulus) by producing a preventative (or welcoming) reaction. The decrease in CR onset latency has been observed in a wide variety of procedures, including both human and rabbit eyelid conditioning. In general, onset latencies reach a final asymptotic value of one-half to two-thirds the length of the ISI, depending on the length of the ISI (Millenson et al., 1977).

Adaptive Signal Processing

If we view the (to be) conditioned stimuli as input signals and the desired response topography as a desired output signal, then we can view the problem of CR generation as a problem in adaptive signal processing. That is, what we seek is an *adaptive filter* that will convert the input signals (the

CSs) into the desired output signal (the CR). The term *filter* applies to any device that processes incoming signals in order to eliminate noise, identify signals as belonging to a specific class, or predict some other input signal. Adaptive filters are those filters that design their adjustment settings by iteratively measuring the statistical properties of the environment, (i.e., the adaptive element's input and output signals). The design of adaptive filters is the basis of adaptive signal processing, a field pioneered by Bernard Widrow and colleagues (Widrow & Stearns, 1985). Adaptive filters based on the LMS algorithm have enjoyed great commercial success in a wide variety of signal-processing applications. They are used, for example, in long-distance telephone lines to filter out echoes.

It is intriguing to note that three disparate areas of research into adaptive systems — animal learning theory, connectionist backpropagation models of human learning, and adaptive signal processing — all have their roots in the adaptive properties of Widrow and Hoff's (1960) LMS rule. The common roots between animal learning theory and connectionist theories of adaptive networks have already provided significant synergistic insights for the further development of both animal learning theories (Donegan, Gluck, & Thompson, 1989; Gluck & Thompson, 1987; Klopf, 1988; Sutton & Barto, 1981, 1987; Thompson & Gluck, 1989a, 1989b) and human learning theory (Gluck & Bower, 1988a, 1988b). It would seem natural, therefore, to look towards adaptive signal processing theories as another source of insights and developments that might apply to the other two areas, animal learning theory and connectionist network theories. Widrow and Winter (1988) illustrated a number of ways in which developments in adaptive filtering and connectionist adaptive networks can be conjoined.

Might theories of adaptive filters and adaptive signal processing be used to extend models of animal learning theory? Theoretical and practical developments in adaptive signal processing have shown how the static predictive properties of the LMS rule can be extended to real-time problems in signal classification and production (Widrow & Stearns, 1985). Given the common algorithmic bases for animal learning theory and adaptive filters, it is natural to ask: To what extent can we view adaptive filters as a model of conditioned response topography?

The LMS Spectrum Analyzer. One approach to developing adaptive filters exploits a formal connection between the discrete Fourier transform (DFT) and the LMS algorithm. This approach, called an "LMS spectrum analyzer" is described by Widrow and colleagues (Widrow, 1987; Widrow, Baudrenghien, Vetterli, & Titchener, 1987). It uses a set of N periodic complex "phasors" such as sine waves of various frequencies and phases (see Fig.4.7). The phasors are weighted and summed to generate a desired signal using an adaptive linear combiner (ALC). The weights are adapted ac-

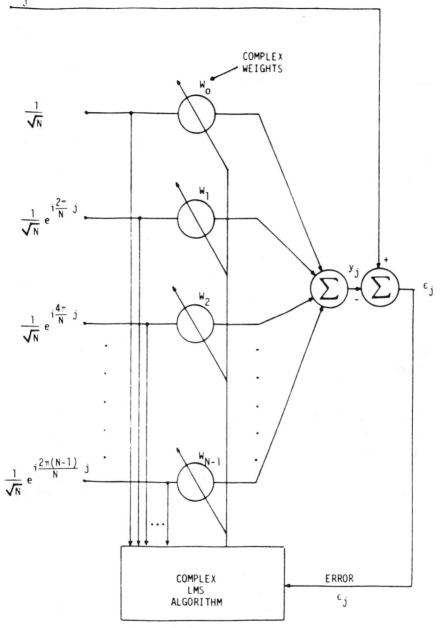

FIG. 4.7. The LMS spectrum analyzer. From "A Fundamental Relationship Between the LMS Algorithm and the Discrete Fourier Transmission" by B. Widrow, 1987, *Proceedings of the IEEE International Symposium on Circuits and Systems,* Philadelphia, PA, May 4–7. Reprinted with permission.

cording to the Widrow–Hoff/LMS that, as described earlier, is equivalent to the Rescorla–Wagner rule. The system attempts to realize a best (least-squared) fit between this reconstructed signal and a desired output signal. Widrow (1987) showed how it is possible to compute a signal's discrete Fourier transform by making use of the LMS adaptive algorithm in this manner.

An LMS Spectrum Analyzer Model of Response Topography.   To develop an adaptive filter model of response topography we begin by assuming that the onset of the conditioned stimulus (CS) generates a collection of input signals to the LMS algorithm. These signals might resemble the sine waves of varying phase and frequency used in the traditional application of the DFT. In our preliminary simulations of an LMS spectrum analyzer model of conditioned response topography, we allowed the onset of the CS to give rise to 120 such input signals. These signals range in frequency from 1 to 30 cycles per trial, with phases of 0, $\pi/2$, π, $3\pi/2$. As a first approximation to a desired CR, we used the temporal pattern of the US input as the desired output. The resulting simulations, shown in Fig.4.8, illustrate how the Rescorla–Wagner/LMS algorithm can build an approximately correct CR given this temporal representation of the CS and US input signals (we review later the clear and obvious limitations of this model). In these simulations, a single trial was modeled as 100 discrete time steps with the onset of the conditioned stimulus (CS) occurring at time step 1 and the unconditional stimulus (US) occurring between time steps 49 and 51, inclusively. A training trial consisted of sweeping through each of these time steps, taking the current value of each of the input lines as the inputs and the current value of the US as the desired CR output, and then updating the 120 weights according to the Rescorla–Wagner/LMS algorithm. Thus, a single training trial involved $100 \times 120 = 12,000$ weight updates. The top line of Fig.4.8a shows the desired output (equivalent to the US) and the following lines show the development of the CR over training trials using input signals that varied between $+1.0$ and -1.0 and a learning rate (β in equation 3) of .003. The model accurately simulates the fact that the CR peak occurs at the time of the UR peak (item 1).

This model employs a distributed representation of the conditioned response in that all the input lines are used to varying degrees such that no single synapse or input line is necessary or sufficient for the response to occur. Changes in the number or frequency range of the inputs result in graceful degradation or improvement in performance, better performance corresponding to a larger number of inputs with a greater range of represented frequencies. We note, however, that it is not critical that the inputs be so regular or periodic as the sine waves used in the simulation shown in Fig. 4.8a. Rather, the inputs need only be sufficiently rich, varied, and complex to form a complete set for "building", through linear combination, the range of desired output signals. Fig.4.8b shows the result of using complex inputs formed from the 120 sine wave input signals by random summation of various phases and frequencies. Each complex input was constructed from a distinct randomly weighted sum of each of the 120 simple sine waves. The learning rate, β, for this simulation was .02.

Figure 4.9 shows a simulation of a peak shift experiment. The axes and simulation parameters are the same as in Fig.4.8, but a learning rate of .007 was used. Following training at an ISI of 33 cycles, the system was shifted to training with an ISI of 66 cycles. As desired, the shift occurred not through a smooth interpolative change but rather with a decrease in response probability (amplitude) at the first ISI and a simultaneous increase in the response probability (amplitude) at the second ISI.

Figure 4.10b shows a simulation of a mixed-ISI training paradigm, analogous to the Millenson and colleagues (1977) study illustrated in Fig.4.10a. As desired, a double-peaked response results (item 3).

The LMS spectrum analyzer model of response topography accounts for the most salient aspect of the conditioned response: the locus of the CR peak coinciding with the locus of the US (item 1). It also accounts for two other important aspects of the conditioned response: The discrete CR peak shift with ISI change (item 2), and the double-peak CR with mixed ISI training (item 3). It does not, however, account for two other very important phenomena of response topography. First, the model does not account for the ISI "window of eligibility", which progressively retards conditioning if the conditioned stimulus (e.g., a tone CS) preceded the unconditional stimulus (e.g., an airpuff US) by less than approximately 50 ms or more than about 600 ms (item 4). Second, the model does not account for the fact that while the peak eyeblink CR remains consistently at the locus of the airpuff US, the onset of the eyeblink CR gradually moves forward in time, and becomes larger, over the course of training (item 5).

Given the obvious limitations of this simple adaptive filter model of response topography, how should we view the model and what purpose does it serve? There are two advantages to beginning by formulating this simple model and understanding its strengths and limitations. First, the model represents the extent to which the topography of the conditioned response can be explained by an existing trial-level model (the Rescorla–Wagner model) with additional assumptions made only about the nature of the stimulus representation. Within this framework, the model can be seen to be limited to characterizing the initial form of the CR for optimal ISIs.

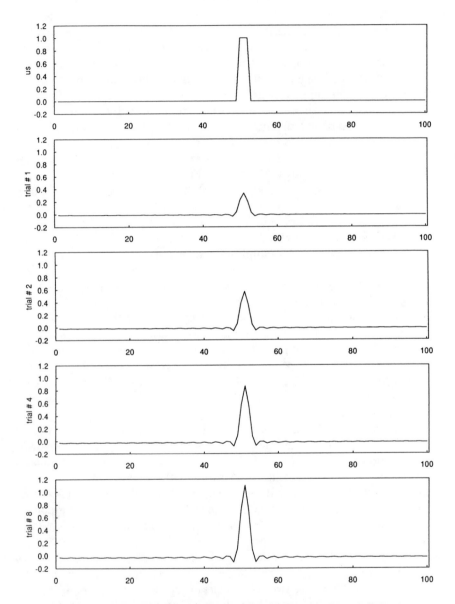

FIG. 4.8. (a) Simulation of basic conditioned response simulation output with simple sinusoidal inputs. Graphs show output (CR) vs. time (cycles). Top graphs shows the US/UR which is used as the training signal. Successive graphs show CR development over a series of learning trials. (b) Simulation of basic conditioned response simulation output using complex inputs formed by assigning to each complex input a distinct randomly weighted sum of the 120 simple inputs. The learning rate (β) used was .02.

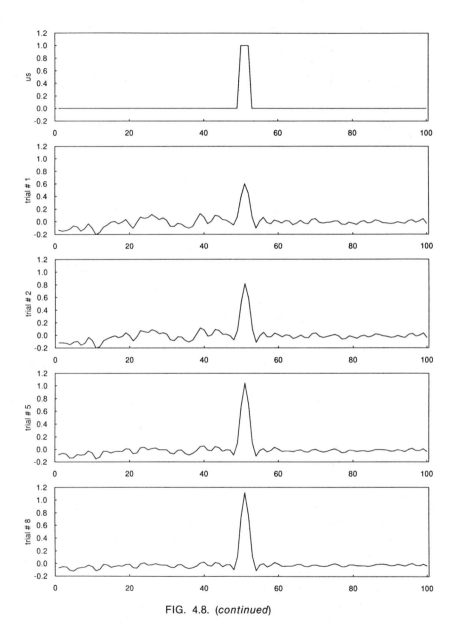

FIG. 4.8. (*continued*)

That is, when the stimulus representation assumptions of the Rescorla–Wagner model are extended as previously described, the temporal version of the Rescorla–Wagner model can capture the predictive aspects of conditioned response topography (items 1, 2, & 3), but not the adaptive nature of the response (items 4 & 5).

A second advantage of this limited model of conditioned response topography, is that it allows us to make a direct and formal connection between classical conditioning and VOR adaptation: two simple forms of motor learning, both of which have been neurobiologically localized within the cerebellum (Thompson, 1986; Ito, 1982, 1985).

Adaptive Signal Processing and the Adaptive-VOR

The vestibulo-ocular reflex (VOR) generates compensatory eye movements so as to maintain stable retinal images during movement of the head (see Fig. 4.11). Under normal conditions, these compensatory eye movements are achieved by rotating the eyes at the same speed as the head but in the opposite direction; thus, the eyes remain clearly focused on the same object as before the head movement. However, the VOR may be forced to adapt its behavior to accommodate changing conditions brought about naturally by cell loss, disease, and aging, or artifically in the laboratory by special glasses that alter the visual fields. The ability of the cerebellum to detect and repair this "dysmetria" that would otherwise cause motor incoordination indicates that more than a simple open loop control system is involved; feedback as to the accuracy of the eye movements is clearly being provided to the cerebellum by the visual system. Thus, a slip of the retinal image signals the cerebellum to recalibrate the VOR. This recalibration signal must indicate the exact nature of the necessary change in the VOR, for example, how much of an increase or decrease in the gain will correctly recalibrate the reflex.

Robinson (1976) performed a study that clearly illustrates this adapting behavior of the VOR as well as the critical role of the cerebellum in instigating this behavior. He first performed numerous experiments to determine the adaptibility of the VOR by chronically attaching left/right reversing prism glasses on five of the seventeen cats involved in the experiment. The cats were then rotated in the test apparatus so as to force the VOR to adapt to the disruption of the cooperation between head and eye movements. Robinson found that such a disruption of the retinal image caused modifiable adaptive changes to occur very rapidly. In four out of the five cats, the eye movements reversed direction in order to adapt to the change in visual fields.

After illustrating the excellent adaptive abilities of the VOR, Robinson

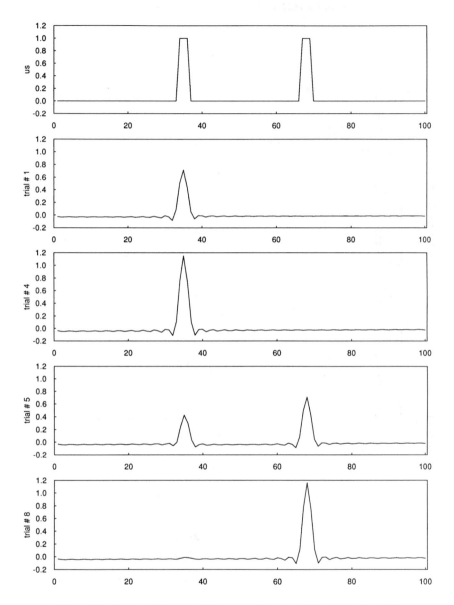

FIG. 4.9. Peak shift simulation results. In trials 1–4, the US occurred at cycle 33. At trial 5 the US shifted to cycle 66 and remained there for the duration of the simulated training session. This ISI shift prompted the production of a new CR peak at cycle 66 and the extinction of the old peak at cycle 33.

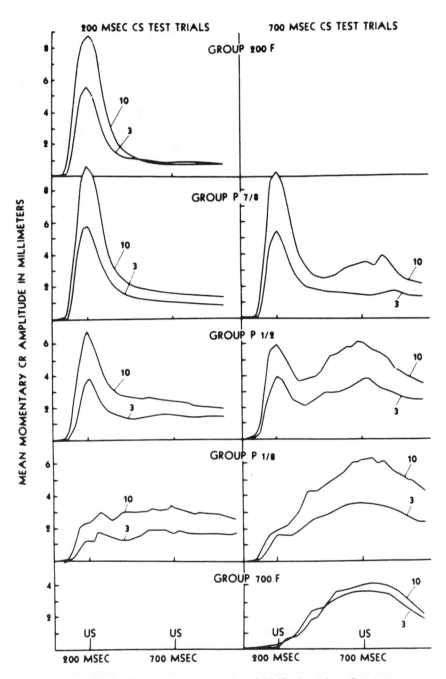

FIG. 4.10. (a). The mean topography of NMRs based on five test trials on days 3 and 10 for 200 and 700 ms CS durations. The mean membrane extension in milimeters is presented as a function of CS onset in milliseconds.

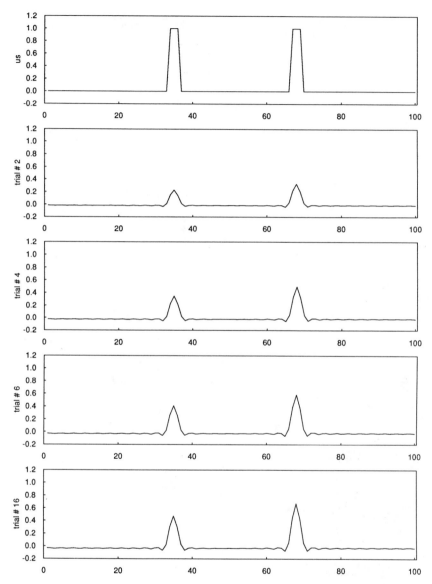

(b). Simulation of an analogue of the Millenson et al. experiment. Training trials alternatively used 33 and 66 cycle ISIs. Output is shown after each trial. The response is double-peaked with later response being larger because the output was calculated subsequent to a 66-ISI trial. (a) from "Classical Conditioning of the Rabbits' Nictitating Membrane Response Under Fixed and Mixed CS-US Intervals" by J. R. Mittenson, E. J. Kehoe, and I. Gormezano, 1977, *Learning and Motivation, 8.* Copyright 1977 by Academic Press. Reprinted with permission.

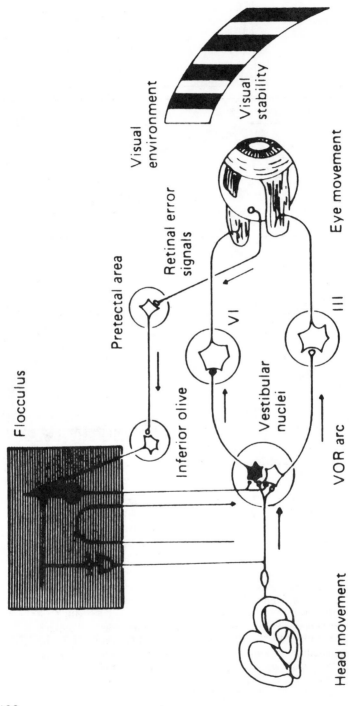

Flocculus

Pretectal area

Retinal error signals

Visual environment

Visual stability

Inferior olive

VI

Vestibular nuclei

III

Eye movement

Head movement

VOR arc

FIG. 4.11. Neuronal diagram for the floccular control system of the VOR. III, VI=Oculomotor and abducens nuclei. From "Cerebellar Plasticity as the Basis of Motor Learning." In D. Eccles (Ed.), *Recent Achievements in Restorative Neurology 1: Upper Motor Neuron Functions and Dysfunctions,* 1985, Basel: S. Karger. Copyright 1985. Reprinted with permission.

sought to determine the role of the cerebellum, in particular the vestibulo-cerebellum, in controlling these changes. Robinson (1977) defined the vestibulocerebellum as "the flocculi, the ventral paraflocculi, the lateral third of the dorsal parraflocculi, the nodulus, uvula, the lower half of lobe VIII, and the lower three or four lobules of the paramedian lobules" (p. 961). Robinson found the vestibulocerebellum to be critical in the maintenance of the VOR. After vestibulocerebellar leisions, the VOR remained unchangeable no matter what was done to them. The cats showed no response to prism glasses after the surgery—except, of course, severe incoordination. Furthermore, the plastic changes that had occurred in the five cats who wore the prism glasses before surgery were completely abolished after the surgery. This study indicates that the vestibulocerebellum is necessary to produce and maintain the large plastic changes that are observed in the VOR when it must adapt to changes in the visual field.

Subsequent work by Ito and colleagues further established that the flocculus region of the vestibulocerebellum is critical for this adaptation. The primary vestibular fibers project to the flocculus as mossy fibers, much as conditioned stimulus (CS) information does in eyelid conditioning. The flocculus also receives climbing fibers from the retina that according to Ito (1982), contain error information about retinal slip: the discrepancy between the image that ought to project to the fovea (i.e., a stable image) and the "erroneous" image that does project to the fovea.

It should be noted that the precise locus or loci of neuronal plasticity that code adaptation of the VOR is still a matter of debate. Ito (1987) and associates argued for cerebellar cortex of the flocculus whereas Lisberger (1984), for example, argues for vestibular nuclei. Both agree that the cerebellar cortex of the flocculus is necessary for adaptation of the VOR. In the eyelid conditioning paradigm, evidence to date is consistent with memory trace location in cerebellar cortex, interpositus nucleus or both. The medial vestibular nucleus can be considered a deep cerebellar nucleus (displaced to the brain stem) in term of its connections, for example, monosynaptic projection of Purkinje cell axons. So both hypotheses regarding the locus of VOR plasticity are consistent with the evidence regarding loci of neuronal plasticity in eyelid conditioning.

Fujita's Model

Fujita (1982a, 1982b) proposed an "adaptive filter" model of the cerebellum to formally account for the adaptive abilities of the VOR. While modulating the VOR, Purkinje cells are presumed to receive sinusoidal input of various phases from the mossy fibers via the granule cells and parallel fibers. Within Fujita's model, the Purkinje cells learn to respond selectively to the various phase versions until they only respond to a very specific combination of inputs; that is to say, they adjust the synaptic weights on the parallel fiber inputs so that when summed at the Purkinje cell, the desired output is produced. It becomes clearer in the following review of Fujita's model that the critical "adaptive filtering" presumed to take place at the parallel fiber–Purkinje cell synapses is equivalent to Widrow's "LMS spectrum analyzer." Thus, Fujita's "LMS spectrum analyzer" model of Purkinje cells, and their role in VOR adaptation, is formally equivalent to the simple real-time extension of the Rescorla-–Wagner model reviewed earlier.

Before describing the details of Fujita's adaptive filter model, we review the general anatomy of the cerebellum shown in Fig.4.4. The cerebellar cortex is composed of five different types of neurons: granule, Golgi, Purkinje, basket, and superficial stellate cells. It receives two sets of afferent fibers, climbing fibers and mossy fibers, and sends out one type of efferent fiber, Purkinje cell axons, to the vestibular nucleus. The mossy fibers enter the cerebellum and synapse with the granule cells whose axons continue to ascend into the molecular layer of the cortex where they become parallel fibers. The Purkinje cells have fanlike dendritic branches that are perpendicular to the parallel fibers and form crossover synapses with them. The dendrites of the Golgi cells cover an enormous spread such that they are excited by both the mossy fiber inputs at the bottom of the cerebellum and the parallel fibers at the top. Golgi axons then form extensive inhibitory synapses with the granule cells.

In Fujita's adaptive filter model, Purkinje cells are presumed to perform a filtering function on the basis of multiple pairs of input signals and corresponding desired output signals. The Golgi cells are postulated to work as phase lag elements that act as a leaky integrator with a time constant of a few seconds. The output from this network, that is, the parallel fiber signals, would then represent different versions of compensators at different phase lags, depending on the relative weights of the inputs. The outputs of the parallel fiber signals are gathered together through various synaptic connections, which possess modifiable weights, to form the desired Purkinje cell output, that is, the final signal. The main idea behind Fujita's adaptive filter model is easily understood if one thinks of the mossy fiber inputs as individual sine waves with different phases and frequencies. The cerebellum learns to sum these various waves to produce a specific response curve (see Fig.4.7).

As shown in Fig.4.12, we can denote a particular mossy fiber input with the function $u(t)$, which represents the rate of impulses fired per second at time t. When $u(t)$ enters the cerebellum, it is first acted upon by some transducer (let F_j be the function of the transducer) so as to produce a linearly independent set of signals, the parallel fiber signals: $x_1(t), x_2(t), \ldots x_m(t)$. Thus, $x_j(t) = F_j(u(t))$. These individual parallel fiber signals are

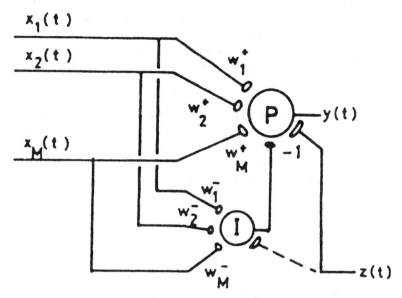

FIG. 4.12. Fujita's adaptive filter model of the cerebellum showing the circuit for a Purkinje cell: P and I denote a Purkinje cell and an inhibitory neuron, respectively. A connection weight between P and I is assumed to take the value of -1. A climbing fiber signal $z(t)$ is also provided to a Purkinje cell which functions as a "teacher signal" to adjust a modifiable weight $w_j{}^+ (j=1,2,3,\ldots M)$. The collateral of the climbing fiber to the inhibitory neuron is assumed not to modify the weight and therefore is designated by a broken line. From "Adaptive Filter Model of the Cerebellum" by M. Fujita, 1982, *Biological Cybernetics, 45,* Fig. 4. Copyright 1982. Reprinted with permission.

combined through adjustable weights to form the final signal, the output of the Purkinje cell. Therefore, the output of the Purkinje cell is equal to the sum of the weighted values of the parallel fiber inputs. These values are equal to $x_j(t)$, the impulses at time t, multiplied by the weights of the corresponding synapses, w_j. If $y(t)$ denotes the output signal of the Purkinje cell, then $y(t) = w_j x_j(t)$. It is necessary to note that not all the parallel fiber inputs to the Purkinje cells possess positive weights. Some signals from the golgi-granule cell system do not reach the Purkinje cells directly but instead pass through inhibitory interneurons — basket and superficial stellate cells — on their way to synapsing with the Purkinje cells. When these signals arrive at the Purkinje cell synapse they have been multiplied by "negative" weights, w_j-, and are inhibitory signals.

As illustrated in Fig. 4.12, the weights assigned to the individual parallel fiber signals are adaptive and plastic. They are adjustible depending on the desired output, c(t), and how close the actual output of the Purkinje cells, y(t), is to this desired output.

Fujita (1982a), in a formal elaboration of the models first proposed by Marr (1969) and Albus (1971), presumed that the climbing fiber afferent inputs into the cerebellum, which originate in the inferior olive and form powerful excitatory synapses with the Purkinje cells, are responsible for the learning capabilities of the adaptive filter. In other words, the mossy fiber afferents carry the information to be processed by the cerebellum and the climbing fiber afferents carry "teaching signals" to the Purkinje cells. The activity of the climbing fiber inputs at time t, denoted by $Z(t)$, is determined by the discrepancy between the actual and desired Purkinje cell output relative to its spontaneous discharge rate. That is,

$$Z(t) = z_0 + z(t), \tag{4}$$

where z_0 is equal to this spontaneous discharge rate. Thus, $z(t)$ represents the deviational part of the climbing fiber impulse rate relative to its normal discharge rate. If the Purkinje cell output at time t is y (t) and the desired output is c (t), then

$$z(t) = y(t) - c(t), \tag{5}$$

the discrepancy between the actual and desired Purkinje cell output. Thus, when $Z(t) > z_0, z(t)$ is positive and $y(t) > c(t)$, and the climbing fiber signals a required decrease in the synaptic weight of the jth parallel fiber, so as to decrease the value of y(t). When $Z(t) < z_0$ it signals that an increase is needed in synaptic weight. The amount of weight change that occurs is proportional to the product of the jth parallel fiber's impulse rate, $x_j(t)$, and $z(t)$, the deviational part of $Z(t)$ from z_0. In Fujita (1982a), his equation 2.4 (and 2.21), specify that the change in synaptic weight, $w_j(t)$, will be controlled by

$$\Delta w_j(t) = -\epsilon z(t) x_j(t) dt \tag{6}$$

where ϵ is a proportionality constant.

Correspondence between Fujita and Rescorla-Wagner

Expanding the terms of equation 6 of Fujita's cerebellar model of VOR adaptation, we can expand the z(t) term via equation 5 rewriting this continuous function as a difference equation,

$$\Delta w_j(t) = -\epsilon[y(t) - c(t)] x_j(t). \tag{7}$$

To see more clearly the correspondence to the Rescorala–Wagner/LMS rule of equation 3 of Table 4.4 and Fujita's Purkinje cell synaptic learning rule of equation 6 (2.4 in Fujita, 1982a), we can equate Fujita's proportionality constant ϵ, with the learning rate β in equation 3; the actual output of the Purkinje cells, $y(t)$, with the summed strength of all conditioned stimulus (CSs) present, that is, the conditioned response (CR), $\sum_{j=1}^{n} w_j a_j$; the desired Purkinje cell output, $c(t)$, with λ, which indicates the presence or absence of US in equation 3; the incoming parallel fiber activation $x_j(t)$ with a_i which represents the presence or absence of the conditioned stimulus (CS), to yield (with some rearrangment of terms),

$$\Delta w_i = \beta a_i (\lambda - \sum_{j=1}^{n} w_j a_j)$$

the Rescorla–Wagner/LMS model of classical conditioning.

Biological Correspondences Between Conditioning and VOR Studies

A close parallel can be drawn between the error signaling role of the climbing fibers in adaptation of the VOR and the reinforcing or teaching role of the climbing fibers in classical conditioning. In the latter paradigm, onset of the US consistently evokes climbing fiber responses (complex spikes) in appropriate Purkinje cells prior to training. In the well-trained animal, US onset rarely evokes climbing fiber responses. The climbing fiber response of Purkinje cells can thus be viewed as an error; if no behavioral CR occurs prior to US onset (beginning of training) the climbing fiber response occurs (error). If, in a well-trained animal, a robust CR does occur

TABLE 4.4
Learning Rules

Model	Associative Changes	Equation
Rescorla–Wagner Reinforced	$\Delta V_i = \alpha_i \beta_1 (\lambda - \sum_{s \in S} V_s)$	1
Nonreinforced	$\Delta V_i = \alpha_i \beta_2 (\lambda - \sum_{s \in S} V_s)$	2
LMS	$\Delta w_i = \beta a_i (\lambda - \sum_{j=1}^{n} w_j a_j)$	3

Note. $\Delta w_i, \Delta V_i$ = Change in associative strength of CS_i, $\sum_{s \in S} V_s = \sum_{j=1}^{n} w_j a_j$ = Summed strength for all CSs present. λ = Indicates presence (1) or absence (0) of US. a_j = Indicates presence (1) or absence (0) of CS. β, β_1, β_2 = Learning rate parameters (US dependent). α_i = Learning rate parameter (CS dependent).

prior to US onset, the animal has not committed an error but instead has successfully predicted the occurrence of the US; and the climbing fiber response does not occur. This result can be accounted for at the level of the cerebellar-brain stem circuit by the existence of descending (efferent) pathways from the interpositus that act to inhibit US activation of the climbing fibers (see Fig. 4.13; Thompson, 1986). Prior to learning, interpositus neurons (and their efferents) are not activated on the CS period; in a well-trained animal they are massively activated. We adopt the assumption that the relative degree of activation of climbing fibers by US onset is the reinforcing event that determines the amount of associative strength that will accrue on a given trial. Within this circuit-level framework, the descending inhibitory system provides a circuit-level instantiation of a fundamental aspect of the Rescorla–Wagner formulation; the inverse relation between the amount of associative strength that accrues on a given trial and the preexisting strength of the association.

Summary

Two quite different behavioral forms of learning, classical conditioning of discrete behavioral responses and adaptation of the VOR, have converged quite remarkably toward a common neural substrate. The cerebellum and its associated brain stem circuitry are necessary and sufficient for both forms of behavioral plasticity. In both paradigms a key event is a depression in the frequency of firing of Purkinje cells as a result of training or adaptation. A decrease in Purkinje cell firing will yield an increased neuronal response in interpositus (classical conditioning) or in vestibular nuclei (VOR adaptation), which increases the probability of a behavioral response.

Temporal Coarse Coding
and Distributed Representations

Despite the formal theoretical convergence between conditioning and VOR adaptation already described, there appears to be a major empirical discrepancy at the neuronal level between the two forms of behavioral plasticity. Conjuctive stimulation of climbing fibers with parallel fibers yields a long-term depression (LTD) of the parallel fiber–Purkinje cell synapse efficacy. The long-term depression effect has been reported when mossy fiber activation (the CS analogue) precedes climbing fiber activation (the US analogue) by 20 ms, with simultaneous activation, and when the climbing fiber activation precedes mossy fiber activation by up to 375 ms. These temporal parameters are clearly quite different than those necessary to establish behavioral conditioned responses (CRs). With peripheral CSs and USs or with direct electrical stimulation of mossy fibers as the conditioned stimulus and climbing fibers as the unconditional stimulus

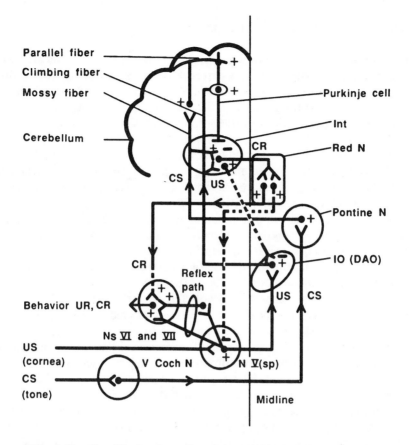

FIG. 4.13. Simplified schematic of hypothetical memory trace circuit for discrete behavioral responses learned as adaptation to aversive events. The US (corneal airpuff) pathway seems to consist of somatosensory projections to the dorsal accessory portion of the inferior olive (DAO) and its climbing fiber projections to the cerebellum. The tone CS pathway seems to consist of auditory projections to the cerebellum. The efferent (eyelid closure) CR pathway projects from the interpositus nucleus (Int) of the cerebellum to the red nucleus (Red N) and via the descending rubral pathway to act ultimately on motor neurons. The red nucleus may also exert inhibitory control over the transmission of somatic sensory information about the US to the inferior olive (IO) and there is also a direct inhibitory pathway from the interpositus nucleus to the inferior olive, so that when an eyeblink CR occurs there is likely to be inhibition of US activation of climbing fibers. Evidence to date is most consistent with storage of the memory traces in localized regions of cerebellar cortex and possibly interpositus nucleus as well. Pluses indicate excitatory and minuses inhibitory synaptic action. Additional abbreviations: N V (sp), spinal fifth cranial nucleus; N VI, sixth cranial nucleus; N VII, seventh cranial nucleus; V Coch N, ventral cochlear nucleus. Adapted from Thompson (1986).

(Steinmetz, Lavond, & Thompson, 1989), the CS onset (mossy fiber activation) is effective only if it precedes US onset (climbing fiber activation) by approximately 70 ms. Thus, at the behavioral level we have a precisely timed motor movement, whereas at the neuronal level we have synapses whose temporal specificity for plasticity is, at best, very coarse.

This result is by no means novel within the literature on biological systems. Animals commonly reveal a behavioral degree of stimulus resolution and specificity that is not observed at the neuronal level (Baldi & Heiligenberg, 1988). Bats, for example, use time delays for the return of echoes to discriminate the distances between different targets. At the behavioral level, bats can discriminate differences in distance as small as 1 to 1.5 cm, which correspond to associated echo delays of .06 to .09 ms. At the neuronal level, however, the sensitivity of neurons in the bat auditory cortex is very broadly tuned over a wide range of delays, with near neighbors differing, at best, by .13 ms (Suga & Horikawa, 1986).

A particularly striking example of unit coarse coding yielding a very precise behavioral outcome is seen in the work of Georgopoulus, Schwartz, and Kettner (1986). They trained monkeys to reach from a center hold position to any one of eight different locations in three-dimensional space, signaled by target light, and recorded the activity of single neurons in the arm area of motor cortex. Eighty percent of the neurons studied exhibited some degree of directional tuning; that is, they responded more with reaching in some directions than others. But each individual unit had very poor selectivity, they typically responded to some degree with movement in any direction. The actual direction of arm movement of the hand could not be predicted with any degree of precision from any given unit. A neuronal population vector was computed and summed over all the units for each direction of movement. This population vector predicted the exact direction of arm movement with a high degree of precision. This result illustrates how a behavioral variable could be uniquely represented in a neuronal ensemble whose constituent neurons are not very specific for that variable.

Similar results have been described for neural coding of direction of saccadic eye movements in the pontine reticular formation (Henn & Cohen, 1976), coding of the direction of head tilt in vestibular neurons (Schor, Miller, & Tomko, 1984), coding of the direction of body motion relative to neck or head motion relative to body in spinal interneurons (Wilson, Ezure, & Timerick, 1984), for the prediction of the direction of the upcoming movement of a visual stimulus, even before the movement occurs, by neurons in motor cortex (Crutcher, Schwarz, & Georgopoulos, 1985) and for prediction of the direction of movement of a stimulus in the visual field by neurons in the posterior parietal cortex (Steinmetz, Motter, Duffy, & Mountcastle, 1987).

Recently, Lee, Rohrer, and Sparks (1988) showed that the coding for eye movement in the superior colliculus is also represented by distributed patterns of firing. Lee and colleagues showed that when a subset of neurons is deactivated, the eye movement misses the intended target by the resultant vector obtained by summing the central eye-movement sensitivities of all the deactivated units. This demonstrates that a large population of neurons is responsible for the coding of simple eye movements (Sejnowski, 1988).

Coarse Coding and Hyperacuity

Throughout a wide range of behavioral paradigms and biological systems, systems of broadly (i.e., coarsely) tuned neurons yield a degree of behavioral specificity far beyond the capability of the individual neurons, a phenomenon known as "hyperacuity". This suggests that individual neurons represent stimulus information in a *coarse coding* scheme, whereby stimulus variables are represented by distributed patterns of activity over a large number of neurons (Hinton, McClelland, & Rumelhart, 1986; Kienker, Sejnowski, Hinton, & Schumaker, 1986; Sejnowski, 1988). The theoretical properties of coarse coding and hyperacuity have been explored and analyzed by Heiligenberg (1987) and Baldi and Heiligenberg (1988). Their analyses illustrate, through simulations and analytic results, how ordered representations of stimulus variables in neuronal maps can be broadly tuned (i.e., have poor resolution) yet still yield stimulus resolution at the behavioral level far exceeding that observed at individual sensory neurons. Within their model, a bank of filters is presumed to be tuned to progressively higher ranges of a continuous stimulus variable, x. The sensitivity of each filter element, k, is presumed to be bell-shaped with a peak value at its center, C_k, and with a width specified by d, such that the resulting activation of the neuron is given by

$$f_k(x,d) = e^{-\left[\frac{x-c_k}{d}\right]^2}. \tag{8}$$

For any value of the stimulus variable x, each sensor contributes to a global "pool," $G(x,d)$, in proportion to its activation, $f_k(x,d)$ and its rank, k. Heiligenberg (1988) demonstrated that the resulting "behavioral acuity" function, $G(x,d)$, becomes monotonic in x for sufficiently large values of the width parameter, d. This demonstrates that high behavioral resolution can be obtained by using sufficiently many broadly tuned elements with comparatively poorer resolution. This model is relatively immune to inaccuracies in the arrangements. For example, random variations ("noise") in either the synaptic strengths of the elements or in the spacial center, C_k, of the individual unit response profiles cause minimal distruption to the system's global performance. These results illustrate that with broadly tuned units, synaptic strengths require less accurate settings. A further implication of this robustness to random noise is an implicit tolerance to failures of individual units. Such failures, or "lesions," may be behaviorally undetectable, causing only marginal decreases in the system's performance (Heiligenberg, 1987, p. 630).

Temporal Coarse Coding and the Cerebellum

If the ultimate sensory precision of a distributed/coarse coded system can far exceed the precision of any individual element, this may also apply to the temporal specificity of the cerebellar control of motor learning. To evaluate this possibility we have modified our adaptive filter model of response topography so that the "conditionability" of the synapse decays slowly after CS and US presentation. This decay of eligibility was implemented by passing the feedback (US) through a leaky integrator so that the effective US was smeared in time.

Thus, at the unit (synaptic) level, conjunctive stimulation within a wide temporal proximity will yield "plasticity." The results can be seen in Fig. 4.14. and should be compared with Fig. 4.8b; note that the asymptotic response topography looks about the same, even slightly smoother. As desired, the locus of the eyeblink is right on target with the US, in spite of the "coarseness" of the temporal plasticity. Though the UR is smoother overall, the temporal accuracy of the UR peak is maintained as desired.

DISCUSSION

We began this chapter by reviewing three relevant bodies of literature: the behavioral paradigm of classical (Pavlovian) conditioning, the work of Thompson and colleagues in identifying the neuronal substrates for the acquisition of the conditioned eyeblink response, and the relevant formal models of conditioning behavior. In the second half of the chapter, we tried to do three things. First, we saw how the Rescorla–Wagner model of classical conditioning can be extended to account for the temporal specificity of the initial form of the conditioned response (CR) for optimal ISIs. This model is based on well-known and well-understood theories of adaptive signal processing and adaptive filters. Thus, when the stimulus representation assumptions of the Rescorla–Wagner model are extended using constructs from theories of adaptive signal processing, this real-time extention of the Rescorla–Wagner model can capture the predictive aspects of conditioned response topography but not the adaptive nature of the response. Second, we saw how this model of classical conditioning can be formally mapped onto Fujita's (1982) model of the adaptive component of the vestibulo-ocular reflex (VOR). Both of these models are based on LMS

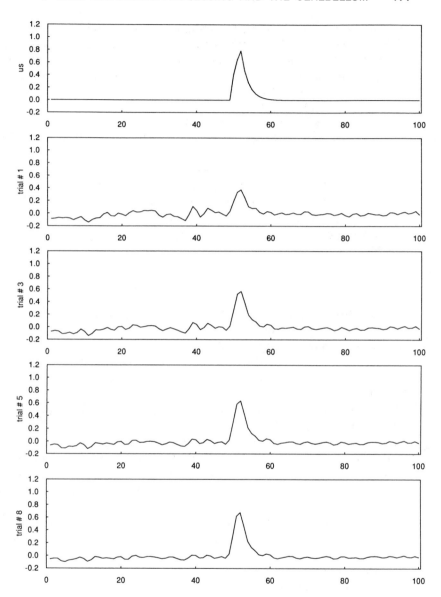

FIG. 4.14. CR topography with coarse temporal sensitivity. See text for further details.

spectrum analyzers that are performing the equivalent of an iterative approximation of the discrete Fourier transform of the desired response. Fujita's adaptive filter model has been adopted by Ito and colleagues as one model of how Purkinje cells in the cerebellar cortex might control the adaptive VOR. Thus, at a theoretical level we see the beginnings of a potential reconciliation of VOR adaptation and conditioning theories of the cerebellum. Third, we saw that when the temporal sensitivity of the units (synapses) is coarse and broadly tuned rather than precisely tuned, the model exhibits smoother topography, precise temporal loci, and improved noise tolerance. The advantage of coarse coding in distributed representation systems is well known, especially in models of sensory systems. It is especially relevant here because Ito has shown that plasticity at parallel fiber–Purkinje cell synapses in the cerebellar cortex is only coarsely sensitive to temporal parameters. This result has previously been taken to be inconsistent with the supposition that parallel fiber–Purkinje cell plasticity mediates the precise temporal characteristics of the conditioned response. Within the context of an adaptive filter model of conditioning, we can see that Ito's empirical results are consistent with a cerebellar model of conditioning.

Alternative Models

An alternative approach to account for the fact that the peak of the CR develops at the time of onset of the US is to make use of a "tapped delay line." This notion supposes that the CS activates different input (CS afferent) lines at successively later times throughout the CS period. Moore and colleagues (Desmond & Moore, 1988; Moore & Blazis, 1989) proposed a number of models for conditioned response topography that extend the Sutton and Barto (1981) model through the use of a common engineering solution to the problem of temporal specificity: tapped delay lines. Although it is true that different parallel fibers have different conduction times, these differences can account at most for a few milliseconds of the CS-US onset interval, not for the requisite hundreds of millisecond range over which the CR peaks at US onset. Further, a click stimulus at the beginning of the CS interval is an effective CS—the CS does not need to extend throughout the CS period. Indeed, brief electrical stimulation of the mossy fibers over a 5 ms period at the beginning of the CS period is an effective CS (Logan et al., 1985). Thus, as a biological model of the temporal specifity of the conditioned response, what little evidence exists for tap-lines is negative.

General Discussion

We have seen in recent years a great surge of interest across the disciplines of cognitive psychology, computer science, and neurobiology in understanding the information-processing capabilities of adaptive networks consisting of interconnected, neuron-like computing elements. These connectionist and parallel-distributed processing models are notable for their computational power and resemblance to psychological and neurobiological processes (e.g., Ackley, Hinton, & Sejnowski, 1985; Gluck & Bower, 1988a,b; Hinton & Anderson, 1981; Rumelhart & McClelland, 1986). In essence, this connectionist paradigm in cognitive science represents a return to the original aims of classical learning theory in psychology, namely, understanding human-learning phenomena as emerging from complex configurations of the elementary associative processes, for example, classical conditioning.

The basic processes and phenomena of classical conditioning appear to have reemerged as critical for understanding more complex phenomena of learning and memory (Gluck & Bower, 1988b; Rescorla, 1988). In the context of neuroscience and psychobiology, classical conditioning has also played a fundamental role; it has proved to be the "Rosetta stone" for both invertebrate and vertebrate analyses of the neurobiology of learning and memory (Kandel, 1976; Thompson et al., 1976).

ACKNOWLEDGMENTS

This chapter is based on a talk given in Chicago at the 1988 Annual Conference of the Psychonomic Society. Some of the introductory material in this chapter was adapted from previous papers written with other colleagues, including Donegan, Gluck, and Thompson (1989), Thompson, Lavond, and Donegan (1988), and Gluck and Bower (1988a). For their helpful comments and critiques on earlier drafts of this manuscript, we are indebted to A.J. Annala, Pierre Baldi, Gabor Bartha, Hui-Ling Lou, Dan Rosen, David Rumelhart, and Bernard Widrow. This research was supported by an Office of Naval Research grant (N00014-88-K-0112) to R.F. Thompson and M.A. Gluck, a Sloan Foundation grant to R.F. Thompson, G.H. Bower, and M.A. Gluck, a National Science Foundation grant (BNS-8718300) to R.F. Thompson, and a McNight Foundation grant to R.F. Thompson.

REFERENCES

Ackley, D. H., Hinton, G. E., & Sejnowski, T. J. (1985). A learning algorithm for Boltzmann machines. *Cognitive Science, 9,* 147–169.

Albus, J. S. (1971). A theory of cerebellar function. *Mathematical Biosciences, 10,* 25–61.

Baldi, P., & Heiligenberg, W. (1988). How sensory maps could enhance resolution through ordered arrangments of broadly tuned receivers. *Biological Cybernetics, 59,* 313–318.

Brindley, G. S. (1964). The use made by the cerebellum of the information that it receives from sense organs. *International Brain Research Organization Bulletin, 3,* 80.

Chapman, P. F., Steinmetz, J. E., & Thompson, R. F. (1988). Classical conditioning does not occur when direct stimulation of the red nucleus or cerebellar nuclei is the unconditioned stimulus. *Brain Research, 441,* 97–104.

Cohen, D. H. (1980). The functional neuroanatomy of a conditioned response. In R. F. Thompson, L. H. Hicks, & V. B. Shvyrkov (Eds.), *Neural mechanisms of goal-directed behavior and learning.* New York: Academic Press.

Coleman, S. R., & Gormezano, I. (1971). Classical conditioning of the rabbit's (Oryctolagus cuniculus) nictitating membrane response under symmetrical CS-US interval shifts. *Journal of Comparative and Physiological Psychology, 77,* 447–455.

Crutcher, M. D., Schwartz, A. B., & Georgopoulos, A. P. (1985). Representation of movement direction in primate motor cortex in the absence of immediate movement. *Neuroscience Abstracts, 11(2),* 1273.

Davis, M., Gendelman, T., Gendelman, D. S., Tischler, M., & Kehne, J. H. (1982). Habituation and sensitization of startle reflexes elicited electrically from the brain stem. *Science, 218,* 688–690.

Desmond, J. E., & Moore, J. W. (1988). Adaptive timing in neural networks: The conditioned response. *Biological Cybernetics, 58,* 405–415.

Donegan, N. H., Foy, M. R., & Thompson, R. F. (1985). Neuronal responses of the rabbit cerebellar cortex during performance of the classically conditioned eyelid response. *Neuroscience Abstracts, 11,* 245.8.

Donegan, N. H., Gluck, M. A., & Thompson, R. F. (1989). Integrating behavioral and biological models of classical conditioning. In R. D. Hawkins & G. H. Bower (Eds.), *Computational models of learning in simple neural systems (Volume 22 of the Psychology of Learning and Motivation).* New York: Academic Press.

Donegan, N. H., Lowry, R. W., & Thompson, R. F. (1983). Effects of lesioning cerebellar nuclei on conditioned leg-flexion responses. *Neuroscience Abstracts, 9,* 100.7, 331.

Donegan, N. H., & Wagner, A. R. (1987). Conditioned diminution and facilitation of the UCR: A sometimes-opponent-process interpretation. In I. Gormezano, W. Prokasy, & R. Thompson (Eds.), *Classical conditioning II: Behavioral, neurophysiological, and neuro-chemical studies in the rabbit.* Hillsdale, NJ: Lawrence Erlbaum Associates.

Eccles, J. C. (1977). An instruction-selection theory of learning in the cerebellar cortex. *Brain Research, 127,* 327–352.

Foy, M. R., & Thompson, R. F. (1986). Single unit analysis of Purkinje cell discharge in classically conditioned and untrained rabbits. *Neuroscience Abstracts, 12,* 518.

Fujita, M. (1982a). Adaptive filter model of the cerebellum. *Biological Cybernetics, 45,* 195–206.

Fujita, M. (1982b). Simulation of adaptive modification of the vestibulo-ocular reflex with an adaptive filter model of the cerebellum. *Biological Cybernetics, 45,* 207–214.

Georgopoulos, A. P., Schwartz, A. B., & Kettner R. E. (1986). Neuronal population coding of movement direction. *Science, 233,* 1416–1419.

Gluck, M. A., & Bower, G. H. (1988a). Evaluating an adaptive network model of human learning. *Journal of Memory and Language, 27,* 166–195.

Gluck, M. A., & Bower, G. H. (1988b). From conditioning to category learning: An adaptive network model. *Journal of Experimental Psychology: General, 117(3),* 225–244.

Gluck, M. A., Parker, D. B., & Reifsnider, E. (1988). Some biological implications of a differential-Hebbian learning rule. *Psychobiology, 16(3),* 298–302.

Gluck, M. A., Parker, D. B., & Reifsnider, E. (1989). Learning with temporal derivatives in pulse-coded neuronal systems. In D. Touretzky (Ed.), *Advances in neural information processing systems: Proceedings of the November 1988 Neural Information Processing Systems (NIPS) Conference, Denver, CO.* San Mateo, CA: Morgan Kaufman.

Gluck, M. A., & Thompson, R. F. (1987). Modeling the neural substrates of associative learning and memory: A computational approach. *Psychological Review, 94,* 176–191.

Gormezano, I. (1972). Investigations of defense and reward conditioning in the rabbit. In A. H. Black & W. F. Prokasy (Eds.), *Classical Conditioning II: Current research and theory* (pp. 151–181). New York: Appleton-Century-Crofts.

Gormezano, I., Kehoe, E. K., & Marshal, B. S. (1983). Twenty years of classical conditioning research with the rabbit. *Progress in Psychobiology and Physiological Psychology, 10,* 197-275.

Gormezano, I., Schneiderman, N., Deaux, E., & Fuentes, I. (1962). Nictitating membrane: Classical conditioning and extinction in the albino rabbit. *Science, 138,* 33-34.

Grossberg, S. (1969). On learning of spatiotemporal patterns by networks with ordered sensory and motor components. I. Excitatory components of the cerebellum. *Studies of Applied Mathematics, 48,* 105-132.

Hebb, D. (1949). *Organization of behavior.* New York: Wiley.

Heiligenberg, W. (1987). Central processing of sensory information in electric fish. *Journal of Comparative Physiology A, 161,* 621-631.

Henn, V., & Cohen, B. (1976). Coding of information about rapid eye movements in the pontine reticular formation of alert monkeys. *Brain Research, 108(2),* 307-325.

Hinton, G. E., & Anderson, J. A. (1981). *Parallel models of associative memory.*. Hillsdale, NJ: Lawrence Erlbaum Associates.

Hinton, G. E., McClelland, J. L., & Rumelhart, D. E. (1986). Distributed representations. In D. E. Rumelhart & J. L. McClelland (Eds.), *Parallel distributed processing: Explorations in the microstructure of cognition* (Vol. 1). Cambridge, MA: Bradford Books/MIT Press.

Hull, C. L. (1943). *Principles of behavior.* New York: Appleton-Century-Crofts.

Ito, M. (1974). The control mechansims of cerebellar motor system. In F. O. Schmitt, & R. G. Worden (Eds.), *The neuroscience, third study program.* Boston: MIT Press.

Ito, M. (1982). Cerebellar control of the vestibulo-ocular reflex around the flocculus hypothesis. *Annual Review of Neuroscience, 5,* 275-296.

Ito, M. (1984). *The cerebellum and neural control.* New York: Raven.

Ito, M. (1985). Cerebellar plasticity as the basis of motor learning. In D. Eccles (Ed.), *Recent achievements in restorative neurology 1: Upper motor neuron functions and dysfunctions.* Basel: S. Karger.

Ito, M. (1987). Characterization of synaptic plasticity in the cerebellar and cerebral neocortex. In J. Changeux & M. Konishi (Eds.), *Life sciences research report 38, The neural and molecular bases of learning* (pp. 263-280). New York: Wiley.

Ito, M. (1989). Long term depression. *Annual Review of Neuroscience, 12,* 85-102.

Kamin, L.J. (1969). Predictability, surprise, attention and conditioning. In B.A. Campbell & R. M. Church (Eds.), *Punishment and aversive behavior* (pp. 279-296). New York: Appleton-Century-Crofts.

Kandel, E. R. (1976). *Cellular basis of behavior: An introduction to behavioral neurobiology.* San Francisco, CA: W. H. Freeman.

Kandel, E.R. (1979). Small systems of neurons. *Scientific American, 241(3),* 66-76.

Kapp, B. S., Gallagher, M., Applegate, C. D., & Frysinger, R.C. (1982). The amygdala central nucleus: Contributions to conditioned cardiovascular responding during aversive Pavlovian conditioning in the rabbit. In C. D. Woody (Ed.), *Conditioning: Representation of involved neural functions* (pp. 581-600). New York: Plenum.

Kassel, J., Shambes, G. M., & Welker, W. (1984). Fractured cutaneous projections to the granule cell layer of the posterior cerebellar hemisphere of the domestic cat. *Journal of Comp. Neurology,* 458-468.

Kienker, P. K., Sejnowski, T. J., Hinton, G. E., & Schumaker, L. (1986). Separating figure from ground with a parallel network. *Perception, 15,* 197-216.

Klopf, A. H. (1988). A neuronal model of classical conditioning. *Psychobiology, 16(2),* 85-125.

Kohonen, T. (1977). *Associative memory: A system-theoretic approach.* New York: Springer-Verlag.

Lashley, K. S. (1916). The human salivary reflex and its use in psychology. *Psychological Review, 23,* 446-464.

Lashley, K. S. (1929). *Brain mechanisms and intelligence.* Chicago: University of Chicago Press.

Lavond, D. G., Hembree, T.L., & Thompson, R. F. (1985). Effect of kainic acid lesions of the cerebellar interpositus nucleus on eyelid conditioning in the rabbit. *Brain Research, 326,* 179–182.

Lee, C., Rohrer, W. H., & Sparks, D.L. (1988). Population coding of saccadic eye movements by neurons in the superior colliculus. *Nature, 332,* 357–360.

Lehky, S.R., & Sejnowski, T.J. (1987). Line element model of disparity discrimination. *Investigations of Opth. Visual Science, 28,* 293.

Lehky, S. R., & Sejnowski, T.J. (1988). Model of depth interpolation using a distributed representation of disparity. *Investigations of Opth. Visual Science, 29,* 398.

Lincoln, J.S., McCormick, D.A., & Thompson, R.F. (1982). Ipsilateral cerebellar lesions prevent learning of the classically conditioned nictitating membrane/eyelid response. *Brain Research,* 190–193.

Lisberger, S. G. (1984). The latency of pathways containing the site of motor learning in the monkey vestibulo-ocular reflex. *Science,* 74–76.

Logan, C. G., Steinmetz, J. E., Woodruff-Pak, D. S., & Thompson, R. F. (1985). Short-duration mossy fiber stimulation is effective as a CS in eyelid classical conditioning. *Neuroscience Abstracts, 11(2),* 835.

Lye, R. H., O'Boyle, D. J., Ramsden, R. T., & Schady, W. (1988). Effects of a unilateral cerebellar lesion on the acquisition of eye-blink conditioning in man. *Journal of Physiology (London), 403,* 58P.

Mackintosh, N. J. (1983). *Conditioning and associative learning.* Oxford: Oxford University Press.

Marr, D. (1969). A theory of cerebellar cortex. *Journal of Physiology, 202,* 437–470.

Mauk, M. D., Steinmetz, J. E., & Thompson, R. F. (1986). Classical conditioning using stimulation of the inferior olive as the unconditioned stimulus. *Proceedings of the National Academy of Sciences, 83,* 5349–5353.

Mauk, M. D., & Thompson, R. F. (1987). Retention of classically conditioned eyelid responses following acute decerebration. *Brain Research, 403,* 89–95.

Mazur, J. E., & Wagner, A. R. (1982). An episodic model of associative learning. In M. L. Commons, R. J. Herrnstein & A. R. Wagner (Eds.), *Quantitative Analyses of Behavior: Vol. III. Acquisition.* Cambridge, MA: Ballinger.

McCormick, D. A., Lavond, D. G., Clark, G. A., Kettner, R. E., Rising, C. E., & Thompson, R. F. (1981). The engram found?: Role of the cerebellum in classical conditioning of nictitating membrane and eyelid responses. *Bulletin of the Psychonomic Society, 18(3),* 103–105.

McCormick, D. A., Steinmetz, J. E., & Thompson, R. F. (1985). Lesions of the inferior olivary complex cause extinction of the classically conditioned eyeblink response. *Brain Research, 359,* 120–130.

McCormick, D. A., & Thompson, R. F. (1984a). Cerebellum: Essential involvement in the classically conditioned eyelid response. *Science, 223,* 296–299.

McCormick, D. A., & Thompson, R. F. (1984b). Neuronal responses of the rabbit cerebellum during acquisition and performance of a classically conditioned nictitating membrane-eyelid response. *Journal of Neuroscience, 4,* 2811–2822.

Millenson, J. R., Kehoe, E. J., & Gormezano, I. (1977). Classical conditioning of the rabbit's nictitating membrane response under fixed and mixed CS-US intervals. *Learning and Motivation, 8,* 351–366.

Moore, J. W., & Blazis, D. E. J. (1989). Simulation of a classically conditioned response: A cerebellar neural network implementation of the Sutton-Barto-Desmond model. In J. H. Byrnes & W. O. Berry (Eds.), *Neural models of plasticity: Experimental and theoretical approaches.* New York: Academic Press.

Norman, R. J., Buchwald, J. S., & Villablanca, J. R. (1977). Classical conditioning with auditory discrimination of the eyeblink in decerebrate cats. *Science, 196,* 551–553.

Parker, D. (1985). *Learning logic* (Report #47). Cambridge, MA: Center for Computational Research in Economics and Management Science, MIT.

Parker, D. (1986). A comparison of algorithms for neuron-like cells. In *Proceedings of the neural networks for computing conference.* Snowbird, Utah.

Pavlov, I. (1927). *Conditioned reflexes.* London: Oxford University Press.

Pellionisz, A., & Llinas, R. (1979). Brain modeling by tensor network theory and computer simulation. The cerebellum: parallel processor for predictive coordination. *Neuroscience,* 323–348.

Rescorla, R. A. (1968). Probability of shock in the presence and absence of CS in fear conditioning. *Journal of Comparative and Physiological Psychology, 66,* 1–5.

Rescorla, R. A. (1988). Pavlovian conditioning: It's not what you think it is. *American Psychologist, 43(3),* 151–160.

Rescorla, R.A., & Holland, P.C. (1982). Behavioral studies of associative learning in animals. *Annual Review of Psychology, 33,* 265–308.

Rescorla, R. A., & Wagner, A. R. (1972). A theory of Pavlovian conditioning: Variations in the effectiveness of reinforcement and non-reinforcement. In A. H. Black & W. F. Prokasy (Eds.), *Classical conditioning II: Current research and theory.* New York: Appleton-Century-Crofts.

Robinson, D. A. (1976). Adaptive gain control of vestibulo-ocular reflex by the cerebellum. *Journal of Neurophysiology, 39(5),* 954–969.

Rosenberg, C. R., & Sejnowski, T. J. (1986). The spacing effect on Nettalk, a massively-parallel network. In *Proceedings of the 8th Annual Conference of the Cognitive Science Society.* Amherst, MA.

Rumelhart, D. E., Hinton, G. E., & Williams, R. J. (1986). Learning internal representations by error propagation. In D. Rumelhart & J. McClelland (Eds.), *Parallel distributed processing: Explorations in the microstructure of cognition* (Vol. 1). Cambridge, MA: MIT Press.

Rumelhart, D. E., & McClelland, J. L. (1986). *Parallel Distributed Processing: Explorations in the microstructure of cognition* (vol. 1). Cambridge, MA: MIT Press.

Schneiderman, N. (1972). *Response system divergencies in aversive classical conditioning.* New York: Appleton-Century-Crofts.

Schor, R.H., Miller, A.D., & Tomko, D.L. (1984). Response to head tilt in cat central vestibular neurons I. Direction of maximum sensitivity. *Journal of Neurophysiology, 51(1),* 136–146.

Sejnowski, T. J. (1988). Neural populations revealed. *Nature, 332,* 308.

Solomon, P. R., Lewis, J. L., LoTurco, J., Steinmetz, J. E., & Thompson, R. F. (1986). The role of the middle cerebellar peduncle in acquisition and retention of the rabbits classically conditioned nictitating membrane response. *Bulletin of the Psychonomic Society, 24(1),* 75–78.

Spence, K. W. (1956). *Behavior theory and conditioning.* New Haven, CT: Yale University Press.

Steinmetz, J. E., Lavond, D. G., & Thompson, R. F. (in press). Classical conditioning in rabbits using pontine nucleus stimulation as a conditioned stimulus and inferior olive stimulation as an unconditioned stimulus. *Synapse.*

Steinmetz, J. E., Logan, C. G., Rosen, D. J., & Thompson, J. K. (1987). Initial localization of the acoustic conditioned stimulus projection system to the cerebellum essential for classical eyelid conditioning. *Proceedings of the National Academy of Sciences, 84,* 3531–3535.

Steinmetz, M. A., Motter, B. C., Duffy, C. J., & Mountcastle, V. B. (1987). Functional properties of parietal visual neurons: Radial organization of directionalities within the visual field. *Journal of Neuroscience, 7(1),* 177–191.

Steinmetz, J. E., Rosen, D. J., Woodruff-Pak, D. S., Lavond, D. G., & Thompson, R. F. (1986). Rapid transfer of training occurs when direct mossy fiber stimulation is used as a conditioned stimulus for classical eyelid conditioning. *Neuroscience Research, 3,* 606–616.

Suga, N., & Horikawa, J. (1986). Multiple time axes for representation of echo delays in the auditory cortex of the mustached bat. *Journal of Neurophysiology, 55,* 776–805.

Sutton, R. S., & Barto, A. G. (1981). Toward a modern theory of adaptive networks: Expectation and prediction. *Psychological Review, 88,* 135–170.

Sutton, R. S., & Barto, A. G. (1987). A temporal-difference model of classical conditioning. In *Proceedings of the 9th Annual Conference of the Cognitive Science Society.* Seattle, WA.

Thompson, R. F. (1986). The neurobiology of learning and memory. *Science, 233,* 941–947.

Thompson, R. F. (1988). The neural basis of associative learning of discrete behavioral responses. *Trends in Neuroscience, 11*(4), 152–155.

Thompson, R. F., Berger, T. W., Cegavske, C. F., Patterson, M. M., Roemer, R. A., Teyler, T. J., & Young, R. A. (1976). The search for the engram. *American Psychologist, 31,* 209–227.

Thompson, R. F., Donegan, N. H., Clark, G. A., Lavond, D. G., Madden, J. IV, Mamounas, L. A., Mauk, M. D., & McCormick, D. A. (1987). Neuronal substrates of discrete, defensive conditioned reflexes, conditioned fear states, and their interactions in the rabbit. In I. Gormezano, W. F. Prokasy, & R. F. Thompson (Eds.), *Classical conditioning III: Behavioral, neurophysiological, and neurochemical studies in the rabbit.* Hillsdale, NJ: Laurence Erlbaum Associates.

Thompson, R. F., & Gluck, M. A. (1989a). A biological neural-network analysis of learning and memory. In S. Zournetzer, C. Lau, & J. Davis (Eds.), *An introduction to neural and electronic networks.* New York: Academic Press.

Thompson, R. F., & Gluck, M. A. (1989b). Brain substrates of basic associative learning and memory. In H. J. Weingartner & R. F. Lister (Eds.), *Cognitive neuroscience.* New York: Oxford University Press.

Thompson, R. F., Donegan, N. H., & Lavond, D. G. (1988). The psychobiology of learning and memory. In R. C. Atkinson, R. J. Herrnstein, G. Lindzey, & R. D. Luce (Eds.), *Steven's handbook of experimental psychology* (2nd Ed.). New York: Wiley.

Tischler, M. D., & Davis, M. (1983). A visual pathway that mediates fear-conditioned enhancement of acoustic startle. *Brain Research,276,* 55–71.

Wagner, A. R. (1969). Stimulus selection and a modified continuity theory. In G. Bower, & J. Spence (Eds.), *The psychology of learning and motivation* (Vol. 3). New York: Academic Press.

Wagner, A. R. (1981). SOP: A model of automatic memory processing in animal behavior. In N. Spear, & G. Miller (Eds.), *Information processing in animals: Memory mechanisms.* Hillsdale, NJ: Lawrence Erlbaum Associates.

Wagner, A. R., Logan, F. A., Haberlandt, K., & Price, T. (1968). Stimulus selection in animal discrimination learning. *Journal of Experimental Psychology, 76,* 171–180.

Wagner, A. R., & Rescorla, R. A. (1972). Inhibition in Pavlovian conditioning: Applications of a theory. In R. A. Boakes, & S. Halliday (Eds.), *Inhibition and learning* (pp. 301–336). New York: Academic Press.

Werbos, P. (1974). *Beyond regression: New tools for prediction and analysis in the behavioral sciences.* Unpublished doctoral dissertation, Dept. of Economics, Harvard University, Cambridge, MA.

Widrow, B. (1987). A fundamental relationship between the LMS algorithm and the discrete fourier transform. *Proceedings of the IEEE International Symposium on Circuits and Systems.* Philadelphia, Pennsylvania, May 4–7.

Widrow, B., Baudrenghien, P., Vetterli, M., & Titchener, P. (1987). Fundamental relations between the LMS algorithm and the DFT. *IEEE Transaction on Circuits and Systems, 34.*

Widrow, B., & Hoff, M. E. (1960). Adaptive switching circuits. *Institute of Radio Engineers, Western Electronic Show and Convention, Convention Record,4,* 96–194.

Widrow, B., & Stearns, S. D. (1985). *Adaptive Signal Processing.* Englewood Cliffs, NJ: Prentice-Hall.

Widrow, B., & Winter, R. (1988). Neural nets for adaptive filtering and adaptive pattern recognition. *Computer,* March, 25–39.

Wilson, V. J., Ezure, K., & Timerick, S. J. (1984). Tonic neck reflex of the decerebrate cat: response of spinal interneurons to natural stimulation of neck and vestibular receptors. *Journal of Neurophysiology, 51(3),* 567–577.

Yeo, C. H., Hardiman, M. J., & Glickstein, M. (1985a). Classical conditioning of the nictitating membrane response of the rabbit: I. Lesions of the cerebellar cortex. *Experimental Brain Research, 99–113.*

Yeo, C. H., Hardiman, M. J., & Glickstein, M. (1985b). Classical conditioning of the nictitating membrane response of the rabbit: II. Lesions of the cerebellar nuclei. *Experimental Brain Research, 87–98.*

Zimmer-Hart, C. L., & Rescorla, R. (1974). Extinction of Pavlovian conditioned inhibition. *Journal of Comparative and Physiological Psychology, 86,* 837–845.

5

Elemental Adaptive Processes of Neurons and Synapses: A Statistical/Computational Perspective

William B Levy, Costa M. Colbert, and Nancy L Desmond

Department of Neurological Surgery and the Neuroscience Program University of Virginia School of Medicine

INTRODUCTION[1]

From the biological vantage, there are a variety of neuronal modifications and, in an independent and parallel way, there are a variety of ways to relate such modifications to the behavior of neuronal networks and of entire organisms. Several years ago, we (Levy & Desmond, 1985b) presented a view of synaptic modification, built around associative synaptic modification, which tried to communicate with both experimental biologists and network theoreticians. As with many of the chapters in the present volume, we were greatly struck by the fact that such associative modification was relevant to both pattern recognition problems (see also Levy, 1982; Levy & Steward, 1979) and to the developmental process of synaptic competition.

Our tack here, however, is somewhat different. In this chapter, we attempt to unify and interrelate a disparate set of biological observations of neuronal modification. This unification is obtained by considering fundamental aspects of probability and statistics rather than by just considering

---

[1]We use the phrase *synaptic modification* to mean modification of the strength of the connection between two neurons. *Associative synaptic modification* means a synaptic modification resulting from the approximate coactivity, in time and space, of the pre- and postsynaptic elements that form the synapse. *Neuronal modification* encompasses synaptic modification but also includes changes in a neuron that are not localized to a specific synapse on that neuron. *Potentiation* and *depression* describe a synaptic change as either a strengthening or weakening, respectively, of the influence of that synapse on its postsynaptic element. A *postsynaptic element* is often thought of as a neuron, but it may also mean a portion of a neuron, e.g., a dendritic segment.

the experimental paradigms used to induce the biological phenomenology. More specifically, we use the framework of prediction based on the computation of probabilities from stored statistics to interrelate different forms of neuronal modification. Although this unification is useful in its own right, it also (a) implies testable working hypotheses about neuronal function for the experimental neurobiologist and (b) creates a context that allows network theoreticians to incorporate the biological observations discussed here into computationally oriented models of network function.

The Hippocampus

Because most research on associative synaptic modification has been done in the hippocampus and because our own experimental research and network models have concentrated on the hippocampus, much of our discussion refers to observations obtained in this structure. It is in the hippocampus that activity-dependent, long-lasting synaptic modification, called long-term potentiation (LTP), was first identified (Bliss & Lomo, 1973), and it is here also that the coactivity requirement that produces associative synaptic modification was confirmed (Levy & Steward, 1979; McNaughton, Douglas, & Goddard, 1978). How the properties of the hippocampus facilitated identification of these synaptic phenomena is discussed in the final section on biological support for the modification rules.

There are other reasons the hippocampus is an attractive system for study. For one, the hippocampus is an important brain region in its own right and needs to be understood just for that reason. In addition, the relative simplicity of hippocampal anatomy and the various types of modifiability that are easily studied there make the hippocampus an attractive model system. Despite its simplicity, the hippocampus shares many similarities with the neocortex, particularly at the cellular level. For example, it appears that many of the cellular processes involved in visual cortical modification (see Bear & Cooper, chap. 2 in this volume) exist in the hippocampus as well. Such similarities justify the emphasis on the hippocampus as a model system.

Figure 5.1 schematically depicts the major extrinsic input to the hippocampus, the entorhinal cortex (EC), the major subdivisions of the hippocampus, and the connections between these hippocampal regions. For details of hippocampal anatomy, see the recent review by Amaral (1987).

What Does the Hippocampus Do?

A variety of theories of hippocampal function have been published regularly since 1952, and it would be easy to cull 30 or even 50 different

FIG. 5.1. The major subdivisions of the hippocampus are areas CA1, CA3, and the dentate gyrus (DG). The major inputs to these hippocampal subdivisions are indicated by the lines and arrows. The arrows indicate monosynaptic connections and the direction of signal propagation. The major extrinsic input to the hippocampus originates in 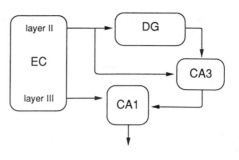 the entorhinal cortex (EC). The axons of neurons in layer II of the EC project to the DG and CA3 regions of the hippocampus; the axons of neurons in layer III of the EC project to the CA1 region of the hippocampus.

explanations of hippocampal function from these theories. Our own hypothesis that the hippocampus functions as a prediction-generating device appears elsewhere (Levy, 1989), and we encourage the reader to examine the theory set forth there. The reader should also examine chapter 1 in this volume by McNaughton and Nadel for a related but alternate view of hippocampal function.

For the purpose of the current chapter, however, we need only suppose that the hippocampus, particularly the area known as CA1 (see Fig. 5.1), generates predictions about events in the future. The generation of predictions is by no means exclusive to the hippocampus and what is discussed here can be hypothesized to occur in many different brain regions. Thus it is the general problem of prediction generation by neurons, rather than the objective of predictions made by the hippocampus, which is the embarkation point of this chapter.

Chapter Overview

This chapter considers formulations of adaptive modifications that lead to the storage of statistics. The framework of prediction of future events by neurons and the fact that an associatively modifiable synapse can store something like the correlation between the activities of its pre- and postsynaptic elements orient our thinking. The prediction issue and the existence of associative modifiablity lead us to consider the possibility that other neuronal modifications may generate stored statistics. This line of thought then leads to questions such as, "Does a neuron, whose job is to generate a prediction, combine these statistics so as to produce appropriate probabilities?"

There are three main sections in this chapter. The first part introduces our notation and describes the basic and well-known mathematics of probabilistic predictions based on averages. Here we remind the reader how statistics that are averages may be combined to generate predictions. The point is that a neuron may do likewise. If a neuron can store a particular set of statistics and can implement the computations implied by maximum entropy inference, then a neuron will produce mathematically rigorous probabilities.

The second portion of the chapter discusses how various adaptive modifications that are similar to those observed experimentally can be used to store the statistics discussed in the next section. This section discusses three rules describing neuronal modification that reflect the necessarily local information available to the neuron, and relates these rules to the generation of three specific statistics. It also considers how such modifications must interact if a neuron is to generate the computation developed from the maximum entropy principle.

The final section goes into more biological detail and points out the experimental observations that inspire our thesis — statistics are encoded as synaptic and neuronal modifications. This section relates the biological observations to the adaptive processes presented in the section discussing averaging. Specifically, the biological evidence suggests that the three statistics are encoded via associative modification, via the modification of neuronal excitability, and via the neuronal and synaptic modifications associated with low-frequency synaptic activation. All three forms of neuronal modifications exist in the hippocampus.

OUR PERSPECTIVE: PREDICTION USING PROBABILITIES BASED ON STORED STATISTICS

As mentioned earlier, the framework used here to unify the biological observations derives from fundamental aspects of probability and statistics.

There are two reasons for the attraction of probability theory. First, as Golden (unpublished manuscript) recently pointed out, probability theory is the uniquely correct, and standard, formulation of a finite, continuously valued logic (Cox, 1946, 1979). Furthermore, most of the computational problems addressed by neural networks can be described within the framework of probability theory. Statistical inference offers a similar motivation.

The ideas of describing neural activity in terms of probabilities, of representing probabilities in terms of neural activity, and of storing statistics at synapses to generate probabilities came early to neural network theory thanks to Rosenblatt (1962). The idea of storing a statistic at a synapse was used, sometimes implicitly and sometimes explicitly, by many of the early theorists who followed Rosenblatt (e.g. Amari, 1977; Anderson, Silverstein, Ritz, & Jones, 1977; Grossberg, 1987; Kohonen, Lehtiö, & Rovamo, 1974; Willshaw & von der Malsburg, 1976). In the work of Geman (1981), the nature of averaging processes at synapses is made explicit as a central theme of synaptic modification and is made rigorous in its treatment. Our own experimental work on synaptic modification and our orientation derive from the perspectives of these and other theorists. As seen later, the issue of averaging (i.e., forming statistics) is no less fundamental than the associative modification principle generally attributed to Hebb (1949).

Statistical Inference and the Generation of Probabilities

In order to understand our perspective on adaptive modifications, we remind the reader of some procedures, known to Bayes and the Bernoullis, for generating probabilities from statistics.

Statistics Imply Probability Distributions

A statistic, in the form of an average (or equivalently an expectation or a moment), can imply a probability distribution. For example, consider the problem of predicting the outcome of a coin flip that must come out as either heads or tails. Let $Z=1$ stand for a head and $Z=0$ stand for a tail. If we know the relative frequency of heads, call it $E[Z]$ for expected value of Z, then we immediately can infer the probability distribution of all possible outcomes:

$$P(Z) = E[Z]^Z(1 - E[Z])^{(1-Z)}. \tag{1}$$

There are only two possible outcomes for Z (i.e., Z is a binary variable); thus it is easy to write the probabilities of all (i.e., both) possible values of Z covered by the distribution $P(Z)$:

$$P(Z = 1 = \text{head}) = E[Z]^1(1 - E[Z])^0 \tag{2}$$

and

$$P(Z = 0 = \text{tail}) = E[Z]^0(1 - E[Z])^1. \tag{3}$$

There is a particularly interesting fact about the general procedure for inferring a distribution from a set of expectations. Given a particular set of expectations over the variable X, where the members of this set are just those expectations available to the computation (or, for the purposes here, available to a neuron), and given a description of all possible configurations of the variable X (the support of the distribution, for those knowledgeable in probability theory), there is an axiomatically derived procedure that produces a unique probability distribution $P(X)$ consistent with the averages. This procedure is the minimum relative entropy procedure (MRE) of Shore and Johnson (1980), a generalization of Jaynes' (1979) maximum entropy procedure. Though it is not yet known if a neuron creates a computation consistent with this procedure, we have postulated that it does (Levy, 1989) and follow through with this postulate here in order to create the context of neurons that use averages to compute probabilities.

Bayes' Equation and Averages are Useful for Computing Probabilities

A general statement of the prediction problem is: Given information about the occurrence of some event, what can we infer about the occurrence of another, possibly related event? For instance, suppose we are supplied with the information that the Giants will play the Dodgers this week. What is the probability that the Giants will win? In order to remind readers of Bayes' theorem and to introduce some notation, we continue this example in depth before shifting to the context of a neuron predicting its own future activity. Those readers familiar with Bayes' theorem and conditional probabilities may wish to just skim this section to pick up the notation.

Let X be all possible contests the Giants might enter, and let the specific contest between the Giants and the Dodgers be designated $X=x$. Let Z be the outcome of a game with $Z=1$ a victory for the Giants. Then $P(X=x)$ is the probability that the Giants play the Dodgers; $P(Z=1)$ is the probability that the Giants win regardless of whom they play; and $P(Z=1|X=x)$ is the probability that the Giants win when they play the Dodgers.

The definition of a conditional probability is

$$P(Z|X) = \frac{P(Z,X)}{P(X)} . \tag{4}$$

From equation 4 and from the fact that Z is a binary variable, we can write several equivalent expressions for the probability that the Giants win when they play the Dodgers:

$$P(Z=1|X=x) = \frac{P(X=x|Z=1)P(Z=1)}{P(X=x)}$$

$$= \frac{P(X=x|Z=1)P(Z=1)}{P(X=x,Z=1) + P(X=x,Z=0)}$$

$$= \frac{P(X=x|Z=1)P(Z=1)}{P(X=x|Z=1)P(Z=1) + P(X=x|Z=0)(1 - P(Z=1))} . \tag{5}$$

The last expression is just Bayes' theorem. The terms necessary for the computation of $P(Z=1|X=x)$ via Bayes' theorem are:

$P(Z=1)$ the probability the Giants win no matter whom they play;

$P(X=x)$ the probability the Giants play the Dodgers;

$P(X=x|Z=1)$ the probability the Giants played the Dodgers given that the Giants have won; and

$P(X=x|Z=0)$ the probability the Giants played the Dodgers given that the Giants have lost.

Thus, equation 5 tells us how to use some conditional probabilities, $P(X|Z)$, to compute another conditional probability, $P(Z|X)$.

Those unfamiliar with Bayes' theorem sometimes find it paradoxical that predictions are generated by this "inversion" of conditional probabilities (i.e., using $P(X=x|Z=1)$ to compute $P(Z=1|X=x)$). They often ask "Why not just learn $P(Z=1|X=x)$ and forget about the calculation of all those other probabilities?"

Learning the desired probabilities directly is perfectly reasonable, and preferable, for the example just given because X, the set of possible games against teams in the league, is not very large. One just compiles statistics as the teams play throughout the season. For problems faced by neural networks, however, X includes an incredibly large number of possibilities, most of which will occur rarely or never at all. For this reason it is often impossible to compute the desired probabilities directly.

We believe that the Bayesian inversion and the computations consistent with minimum relative entropy inference are forced on a neural network by the combinatorial explosion of possibilities that may occur.

Consider the following example. Suppose there is a network with 1,000 neurons whose individual outputs are either fire or not fire. Let X be a vector with 1,000 binary elements, X_i, $i=1, 2, \ldots, 1000$, that each correspond to the output of one neuron. Considering all the combinations of neurons that might be firing at a particular time, the vector X could take on $2^{1,000}$ different configurations. Now, let Z_j be a binary valued variable, for example, a threshold event in another neuron j. Because there are so many possible configurations of x, any one prediction $P(Z_j=1|X=x)$ is unlikely to be well sampled, if sampled at all. That is, any particular configuration, x, is unlikely to occur very often, so reliable statistics about the probability of Z_j given different configurations x in X will be difficult to compile. On the other hand, as in the previous example, we can use summary statistics, in this case $E[X_i|Z_j=1]$, $i=1, 2, \ldots, 1000$, to infer any of the points covered by the probability distribution $P(X|Z_j=1)$. In this situation, the MRE procedure of Shore and Johnson (1980) says that the probability is constructed as if the variables X_i conditioned on Z_j are independent:

$$P^*(X=x|Z_j=1) = \prod_i P^*(X_i=x_i|Z_j=1) \tag{6}$$

$$= \prod_i E[X_i|Z_j=1]^{x_i}(1 - E[X_i|Z_j=1])^{(1 - x_i)}. \tag{7}$$

$P^*(\ )$ denotes a probability inferred by the MRE procedure rather than the actual probability, $P(\ )$, itself. Equation 7 shows how each term i in the multiple product of the right-hand side of equation 6 is a selected probability, depending on x_i, from the probability distribution $P^*(X_i|Z_j=1)$. A similar equation can be written for $P^*(X_i|Z_j=0)$.

Considering the fundamental importance of Bayes' approach to the generation of predictions, it is not surprising that Bayes' procedure, or some part of it, appears in many neural network theories, for example, Minsky and Papert (1969), Hinton and Sejnowski (1983), Tank and Hopfield (1986), Golden (unpublished manuscript), and Levy (1989).

The next step takes the last version of equation 5 and substitutes using: the left-hand side of equation 6; the related form conditioned instead on $Z_j=0$; and $E[Z_j]$ after noting the equivalence $E[Z]=P(Z=1)$ when Z_j is binary. As a result

$$P^*(Z_j=1|X=x) = \frac{E[Z_j]P^*(X=x|Z_j=1)}{E[Z_j]P^*(X=x|Z_j=1) + (1 - E[Z_j])P^*(X=x|Z_j=0)}$$

$$\tag{8}$$

We hypothesize that computations like equation 8 are performed in each of the primary hippocampal CA1 neurons, j. Inputs i, the afferents from the CA3 region to CA1, at time t predict the probability of a thresholded event Z_j generated slightly later in time by another set of inputs, specifically those from the entorhinal cortex (EC) to each CA1 neuron j. The event Z_j might be, for example, a dendritic or a somatic spike.

For the purposes of this chapter, the importance of Bayes' equation, specifically the form given as equation 8, lies in its focus on three particular probability distributions. More specifically, equation 8 focuses attention on three statistics (see Table 5.1), each of which implies, via MRE, a probability distribution.

TABLE 5.1
Three Statistics and Their Corresponding MRE-inferred Probability
Distributions

Statistic	Inferred Probability Distribution
$E[X_i\|Z_j=1]$	$P^*(X_i=x_i\|Z_j=1)$ for any allowed value x_i
$E[X_i\|Z_j=0]$	$P^*(X_i=x_i\|Z_j=0)$ for any allowed value x_i
$E[Z_j]$	$P^*(Z_j)$ for any allowed value Z_j

Statistics imply probability distributions as described in the text. X_i is the transient activity of the cell named i that is presynaptic to cell j; together they form the ij synapse. The variable Z_j indicates whether or not cell j, or some relevant portion of j, surpasses a threshold level of excitation. $E[X_i|Z_j=1]$ is the expected value of the ith afferent given the threshold is exceeded in cell j; $E[X_i|Z_j=0]$ is the expected value of the ith afferent given the threshold is not exceeded in cell j; and $E[Z_j]$ is the expectation that cell j exceeds the threshold. $P^*(\ )$ is an MRE-inferred probability.

Let us now consider the adaptive processes of neurons and synapses that might generate these statistics.

STORING STATISTICS AT NEURONS AND SYNAPSES

This section presents three distinct modification rules that result in the computation and storage of the three statistics in Table 5.1. The first two modification rules describe associative synaptic modifications that we postulate occur independently at each synapse. To identify this bipartite characteristic of each synapse, we subdivide synaptic strength w_{ij} into w_{ij}^+ and w_{ij}^-. The third modification rule describes two nonassociative modification processes that depend on the activity history of the neuron rather than the history of the individual synapses. This section also describes how these modification rules translate into the statistics of Table 5.1, and how they combine to produce the appropriate computation of probabilities.

$E[X_i|f(y_j)=1]$: Synaptic LTP and LTD Store a Correlation

The synaptic modification rule that produces the first statistic is derived from observations of long-term synaptic potentiation and depression (see the section on experimental support for details and references). The longevity of potentiation and depression are equivalent when tested in the intact animal, and there exist individual experiments that show no evidence of decay of either process even when followed for hours. The induction of either potentiation or depression requires the same event — powerful net postsynaptic excitation. Weak presynaptic activity, on the other hand, produces no consistent long-term change of synaptic efficacy. In addition, given a constant level of input, the amount of potentiation and depression are limited so that synaptic strength converges to an asymptotic value.

The required postsynaptic event has characteristics that imply that postsynaptic excitation, call it y_j, translates into a permissive postsynaptic process in a highly nonlinear manner. For the sake of generality this nonlinear translation is indicated as $f(y_j)$. The exact form of this nonlinearity is not known. Some occasionally prefer a sigmoidal function (e.g., Grossberg, 1987; Hopfield, 1984); however, here we will always need the step function so that $f(y)$ yields only values in the set $\{0,1\}$ (i.e., the permissive event is all-or-none and $Z_j \equiv f(y_j)$).

Figure 5.2 gives a simplified description of the experimental conditions that produce the long-term synaptic modifications most related to the rule suggested by Hebb (1949). Pre- and postsynaptic activity are interpreted as either off or on.

Note in Fig. 5.2 that only one type of noncorrelation $\{X_i=0, Z_j=1\}$ and one type of correlation $\{X_i=1, Z_j=1\}$ result in the modification of w_{ij}^+.

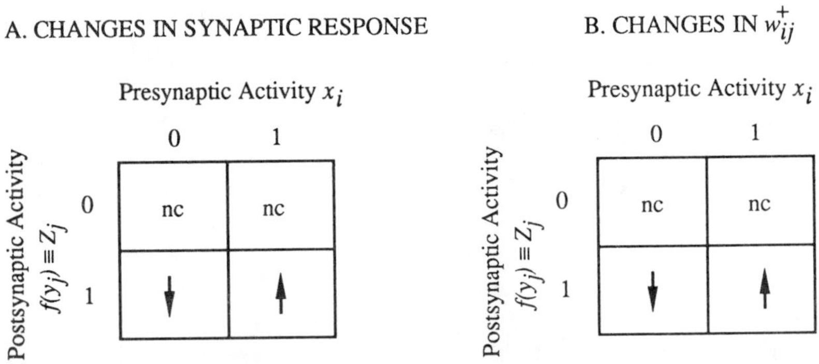

A. CHANGES IN SYNAPTIC RESPONSE   B. CHANGES IN w_{ij}^+

FIG. 5.2. Contingency tables for associative long-term potentiation/depression of synaptic efficacy. A, the contingency table of the qualitative changes observed in the evoked synaptic response. B, the contingency table of the qualitative changes of w_{ij}^+. The four quadrants of each table express the possible activity contingencies which may lead to changes in synaptic efficacy. 0 and 1 indicate, respectively, inactivity and activity. The changes in synaptic efficacy resulting from each of the four possible combinations of presynaptic activity, x_i, and postsynaptic activity, $f(y_j)$, are indicated as follows: nc, no change in synaptic efficacy; ↓, decreased synaptic efficacy; and ↑, increased synaptic efficacy. Hebb's (1949) postulate is the increased efficacy indicated in the lower right quadrants. Note that modification in either direction requires postsynaptic activity, and that the direction of changes of the observed response (A) and w_{ij}^+ (B) are the same.

Because both modifications require $Z_j = 1$, we call this event permissive for modification of w_{ij}^+.

The simplest form of the synaptic modification rule consistent with the electrophysiological observations previously summarized in Fig. 5.2A is

$$w_{ij}^+(t+1) = w_{ij}^+(t) + \Delta w_{ij}^+(t, t+1) \tag{9}$$

where

$$\Delta w_{ij}^+(t, t+1) = \epsilon f(y_j(t))(cx_i(t-\eta) - w_{ij}^+(t)). \tag{10}$$

In these equations, i corresponds to one particular presynaptic afferent and j corresponds to one particular postsynaptic neuron (see Fig. 5.3). Given the assumption that an afferent contacts a postsynaptic neuron no more than once, the pair ij uniquely specifies one particular synapse. w_{ij}^+ is the part of the synaptic strength (or efficacy, or weight) of the synapse ij dependent on $f(y_j) = 1$ for modification. Δw_{ij}^+ is the change in this part of the strength of

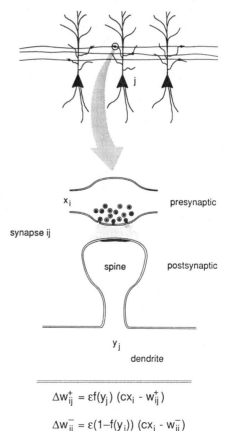

FIG. 5.3. The variables in the modification equations and their hypothesized neuronal locations. The upper panel provides a more macroscopic view of several axons, including i, coursing by or forming a synapse on several neurons, including j. One such synapse, ij, is exploded in the lower panel. x_i corresponds to the activity of axon i. y_j corresponds to the excitation of the dendritic segment of neuron j on which a spine makes a synapse with axon i. The two synaptic modification equations (w_{ij}^- and w_{ij}^+) for a synapse ij are listed at the bottom. Δ is read as 'change of', ϵ and c are positively valued and essentially constant over the timeframe of synaptic activity described by these two equations. See text for more details.

$$\Delta w_{ij}^+ = \epsilon f(y_j) (cx_i - w_{ij}^+)$$

$$\Delta w_{ij}^- = \epsilon(1-f(y_j)) (cx_i - w_{ij}^-)$$

synapse *ij*. y_j corresponds to the relevant (i.e., local dendritic) net excitatory activation of postsynaptic neuron *j*. x_i corresponds to the presynaptic activation of afferent *i*. *t* is a point in time, $(t, t+1)$ is the interval between *t* and $t+1$, and η is a positive constant in units of time meant to capture the fact that the relevant activity of x_i precedes but does not follow activation of y_j. ϵ is a positive value between zero and one that adjusts the magnitude of the change in efficacy during a given time interval. ϵ is often assumed to be a constant, but recent evidence indicates that it is a variable (Levy & Burger, 1987a). c is a positive constant of units which produce matching units of cx_i and w_{ij} (similar constants appear in later equations without explanation). In what follows, all arguments *t* will be left implicit.

In contrast to theories that allow both positive and negative values for the variables corresponding to activation, we strictly confine y_j and x_i to nonnegative values. x_i, for example, can be thought of as the frequency of afferent firing or simply as on or off. The function *f* is a nonnegative, nondecreasing function, so that increasing y_j produces monotonically increasing values of $f(y_j)$.

Note that equation 10 is consistent with the contingency tables of Fig. 5.2 because they both predict depression when $f(y_j) > 0$ and $x_i = 0$, while they predict no change when $f(y_j) = 0$ no matter what the value of x_i.

The difference term, $(cx_i - w_{ij}^+)$, insures that w_{ij}^+ will never be less than zero or greater than the largest value of cx_i. Moreover, this term causes convergence to be asymptotic in nature. The equation guarantees that the strength of any existing synapse is greater than zero because zero would only be approached asymptotically. However, positing a discontinuity near zero by which a synapse is removed is a sensible postulate from a developmental-biological perspective. ϵ controls the rate of convergence and the approximation error of the convergence.

The Relationship of Equation 10 to the Storing of a Statistic

This section discusses how the synaptic efficacy w_{ij}^+ of equations 9 and 10 encodes the first of the desired statistics in Table 5.1. We begin by averaging both sides of equation 10. (To do so assumes some properties of the activity of x_i and y_j. These assumptions are beyond the scope of this chapter, namely, that x_i and y_j are stochastic, ergodic, and that suitable stationarity exists [Geman, 1981]):

$$E[\Delta w_{ij}^+] = E[\epsilon f(y_j)(cx_i - w_{ij}^+)]. \tag{11}$$

We can bring the constants out of the expected value and distribute the sums,

$$E[\Delta w_{ij}^+] = \epsilon c E[f(y_j)x_i] - \epsilon E[w_{ij}^+ f(y_j)]. \tag{12}$$

When ϵ is small, w_{ij}^+ itself is almost constant and approximately independent of $f(y_j)$ so that the last term is satisfactorily approximated as

$$\epsilon E[w_{ij}^+ f(y_j)] \cong \epsilon w_{ij}^+ E[f(y_j)]. \tag{13}$$

Under the stated assumptions of stationarity and ergodicity, $E[\Delta w_{ij}^+] \to 0$, so we can rewrite equation 12 as

$$0 \cong \epsilon c E[f(y_j)x_i] - \epsilon w_{ij}^+ E[f(y_j)]. \tag{14}$$

Solving for w_{ij}^+ gives

$$w_{ij}^+ \cong \frac{E[f(y_j)x_i]}{E[f(y_j)]}, \tag{15}$$

where we have taken $c = 1$; moreover, the approximation is exact in the limit $\epsilon \to 0$.

Suppose some threshold level of postsynaptic activation must occur in order for any synaptic modification to occur (e.g., Amari, 1977). That is,

$$f(y_j) = \begin{bmatrix} 0 & \text{for } y_j \text{ below threshold} \\ 1 & \text{for } y_j \text{ equal to or above threshold.} \end{bmatrix} \tag{16}$$

Because $f(y_j)$ thus defined is a binary process,

$$E[f(y_j),x_i] = E[f(y_j)=1,x_i] + E[f(y_j)=0,x_i], \tag{17}$$

but note that

$$E[f(y_j)=0,x_i] = 0. \tag{18}$$

Thus, the only nonzero expectations are conditional on $f(y_j)=1$, and equation 15 becomes

$$w_{ij}^+ \cong \frac{E[X_i,f(y_j)=1]}{E[f(y_j)=1]} = E[X_i|f(y_j)=1], \tag{19}$$

which just encodes the first conditional expectation of Table 5.1 as a synaptic strength.

Incompatible Equations

The following associative synaptic modification equations preserve the basic Hebbian notion that synaptic modification is a function of pre- and postsynaptic coactivity (the lower right quadrant of the contingency tables in Fig. 5.2); however, each of these equations fails to predict all quadrants of Fig. 5.2. Consider the following modification rules where $g(x_i)$ is a nonnegative, nondecreasing function of presynaptic activation, $f(y_j)$ is a nonnegative, nondecreasing function of postsynaptic activation, and b is a positive constant. Each variable is considered to be greater than or equal to zero.

$$\Delta w_{ij}^+ = f(y_j)g(x_i) - b \qquad (20)$$

The $- b$ term, which stands apart from the other terms of equation 20, predicts spontaneous decay that is independent of both pre- and postsynaptic activity. The equation also predicts unbounded changes of synaptic strength. That is, as long as either the pre- or the postsynaptic term is zero, the synaptic weight continues to decrease toward $- \infty$. Likewise, any activity conditions that initially cause potentiation continually yield more potentiation. Although it could be argued that the physical realization of the rule might prevent an unbounded decrease by imposing the constraint, $\max \geq w_{ij}^+ \geq 0$ (where max is some fixed, finite positive value), the more important experimental observation is that long-term depression is an actively triggered, rather than a spontaneous, continually ongoing, process (Levy & Steward, 1979, 1983; Levy, Brassel, & Moore, 1983; King & Levy, 1986) as implied by the activity independent term $(- b)$.

Another modification rule that does not fit the electrophysiological data but that does require a permissive postsynaptic event for long-term depression is

$$\Delta w_{ij}^+ = f(y_j)(x_i - b). \qquad (21)$$

Equation 21 is very similar to equation 10, but the subtracted term is the constant b, rather than a function of the synaptic efficacy itself, w_{ij}^+. As a result, equation 21 lacks suitable convergence properties. Specifically, in environments with $f(y_j) > 0$ and x held constant, as is often the case in long-term potentiation/depression experiments, synaptic efficacy is predicted to continually change when, in fact, it approaches an asymptotic value (Levy et al., 1983; Lopez, Burger, & Levy, 1985). Thus, although equation 21 predicts the initial phases of potentiation and depression correctly, it erroneously implies that there are no limits to either potentiation or depression.

A third modification equation that is inconsistent with experimental results is

$$\Delta w_{ij}^+ = (f(y_j) - b)g(x_i).\tag{22}$$

Equation 22 implies that changes in synaptic efficacy only occur when there is presynaptic activity, a prediction that is not consistent with the experimental observations (Wilson, Levy, & Steward, 1979; Lopez, Burger, Dickstein, Desmond, & Levy, submitted). Furthermore, equation 22 implies that the level of postsynaptic activity dictates whether potentiation or depression will occur. For example, this equation predicts that weak presynaptic activity in the absence of postsynaptic activity should decrease synaptic efficacy. Neither prediction, however, is consistent with experimental observations in the hippocampal dentate gyrus (see the section discussing experimental support).

Equation 10 then is the candidate elemental associative long-term synaptic modification rule that best describes experimentally observed long-term potentiation/depression. Furthermore, this rule encodes the statistic $E[X_i|Z_j=1]$, one of the three types of statistics required to compute equation 8.

The next section proposes an elemental modification to store $E[X_i|Z_j=0]$, the second statistic of Table 5.1 required to compute a prediction via equation 8.

$E[X_i|f(y_j)=0]$:
Short-term Synaptic Depression Stores a Correlation

In the associative paradigm, there are two noncorrelation contingencies $\{x_i=0, f(y_j)=1\}$, presynaptic inactive with postsynaptic active, and $\{x_i=1, f(y_j)=0\}$, presynaptic active with postsynaptic inactive. Although there is no a priori reason to believe that one of these noncorrelation contingencies is more important than the other, only the noncorrelation $\{x_i=0, f(y_j)=1\}$ seems to modify synaptic strength (see contingency tables of Fig. 5.2 and equation 10). Some theoreticians would prefer a synaptic modification rule in which the noncorrelation $\{x_i=1, f(y_j)=0\}$ is somehow encoded as well.

Until just recently we have been unable to answer this comment satisfactorily except to note that our ideas are driven by experimental observations. However, we now propose a candidate process for encoding the noncorrelation, $\{x_i=1, f(y_j)=0\}$. This not-so-new process, which includes the biological phenomenon of low-frequency depression, goes by the name of synaptic habituation because of its paradigmatic similarity to behavioral habituation.[2]

---

[2]Note added in proof: Stanton and Sejnowski (*Nature 339* (1989) 215–218) reported a synaptic depression in CA1 which may correspond to our Δw_{ij}^- rule and which may depend on hippocampal theta.

The identification of synaptic habituation in isolated systems (e.g., in the hippocampus, Alger & Teyler, 1976; or in the frog spinal cord, Farel & Thompson, 1972) comes by way of the paradigmatic definition of habituation developed by Thompson and Spencer (1966). The section on experimental support below discusses most of the nine characteristics comprising this definition. For now, we need only point out three of these characteristics: (1) repeated activation of weakly excitatory inputs depresses synaptic strength in an exponential fashion; (2) repeated activation of powerfully excitatory inputs does not lead to synaptic depression; and (3) there is spontaneous recovery from the synaptic depression evoked by repeated presynaptic activation (i.e., characteristic 1).

The possible relevance of a subset of the synaptic habituation phenomena to the context of this chapter may be more easily appreciated in Fig. 5.4A. This figure presents a contingency table of the conditions that produce associative modification based on synaptic habituation. Pre- and postsynaptic activity (x_i and $f(y_j)$, respectively) are interpreted as either off or on.

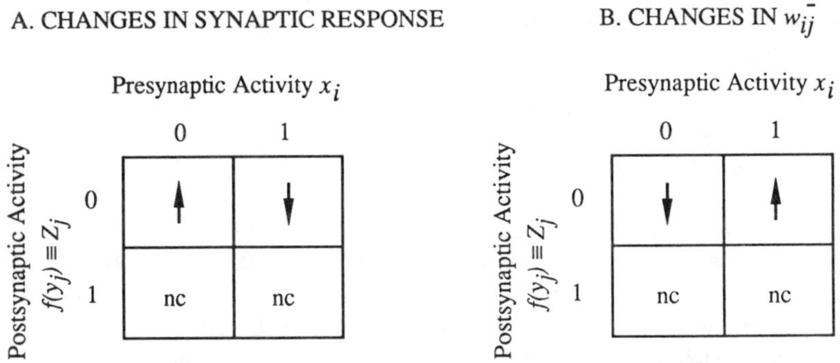

A. CHANGES IN SYNAPTIC RESPONSE   B. CHANGES IN w_{ij}^-

FIG. 5.4. Contingency tables for short-term synaptic modification. A, contingency table of the qualitative changes observed in the evoked synaptic response. B, contingency table of the qualitative changes in w_{ij}^-, the synaptic weakening variable. The four quadrants of each table express the possible activity contingencies which may lead to synaptic changes. 0 and 1 indicate, respectively, inactivity and activity. The outcomes resulting from each of the four possible combinations of presynaptic activity, x_i, and postsynaptic activity, $f(y_j)$, are: nc, no change in synaptic efficacy; ↓, decreased synaptic efficacy; and ↑, increased synaptic efficacy. For these short-term changes, note that modification requires postsynaptic *inactivity*, which is just the opposite of Fig. 5.2. Moreover, in contrast to Fig. 5.2, the direction of changes of w_{ij}^- and the evoked synaptic response differ because an increase in the variable w_{ij}^- corresponds to a decrease in the magnitude of the evoked synaptic response.

The upper left-hand quadrant in the contingency table of Fig. 5.4A, no presynaptic or postsynaptic activity, shows an increase in synaptic strength. This is the spontaneous recovery process. The upper right-hand quadrant is the depression observed following repeated presynaptic activation. Although no change operations in the lower half of this contingency table are consistent with no habituation to high-intensity stimulation (characteristic 2), these no change operations have no experimental support or refutation when the technical details of the experimental systems are considered (see the section on experimental support below for details). Even though the experimental phenomena which correspond to each of the four quadrants of the contingency table in Fig. 5.4A are not fully documented, the observed experimental observations do fit this table (Alger & Teyler, 1976; Harris, Lasher, & Steward, 1978). Thus it is appropriate to consider the possibility of an associative modification rule complementary to equation 10.

Viewing the contingency table of Fig. 5.4A in the abstract invites comment about the remarkable similarity, and complementarity, to the contingency relationship of Fig. 5.2A. It could even be argued that what appears to be the short-term nature of synaptic habituation results from viewing the upper left-hand quadrant of the contingency table of Fig. 5.4A as the dominant and normal activity state of the system (as it indeed is in the hippocampus and neocortex). Within any one absolute refractory period, any pair of pre- and postsynaptic elements is most likely to be silent in these cortical regions. Whether a modification is viewed as long-term potentiation or as decay of depression just depends on the normal baseline synaptic strength and activity levels of the system.

The complementary nature of these two contingency tables is, of course, the main point here. Together they describe a particular change in synaptic strength for each of the four possible associative activity contingencies at a synapse.

Given this intuitive understanding of synaptic habituation and its relationship to long-term potentiation/depression, we now consider a pair of equations that describes the contingencies of synaptic modification of Fig. 5.4A, and that produces the second statistic in Table 5.1. The complementary associative encoding equations are:

$$w_{ij}^-(t+1) = w_{ij}^-(t) + \Delta w_{ij}^-(t,t+1) \tag{23}$$

where

$$\Delta w_{ij}^-(t,t+1) = \epsilon[1 - f(y_j(t))][c_2 x_i(t-\eta) - w_{ij}^-(t)]. \tag{24}$$

w_{ij}^- is a synaptic weakening factor which, along with w_{ij}^+, constitutes the net synaptic efficacy. When w_{ij}^- grows larger, the evoked synaptic response decreases, as described by the contingency table of Fig. 5.4B. A hypothetical interaction between w_{ij}^+ and w_{ij}^- is discussed later.

By an analysis of equation 24, similar to that for w_{ij}^+ (see the section discussing equation 10; p.198), the w_{ij}^- part of synapse ij converges in the limit as

$$w_{ij}^- \rightarrow E[X_i|f(y_j)=0].$$ (25)

Each synapse ij, then, encodes two statistics: the conditional expectation of X_i given $f(y_j)=1$, namely

$$w_{ij}^+ \rightarrow E[X_i|f(y_j)=1],$$ (26)

and the conditional expectation of X_i given $f(y_j)=0$, namely

$$w_{ij}^- \rightarrow E[X_i|f(y_j)=0].$$ (27)

In order to understand the combined synaptic action of the asymptotic values of w_{ij}^+ and w_{ij}^- in the context of equation 8, we first note that, for binary valued X_i, equation 7 and its equivalent for $Z_j=0$ are, respectively,

$$P^*(X|Z_j=1) = \prod_i (w_{ij}^+)^{x_i}(1-w_{ij}^+)^{(1-x_i)}$$ (28)

and

$$P^*(X|Z_j=0) = \prod_i (w_{ij}^-)^{x_i}(1-w_{ij}^-)^{(1-x_i)},$$ (29)

where $f(y_j)$ is binary valued so that Z_j substitutes for $f(y_j)$. Then, substituting equations 28 and 29 into equation 8 and dividing the numerator and denominator of equation 8 by equation 28 gives

$$P^*(Z_j|X=x) = \frac{E[Z_j]}{E[Z_j] + (1-E[Z_j])\prod_i D_{ij}} \quad \text{where}$$ (30)

$$D_{ij} = \left[\frac{w_{ij}^-}{w_{ij}^+}\right]^{x_i} \left[\frac{(1-w_{ij}^-)}{(1-w_{ij}^+)}\right]^{(1-x_i)}$$ (31)

Equation 31 helps us to understand how alterations of w_{ij}^+ and w_{ij}^- affect the Bayes/MRE generated probability, $P^*(Z_j=1|X)$. Because the terms D_{ij}

are in the denominator and are positive, equation 30 increases as a w_{ij}^+ increases or as a w_{ij}^- decreases, provided that x_i is nonzero (i.e., the ith afferent is active).

The Normalization Postulate

One particularly important point is implied by the right-hand side of equation 31. Specifically, there is an aspect of synaptic strength that affects the output $P^*(Z_j = 1 | X = x)$ but that is not dependent on synaptic activity. This point is more obvious if we rewrite equation 31 as

$$D_{ij} = \left[\frac{(1 - w_{ij}^-)}{(1 - w_{ij}^+)} \right]^1 \left[\frac{w_{ij}^-(1 - w_{ij}^+)}{w_{ij}^+(1 - w_{ij}^-)} \right]^{x_i} \tag{32}$$

and note the term raised to the first power. As a result of this term, synaptic modification of each synapse ij is predicted to modify cell activation (i.e., the output $P^*(Z_j = 1 | X)$) even when any particular ith input is inactive (i.e., $x_i = 0$). Another prediction follows whenever there are long-term modifications controlled by equations 9 and 10: when some synapses ij on cell j are potentiated (i.e., some w_{ij}^+ increase), while many more synapses are simultaneously depressed (i.e., some other w_{ij}^+ decrease), the excitability of cell j will appear to increase. This increase will be seen whenever excitability is tested by activating just the potentiated synapses. This prediction and a similar prediction involving w_{ij}^- will be compared with experimental observations in the section on modification of postsynaptic excitability.

We note that this prediction about cell excitability does not depend on X_i restricted to binary values, because a similar term will always be present when probabilities are inferred by the MRE method. This term, raised to the first power, is a normalization term of the distribution function so we call the above prediction the normalization postulate.

So far, then, there is evidence for two of the three statistics in Table 5.1.

$E[f(y_j)]$:
Control of Cell Excitability Stores the
Unconditioned Distribution

Depending on one's viewpoint, control of excitability can be thought of as control of the probability of cell firing, control of the threshold for cell firing, control of the number of action potentials produced by a given amount of synaptic depolarization and so forth. Here we consider a process that has the appearance of a threshold change and a process that supports threshold modification—short-term changes in cell excitability and the formation of new excitatory synapses, respectively.

The hypothesis is, first, that the formation of additional excitatory synapses ij keeps the activity level of cell j from dropping so low that the cell is both wasted as a useful computational element and from dropping so low that the short-term regulation process does not properly exert its control function. Second, the hypothesis is that short-term modification of the excitability of cell j encodes the statistic of the prior distribution, $E[Z_j]$.

Let v_j be the process controlling excitability of neuron j. Then a modification rule that produces the desired statistic is

$$v_j(t+1) = v_j(t) + \Delta v_j(t,t+1) \tag{33}$$

where

$$\Delta v_j(t,t+1) = \epsilon(c_3 f(y_j(t)) - v_j(t)). \tag{34}$$

By an analysis similar to that in the section on $E[X_i | f(y_j) = 1]$, as $t \to \infty$ these two equations produce $v_j \to E[f(y_j)]$, the third statistic in Table 5.1.

From the experimental viewpoint, equations 33 and 34 predict that excitatory activation of postsynaptic cell j induces a short-term potentiation of cell firing followed by a decay of this potentiation because, as noted earlier, $f(y_j)$ is zero most of the time in the hippocampus. In fact, excitatory conditioning stimulation induces a short-term increase in cell excitability whether or not this stimulation is sufficient to induce long-term potentiation (Abraham & Bliss, 1985). Because this process of increased excitability goes to an asymptotic value in an orderly way, and because this modification is short term, some process like equations 33 and 34 seems plausible.

Another process could work, at least intuitively, in concert with this rapid increase in cell excitablity. Such a process would allow each cell to regulate its average level of firing to some preset value (see Levy & Desmond, 1985b for discussion). The proposed mechanism for this regulation is the formation of new excitatory synapses. If this hypothesis is true, then terms such as $E[Z_j] = P(f(y_j) = 1)$ can be approximately built into each cell. Of course, such a mechanism would have only limited accuracy because increasing the number of excitatory synapses is probably a much slower process than changing synaptic strength via equations 10 and 24 (see the section on Synaptogenesis later; p.227). One particular advantage of the new synapse rule is that all postsynaptic cells j would tend to have the same Shannon entropy. This adaptation would prevent individual neurons from being underutilized, in the sense that each neuron would carry its share of the network's representational information (see Levy, 1989, for a discussion of representational information).

Table 5.2 summarizes this section by juxtaposing each statistic of Table 5.1 with the underlying neuronal modification hypothesized in this section.

TABLE 5.2
Modifiable Neuronal Variables Store the Statistics of Table 5.1

Statistic	Variable	Locus	Biological Phenomenon
$E[X_i\|Z_j=1]$	w_{ij}^+	synaptic[†]	long-term potentiation/depression
$E[X_i\|Z_j=0]$	w_{ij}^-	synaptic[†]	low-frequency depression/spontaneous recovery
$E[Z_j]$	v_j	cell excitability	ITTO curve shifts, synaptogenesis

Neurons store the statistics of Table 5.1 at various loci. X_i is the transient activity of the cell labelled i, which is presynaptic to cell j; together they form synapse ij. Z_j is whether or not cell j, or some relevant portion of j, surpasses a threshold level of excitation. $E[X_i|Z_j=1]$ is the expected value of the ith afferent given the threshold is exceed in cell j; $E[X_i|Z_j=0]$ is the expected value of the ith afferent given the threshold is not exceeded in cell j; and $E[Z_j]$ is the expectation that cell j exceeds the threshold. The variables w_{ij}^+ and w_{ij}^- together are the net synaptic efficacy of synapse ij. The variable v_j is the process controlling the excitability of cell j. [†]As pointed out in the text (cf. equation 32 and its associated discussion) there is a cell excitability shift associated with these two modification processes which need not have a synaptic locus.

EXPERIMENTAL SUPPORT FOR THE MODIFICATION RULES

This section sets forth some of the experimental results that suggest the neuronal modification equations discussed in the previous section. This section is organized into three parts. The first part examines biological evidence for equation 10, the synaptic modification rule hypothesized to control w_{ij}^+. The next part examines biological evidence for equation 24, the synaptic modification rule hypothesized to control w_{ij}^-. The final part reviews the evidence for processes controlling cell excitability parameters, v. This part is less straightforward than the previous two because no experiments specifically address the hypothesis put forth here of prediction generation in CA1. Even so, the available observations qualitatively support the ideas in the previous two sections that require excitability changes.

Associative Long-term Potentiation/Depression

The initial report (Bliss & Gardner-Medwin, 1973; Bliss & Lomo, 1973) of long-term potentiation (LTP) of the response evoked in the dentate gyrus (DG) by activation of the entorhinal cortical (EC) input to the DG was immediately appreciated as a breakthrough observation. This appreciation occurred because of the longevity of the increased strength of the activated synapses. That is, the length of time the response modifications persisted could be measured in days (Douglas & Goddard, 1975), whereas the length of time the conditioning stimulation was applied was measured in seconds or less. This longevity meant that there was now a viable model, even a hypothesis, of the cellular substrate of long-term memory.

The next important discovery was by McNaughton and colleagues (1978), who showed that LTP has some type of associative requirement by virtue of its dependence on stimulus intensity. Low-intensity conditioning stimulation did not induce LTP, but high-intensity stimulation, which presumably activated more excitatory afferents, did produce LTP. A similar result was obtained in a quite different way by Wilson, Levy, and Steward (1979). Conditioning the contralateral EC input, which makes very few synapses in the DG (see Fig. 5.5 below), did not evoke LTP of the contralateral EC-DG response. However, if the strength of innervation of the contralateral EC-DG pathway was increased via a lesion that results in a reactive formation of new synapses, then conditioning of this sprouted contralateral EC-DG pathway would induce LTP of its own response. Therefore, the induction of LTP would seem to require powerfully depo-

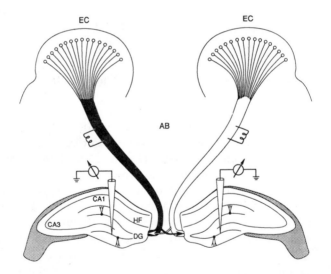

FIG. 5.5. The bilateral projections from the left and right entorhinal cortices (EC) to the left and right dentate gyri (DG). Shaded and open bundles indicate the axon bundles from the left and right EC, respectively, the so-called angular bundles (AB). Note that the ipsilateral EC-DG projection is considerably larger than the contralateral EC-DG projection. The stimulation and recording sites in a typical EC-DG experiment are schematically depicted by the inductor coil and pipette respectively. HF, hippocampal fissure; the major hippocampal subdivisions are denoted as in Fig. 5.1.

larizing conditioning stimulation. Powerful postsynaptic depolarization occurs when a sufficient number of excitatory synapses are activated.

A long-term depression (LTD), or long-lasting decrease in synaptic strength, was also observed in the EC-DG system (see Fig. 5.6 below). LTP and LTD share many characteristics. Not only can LTD be induced prior to experimentally induced LTP (Burger & Levy, 1983), but it is also capable of *erasing* previously induced long-term potentiation (Levy & Steward, 1979). Long-term depression thus appears to be an actively induced process and not a passive decay of LTP. Importantly, LTD has a longevity equal to the longevity of LTP (Burger & Levy, 1983). Furthermore, the same permissive event controls the induction of both LTP and LTD, namely, powerfully excitatory postsynaptic activation (Burger & Levy, 1987; Levy & Burger, 1987b; Levy & Steward, 1979). Finally, the interactions that control the induction of LTP and LTD are spatially (White, Levy, & Steward, 1988) and temporally (Levy & Steward, 1983) constrained.

In the remainder of this section, we explain the observations and the controls inherent in the bilateral EC-DG system that have allowed this system to be so useful for studying the rules of synaptic modification and the temporal meaning of associativity. These experimental observations may be interpreted in terms of an equation governing excitatory synaptic modification. Such an equation was presented in 1982 (Levy, 1982) and remains essentially unchanged to the present. Finally, we briefly comment on the cellular bases of associative synaptic modification.

System Considerations

A variety of experimental preparations is used to understand long-term synaptic modifications including the sophisticated methods of intracellular neurophysiology (e.g., Barrionuevo & Brown, 1983; Malinow & Miller, 1986; Taube & Schwartzkroin, 1988a, b). These methods are superb for understanding the cellular and molecular bases of associative long-term potentiation. However, in order to understand synaptic modification in a way most useful for the modeling of neural networks, we use a relatively old methodology that forces us to rely on the variety and implications of the control experiments (see Levy & Desmond, 1985a for discussion of these controls) rather tha.. the elegance of the experimental techniques (e.g., intracellular conductance measurements) to make inferences about the underlying changes and the activity dependence of these changes. We chose the intact acute preparation because it is our aim to relate our work to the hippocampus as a functioning network. In this light, it is important to reproduce the entire phenomenology of long-term potentiation and long-term depression using the most physiologically relevant stimulus. That is, because synaptic activation provides the postsynaptic permissive event for synaptic modification in a functioning brain, we use this variable in our studies rather than current passed through an intracellular microelectrode.

In order to study the rules of associative long-term modification and to distinguish among some of the algebraic forms theorized to represent these rules, an experimental system must permit a clear distinction between the stimuli that control, in an essentially independent manner, the pre- and postsynaptic terms of an associative modification rule. Thus, there are certain requirements for an experimental system such as two different inputs. These two input systems should have no shared afferents nor should paired stimulation recruit additional active afferents. In addition, one of the input systems must be rather weak so as not to show self-potentiation. This weak input represents the presynaptic afferent i. The second input, the strong input, must activate a powerfully depolarizing postsynaptic excitation which produces large values of y_j. As described in the next two sections, the bilateral EC-DG system provides such an experimental system.

Basic Anatomy and Physiology

The EC-DG system consists of a bilateral monosynaptic excitatory projection arising from the layer II stellate cells of the entorhinal cortex (see Fig. 5.5). These EC axons form the angular bundle as it courses anteriorly and dorsally, and then synapse on the granule cell dendrites in the outer two-thirds of the DG molecular layer (Blackstad, 1958; Hjorth-Simonsen & Jeune, 1972; Lorente de Nó, 1934; Ramon y Cajal, 1968; Steward & Scoville, 1976). EC axon collaterals project to the contralateral DG where they also synapse in the outer two-thirds of the molecular layer (Steward, 1976; Steward & Scoville, 1976). The vast majority ($> 93\%$) of the synapses in the outer two-thirds of the DG molecular layer are EC-DG synapses, and roughly 5% of these synapses are contralateral EC-DG synapses (Steward & Vinsant, 1983). By using such an anatomically homogeneous system and by studying only the earliest phase of this monosynaptic response, we can be confident that any synaptic modification observed reflects changes in the system of interest.

A stimulating electrode can be placed in the angular bundle so that a current pulse through the electrode sends action potentials along the EC axons to both dentate gyri (see Fig. 5.5). A recording electrode placed in the DG molecular layer or granule cell layer records the extracellular field potential response of the granule cells to a test pulse. That is, the response of a population of granule cells is observed via the electric field produced by current flowing into or out of these cells. A measurable field exists and is interpretable because of the extraordinarily homogeneous orientation of the granule cells and their dendrites. The potential recorded by the electrode is just the summation of the synaptic current of many cells having the same orientation. Thus the field potential generated by these cells and their synapses constitutes an average response with individual deviations smoothed. This field response is referred to as a population excitatory postsynaptic potential (pEPSP). The initial slope or the magnitude of the pEPSP evoked by a single test pulse is a measure of the average synaptic efficacy.

When enough granule cells fire synchronously, then another response, the population spike, is superimposed on the pEPSP. This cell firing can be distinguished from the synaptic response because of its opposite polarity and because it occurs somewhat later in time. When the cells fire synchronously, as is usually the case in the experimental test situation, the number of cells firing can be qualitatively expressed as the magnitude of the population spike.

Experimental Observations of LTP and LTD

In the context of associative modification rules, synaptic LTP and LTD correspond, respectively, to positive and negative changes in w_{ij}^+. Both LTP and LTD can be demonstrated in the intact bilateral EC-DG system (see Fig. 5.6). However, we first consider the simpler experiments that use only a single pathway.

A single ipsilateral EC-DG projection is stimulated with a train of high-frequency pulses, for example, eight pulses at 400 Hz. The ipsilateral EC-DG synapses may or may not show long-term potentiation after this conditioning train. If the intensity of the stimulus pulses is low, then a relatively small proportion of the EC axons fire action potentials, and no change in synaptic efficacy occurs. If this experiment is repeated with increasing intensities, we eventually reach an intensity where the synaptic efficacy w_{ij}^+ increases and long-term potentiation occurs. This abrupt transition is referred to as the intensity effect (McNaughton et al., 1978; Wilson, Levy, & Steward, 1981) and is predicted by associative modification rules in the following way. At low intensities, the convergent presynaptic activity is insufficiently strong to produce a postsynaptic event. Apparently this postsynaptic event requires a threshold amount of excitation for its activation. The $f(y_j)$ term in equation 10 is zero up to the threshold level of excitation, and no change in synaptic efficacy can occur until this threshold is achieved.

Now, consider a single contralateral EC-DG projection where the recording electrode is placed contralateral to the stimulating electrode. Because the contralateral projection comprises at most 5% of the synapses in the outer two-thirds of the molecular layer (Steward & Vinsant, 1983), the postsynaptic activation and, correspondingly, the pEPSP evoked by stimulation of the contralateral EC-DG pathway are smaller than for the

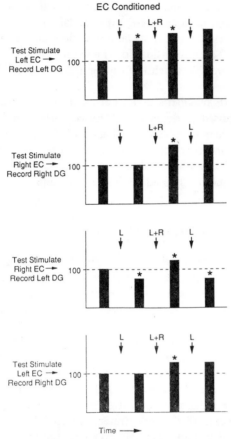

EC Conditioned

Test Stimulate
Left EC →
Record Left DG

Test Stimulate
Right EC →
Record Right DG

Test Stimulate
Right EC →
Record Left DG

Test Stimulate
Left EC →
Record Right DG

Time →

FIG. 5.6. LTP and LTD in the bilateral EC-DG system (see also Levy & Steward, 1979). The four test responses arise from the four possible combinations of the two EC stimulating and two DG recording electrodes illustrated in Fig. 5.5. The top two graphs depict the two strong ipsilateral EC-DG test responses and the bottom two graphs depict the two weak contralateral EC-DG test responses. The time axis is the same for all four responses because the right and left EC receive alternating test stimulation. The initial bar in each graph represents the average baseline response of that graph (100%). The next bar shows the average response that follows brief, high-frequency conditioning of the left EC (L). The third bar indicates the response amplitude after brief, high-frequency paired conditioning of the left and right stimulating electrodes (L + R). The final bar in each graph indicates the average response after brief, high-frequency conditioning of the left EC again. Bars extending above the 100% line indicate potentiation of the tested response; those bars below the 100% line indicate depression. Note that the contralateral response evoked by stimulating the right EC and recording from the left DG is depressed following activation of the converging ipsilateral EC input (L) alone. Paired conditioning stimulation (L + R), however, results in potentiation of this same contralateral response. Asterisks indicate statistically significant changes of the tested response compared to the preceding response.

ipsilateral EC-DG projection. If we repeat the intensity experiment, we find that, no matter how powerful the stimulus intensity, the contralateral synapses never potentiate (Levy & Steward, 1979; see Fig. 5.6). That is, there are too few contralateral afferents to cause postsynaptic activation [$f(y_j)$] sufficient for modification of the contralateral synapses. If the contralateral pathway is enlarged, however, either by induced sprouting or by using a strain of rats in which the projection is normally larger, the intensity effect is in fact observed in the contralateral EC-DG system (Wilson et al., 1979; Wilson, Pang, & Rose, 1987; personal observations).

These simple intensity experiments imply that there is a requirement for sufficiently powerful postsynaptic excitation in order to induce LTP.

Now consider the situation in which the EC-DG projections from both sides of the brain converge on the granule cells in one DG (see Fig. 5.5). Because the two pathways originate on opposite sides of the brain, they can be stimulated independently and unambiguously without recruitment of other afferents. Thus, postsynaptic activity in the DG can be controlled via ipsilateral EC stimulation, and, for a particular set of synapses, presynaptic activity can be manipulated through stimulation of the contralateral EC-DG projection. The contralaterally evoked pEPSP is the measure of altered synaptic efficacy that is of interest here.

Do the contralateral EC-DG synapses, which cannot themselves cause sufficient postsynaptic activation to permit their own modification, modify when the postsynaptic cells are activated via ipsilateral EC stimulation? If both projections are conditioned simultaneously, the contralateral EC-DG synapses potentiate, i.e., $\Delta w_{ij}^+ > 0$ (Levy & Steward, 1979; see Fig. 5.6). However, if only the ipsilateral projection is conditioned, the contralateral synapses depress, i.e., $\Delta w_{ij}^+ < 0$ (Burger & Levy, 1983; Levy & Steward, 1979; see Fig. 5.6). Activation of the contralateral afferents alone produces no long-term change on average. These results are summarized in the contingency table of Fig. 5.2B for Δw_{ij}^+ and in Fig. 5.6.

The nonlinear nature of the postsynaptic permissive event for modification is underscored using the bilateral EC-DG system. By manipulating both stimulus frequency and intensity (i.e., the number of active afferents), we have shown a nonlinear relationship between the amount of long-term modification (both LTP and LTD) of the convergent contralateral pathway and the intensity or frequency of the ipsilateral stimulation providing the postsynaptic permissive event (Burger & Levy, 1987; Levy & Burger, 1987b). These results are translated as a nonnegative, nondecreasing, nonlinear $f(y_j)$ term in equation 10.

From anatomical and physiological observations of the EC-DG system, it is possible to infer that synaptic modification occurs on a synapse-by-synapse basis (see Levy & Desmond, 1985a; Lopez, Burger, Dickstein, Desmond, & Levy, submitted, for more details). Anatomically, the ipsilateral and contralateral EC-DG synapses are not spatially segregated but appear randomly intermingled (Davis, Vinsant, & Steward, 1988). Given the percentage of contralateral synapses and the density of synapses on the granule cell dendrites, there is roughly one contralateral synapse for every nineteen ipsilateral synapses in a cube approximately 2.5 μm on a side. Physiologically, we can depress the contralateral synapses while simultaneously potentiating the abundant neighboring ipsilateral synapses (Levy & Desmond, 1985a; Levy & Steward, 1979; Lopez et al., submitted). Several other dissociated changes between neighboring ipsilateral and contralateral synapses (see Levy & Desmond, 1985a; Lopez et al., submitted) indicate the independent modifiability of the EC-DG synapses. Furthermore, given postsynaptic activation due to concurrent stimulation of the ipsilateral projection, the contralateral synapses potentiate no matter how low the contralateral stimulus intensity (as long as the contralateral pEPSP can be seen above the noise level). If we extrapolate to an intensity so low that only a single contralateral afferent fires, then we would expect only that single synapse to potentiate in the test system. Therefore, we believe that the results obtained by studying the population of synapses activated by the contralateral projection are directly applicable to the behavior of individual synapses.

From these experiments, we can begin to infer the actual form of an associative modification rule. Recall that modification occurs only with a sufficient amount of postsynaptic activation. When postsynaptic activation does occur, the sign of the modification depends on the level of presynaptic activity. By treating the presynaptic variable as stimulus frequency, we (Levy, Brassel, & Moore, 1983) have been able to crudely titrate a balance point between potentiation and depression. In other words, we found (a) a contralateral conditioning frequency greater than zero pulses per second, which still depressed the contralateral response when paired with a powerfully depolarizing postsynaptic activation and (b) a contralateral conditioning frequency less than 400 pulses per second, which still permitted potentiation of the contralateral response. The balance point was about 80-120 pulses per second depending on train length. These results are consistent with the presynaptic term x_i controlling the sign of the modification equation, that is, this term controls whether Δw_{ij}^+ is positive or negative. (Without disagreeing with this last comment, we note that there are alternative interpretations as to whether frequency is the relevant presynaptic variable, e.g., Colbert & Levy, 1988.)

We can write an equation such as

$$\Delta w_{ij}^+ = \epsilon f(y_j)(x_i - b) \tag{35}$$

to fit these observations, where ϵ is a small positive constant, y_j is postsynaptic activity, f is a nonnegative monotone function, x_i is presynaptic activity, and b is a function that produces a balance point between potentiation and depression. If presynaptic activity (x_i) is greater than b, then LTP occurs. If x_i is less than b, then LTD occurs. If x_i equals b, then no change occurs.

Associative modification in the EC-DG system has several other properties that influence the form of the modification equation. With repeated conditioning stimulation, the synaptic weight reaches an asymptotic level (Lopez et al., 1985). The asymptotic properties of the conditioning stimulation that induces LTP and LTD are well-known and are intuitively required for any imaginable physiological system. The asymptotic observations are just that repeated conditioning stimulation of the same type becomes less and less effective so that asymptotic levels of potentiation and depression are achieved. The asymptotic effect is best ascribed not to ϵ and not to $f(y_j)$ but to a term that involves the presynaptic variable x_i. This conclusion follows because neighboring and convergent synapses can be driven to an asymptotic level of efficacy while nearby or collateral synapses remain modifiable. That is, so long as synapses are still changing, ϵ, which is a modifiable variable shared by all synapses, and $f(y_j)$, which is a modifiable variable shared only by the synapses on postsynaptic unit j, must be nonzero. Therefore, b is not a constant but a variable which in some way ensures suitable asymptotic behavior. The simplest such variable is w_{ij}^+ itself, thus giving the term $(cx_i - w_{ij}^+)$ where c is some constant with the appropriate units so that the terms being subtracted, cx_i and w_{ij}^+, are in the same units. Under this hypothesis, then, the asymptotic convergence of potentiation and depression to an equilibrium value is controlled by the difference between a presynaptic term and a term that is a function of the synaptic strength itself.

Even though this difference term, $(cx_i - w_{ij}^+)$, explains the asymptotic property of associative modification, the term does not seem to be the only one controlling the rate of modification. We are moved to this conclusion by the following experimental observation. More conditioning stimulation is required to fully reverse either LTP or LTD than is predicted by this difference term (note graphs in Levy & Steward, 1979, 1983; Lopez et al., 1985; White et al., 1988). In particular, this difference term, by itself, predicts that reversibility depends only on the extant synaptic strength, w_{ij}^+. However, a repetition of identical conditioning stimulation, e.g., potentiating stimulation, makes it more difficult to modify synapses, e.g., depress them in this example. This loss of modifiability occurs even though the later trains of repetitive conditioning do not change appreciably the measured response (Burger & Levy, unpublished observations). Although quantifying the size of the changes may be problematic because only a fraction of the activated synapses are on cells that receive the appropriate permissive event, modifiability seems to decrease with successive conditioning trains. If this decrease is true, then the situation might correspond to variation of the variable ϵ. Thus, we now see how equation 10

$$\Delta w_{ij}^+ = \epsilon f(y_j)(cx_i - w_{ij}^+)$$

has some experimental justification.

A Temporal Definition of Association

By its very definition, a network that predicts must learn sequences. A unidirectional temporal window for associative modification provides a means to encode the statistics of very short sequences of events (see Fig. 5.7 for an example of short sequences). That is, if the associative window covers an interval of time, then the probabilities inferred from the encoded correlations can relate events that occur in sequence, not just events that occur simultaneously.

Recall the probability distribution that is the desired prediction

$$P^*(Z_j(t) = 1 | X(t - \eta)) \tag{36}$$

with $(t - \eta)$ some time before t. As described by equation 8, line 36 can, in part, be calculated from terms of the form:

$$P^*(X_i(t - \eta) | Z_j(t) = 1).$$

To obtain such a probability, it would be useful to have a synaptic modification rule in which the synaptic weight w_{ij}^+ converges to

$$E[X_i(t - \eta) | Z_j(t) = 1]. \tag{37}$$

In fact, equations 9 and 10 have been written to produce just this result. Although the experimental results support a rather similar temporal window, the observed window is longer than that implied by equation 10. Instead, for associative potentiation to occur, the presynaptic event must either coincide with the postsynaptic event or precede the postsynaptic event by no greater than the inverval η.

Such a polarized temporal window for associative modification has been observed experimentally in both the EC-DG (see Fig. 5.7) and the hippocampal CA1 systems. In the EC-DG system, the presynaptic event must precede the postsynaptic event by an interval of 0-20 ms for associative potentiation to occur (Levy & Steward, 1983). If the presynaptic event immediately follows the postsynaptic event, however, associative depression occurs (Levy & Steward, 1983). Associative depression also occurs if the presynaptic event precedes the permissive event by too long an interval, for example, 150 ms (Levy & Steward, 1983). In the case of associative modification of the CA3-CA1 synapses, however, the EC input to CA1 provides the permissive event, Z_j, for modification of the CA3-CA1 synapses. The presynaptic event at the CA3-CA1 synapses must precede the permissive event at the EC-CA1 synapses by 0-10 ms if the CA3-CA1 synapses are to potentiate (Levy, 1988; Moore & Levy, 1986).

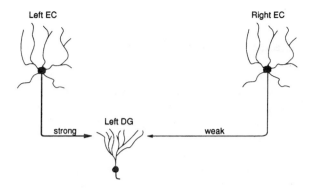

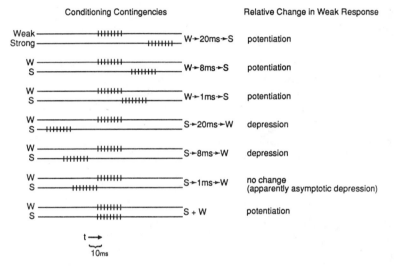

FIG. 5.7. The temporal contingencies of potentiation and depression in the EC-DG system (see Levy & Steward, 1983). The strong input is the projection from the entorhinal cortex (EC) to the ipsilateral dentate gyrus (DG), and the weak input is the contralateral EC projection to this same DG (see also Fig. 5.5). The conditioning contingencies are drawn to scale in the time domain. Conditioning of each pathway consists of eight pulses. When conditioning stimulation of the weak input precedes that of the strong input or occurs simultaneously, there is potentiation of the weak response (i.e., the contralateral EC-DG response). If conditioning of the strong input precedes that of the weak input, depression of the weak response results. The asymptotic depression following the sixth conditioning contingency is inferred from other experiments, which show that this temporal contingency (strong then, after 1 ms weak) does indeed cause depression. W stands for weak (converging contralateral stimulation); S stands for strong (converging ipsilateral stimulation). The time indicated between the arrows is the interval between the last pulse of the first conditioning train and the first pulse of the second conditioning train.

Cellular Events in Associative Modification

Studies of the morphological correlates of LTP in the EC-DG system have provided biological observations pertinent to the development of synaptic modification rules. First, these studies indicate that the changes are synaptic in nature. Moreover, a variety of morphological data indicates that LTP involves the modification of existing excitatory synapses rather than the de novo formation of additional excitatory synapses.

Following the induction of LTP in the EC-DG system, there is no overall increase in the number of synapses with LTP (Desmond & Levy, 1986a). However, simultaneously, the number of axospinous synapses in one subclass, the concave spine synapses, increases with LTP, whereas the number of axospinous synapses in another subclass, the nonconcave spine synapses, decreases with LTP (Desmond & Levy, 1983, 1986a). Although these results may be interpreted as de novo synaptogenesis of concave spine synapses simultaneous with the elimination of nonconcave spine synapses, such an interpretation is difficult to reconcile with the time course of the morphological changes. The altered numbers of spine synapses are evident 2 minutes after the final conditioning train (Desmond & Levy, 1986a). A more parsimonious interpretation of the results, and one perhaps more consistent with the observed time course, is that there is an interconversion of existing nonconcave spine synapses into concave spine synapses with LTP (Desmond & Levy, 1986a; see Fig.5.8). The concave synapses thus represent the recently potentiated population of synapses (see Desmond & Levy, 1988a, for review).

Morphologically, synaptic potentiation is hypothesized to be synaptic enlargement. The concave spine synapses are larger synapses than the nonconcave synapses. Individual potentiated synapses have larger postsynaptic density surface areas, larger appositions of the pre- and postsynaptic membranes, and more front-line synaptic vesicles along the presynaptic membrane (Desmond & Levy, 1986b, 1986c, 1988b). These observations are consistent with the hypothesis that the associative long-term modifications previously described are modifications of existing synapses of the type implied by equation 10.

Role of N-methyl-D-aspartate (NMDA) Receptor-channels in Associative Synaptic Modification

By almost all accounts, the NMDA receptor complex is the cellular mechanism that produces the associative requirement for the induction of LTP (Holmes & Levy, 1988; Wigstrom & Gustafsson, 1985; see Wigstrom

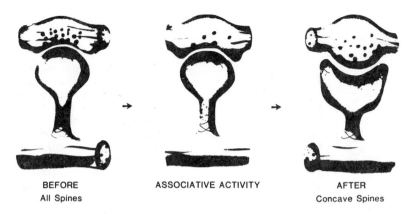

| BEFORE | ASSOCIATIVE ACTIVITY | AFTER |
| All Spines | | Concave Spines |

FIG. 5.8. The interconversion hypothesis. The hypothesis explains the increased number of concave spines in the activated region of the dentate molecular layer following LTP-inducing conditioning stimulation with no corresponding increase in the total number of spine synapses there. Before synaptic potentiation, a dendritic spine head is nonconcave. With brief, high-frequency activity, vesicle fusion occurs and the presynaptic membrane expands (middle frame). At those synapses where the postsynaptic neuron is active concurrently with the presynaptic activity, associative potentiation occurs. The postsynaptic apposed membrane expands at the potentiated synapses, stabilizing the presynaptic membrane expansion. The potentiated spine heads may convert from nonconcave to concave in shape via condensation of additional cytoskeleton in these spine heads. From "Anatomy of Associative Long-term Synaptic Modification." In P. W. Landfield and S. A. Deadwyler (Eds.), *Long-term Potentiation: From Biophysics to Behavior,* 1988, New York: Alan R. Liss. Copyright 1988 by Alan R. Liss, Inc. Reprinted by permission.

& Gustafsson, 1988, for review; on the other hand, see Gamble & Koch, 1987). Recall that associative LTP requires the pairing of two events: presynaptic activity with postsynaptic activity. The NMDA receptor has a characteristic that endows it with the ability to associate pre- and postsynaptic coactivity. Both presynaptic transmitter release and postsynaptic depolarization are required to activate NMDA receptor channels (see Fig. 5.9 for schematic illustration; Dingledine, 1983; MacDermott, Mayer, Westbrook, Smith, & Barker, 1986). Because the NMDA receptor-channel requires both depolarization and transmitter, and because the transient spine depolarization activated by transmitter alone is not sufficient to activate the NMDA receptor-channel, the spine has the capacity to distinguish between (a) its own transient, receptor-driven depolarization due specifically to activity of its presynaptic component and (b) the paired event

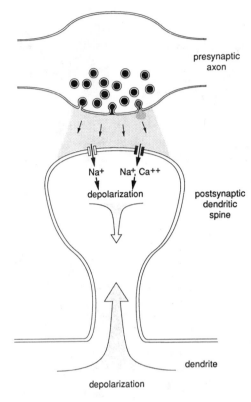

FIG. 5.9. The molecular basis of associative synaptic modification. The presynaptic axon is drawn to indicate a state of transmitter release; the stippling and small arrows indicate the diffusion of transmitter from synaptic vesicles to the postsynaptic membrane where it binds to its receptors. The strong dendritic depolarization (large arrow entering spine) is necessary to activate fully the Na^+ and Ca^{++} influx mediated by the NMDA receptor-channel (solid receptor-channel). This dendritic depolarization arises from synaptic activity elsewhere on the cell. The unshaded and solid channels through the spine head membrane indicate, respectively, nonNMDA and NMDA receptor-channels.

of synaptic activation and dendritic depolarization. It is generally held that high-frequency multiafferent activity provides the required dendritic depolarization (Herron, Lester, Coan, & Collingridge, 1986; Holmes & Levy, 1988).

The time course of the conductance event related to the NMDA receptor channel may well explain the timing characteristics of associative LTP in the EC-DG system (Levy & Steward, 1983). This conductance event has a 10- to 100-fold longer lifetime than the quisqualate receptor channel (Ascher, Bregestovski, & Nowak, 1988; Jahr & Stevens, 1987; Nowak, Bregestovski, Ascher, Herbet, & Prochiantz, 1984), the receptor channel activated by transmitter alone. Prolonged NMDA receptor activation can thus await the facilitating postsynaptic depolarization induced by more extensive synaptic activation. In evaluating the timing requirements for synaptic modification as a function of pre- and postsynaptic activity, Levy and Steward (1983) found that the presumptive dendritic depolarization, when staggered by as much as 37.5 ms from presynaptic activity, must follow and cannot precede synaptic activation if LTP is to occur (see Fig. 5.7).

Synaptic Habituation

As shown in Fig. 5.10, the modification rule for w_{ij}^- is complementary to the rule governing w_{ij}^+. Evidence to support a complementary synaptic weight rule w_{ij}^- derives from the well-known phenomenon of synaptic habituation. To promote a unified definition of the phenomenon, Thompson and Spencer (1966) defined synaptic habituation according to nine paradigmatic criteria met by the experimental systems then commonly accepted as models of behavioral habituation. This definition provided a uniform means to identify and parametrically investigate habituation in other experimental systems (e.g., Carew & Kandel, 1973; Farel & Thompson, 1972) including the EC-DG system in the hippocampal slice preparation (Teyler & Alger, 1976).

The following discussion considers whether the experimental observations of Teyler and Alger (1976) in the EC-DG system of the hippocampal slice are consistent with the outcomes predicted by the synaptic modification rules discussed earlier. Their experimental observations were either replicated or not tested in vivo by Harris and colleagues (1978). First, we consider the observations suggesting the existence of a modification that is conditioned on postsynaptic inactivity, specifically equation 24. We then interpret the remaining observations in terms of both equations 10 and 24.

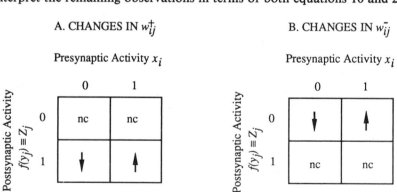

FIG. 5.10. Contingency tables for modification of synaptic efficacy. The tables for w_{ij}^+ (A) and for w_{ij}^- (B) qualitatively express the activity dependence of the two synaptic modification rules, $\Delta w_{ij}^+ = \epsilon f(y_j)(cx_i - w_{ij}^+)$, equation 10, and $w_{ij}^- = \epsilon(1 - f(y_j))(cx_i - w_{ij}^-)$, equation 24. Note that the two tables are complementary so that each contingency of presynaptic (x_i) and postsynaptic activity ($f(y_j)$) determines a unique synaptic modification. 0 and 1 indicate, respectively, inactivity and activity. The changes in synaptic efficacy resulting from each of the four combinations of presynaptic and postsynaptic activity are indicated as follows: nc, no change in synaptic efficacy; ↓, decreased synaptic efficacy; and ↑, increased synaptic efficacy.

Finally, we consider why synaptic habituation has not yet been observed at the hippocampal CA3-CA1 synapses.

Criterion 1 requires exponential depression of synaptic efficacy. Low-frequency, low-intensity stimulation was presented to the EC-DG afferents, and the DG response decreased exponentially with the number of stimulations. Similarly, the form of the rule for w_{ij}^- converges exponentially given a constant input, as shown in the section on $E[X_i|f(y_j) = 0]$.

Criterion 2 requires that spontaneous recovery occur after terminating the low-frequency, low-intensity stimulation just described. As an experimental manipulation, spontaneous recovery is just $\{f(y_j)=0, x_i=0\}$ because removing the stimulation yields inactivity of both the pre- and postsynaptic elements. By equation 24, w_{ij}^- should decrease asymptotically to a positive value with paired pre- and postsynaptic inactivity, corresponding to a recovery from habituation.

Criterion 4 requires that responses to high-intensity stimulation habituate less than responses to low-intensity stimulation. In fact, the EC-DG response to low-frequency, high-intensity stimulation did not habituate. Because this stimulus induces postsynaptic activation, the experiment produces the contingency $\{f(y_j)=1, x_i=1\}$, which specifies no change in w_{ij}^- by equation 24. Moreover, this contingency specifies, by equation 10, an increase in w_{ij}^+; indeed, in an occasional animal, potentiation was observed.

Criterion 5 requires that the degree of response habituation increase with increasing stimulus frequency. The degree of response habituation increased with increasing stimulus frequency up to the frequency at which the response began to potentiate. This result must be considered in relation to equation 24 in two ways. First, consider only those stimulus frequencies that lead to habituation. According to equation 24, w_{ij}^- converges to the average of the presynaptic activation x_i when $f(y_j)=0$. Equation 24 thus predicts increasing values of w_{ij}^- and greater habituation with increasing stimulus frequency. Second, for those stimulus frequencies inducing LTP, the specific combination of frequency and intensity presumably leads to postsynaptic activation, i.e., $f(y_j)=1$. With $f(y_j)=1$, equation 24 predicts no change in w_{ij}^-, but equation 10 predicts an increase in w_{ij}^+ (i.e., potentiation of synaptic efficacy).

Criterion 6 requires that recovery time increase with increasing duration of the habituating stimulation even though an asymptotic level of habituation has been reached. After an asymptotic level of habituation was reached following low-frequency, low-intensity stimulation, the experiments investigated the effect of continued stimulation for various time intervals. The time necessary for spontaneous recovery increased with the duration of low-frequency stimulation. This increased time for recovery forces us to posit a decrease in ϵ when the input, x_i, to the cell j is relatively constant. A change in ϵ would have no effect on the asymptotic value of

w_{ij}^-, only on its rate of convergence, so the data are consistent with this hypothesized change in ϵ.

Criterion 3 requires that repeated exposure to the habituating stimulus result in greater, more rapid habituation to subsequent stimuli. The experiments repeated the paradigms of criteria 1 and 2 at intervals, and responses to subsequent stimuli habituated more rapidly than to the first stimulus. However, only the rate and not the degree of habituation appeared to increase. If only the rate of habituation changes, and if there are no confounding effects due to insufficient recovery from habituation (as may have been the case in this experiment), then the results may be interpreted as an increase in ϵ. An increase in ϵ might be expected because, unlike the paradigm of criterion 6, the input to the cell alternates between low-frequency stimulation and no stimulation rather than remaining constant. There is no compelling reason to believe, however, that control of ϵ exists in the hippocampal slice which lacks modulated inputs from the septal and monoaminergic systems. Thus, we are somewhat at a loss to explain this observation.

Criteria 7 and 8 combine habituating and high-frequency, so-called sensitizing, stimulation and thus include contingencies relevant to modification of w_{ij}^+ as well as to w_{ij}^-. As mentioned earlier, we have no experimental evidence to support how w_{ij}^+ and w_{ij}^- are combined to form the synaptic efficacy that is observed experimentally. For the present discussion, we need only require that the observed synaptic efficacies increase with increasing w_{ij}^+ and decrease with increasing w_{ij}^-.

Criterion 7 requires that a sensitizing stimulation given during a period of habituating stimulation induce recovery. Partial recovery of a response depressed by low-frequency stimulation resulted from a high-frequency sensitizing stimulation. This recovery is consistent with an increase in w_{ij}^+ causing an increase in synaptic efficacy.

Criterion 8 requires that subsequent sensitizing stimuli result in less recovery from habituation. The paradigm of criterion 7 was repeated with high-frequency sensitizing stimuli interspersed among low-frequency habituating stimuli. Successive high-frequency stimulation produced increasingly less recovery of the habituated response.

Within the regime of equations 10 and 24, subsequent sensitizing stimulation would be less effective at inducing recovery from habituation because w_{ij}^+ converges to an asymptotic value.

The observations just discussed support the idea that the complementary synaptic weight rule, equation 24, exists and produces a weight that reflects the average presynaptic activity conditioned on postsynaptic inactivity. Interpretation of the experimental observations, however, is limited by a lack of knowledge of the contributions and interactions of w_{ij}^+ and w_{ij}^- to the observed synaptic efficacy. For example, the sensitizing stimulation used to document criterion 8 might well induce substantial potentiation if given in the absence of a habituating stimulus. Thirty seconds after the last habituating stimulus, however, synaptic efficacy returned to approximately its initial value, implying an absence of the expected increase in w_{ij}^+. Further work is thus needed to sort out the contributions of the w_{ij}^+ and w_{ij}^- terms to the overall synaptic efficacy and its modification.

Although Teyler and Alger (1976) documented in the EC-DG systemeight of the nine criteria defining synaptic habituation, its *sine qua non*, low-frequency depression, does not seem to exist at those synapses where our theories most need it—the CA3-CA1 synapses. In both the CA1 and CA3 regions, low-frequency stimulation leads to potentiation rather than to synaptic habituation (Alger & Teyler, 1976). There are at least three explanations why synaptic habituation has not been found at the CA3-CA1 synapses besides the explanation that it doesn't exist. First, the stimulation used to test this system was too powerful, thereby leading to postsynaptic activation and potentiation rather than synaptic habituation. Second, there is something aphysiological about the hippocampal slice preparation; for example, it is to some extent calcium-incompetent, its presynaptic structures leak transmitter, or it is hyperexcitable and thus too readily shows LTP. Finally, it is possible that a nonspecific system, whose activity is permissive for synaptic habituation (e.g., ϵ in equation 24), is lost in the in vitro experimental method (see footnote 2).

Modification of Postsynaptic Excitability

In this section we consider the experimental evidence that a neuron can regulate its own level of excitation as a function of its history of activity. This section has three parts. Part one considers the modification of excitability due to a change in the way synaptic excitation is translated into cell firing. Part two considers some of the cellular and molecular processes that could support such changes in cell excitability. Part three considers a very different set of mechanisms for controlling cell excitability: the formation of new synapses and the activity contingencies that define the different roles played by axons and dendrites in forming new synapses.

This part of the biological support section differs in its organization and concerns from the preceding two parts. First, although experimental results qualitatively support the ideas in the section on storing statistics, no direct evidence is available for formulating equations of cell excitability. Second, the discussion considers two distinct types of mechanisms that could affect regulation of the excitability term $E[Z_j]$. Third, and partially overlapping with the discussion concerning the regulation of $E[Z_j]$, is the evidence that something like the terms $\prod_i(1 - w_{ij}^+)$ and $\prod_i(1 - w_{ij}^-)$ control the translation of synaptic activity into cell firing. These last two terms, implicit in equation 8, are made explicit in equation 32 as effects on probability $[P^*(Z_j = 1 | X)]$ independent of synaptic activity (X_i).

Long- and Short-term Excitability Shifts with Activation

From the beginning of studies of LTP in the hippocampus (Bliss & Lomo, 1973), it has been observed that induction of LTP often results in more potentiation of the population spike than can be explained by the increased synaptic current of the potentiated pEPSP. That is, potentiation of cell excitability, such as lowering the threshold for cell firing, occurs in addition to potentiation of synaptic current.

In order to measure this increased cell excitability, it is necessary to correct for the increased synaptic current of the test response. To perform such a measurement, population spike magnitude is commonly plotted against pEPSP magnitude at a variety of stimulation intensities (see Fig. 5.11) producing a curve called the pEPSP converted to spike (E-S) curve or the input-translated-to-output (ITTO) curve. Changes in excitability (see Fig. 5.11) are evident as a shifting of the curve to the left (i.e., an increased population spike for a given pEPSP slope) or to the right (i.e., a decreased population spike for a given pEPSP slope).

Systematic investigation of the phenomenon of altered cell excitability has dissociated long-term potentiation of the population spike from concurrent long-term potentiation of the pEPSP (Abraham & Goddard, 1983; Taube & Schwartzkroin, 1988a; Wilson et al., 1979, 1981). Conversely, potentiation of the pEPSP can be induced in excess of that of the population spike (Brassel, Levy, & Steward, 1983; Kairiss, Abraham, Bilkey, & Goddard, 1987; Levy, 1984) by concurrent stimulation of other pathways. Therefore, the conversion of synaptic current to cell firing is apparently an independently modifiable parameter of the neuron and may be controlled by a number of different processes.

Short-term increases in cell excitability may occur as well (Abraham & Bliss, 1985). Presentation of low-frequency stimuli immediately caused an

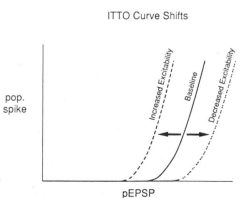

FIG. 5.11. ITTO curves are used to assess cell excitability changes. An input-transformed-to-output (ITTO) curve plots the population spike (pop. spike) against the population EPSP (pEPSP). pEPSP size is varied by varying stimulation intensity. When the ITTO curve shifts to the left, cell excitability has increased. That is, given a shift left, comparing ITTO curves before and after conditioning shows that a given size pEPSP evokes a larger pop. spike. Conversely, when the ITTO curve shifts to the right, cell excitability has decreased.

increase in cell excitability even though the synaptic test response depressed. As documented by ITTO measurements, this altered excitability reached an asymptotic value and remained there for the entire period of low-frequency stimulation. On ceasing this stimulation, cell excitability returned to its prestimulation value.

As discussed in the section on $E[f(y_j)]$ (see p. 205), both short- and long-term changes in excitability play a role in the generation of probabilities. According to the normalization postulate discussed earlier (p. 205), changes in the values of any w_{ij}^+ or any w_{ij}^- will modify the excitability of a cell, whether or not the afferent i is part of the test pathway (i.e., whether or not $x_i > 0$). It is noteworthy that the ITTO shifts experimentally induced by LTP paradigms are long-term, just as the associative synaptic modifications w_{ij}^+ are long-term. Moreover, ITTO shifts induced by a low-frequency depression paradigm are short-term, just as the associative synaptic modifications of w_{ij}^- are short-term. In both cases, neuronal excitability increases. Moreover, these experimental results are consistent with the computation of probabilities by equation 30 although both results require careful analysis.

First, let us consider a low-frequency depression paradigm. Equation 24 indicates that, low-frequency depression, w_{ij}^- grows larger for the activated and tested synapses (i.e., the contingency $\{x_i = 1, f(y_j) = 0\}$). The unactivated synapses are not changing because (a) w_{ij}^- for these unstimulated synapses are at their asymptotic values and (b) $\{x_i = 0, f(y_j) = 0\}$ is the usually occurring contingency. If each w_{ij}^- of the test system grows larger, then the product $\prod_i (1 - w_{ij}^-)$ becomes smaller. Noting that this product is always positive, we inspect equation 38 (derived from equations 30 and 32) and see that, if $\prod_i (1 - w_{ij}^-)$ decreases, $P^*(Z_j = 1 | X = x)$ increases.

$$P^*(Z_j | X = x) = \frac{1}{1 + \dfrac{(1 - E[Z_j])}{E[Z_j]} \prod_i \left[\dfrac{(1 - w_{ij}^-)}{(1 - w_{ij}^+)}\right]^1 \left[\dfrac{w_{ij}^-(1 - w_{ij}^+)}{w_{ij}^+(1 - w_{ij}^-)}\right]^{x_i}} \tag{38}$$

Thus, increased cell excitability, as measured by an ITTO curve shift, should accompany low-frequency depression.

The analysis of the shift in cell excitability associated with LTP is slightly different. The difference arises from the fact that unactivated synapses (i.e., ij such that $\{x_i = 0, f(y_j) = 1\}$) do not remain unchanged, but instead depress by equation 10. (By our estimates there are 5 to 500 times as many inactive synapses as active synapses during LTP-inducing conditioning stimulation.) Therefore, we propose that most w_{ij}^+ decrease and therefore, the product, $\prod(1 - w_{ij}^+)$ over all synapses, increases. The increase in this product decreases the denominator of equation 38, so that $P^*(Z_j = 1 | X = x)$ increases. Thus, the hypothesis is consistent with the observed increases in cell excitability.

Rather than synaptic experiments that condition and test the same input, our theory actually needs heterosynaptic evidence for modification of $E[Z_j]$ using the EC-CA1 pathway for conditioning and the CA3-CA1 pathway for testing. Specifically, we predict increased CA1 cell excitability to CA3 test pulses following high-frequency, or high-intensity, conditioning stimulation of the EC-CA1 pathway.

Possible Subcellular Mechanisms

Either an intrinsic, subcellularly controlled mechanism or an extrinsic, local circuit-controlled mechanism could underlie changes in cell excitability. An intrinsic mechanism would imply that each neuron can alter its probability of firing independently of neighboring neurons, whereas an extrinsic, nonassociative, or global activation mechanism would imply that all neurons adapt essentially equally or, perhaps, adapt in a cell-specific manner via associative synaptic modification of inhibitory synapses.

The intrinsic mechanisms altering cell excitability could be either synaptically or nonsynaptically located. The possibilities include a variety of known K^+ or Cl^- conductances, including both voltage-dependent and nonvoltage-dependent processes (Hvalby, Reymann, & Andersen, 1988; Madison, Malenka, & Nicoll, 1986; see Nicoll, 1988, for review). Modification of such conductances by phorbol esters (Malenka, Madison, & Nicoll, 1986) and direct protein kinase C injection into cells (Hu, Hvalby, Walaas, Albert, Skjeflo, Andersen, & Greengard, 1987) shows the plausibility of these conductances for mediating short- and long-term changes in cell excitability.

Another class of modifications may involve feedback and feedforward inhibitory systems. Even though there are too few interneurons (Seress & Pokorny, 1981) to control individually the excitability of the granule cells in the EC-DG system as required by equation 8, inhibitory synapses could be adjusted individually via an associative modification equation governing inhibitory synapses (see Levy & Desmond, 1985b, for a proposal of such an equation).

Synaptogenesis

There may well be a very different means for increasing the activity of a neuron, namely the formation of new excitatory synapses. As before (Levy & Desmond, 1985b), we advocate a postsynaptic growth rule which makes the formation of new synapses a function of the level of postsynaptic activity. The general idea of this growth rule is that new excitatory input should, in the physiological situation, compensate for an overall paucity of correlated activity converging on a particular cell. That is, the formation of new synapses should eventually raise the average level of firing of such a cell by increasing the probability of convergent coactivity of some of its inputs. A relatively inactive cell would remain receptive to the formation of new synapses until its activity increases to some genetically programmed and/or dynamically controlled level.

The work of Wolff and colleagues provides the strongest evidence for an inverse relationship between postsynaptic activity and receptivity for new innervation. Treating the adult rat superior cervical ganglion, a cholinergic parasympathetic ganglion of the peripheral autonomic nervous system, with the inhibitory neurotransmitter γ-aminobutyric acid (GABA) or the inhibitory substance sodium bromide, decreases cell firing and, with some delay, increases both the number of free postsynaptic densities (Wolff, Joo, Dames, & Feher, 1979, 1981) and the amount of extrasynaptic membrane surface area (Wolff, Joo, & Dames, 1978). The free postsynaptic densities increase in number without any sign of afferent degeneration, supporting the claim that these postsynaptic densities are precursors of synapses rather than degeneration products, and are thus a measure of the neurons' receptivity to new innervation. Moreover, such structures are not just a special property of the peripheral nervous system because free postsynaptic densities normally occur in at least some regions of the central nervous system (e.g., Spacek, 1982; Spacek & Lieberman, 1974).

Whether these new free postsynaptic densities are the actual postsynaptic components of new synapses, and whether new synapses form specifically at these sites is unknown, but the number of free postsynaptic densities decreases as new innervation of the ganglion cells occurs. Cutting the cholinergic hypoglossal nerve and suturing it near the superior cervical ganglion creates a situation for observing the receptivity for new innervation of the ganglion cells. In the absence of inhibitory agents such as GABA or sodium bromide (i.e., the ganglion cells are firing normally), the hypoglossal nerve fails to make new synapses with the ganglion cells, reconnecting instead to the surrounding musculature (Wolff et al., 1981). In the presence of GABA or sodium bromide, the hypoglossal nerve produces new synapses in the ganglion that appear functional both electrophysiologically (Wolff et al., 1979) and by assays of receptor numbers and enzymatic activity (Balcar, Erdo, Joo, Kasa, & Wolff, 1987). Under this condition, as the total number of synapses per unit area increases with time, the number of free postsynaptic densities decreases. This is perhaps the strongest evidence to date that a postsynaptic growth rule is functioning in neurons.

In these experiments GABA was typically infused for days to weeks before studying the ganglion. The earliest evidence of free postsynaptic densities can be seen after 2 hours of GABA infusion (Wolff et al., 1981). Compared to the 20 ms bound defining associative activity in the hippocampus (Levy & Steward, 1983), production of free postsynaptic densities requires a condition lasting 10^5-fold longer. Therefore, synaptogenesis is better considered in a somewhat different light than the other modifications producing the statistics in Table 5.1 because such regulation of a cell's average activity is on a much slower time scale. Moreover, this slow time course is not altogether bad because the synaptic strengths could begin showing large oscillations in a stationary environment if the postsynaptic growth rule were to have a time constant similar to the time constant of the associative modification rule for Δw_{ij}^+ (unpublished computer simulations).

A similar relationship between postsynaptic activity and new innervation exists at the neuromuscular junction. Reinnervation of denervated adult muscle by the same or foreign nerves (Aitken, 1950; Elsberg, 1917; Lomo & Slater, 1978, 1980) also requires postsynaptic inactivity. Normal presynaptic activity as well as direct postsynaptic stimulation suffice to prevent extrajunctional sensitivity to neurotransmitter (Lomo & Slater, 1980), to allow developing muscle to express adult rather than fetal receptor types (Brenner, Lomo, & Williamson, 1987), and to trigger the loss of ectopic junctions and acetylcholine receptor clusters in previously inactive muscle (Lomo, Pockett, & Sommerschild, 1988).

There may also be a complementary process for synapse removal. Levy and Desmond (1985b) pointed out that synaptic removal might result from the depression commanded by equation 10 when depression has driven synaptic strength nearly to zero. Removal can be envisioned in two phases. Equation 10 lowers synaptic strength by making the synaptic interface smaller and smaller until the presynaptic element is eventually separated from the postsynaptic element, and then the postsynaptic site receptive for innervation is destroyed. In developing systems, the phenomenon of synapse removal is well known (e.g., Lichtman, 1977; Redfern, 1970; Ronnevi & Conradi, 1974; see Purves & Lichtman, 1980, for review).

Synapse removal may be part of the regulated process that we are calling receptivity for innervation; an example of this might be dendritic retraction during extreme activation. Application of glutamate, the presumptive transmitter, to the tissue culture medium in which hippocampal pyramidal neurons are growing reduces the rate of dendritic outgrowth and causes dendritic retraction in some cases (Mattson, Dou, & Kater, 1988; see Mattson, 1988, for review). Such a result is consistent with the proposed role of the postsynaptic cell in controlling the formation of new synapses.

There is less direct evidence for a process that keeps individual cell activity from growing too large via modification of inhibitory connections. Systems of neurons that are overly active, for example in epileptic brain, tend to develop additional inhibition (Liebowitz, Pedley, & Cutler, 1978; Tuff, Racine, & Adamec, 1983a; Tuff, Racine, & Mishra, 1983b; Valdes, Dasheiff, Birmingham, Crutcher, & McNamara, 1982). These studies, however, are not able to distinguish between more inhibitory innervation and stronger existing inhibitory synapses.

CONCLUDING THOUGHTS

In this chapter the framework of prediction has interrelated a diverse group of biological observations. The essence of the chapter is found in Tables 5.1 and 5.2 and in equations 10 and 24. Figure 5.10 qualitatively illustrates both equations as contingency tables. Both long-term and short-term synaptic modifications find a place within the prediction framework. One novel observation is that the cell excitability changes accompanying such synaptic modifications fit the requirements of probability generation (equation 8). The theory presented here also has its weaknesses. Clearly the weakest part of the theory concerns the excitability changes discussed at the end of the last section. Even with these weaknesses, it is our hope that this chapter will stimulate network theoreticians to consider alternative theories that incorporate these nonassociative phenomena and, at the same time, will stimulate some neurobiologists to perform experiments to disprove or extend the ideas presented here.

ACKNOWLEDGMENTS

Supported by NIH RO1 NS15488 and NIMH RSDA MH00622 to WBL and by the Department of Neurological Surgery, Dr. John A. Jane, Chairman. CMC was supported by MSTP training grant NIH 5T32 GM0726713.

REFERENCES

Abraham, W. C., & Bliss, T. V. P. (1985). An analysis of the increase in granule cell excitability accompanying habituation in the dentate gyrus of the anesthetized rat. *Brain Research, 331*, 303–313.

Abraham, W. C., & Goddard, G. V. (1983). Asymmetric relationships between homosynaptic long-term potentiation and heterosynaptic long-term depression. *Nature, 305*, 717–719.

Aitken, J. T. (1950). Growth of nerve implants in voluntary muscle. *Journal of Anatomy, 84*, 38–49.

Alger, B. E., & Teyler, T. J. (1976). Long-term and short-term plasticity in the CA1, CA3, and dentate regions of the rat hippocampal slice. *Brain Research, 110*, 463–480.

Amaral, D. G. (1987). Memory: Anatomical organization of candidate brain regions. In F. Plum (Ed.), *Handbook of physiology. Section I: The nervous system* (Vol. 5, Pt 1, pp. 211–294). New York: Oxford University Press.

Amari, S.-I. (1977). Neural theory of association and concept-formation. *Biological Cybernetics, 26*, 175–185.

Anderson, J. A., Silverstein, J. W., Ritz, S. A., & Jones, R. S. (1977). Distinctive features, categorical perception, and probability learning: Some applications of a neural model. *Psychological Review, 84*, 413–451.

Ascher, P., Bregestovski, P., & Nowak, L. (1988). N-Methyl-D-aspartate-activated channels of mouse central neurones in magnesium-free solutions. *Journal of Physiology, 399*, 207–226.

Balcar, V. J., Erdo, S. L., Joo, F., Kasa, P., & Wolff, J. R. (1987). Neurochemistry of GABAergic system in cerebral cortex chronically exposed to bromide in vivo. *Journal of Neurochemistry, 48,* 167–169.

Barrioneuvo, G., & Brown, T. H. (1983). Associative long-term synaptic potentiation in hippocampal slices. *Proceedings of the National Academy of Sciences USA, 80,* 7347–7351.

Blackstad, T. W. (1958). On the termination of some afferents to the hippocampus and fascia dentata. *Acta Anatomica (Basel), 35,* 202–214.

Bliss, T. V. P., & Gardner-Medwin, A. R. (1973). Long-lasting potentiation of synaptic transmission in the dentate area of the unanaesthetized rabbit following stimulation of the perforant path. *Journal of Physiology, 232,* 357–374.

Bliss, T. V. P., & Lomo, T. (1973). Long-lasting potentiation of synaptic transmission in the dentate area of the anaesthetized rabbit following stimulation of the perforant path. *Journal of Physiology, 232,* 331–356.

Brassel, S., Levy, W. B, & Steward, O. (1982). Feed-forward inhibition and the regulation of cell discharge following long-term potentiation. *Society for Neuroscience Abstracts, 8,* 740.

Brenner, H. R., Lomo, T., & Williamson, R. (1987). Control of end-plate channel properties by neurotrophic effects and by muscle activity in rat. *Journal of Physiology, 388,* 367–381.

Burger, B. S., & Levy, W. B (1983). Shared characteristics of potentiation and depression in the EC-DG system. *Society for Neuroscience Abstracts, 9,* 1221.

Burger, B. S., & Levy, W. B (1987). A frequency-dependent threshold-like effect controls both LTP and LTD. *Society for Neuroscience Abstracts, 13,* 974.

Carew, T. J., & Kandel, E. R. (1973). Acquisition and retention of long-term habituation in Aplysia: correlation of behavioral and cellular processes. *Science, 182,* 1158–1160.

Colbert, C. M., & Levy, W. B (1988). What is the code? *Proceedings of the International Neural Network Society, 1,* 246.

Cox, R. T. (1946). Probability, frequency, and reasonable expectation. *American Journal of Physics, 14,* 1–13.

Cox, R. T. (1979). Of inference and inquiry, an essay in inductive logic. In R. D. Levine & M. Tribus. (Eds.), *The maximum entropy formalism* (pp. 119–167). Cambridge, MA: MIT Press.

Davis, L., Vinsant, S. L., & Steward, O. (1988). Ultrastructural characterization of the synapses of the crossed temporodentate pathway in rats. *Journal of Comparative Neurology, 267,* 190–202.

Desmond, N. L, & Levy, W. B. (1983). Synaptic correlates of associative potentiation/depression: An ultrastructural study in the hippocampus. *Brain Research, 263,* 21–30.

Desmond, N. L, & Levy, W. B. (1986a). Changes in the numerical density of synaptic contacts with long-term potentiation in the hippocampal dentate gyrus. *Journal of Comparative Neurology, 253,* 466–475.

Desmond, N. L, & Levy, W. B. (1986b). Changes in the postsynaptic density with long-term potentiation in the dentate gyrus. *Journal of Comparative Neurology, 253,* 476–482.

Desmond, N. L, & Levy, W. B. (1986c). More front-line synaptic vesicles with long-term synaptic potentiation in the hippocampal dentate gyrus. *Society for Neuroscience Abstracts, 12,* 504.

Desmond, N. L, & Levy, W. B. (1988a). Anatomy of associative long-term synaptic modification. In P. W. Landfield & S. A. Deadwyler (Eds.), *Long-term potentiation: From biophysics to behavior* (pp. 265–305). New York: Alan R. Liss.

Desmond, N. L, & Levy, W. B. (1988b). Synaptic interface surface area increases with long-term potentiation in the hippocampal dentate gyrus. *Brain Research, 453,* 308–314.

Dingledine, R. (1983). N-methyl aspartate activates voltage-dependent calcium conductance in rat hippocampal pyramidal cells. *Journal of Physiology, 343,* 385–405.

Douglas, R. M., & Goddard, G. V. (1975). Long-term potentiation of the perforant path-granule cell synapse in the rat hippocampus. *Brain Research, 86,* 205–215.

Elsberg, C. A. (1917). Experiments on motor nerve regeneration and the direct neurotization of paralyzed muscles by their own and foreign nerves. *Science, 45,* 318–320.

Farel, P. B., & Thompson, R. F. (1972). Habituation and dishabituation to dorsal root stimulation in the isolated frog spinal cord. *Behavioral Biology, 7,* 37–45.

Gamble, E., & Koch, C. (1987). The dynamics of free calcium in dendritic spines in response to repetitive synaptic input. *Science, 236,* 1311–1315.

Geman, S. (1981). The law of large numbers in neural modelling. *SIAM American Mathematical Society Proceedings, 13,* 91–105.

Golden, R. M. *A unified framework for connectionist systems.* Unpublished manuscript.

Grossberg, S. J. (1987). *The adaptive brain I.* Amsterdam: Elsevier.

Harris, E. W., Lasher, S. S., & Steward, O. (1978). Habituation-like decrements in transmission along the normal and lesion-induced temporodentate pathways in the rat. *Brain Research, 151,* 623–631.

Hebb, D. O. (1949). *The organization of behavior.* New York: Wiley.

Herron, C. E., Lester, R. A. J., Coan, E. J., & Collingridge, G. L. (1986). Frequency-dependent involvement of NMDA receptors in the hippocampus: a novel synaptic mechanism. *Nature, 322,* 265–268.

Hinton, G. E., & Sejnowski, T. J. (1983). Optimal perceptual inference. *Proceedings IEEE Conference on Computer Vision and Pattern Recognition,* 418–453.

Hjorth-Simonsen, A., & Jeune, B. (1972). Origin and termination of the hippocampal perforant path in the rat studied by silver impregnation. *Journal of Comparative Neurology, 144,* 215–232.

Holmes, W. R., & Levy, W. B. (1988). Calcium influx through NMDA-receptor channels modeled in a hippocampal dentate granule cell. *Society for Neuroscience Abstracts, 14,* 564.

Hopfield, J. J. (1984). Neurons with graded response have collective computational properties like those of two-state neurons. *Proceedings of the National Academy of Sciences USA, 81,* 3088–3092.

Hu, G.-Y., Hvalby, O., Walaas, S. I., Albert, K. A., Skjeflo, P., Andersen, P., & Greengard, P. (1987). Protein kinase C injection into hippocampal pyramidal cells elicits features of long term potentiation. *Nature, 328,* 426–429.

Hvalby, O., Reymann, K., & Andersen, P. (1988). Intracellular analysis of potentiation of CA1 hippocampal synaptic transmission by phorbol ester application. *Experimental Brain Research, 71,* 588–596.

Jahr, C. E., & Stevens, C. F. (1987). Glutamate activates multiple single channel conductances in hippocampal neurons. *Nature, 325,* 522–525.

Jaynes, E. T. (1979). Where do we stand on maximum entropy? In R. D. Levine & M. Tribus (Eds.), *The maximum entropy formalism* (pp. 15–118). Cambridge, MA: MIT Press.

Kairiss, E. W., Abraham, W. C., Bilkey, D. K., & Goddard, G. V. (1987). Field potential evidence for long-term potentiation of feed-forward inhibition in the rat dentate gyrus. *Brain Research, 401,* 87–94.

King, M. A., & Levy, W. B. (1986). Heterosynaptic depression of hippocampal CA3 afferents to CA1 accompanies long-term potentiation of convergent entorhinal afferents. *Society for Neuroscience Abstracts, 12,* 505.

Kohonen, T., Lehtiö, P., & Rovamo, J. (1974). Modelling of neural associative memory. *Annales Academiae Scientiarum Fennicae A, 167,* 1–18.

Levy, W. B. (1982). Associative encoding at synapses. *Proceedings of the Fourth Annual Conference of Cognitive Science Society,* 135–136.

Levy, W. B. (1984). Long-term reversible changes in the translation of synaptic current into cell firing. *Society for Neuroscience Abstracts, 10,* 77.

Levy, W. B. (1988). A theory of the hippocampus based on reinforced synaptic modification in CA1. *Society for Neuroscience Abstracts, 14,* 168.

Levy, W. B. (1989). A computational approach to hippocampal function. In R. D. Hawkins

& G. H. Bower (Eds.), *Computational models of learning in simple neural systems* (pp. 243-305). Orlando, FL: Academic Press.

Levy, W. B, Brassel, S. E., & Moore, S. D. (1983). Partial quantification of the associative synaptic learning rule of the dentate gyrus. *Neuroscience, 8,* 799-808.

Levy, W. B, & Burger, B. (1987a). Electrophysiological observations which help describe an associative synaptic modification rule. *IEEE First Annual International Conference on Neural Networks, 4,* 11-15.

Levy, W. B, & Burger, B. (1987b). An intensity-dependent threshold-like effect controls both LTP and LTD. *Society for Neuroscience Abstracts, 13,* 974.

Levy, W. B, & Desmond, N. L. (1985a). Associative potentiation/depression in the hippocampal dentate gyrus. In G. Buzsaki & C. H. Vanderwolf (Eds.), *Electrical activity of the archicortex* (pp. 359-373). Budapest, Hungary: Akademiai Kiado.

Levy, W. B, & Desmond, N. L. (1985b). The rules of elemental synaptic plasticity. In W. B Levy, J. Anderson, & S. Lehmkuhle (Eds.), *Synaptic modification, neuron selectivity and nervous system organization* (pp. 105-121). Hillsdale, NJ: Lawrence Erlbaum Associates.

Levy, W. B, & Steward, O. (1979). Synapses as associative memory elements in the hippocampal formation. *Brain Research, 175,* 233-245.

Levy, W. B, & Steward, O. (1983). Temporal contiguity requirements for long term associative potentiation/depression in the hippocampus. *Neuroscience, 8,* 791-797.

Lichtman, J. W. (1977). The reorganization of synaptic connexions in the rat submandibular ganglion during post-natal development. *Journal of Physiology, 273,* 155-177.

Liebowitz, N. R., Pedley, T. A., & Cutler, R. W. P. (1978). Release of gamma-aminobutyric acid from hippocampal slices of the rat following generalized seizures induced by daily electrical stimulation of entorhinal cortex. *Brain Research, 138,* 369-373.

Lomo, T., Pockett, S., & Sommerschild, H. (1988). Control of number and distribution of synapses during ectopic synapse formation in adult rat soleus muscles. *Neuroscience, 24,* 673-686.

Lomo, T., & Slater, C. R. (1978). Control of acetylcholine sensitivity and synapse formation by muscle activity. *Journal of Physiology, 275,* 391-402.

Lomo, T., & Slater, C. R. (1980). Acetylcholine sensitivity of developing ectopic nerve-muscle junctions in adult rat soleus muscles. *Journal of Physiology, 303,* 173-189.

Lopez, H., Burger, B., Dickstein, R., Desmond, N. L., & Levy, W. B. *Long-term potentiation and long-term depression in the hippocampal dentate gyrus: Quantification of dissociable synaptic modification.* Manuscript submitted for publication.

Lopez, H., Burger, B., & Levy, W. B. (1985). The asymptotic limits of long-term potentiation/depression are independently controlled. *Society for Neuroscience Abstracts, 11,* 930.

Lorente de No, R. (1934). Studies on the structure of the cerebral cortex. II. Continuation of the study of the ammonic system. *Journal für Psychologie und Neurologie, 46,* 113-177.

MacDermott, A. B., Mayer, M. L., Westbrook, G. L., Smith, S. J., & Barker, J. L. (1986). NMDA-receptor activation increases cytoplasmic calcium concentration in cultured spinal cord neurones. *Nature, 321,* 519-522.

Madison, D. V., Malenka, R. C., & Nicoll, R. A. (1986). Phorbol esters block a voltage-sensitive chloride current in hippocampal pyramidal cells. *Nature, 321,* 695-697.

Malenka, R. C., Madison, D. V., & Nicoll, R. A. (1986). Potentiation of synaptic transmission in the hippocampus by phorbol esters. *Nature, 321,* 175-177.

Malinow, R., & Miller, J. P. (1986). Postsynaptic hyperpolarization during conditioning reversibly blocks induction of long-term potentiation. *Nature, 320,* 529-530.

Mattson, M. P., Dou, P., & Kater, S. B. (1988). Outgrowth-regulating actions of glutamate in isolated hippocampal pyramidal neurons. *Journal of Neuroscience, 8,* 2087-2100.

Mattson, M. P. (1988). Neurotransmitters in the regulation of neuronal cytoarchitecture. *Brain Research Reviews, 13,* 179-212.

McNaughton, B. L., Douglas, R. M., & Goddard, G. V. (1978). Synaptic enhancement in fascia dentata: co-operativity among coactive afferents. *Brain Research, 157,* 277–293.

Minsky, M. L., & Papert, S. A. (1969). *Perceptrons.* Cambridge, MA: MIT Press.

Moore, S. D., & Levy, W. B. (1986). Association of heterogeneous afferents produces long-term potentiation. *Society for Neuroscience Abstracts, 12,* 504.

Nicoll, R. A. (1988). The coupling of neurotransmitter receptors to ion channels in the brain. *Science, 241,* 545–551.

Nowak, L., Bregestovski, P., Ascher, P., Herbet, A., & Prochiantz, A. (1984). Magnesium gates glutamate-activated channels in mouse central neurones. *Nature, 307,* 462–465.

Purves, D., & Lichtman, J. W. (1980). Elimination of synapses in the developing nervous system. *Science, 210,* 153–157.

Ramon y Cajal, S. (1968). *The structure of Ammon's horn.* Springfield, IL: Charles C. Thomas.

Redfern, P. A. (1970). Neuromuscular transmission in new-born rats. *Journal of Physiology, 209,* 701–709.

Ronnevi, L.-O., & Conradi, S. (1974). Ultrastructural evidence for spontaneous elimination of synaptic terminals on spinal motoneurons in the kitten. *Brain Research, 80,* 335–339.

Rosenblatt, F. (1962). *Principles of neurodynamics.* Washington, DC: Spartan Books.

Seress, L., & Pokorny, J. (1981). Structure of the granular layer of the rat dentate gyrus. A light microscopic and Golgi study. *Journal of Anatomy, 133,* 181–195.

Shore, J. E., & Johnson, R. W. (1980). Axiomatic derivation of the principle of maximum entropy and the principle of minimum cross-entropy. *IEEE Transactions on Information Theory, IT-26,* 26–37.

Spacek, J. (1982). 'Free' postsynaptic-like densities in normal adult brain: their occurrence, distribution, structure and association with subsurface cisterns. *Journal of Neurocytology, 11,* 693–706.

Spacek, J., & Lieberman, A. R. (1974). Ultrastructure and three-dimensional organization of synaptic glomeruli in rat somatosensory thalamus. *Journal of Anatomy, 117,* 487–516.

Steward, O. (1976). Topographic organization of the projections from the entorhinal area to the hippocampal formation of the rat. *Journal of Comparative Neurology, 167,* 285–314.

Steward, O., & Scoville, S. A. (1976). Cells of origin of entorhinal cortical afferents to the hippocampus and fascia dentata of the rat. *Journal of Comparative Neurology, 169,* 347–370.

Steward, O., & Vinsant, S. (1983). The process of reinnervation in the dentate gyrus of the adult rat: A quantitative electron microscopic analysis of terminal proliferation and reactive synaptogenesis. *Journal of Comparative Neurology, 214,* 370–386.

Tank, D. W., & Hopfield, J. J. (1987). Neural computation by concentrating information in time. *Proceedings of the National Academy of Sciences USA, 84,* 1896–1900.

Taube, J. S., & Schwartzkroin, P. A. (1988a). Mechanisms of long-term potentiation: EPSP/spike dissociation, intradendritic recordings and glutamate sensitivity. *Journal of Neuroscience, 8,* 1632–1644.

Taube, J. S., & Schwartzkroin, P. A. (1988b). Mechanisms of long-term potentiation: A current-source density analysis. *Journal of Neuroscience, 8,* 1645–1655.

Teyler, T. J., & Alger, B. E. (1976). Monosynaptic habituation in the vertebrate forebrain: The dentate gyrus examined in vitro. *Brain Research, 115,* 413–425.

Thompson, R. F., & Spencer, W. A. (1966). Habituation: A model phenomenon for the study of neuronal substrates of behavior. *Psychological Review, 73,* 16–43.

Tuff, L. P., Racine, R. J., & Adamec, R. (1983). The effects of kindling on GABA-mediated inhibition in the dentate gyrus of the rat. I. Paired-pulse depression. *Brain Research, 277,* 79–90.

Tuff, L. P., Racine, R. J., & Mishra, R. K. (1983). The effects of kindling on GABA-mediated inhibition in the dentate gyrus of the rat. II. Receptor binding. *Brain Research, 277,* 91–98.

Valdes, F., Dasheiff, R. M., Birmingham, F., Crutcher, K. A., & McNamara, J. O. (1982).

Benzodiazepine receptor increases after repeated seizures: Evidence for localization to dentate granule cells. *Proceedings of the National Academy of Sciences USA, 79,* 193–197.

White, G., Levy, W. B, & Steward, O. (1988). Evidence that associative interactions between afferents during the induction of long-term potentiation occur within local dendritic domains. *Proceedings of the National Academy of Sciences USA, 85,* 2368–2372.

Wigstrom, H., & Gustafsson, B. (1985). On long-lasting potentiation in the hippocampus: a proposed mechanism for its dependence on coincident pre- and postsynaptic activity. *Acta Physiologica Scandinavica, 123,* 519–522.

Wigstrom, H., & Gustafsson, B. (1988). Presynaptic and postsynaptic interactions in the control of hippocampal long-term potentiation. In P. W. Landfield & S. A. Deadwyler (Eds.), *Long-term potentiation: From biophysics to behavior* (pp. 73–107). New York: Alan R. Liss.

Willshaw, D. J., & von der Malsburg, C. (1976). How patterned neural connections can be set up by self-organization. *Proceedings of the Royal Society of London Series B, 194,* 431–445.

Wilson, R. C., Levy, W. B, & Steward, O. (1979). Functional effects of lesion-induced plasticity: Long term potentiation in the normal and lesion-induced temporodentate circuits. *Brain Research, 176,* 65–78.

Wilson, R. C., Levy, W. B, & Steward, O. (1981). Changes in translation of synaptic excitation to dentate granule cell discharge accompanying long-term potentiation. II. An evaluation of mechanisms utilizing dentate gyrus dually innervated by surviving ipsilateral and sprouted crossed temporodentate inputs. *Journal of Neurophysiology, 46,* 339–355.

Wilson, R., Pang, K., & Rose, G. M. (1987). Characteristics of crossed and multisynaptic pathways from the entorhinal cortex to the contralateral dentate gyrus in unanesthetized rats. *Society for Neuroscience Abstracts, 13,* 975.

Wolff, J. R., Joo, F., & Dames, W. (1978). Plasticity in dendrites shown by continuous GABA administration in superior cervical ganglion of adult rat. *Nature, 274,* 72–73.

Wolff, J. R., Joo, F., Dames, W., & Feher, O. (1979). Induction and maintenance of free postsynaptic membrane thickenings in the adult superior cervical ganglion. *Journal of Neurocytology, 8,* 549–563.

Wolff, J. R., Joo, F., Dames, W., & Feher, O. (1981). Neuroplasticity in the superior cervical ganglion as a consequence of long-lasting inhibition. In F. Joo & O. Feher (Eds.), *Cellular analogues of conditioning and neural plasticity* (pp. 1–9). New York: Pergamon Press.

6

I Thought I Saw It Move: Computing Optical Flow in the Primate Visual System

H. Taichi Wang
Bimal Mathur
Science Center, Rockwell International

Christof Koch
Division of Biology,
California Institute of Technology

COMPUTATIONAL THEORY

One prominent school of thought holds that information-processing systems, whether biological or man-made, should follow essentially similar computational strategies when solving complex perceptual problems, in spite of their vastly different hardware (Marr, 1982). However, it is not apparent how algorithms developed for machine vision or robotics can be mapped in a plausible manner onto nervous structures, given their known anatomical and physiological constraints. In this chapter, we show how one well-known computer algorithm for estimating visual motion can be implemented within the early visual system of primates.

The measurement of movement can be divided into multiple stages and may be performed in different ways in different biological systems. In the primate visual system, motion appears to be measured on the basis of two different systems, termed *short-range* and *long-range* processes (Braddick, 1974, 1980). The short-range process analyzes continuous motion, or motion presented discretely but with small spatial and temporal displacement from one moment to the next (apparent motion; in the human fovea both presentations must be within 15 minutes of arc and with 60–100 *msec* of each other). The long-range system processes larger displacements and temporal intervals. A second, conceptually more important, distinction is that the short-range process uses the image intensity, or some linear filtered version of image intensity (e.g. filtered via a Laplacian-of-Gaussian operator) to compute motion, while the long-range process uses more high level "token-like" motion primitives, such as lines, corners, and triangles (Ullman, 1981). Among short-range motion processes, the two most popular classes of algorithms are the gradient method on the one hand and the correlation, second-order or spatio-temporal energy methods on the other hand. We will discuss this distinction further below.

The problem in computing the optical flow field consists of labeling every point in a visual image with a vector, denoting at what speed and in what direction this point moves (for reviews on motion see Hildreth & Koch, 1987; Horn, 1986; Nakayama, 1985; Ullman, 1981). One limiting factor in any system's ability to accomplish this is the fact that the optical flow computed from the changing image brightness can differ from the actual velocity field. Thus, a perfectly featureless rotating sphere will not induce any optical flow field, even though the underlying velocity field – a geometrical concept – differs from zero. Conversely, if the sphere does not rotate but the light source moves across the scene (e.g., the sun), the computed optical flow will be different from zero even though the velocity field is not (Horn, 1986). We do not deal with this problem further and assume that the system can eliminate moving shadows.

The basic tenet underlying Horn and Schunck's (1981) analysis of the problem of computing the optical flow field from the time-varying image intensity $I(x,y,t)$ falling onto a retina or a phototransistor array is rooted in the fact that the total derivative of the image intensity between two image frames separated by the interval dt is zero: $dI(x,y,t)/dt = 0$. In other words, the image intensity seen from the point-of-view of an observer located in the image plane and moving with the image does not change. This conservation law is strictly satisfied only for translation of a rigid lambertian body. This law will be violated to some extent for other types of movements, such as if the illuminated object has specular components or for rotation around an axis. The question is to what extent this rule will be violated and whether the system built using this hypothesis will suffer from a severe "visual illusion." In an elegant analysis using the Theory of Dynamical Systems, Verri and Poggio (1989) discuss to what extent the smoothed optical flow is qualitatively similar to the underlying velocity field.

Using the chain rule of differentiation, $dI/dt = 0$ can be reformulated as $I_x \dot{x} + I_y \dot{y} + I_t = 0$, where $\dot{x} = dx/dt$ and $\dot{y} = dy/dt$ are the x and y components of velocity V, and $I_x = \partial I/\partial x$, $I_y = \partial I/\partial y$ and $I_t = \partial I/\partial t$ the spatial and temporal image gradients that can be measured from the image. We now have a single linear equation with two unknowns $(\dot{x}, \dot{y})$. Measuring at n different locations does not help in general, because we are then faced with n linear equations in $2n$ unknowns. Additional constraints are needed to unambiguously compute the optical flow field. The inability to measure both components of the velocity vector is also known as the aperture problem. Any system with a finite viewing aperture and the rule $dI/dt = 0$ can only measure the component of motion $-I_t/|\nabla I|$ along the spatial gradient ∇I. The motion component perpendicular to the local gradient remains invisible. In addition to the aperture problem, the initial motion data are usually noisy and may be sparse. That is, at those locations where the local visual contrast is weak or zero, no initial optical flow data exist (the featureless rotating sphere would be perceived as stationary), thereby complicating the task of recovering the optical flow field in a robust manner.

Horn and Schunck (1981) first introduced a "smoothness constraint" to solve this problem. According to the underlying rationale for this constraint, nearby points on moving objects tend to have similar three-dimensional velocities; thus, the projected velocity field should reflect this fact. The algorithm then finds the optical flow field that is as compatible as possible with the measured motion components as well as vary smoothly almost everywhere in the image. The final optical flow field is determined by minimizing a cost functional L:

$$
L(\dot{x}, \dot{y}) = \int\int \left((I_x\dot{x} + I_y\dot{y} + I_t)^2 \right.
$$

$$
\left. + \lambda[(\frac{\partial\dot{x}}{\partial x})^2 + (\frac{\partial\dot{x}}{\partial y})^2 + (\frac{\partial\dot{y}}{\partial x})^2 + (\frac{\partial\dot{y}}{\partial y})^2] \right) \mathrm{dxdy}, \tag{1}
$$

where the parameter λ controls the compromise between the smoothness of the desired solution and its closeness to the data. As discussed further down, the first term represents compatibility of the optical flow with the raw data while the second term enforces smoothness. L is quadratic in $\dot{x}$ and $\dot{y}$ and therefore has a unique minimum. This area-based optical flow algorithm (area-based because its derives motion at a point in the image by taking into account motion in the surrounding area) computes the qualitative correct optical flow field for real images (Horn & Schunck, 1981). The smoothness constraint stabilizes the solution against the unavoidable noise in the measured data.

Using general, domain-independent constraints such as smoothness of the optical flow (as compared to very specific constraints of the type "a red blob at desk-top height is a telephone," popular in early computer vision algorithms) to solve the ill-posed problems of early vision is very common (Poggio, Torre, & Koch, 1985). Thus, smoothness and uniqueness are exploited in the Marr and Poggio (1977) cooperative stereo algorithm, smoothness is used in surface interpolation (Grimson, 1981) and object rigidity is used for reconstructing a three-dimensional figure from motion (structure-from-motion; Ullman, 1979).

Before we continue, it is important to emphasize that the optical flow is computed in two, conceptual separate, stages. In the first stage, an initial estimate of the local motion, based on spatial and temporal image intensities, is computed. Horn and Schuck's method of doing this (using $dI/dt = 0$) belongs to a broad class of motion algorithms, collectively known as gradient algorithms. These exploit the relation between the spatial and the temporal intensity gradient at a given point to estimate the motion field

(Fennema & Thompson, 1979; Hildreth, 1984; Limb & Murphy, 1975; Marr & Ullman, 1981; Yuille & Grzywacz, 1988). A new variant of the gradient method, using $d\,\nabla I/dt = 0$ to compute the initial estimate of local motion, leads to uniqueness of the optical flow (Uras, Girosi, Verri, & Torre, 1989). Alternatively, a correlation or second-order model could be used at this stage for estimating local motion (Adelson & Bergen, 1985; Hassenstein & Reichardt, 1956; Poggio & Reichardt, 1973; Watson & Ahumada, 1985). However, for both principal (e.g., nonuniqueness of initial motion estimate) and practical (e.g., robustness to noise) reasons, all these methods require a second, independent stage where smoothing occurs. Finally, the discontinuities in optical flow, as encountered when objects move across the stationary background or past each other, should be taken into account at this stage to prevent them from being smoothed over (discussed below).

IMPLEMENTATION IN A RESISTIVE NETWORK

It has been shown previously that this type of quadratic variational functional—common in early vision (Poggio et al., 1985)—can be solved using simple electrical networks (Poggio & Koch, 1985). This mapping is based on the key idea that the power dissipated in a linear electrical network is quadratic in the currents or voltages; thus, if the values of the resistances are chosen appropriately, the steady-state voltage distribution in the network corresponds to the minimum of L in equation 1. Data are supplied by injecting currents into the nodes of the network. The resistive network for computing optical flow is shown in Fig.6.1. Here, the voltage in the top part of the network corresponds to the x component of the velocity, whereas the voltage in the bottom grid corresponds to the y component (Hutchinson, Koch, Luo, & Mead, 1988; for an overview see Koch, 1989). The measured temporal and spatial intensity gradients determine the values of the resistances and batteries. The value of the horizontal conductances within both grids is given by λ. Once the network settles into its steady-state—dictated by Kirchhoff's and Ohm's laws—the solution can simply be read off. Efforts are now underway (see, in particular, Harris, Koch, Luo, & Wyatt, 1989) to build such resistive networks for various early vision algorithms in the form of miniaturized circuits using analog, subthreshold Complementary Metal-Oxide-Semiconductor (CMOS) very large scale integrated circuit (VLSI) technology of the type pioneered by Mead (1989).

IMPLEMENTATION IN A NEURONAL NETWORK

We now turn towards a possible neurobiological implementation of this computer vision algorithm. Specifically, we show that a reformulated variational functional equivalent to equation 1 can be evaluated within the known anatomical and physiological constraints of the primate visual

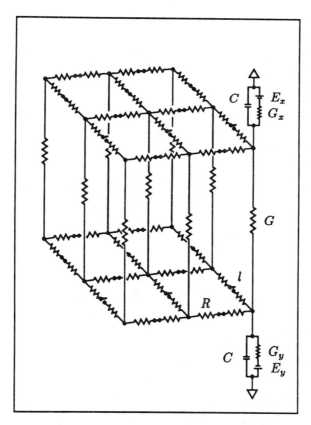

FIG. 6.1. Computing motion in resistive networks. Hybrid network, computing the optical flow in the presence of discontinuities, by finding a local minimum of the functional in equation 1. The voltages in the top grid correspond to the x components of the flow field, $\dot{x}$, and the voltage in the bottom grid to $\dot{y}$. The degree to which voltage spreads depends on the value of the horizontal conductances, given by λ. The values of the vertical conductances connecting both grids as well as the values of the conductances and batteries connected to ground (for clarity, only two such elements are shown) depend on the measured intensity gradients I_x, I_y, and I_t. Binary switches, which make or break the resistive connections between nodes, implement motion discontinuities, since an arbitrary high voltage (velocity) will not affect the neighbouring site across the discontinuity. Adapted from "Computing Motion Using Analog and Binary Resistive Networks" by J. Hutchinson, C. Koch, J. Luo, and C. Mead, 1988, *IEEE Computer, 21,* pp. 52–61.

system and that this formalism can explain a number of psychophysical and physiological phenomena.

The resistive networks already described use *analog* or *frequency* coding (Ballard, Hinton, & Sejnowski, 1983): the x and y components of velocity are given directly by the voltages at the two nodes in the resistive grid (Fig.6.1). If the voltage at any one node doubles, the appropriate component of the velocity doubles. However, neurons in the visual cortex of mammals represent the direction of motion in a very different manner, using many neurons per location such that each neuron codes for motion in one particular direction (Fig.6.3). In this representation, the velocity vector at any point **i,j** in the image, **V(i,j)**, is not coded explicitly but is computed across a population of n such cells, each of which codes for motion in a different direction (given by the unit vector Θ_k). In our model, we assume

$$V(i,j) = \sum_{k=1}^{n} V(i,j,k)\Theta_k. \tag{2}$$

To mimic neuronal responses more accurately, in particular, that cortical cells have a very low tonic discharge rate the output of all our model neurons is half-wave rectified; $f(x)=x$ if $x>0$ and 0 if $x<0$. In other words, if the inhibitory synaptic input exceeds the excitatory one, the neuron, is silent. We then require at least $n=4$ neurons to represent all possible directions of movement. Note that in this representation the individual components $V(i,j,k,)$ are not the projections of the velocity field **V(i,j)** onto the direction Θ_k (except for $n=4$).

Let us now consider a two-stage model for extracting optical flow field (Fig.6.2). In a preliminary stage, we assume that the image $I(i,j)$ is projected onto the image plane and relayed to the first processing stage via two sets of sustained (S) and transient (T) cells:

$$S(i,j) = \nabla^2 G * I(i,j) \tag{3}$$

and

$$T(i,j) = \frac{\partial(\nabla^2 G * I(i,j))}{\partial t}, \tag{4}$$

where G is the two dimensional Gaussian filter (with $\sigma^2=4$ pixels; Marr & Hildreth, 1980; Marr & Ulman, 1981), and the $\nabla^2 G$ function a reasonable approximation to the difference-of-Gaussian–shaped receptive fields of retinal ganglion cells (Enroth-Cugell & Robson, 1966).

In the first processing stage, the local motion information (the velocity component along the local spatial gradient) is measured using n ON–OFF orientation- and direction-selective cells $U(i,j,k)$, each with preferred direc-

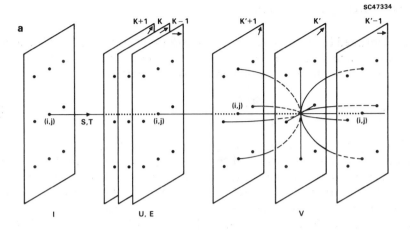

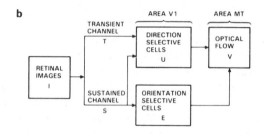

FIG. 6.2. Computing motion in neuronal networks. **(a)** Simple scheme of our model. The image *I* is projected onto a rectangular 64 by 64 retina and sent to the first processing stage via the *S* and the *T* channels. Subsequently, a set of $n = 16$ ON–OFF orientation- and direction-selective (*U*) cells code local motion in *n* different directions. Neurons with overlapping receptive field positions *i,j* but different preferred directions Θ_k are arranged here in *n* parallel planes. The ON subfield of one such *U* cell is shown in Fig.6.9a. The output of both *E* and *U* cells is relayed to a second set of 64 by 64 *V* cells where the final optical flow is computed. The final optical flow is represented in this stage on the basis of a population coding scheme $V(i,j) = \Sigma_{k=1}^{n} V(i, j, k) \Theta_k$, *with n = 16*. Each cell *V* (*i, j, k*) in this second stage receives input from cells *E* and *U* at location *i, j*, as well as from neighboring *V* neurons at different spatial locations. From Wang et al. (1989). **(b)** Block model of a possible neuronal implementation. The *T* and *S* streams originate in the retina and enter primary visual cortex in layer 4Cα and 4Cβ. The output of V1 projects from layer 4B to the middle temporal area (MT). We assume that the ON-OFF orientation- and direction-selective neurons *E* and *U* are located in V1 (or possibly in the output layer of V2 or the superficial input layer of MT), while the final optical flow is assumed to be represented by the *V* units in the deep layers of area MT.

243

tion indicated by the unit vector Θ_k (here the V neurons and the U neurons have the same number of directions and the same preferred directions for the sake of simplicity, even though this is not necessary):

$$U(i,j,k) = \frac{-T(i,j)\nabla_k S(i,j)}{|\nabla S(i,j)|^2 + \epsilon} \tag{5}$$

where ϵ is a constant and ∇_k the spatial derivative along the direction Θ_k. This derivative is approximated by projecting the convolved image $S(i,j)$ onto a simple-type receptive field, consisting of a 1 by 7 pixel positive (ON) subfield next to a 1 by 7 pixel negative (OFF) subfield. Because of the Gaussian convolution in the S cells, the resulting receptive field has an ON subfield of 3 by 9 pixel next to an OFF subfield of the same size (Fig.6.9a shows such a subfield). Such receptive fields are common in the primary visual cortex of cats and primates (Hubel & Wiesel, 1962). We assume that at each location n such receptive fields, each with preferred axis given by Θ_k ($k \in \{1 \ldots n\}$) exist. The cell $U(i,j,k)$ responds optimally if a bar or grating oriented at right angles to Θ_k moves in direction Θ_k. Its output is proportional to the product of a transient cell (T) with a sustained simple cell with an odd-symmetric receptive field ($\nabla_k S$); thus, the response of U is proportional to the magnitude of velocity. Our definition of U differs from the standard gradient model $U = -T/\nabla_k S$, by including a gain control term, ϵ, such that U does not diverge if the visual contrast of the stimulus decreases to zero; thus, $U \rightarrow -T\nabla_k S$ as $\nabla S \rightarrow 0$. Under these conditions of small stimulus contrast, our model can be considered a second-order model, similar to the correlation or spatiotemporal energy models (Adelson & Bergen, 1985; Hassenstein & Reichardt, 1956; Poggio & Reichardt, 1973; Watson & Ahumada, 1985). Thus, our model of local motion detection appears to contain aspects of both gradient and second-order methods, depending on the exact experimental conditions (for a further discussion of this issue, see Koch, Wang, Mathur, Hsu & Suarez, 1989). Finally, as an input to the last, integrating stage we also require a set of ON–OFF, orientation- but not direction-selective neurons:

$$E(i,j,k) = |\nabla_k S(i,j)|. \tag{6}$$

The absolute value operation ($|\cdot|$) insures that these neurons only respond to the amplitude of the spatial gradient, but not to its sign.

We have now progressed from registering and convolving the image in the retina to representing the spatial and temporal image brightness gradients within the first stage of our network. In the second processing stage, we determine the final optical flow field by computing the activity of a second set of cells, V. The state of these neurons — coding for the final optical flow field — is evaluated by minimizing a reformulated version of the functional in equation 1. The first term expresses the fact that the final velocity field should be compatible with the initial data, that is, with the velocity component measured along the local spatial gradient ("velocity constraint line"). In other words, the final velocity field $V(i,j) = \Sigma^n_{k=1} V(i,j,k) \Theta_k$ should be compatible with the local motion term U:

$$L_0 = \sum_{i,j,k} \left(\sum_{k'} V(i,j,k') \cos (k' - k) - U(i,j,k) \right)^2 E^m(i,j,k), \qquad (7)$$

where $\cos (k' - k)$ represents the cosine of the angle between $\Theta_{k'}$ and Θ_k, and $E(i,j,k)$ is the output of an orientaion-selective neuron raised to the mth power. This term ensures that the local motion components $U(i,j,k)$ only have an influence when there is an appropriate oriented local pattern; in other words, E^m prevents velocity terms incompatible with the measured data from contributing significantly to L_0. Thus, we require that the neurons $E(i,j,k)$ do not respond significantly to directions differing from Θ_k. If they do, L_0 will increasingly contain contributions from other, undesirable, data terms. A large exponent m is advantageous on computational grounds, because it will lead to a better selection of the velocity constraint line. For our model neurons (with a half-width tuning of approximately 60°, $m = 2$ gave satisfactory responses. The second term in equation 1 can be reformulated in a straightforward manner by replacing the partial derivatives of $\dot{x}$ and $\dot{y}$ by their components in terms of $V(i,j,k)$ (for instance, the x component of the vector $\mathbf{V(i,j)}$ is given by $\Sigma_k V(i,j,k) \cos\Theta_k$). This leads to

$$L_1 = \sum_{i,j,k,k'} [4V(i,j,k) - V(i-1,j,k) - V(i+1,j,k) - V(i,j-1,k)$$

$$- V(i,j+1,k)] \times \cos (k' - k) V(i,j,k'). \qquad (8)$$

We are now searching for the neuronal activity level $V(i,j,k)$ that minimizes the functional $L_0 + \lambda L_1$. Similar to the original Horn and Schunck's functional equation 1, the reformulated variational functional is quadratic in $V(i,j,k)$, so we can find this state by evolving $V(i,j,k)$ on the basis of the steepest descent rule:

$$\frac{\partial V(i,j,k)}{\partial t} = - \frac{\partial (L_0 + \lambda L_1)}{\partial V(i,j,k)} \qquad (9)$$

The contribution from the L_0 term to the righthand side of this equation has the form:

$$\sum_{k'} \cos(k - k')E^{m}(i,j,k')\left(U(i,j,k') - \sum_{k''} \cos(k' - k'')V(i,j,k'')\right) \quad (10)$$

while the contribution from the L_1 has the form:

$$\lambda\sum_{k'} \cos(k - k')[V(i-1,j,k') + V(i+1,j,k') + V(i,j-1,k') +$$

$$V(i,j+1,k') - 4V(i,j,k')] \quad (11)$$

The terms in equations 10 and 11 are all linear either in U or V. This enables us to view them as the linear synaptic contributions of the U and V neurons towards the activity of neuron $V(i,j,k)$. The lefthand term of equation 9 can be interpreted as a capacitive term, governing the dynamics of our model neurons. In other words, in evaluating the new activity state of neuron $V(i,j,k)$, we evaluate expressions 10 and 11 by summing all the contributions from the V and U of the same location i,j as well as neighboring V neurons and subsequently using a simple numerical integration routine, to compute the new state at time $t + \Delta t$. The appropriate network carrying out these operations is shown schematically in Fig.6.2a.

This neuronal implementation converges to the solution of the Horn and Schunck algorithm as long as the correct constraint line is chosen in equation 7, that is as long as the E^{m} term is selective enough to suppress velocity terms incompatible with the measured data. In the next two sections, we illustrate the behavior of this algorithm by replicating a number of perceptual and electrophysiological experiments.

CORRESPONDENCE TO CORTICAL ANATOMY
AND PHYSIOLOGY

The neuronal network we propose to compute optical flow (Fig.6.2) maps directly onto the primate visual system. Two major visual pathways, the parvo- and the magnocellular, originate in the retina and are perpetuated into higher visual cortical areas. *Magnocellular* cells appear to be the ones specialized to process transient information (such as motion; for reviews see DeYoe & van Essen, 1988; Livingstone & Hubel, 1988), because they respond faster and more transiently and are more sensitive to low-contrast stimuli than parvocellular cells. *Parvocellular* neurons, on the other hand, are selective for form and color. We do not identify our S and T channels with either the parvo- or the magno-pathway because this is not crucial to our model. We require that one set of cell signals edge information, whereas a second population is sensitive to transients. We approximate the spatial receptive field of our retinal neurons using the Laplacian-of-Gaussian operator and the temporal properties of our transient pathway by the first derivative. Thus, the response of our U neurons increases linearly with increasing velocity of the stimulus. This is of course an oversimplification (for instance, neurons are never either pure dc nor do they have an infinitely fast impulse response function) and we are investigating more realistic filter functions.

Both the magno- and the parvocellular pathways project into layer 4C of primary visual cortex. Here the two pathways diverge, magnocellular neurons projecting to layer 4B (Lund et al., 1976). Cells in this layer are orientation- as well as direction-selective (Dow, 1974). Layer 4B cells project heavily to a small but well-defined visual area in the superior temporal sulcus called middle temporal area (MT; Allman & Kass, 1971; Baker et al., 1981; Maunsell & van Essen, 1983a). All cells in MT are direction-selective and tuned for the speed of the stimulus; the majority of cells are also orientation-selective. Moreover, irreversible chemical lesions placed in MT cause striking elevations in psychophysically measured motion thresholds, but have no effect on contrast thresholds (Newsome & Pare, 1988). These findings all support the thesis that area MT is at least partially responsible for mediating motion perception. We assume that the orientation- and direction-selective E and U cells corresponding to the first stage of our motion algorithms are located in layers 4B or 4C in the primary visual cortex, in the output layer of the secondary visual cortex (V2) or possibly in the input layers of area MT, whereas the V cells are located in the deeper layers of area MT. Inspection of the tuning curve of a V model cell in response to a moving bar reveals its similarity with the superimposed experimentally measured tuning curve of the median MT cell of the owl monkey (Fig.6.3).

The structure of our network is indicated schematically in Fig.6.2a. The strengths of synapses between the U and the V neurons and among the V neurons are directly given by the appropriate coefficients in equations 10 and 11. Equation 10 contains the contribution from U and E neurons in primary visual cortex as well as from MT neurons V at the same location i,j but with different oriented receptive fields k''. No spatial convergence or divergence occurs between our U and V modules, although this could be included. The first part of equation 10 gives the synaptic strength of the U to V projection $(\cos (k'-k)E^m(i,j,k)U(i,j,k))$: If the preferred direction of motion of the presynaptic input $U(i,j,k)$ differs by no more than $\pm 90°$ from the preferred direction of the postsynaptic neuron $V(i,j,k)$, the $U \rightarrow V$ projection will depolarize the postsynaptic membrane. Otherwise, it will act in a hyperpolarizing manner because the cos $(k'-k)$ term will be negative. Notice that our theory predicts neurons from all cortical orientation

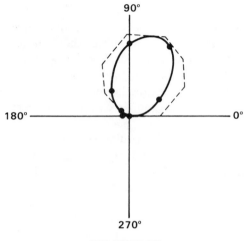

MT NEURON

FIG. 6.3. Polar plot of the median neuron (solid line) in the medial temporal cortex (MT) of the owl monkey in response to a field of random dots moving in different directions (Baker et al., 1981). The tuning curve of one of our model V cells in response to a moving bar is superimposed (dashed line). The distance from the center of the plot is the average response in spikes per second. Both the cell and its model counterpart are direction selective, because motion towards the upper right quadrant evokes maximal response while motion towards the lower left quadrant evokes no response. Figure courtesy of J. Allman and S. Petersen.

columns k projecting onto the V cells, a proposal that could be addressed using anatomical labeling techniques.

The synaptic interaction contains a multiplicative nonlinearity ($U \times E^m$). This veto term can be implemented using a number of different biophysical mechanisms, for instance "silent" or "shunting" inhibition (Koch, Poggio, & Torre, 1982). The smoothness term L_1 results in synaptic connections among the V neurons, both among cells with overlapping receptive fields (same value of i,j) as among cells with adjacent receptive fields (e.g., $i-1,j$). The synaptic strength of these connections acts in either a de- or a hyperpolarizing manner, depending on the sign of cos ($k'-k$) as well as their relative locations (see equation 11).

Let us now discuss the response of MT cells to plaids, a response qualitatively different from the way V1 neurons respond, but similar to the perception of human observers. If two identical sine or square gratings are moved past each other at an angle, human observers perceive the resulting pattern as a coherent plaid, moving in a direction different from the motion of the two individual gratings (Adelson & Movshon, 1982). The direction of the resultant plaid pattern ("pattern velocity") is given by the "velocity space combination rule" and can be computed from knowledge of the local "component velocities" of the two gratings (Adelson & Movshon, 1982; Hildreth, 1984). One such experiment is illustrated in Fig.6.4. A vertical square grating is moved horizontally at a right angle over a second horizontal square grating of the same contrast and moving at the same speed vertically. The resulting plaid pattern is seen to move coherently to the lower righthand corner (Adelson & Movshon, 1982), as does the output of our algorithm. Note that the smoothest optical flow field compatible with the two local motion components (one from each grating) is identical to the solution of the "velocity space combination rule." In fact, for rigid planar motion as occurs in these experiments, this rule as well as the "smoothness constraint" lead to identical solutions, even when the velocity of both gratings differ (illustrated in Figs.6.5a, 6.5b). Notice that the velocity of the coherent pattern is not simply the vector sum of the component velocity (which would predict motion towards the lower right-hand corner in the case illustrated in Figs.6.5a, 6.5b).

If the contrast of both gratings is different, the component velocities are weighted according to their relative contrast. As long as the contrast of the two gratings differ by no more than approximately one order of magnitude, observers still report coherent motion, but with the final pattern velocity biased toward the direction of motion of the grating with the higher contrast (Stone, Mulligan, & Watson, 1988). Because our model incorporates such a contrast-dependent weighting factor (in the form of equation 5), it qualitatively agrees with the psychophysical data (Figs.6.5c, 6.5d).

Movshon, Adelson, Gizzi, and Newsome (1985) repeated Adelson and Movshon's plaid experiments while recording from neurons in striate and extrastriate macaque cortex (see also Albright, 1984). All neurons in V1 and about 60% of cells in MT responded only to the motion of the two individual gratings (component selectivity; Movshon et al., 1985), similar to our $U(i,j,k)$ cell population, whereas about 30% of all recorded MT cells responded to the motion of the coherently moving plaid pattern (pattern selectivity), mimicking human perception. As illustrated in Fig.6.4, our V cells behave in this manner and can be identified with this subpopulation.

An interesting distinction arises between direction-selective cells in V1 and MT. Although the optimal orientation in V1 cells is always perpendicular to their optimal direction, this is true only for about 60% of MT cells (type 1 cells; Albright, 1984; Rodman & Albright, 1989). Thirty percent of MT cells respond strongly to flashed bars oriented parallel to the cells' preferred direction of motion (type 2 cells). These cells also respond best to the pattern motion in the Movshon and colleagues' (1985) plaid experiments. Based on this identification, our model predicts that type 2 cells should respond to an extended bar (or grating) moving parallel to its edge. Even

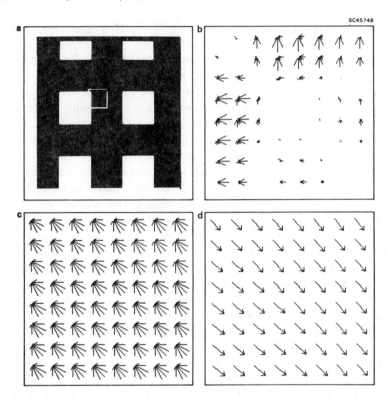

FIG. 6.4. Mimicking perception and single cell behavior. (a) Two superimposed square gratings, oriented orthogonal to each other, and moving at the same speed in the direction perpendicular to their orientation. The amplitude of the composite is the sum of the amplitude of the individual bars. (b) Response of the direction-selective simple cells U to this stimulus. The output of all 16 cells is plotted in a radial coordinate system at each location as long as the response is significantly different from zero; the lengths are proportional to the magnitudes. (c) The output of the V cells using the same needle diagram representation after 2.5 time-constants. (d) The resulting optical flow field, extracted from (c) via population coding, corresponding to a plaid moving coherently towards the lower righthand corner, similar to the perception of human observers (Adelson & Movshon, 1982) as well as to the response of a subset of MT neurons in the macaque (Movshon et al., 1985).

though, in this case, no motion information is available if only the classical receptive field of the MT cell is considered, motion information from the trailing and leading edges will propagate along the entire bar. Thus, neurons whose receptive fields are located away from the edges will eventually (i.e., after several tens of milliseconds) signal motion in the correct direction, even

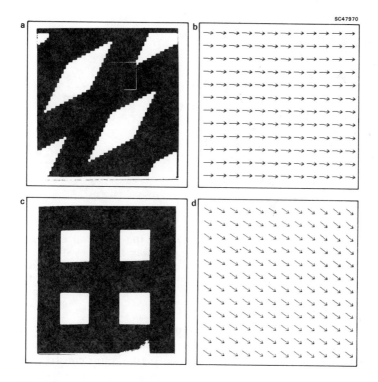

FIG. 6.5.   Additional coherent plaid experiments. **(a)** Two gratings moving towards the lower right (one at −26° and one at −64°), the first moving at twice the speed of the latter. The final optical flow, coded via the V cells, of a 12 by 12 pixel patch (outlined in (a)) is shown in **(b)**, corresponding to a coherent plaid moving horizontally towards the right. The final optical flow is within 5% of the correct flow field. **(c)** Similar to the experiment illustrated in Fig. 6.4, except that the contrast of the horizontal oriented grating only has 75% of the contrast of the vertical oriented grating. The final optical flow **(d)** is biased towards the direction of motion of the vertical grating, in agreement with psychophysical experiments (Stone et al., 1988).

though the direction of motion is parallel to the local orientation. This neurophysiological prediction is illustrated in Figs.6.9a, 6.9b.

Cells in area MT respond well not only to motion of a bar or grating but also to a moving random dot pattern (Albright, 1984; Allman, Miezin, & McGuinness, 1985), a stimulus containing no edges or intensity discontinuities. Our algorithm responds well to random-dot motion, as long as the spatial displacement between two consecutive frames is not too large (Fig.6.6).

The smooth optical flow algorithms we are discussing derive the exact

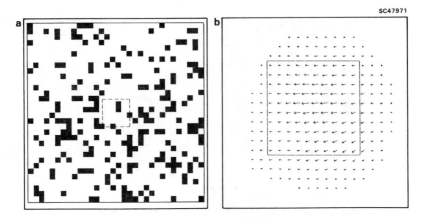

FIG. 6.6 Figure-ground response. **(a)** The first frame of two random-dot stimuli. The area outlined was moved by 1 pixel to the left. **(b)** The final population coded velocity field, signaling the presence of a blob, moving toward the left. The contour of the translated square is projected onto the final optical flow for a comparison

velocity field only if a rigid, Lambertian object moves parallel to the image plane. If an object rotates, the derived optical flow only approximates the underlying velocity field (Verri & Poggio, 1989). Is this constraint reflected in V1 and MT cells? No cells selective to true motion in depth have been reported in primate V1 or MT. Cells in MT do encode information about position in depth, for example, whether an object is near or far, but not about motion in depth, for example, whether an object is approaching or receding (Maunsell & van Essen, 1983b). The absence of cells responding to motion in depth in the primate (but not in the cat; see Cynader & Regan, 1982) supports the thesis that area MT is involved in extracting optical flow using a smoothness constraint, an approach that breaks down for three-dimensional motion. Cells selective to expanding or contracting patterns, caused by motion in depth, or to rotations of patterns within the fronto-parallel plane were first reported by Saito and colleagues (1986), in a cortical area surrounding MT, termed medial superior temporal area (MST). We illustrate the response of our network to a looming stimuli in Fig.6.7. MST receives heavy fiber projections from MT (Maunsell & van Essen, 1983c), consequently it may be possible that motion in depth is extracted on the basis of the optical flow computed in the previous stage.

PSYCHOPHYSICS

We now consider the response of the model to a number of stimuli that generate strong psychophysical percepts. We have already discussed the

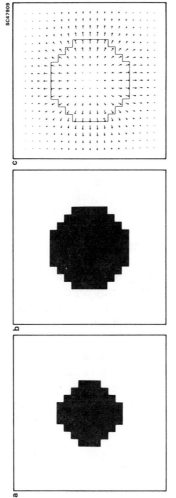

FIG. 6.7. Motion in depth. **(a)** and **(b)** show two images, featuring an approaching circular structure, expanding by one pixel in every direction. **(c)** Even though this type of motion violates the constraint underlying the smoothness assumption, our network computes the qualitative correct solution. Notice the focus of expansion in the middle of the image.

253

plaid experiments (previous section), in which our smoothness constraint leads to the correct, perceived interpretation of coherent motion.

In "motion capture" (Ramachandran & Anstis, 1983), the motion of randomly moving dots can be influenced by the motion of a superimposed low-spatial-frequency grating such that the dots move coherently with the larger contour, that is they are "captured." As the spatial frequency of the grating increases, the capture effect becomes weaker (Ramachandran & Inada, 1985). As first demonstrated by Bülthoff, Little, and Poggio (1989), algorithms that exploit local uniformity or smoothness of the optical flow can explain, at least qualitatively, this optical illusion because the smoothness constraint tends to average out the motion of the random dots in favor of the motion of the neighboring contours (see also Yuille & Grzywacz, 1988). The response of our network—somewhat modified to be able to perceive the low-frequency grating—is illustrated in Figs.6.8c, 6.8d. However, in order to explain the nonintuitive finding that the capture effect becomes weaker for high-frequency gratings, a version of our algorithm that works at multiple spatial scales is required.

Yuille and Grzywacz (1988) showed how the related phenomena of "motion coherence" (in which a cloud of randomly moving dots is perceived to move in the direction defined by the mean of the motion distribution; Williams & Sekuler, 1984) can be accounted for using a specific smoothness constraint. Our algorithm also reproduces this visual illusion quite well (Figs.6.8a, 6.8b). In fact, it is surprising how often the Gestalt psychologists use the words *smooth* and *simple* when describing the perceptual organization of objects (for instance in the formulation of the key law of Prägnanz; Kofka, 1935; Köhler, 1969). Thus, one could argue that these psychologists intuitively captured some of the constraints used in today's computer vision algorithms.

Our algorithm is able to mimic another illusion of the Gestalt psychologists: γ motion (Lindemann, 1922; Kofka, 1931). A figure that is exposed for a short time appears with a motion of expansion and disappears with a motion of contraction, independent of the sign of contrast. Our algorithm responds in a similar manner to a flashed disk (Wang, Mathur, & Koch, 1989). A similar phenomena has previously been reported for both fly and man (Bülthoff & Götz, 1979). This illusion arises from the initial velocity measurement stage and does not rely on the smoothness constraint.

MOTION DISCONTINUITIES

The major drawback of our and all other motion algorithms is the degree of smoothness required, smearing out any discontinuities in the flow field, such as those arising along occluding objects or along a figure-ground

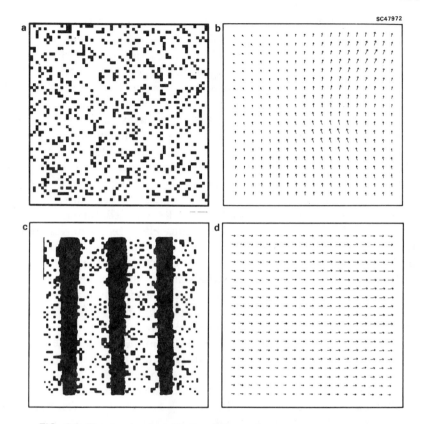

SC47972

FIG. 6.8. Psychophysical illusions. In motion coherence, random dot figures (a) are shown. However, all dots have a common motion component; in this case, all dots have one pixel toward the top, but have a random horizontal displacement component ($\pm 2, \pm 1$ and 0 pixels). **(b)** The final velocity field shows only the motion component common to all dots. Humans observe the same phenomena (Williams & Sekuler, 1984). **(c)** In motion capture, the motion of a low-spatial frequency grating superimposed onto a random-dot display "captures" the motion of the random dots. **(d)** The entire display seems to move towards the right. Human observers suffer from the same optical illusion (Ramachandran & Anstis, 1983).

boundary. Geman and Geman (1984; see also Blake & Zisserman, 1987) proposed a powerful idea to deal with this problem. They introduced the concept of binary line processes that explicitly code for the presence of discontinuities. We adopted the same approach for discontinuities in the optical flow by introducing binary horizontal l^h and vertical l^v line processes representing discontinuities in the optical flow (as first proposed in Koch, Marroquin, & Yuille, 1986). If the spatial gradient of the optical flow between two neighboring points is larger than some threshold, the flow field is broken and the appropriate motion discontinuity at that location is switched on ($l=1$), and no smoothing is carried out. If little spatial variation exists, the discontinuity is switched off ($l=0$). This approach can be justified rigorously using Bayesian estimation and Markov random fields (Geman & Geman, 1984). In our deterministic approximation to their stochastic search technique, a modified, nonconvex version of the variational functional in equation 1 must be minimized (Hutchinson et al., 1988). Domain independent constraints about motion discontinuities, such as that they occur in general along extended contours and that they coexist in general with intensity discontinuities (edges) is incorporated into this approach (Geman & Geman, 1984; Poggio, Gamble, & Little, 1988). As before, some of these constraints may be violated under laboratory conditions (such as when an homogeneous black figure moves over an equally homogeneous black background and the motion discontinuities between the figure and the ground do not coincide with the edges, because there are no edges) and the algorithms suffers an illusion (in this case, computes a zero optical flow field). However, for most natural scenes, these motion discontinuities lead to a dramatically improved performance of the motion algorithm (see Hutchinson et al., 1988).

We have not yet implemented motion discontinuities into the neuronal model. It is known, however, that the visual system uses motion to segment different parts of the scene. A number of authors have studied the conditions under which discontinuities (in either speed or direction) in motion fields can be detected (Baker & Braddick, 1982; van Doorn & Koenderink, 1983; Hildreth, 1984). Van Doorn and Koenderink (1983) concluded that perception of motion boundaries requires that the magnitude of the velocity difference be larger than some critical value, a finding in agreement with the notion of processes that explicitly code for motion boundaries. Recently, Nakayama and Silverman (1988) studied the spatial interaction of motion among moving and stationary waveforms. A number of their results could be reinterpreted in terms of our motion discontinuities.

What about the possible cellular correlate of line processes? Allman, Miezin, and McGuinness (1985) first described cells in area MT in the owl monkey whose true receptive field extended well beyond the classical receptive field as mapped with bar or spot stimuli (see Tanaka et al., 1986, for such cells in Macaque MT). About 40% to 50% of all MT cells have an antagonistic direction-selective surround, such that the response of the cell to motion of a random-dot display or an edge within the center of the receptive field can be modified by moving a stimulus within the surrounding region that is 50 to 100 times the area of the center. The response depends on the difference in speed and direction of motion between the center and the surround, and is maximal if the surround moves at the same speed as the stimulus in the center but in the opposite direction. In brief, these cells become activated if a motion discontinuity exists within their receptive field. In cats, similar cells appear already at the level of area 17 and 18 (Orban & Gulyás, 1988). These authors have speculated as to the existence of two separate cortical systems, one for detecting and computing continuous variables, such as depth or motion, and one for detecting and handling boundaries. Thus, tantalizing hints exist as to the possible neuronal basis of motion discontinuities.

ACCURACY OF REPRESENTATION

Can we say something about the accuracy with which the direction and magnitude of velocity is represented in our network? Neurons are not logical threshold gates, but are devices with statistical behavior, usually characterized by Poisson statistics. Intuitively, as more neurons n code for velocity at each receptive field location, the representation of optical flow should become more accurate. But can this be quantified? And, more interestingly, is the population-coding or vector-sum representation we use (Eq. (2)) more or less accurate than the winner-take-all representation proposed by Bülthoff and his colleagues (1989)? Let us assume that the firing of neurons is a discrete random process, described by Poisson statistics. That is, given an average firing rate p, then the probability that a neuron fires k action potentials in the time interval t is given by

$$p_k(t) = \frac{e^{-pt}(pt)^k}{k!} \tag{12}$$

The variance of firing around the mean rate p is given by $\sigma^2 = pt$. Let us further assume that the firing rates of the neurons are statistically independent processes and that the direction tuning of the neurons is approximated by a cosine function, i.e. $V(\Theta) = V_o cos(\Theta)$. This corresponds to a half-width tuning of $120°$, far broader than the one our V neurons use (see Fig. 6.3). As before, at each location the vector-sum of n half-wave rectified neurons, with an angular resolution of $\delta\Theta = 2\pi/n$, represents the velocity v. The minimum number of neurons required to represent V is $n = 4$. Without loss of generality, we assume that the correct velocity v is along the x axis. We can then define two measures of representation accuracy, namely the relative deviation in the magnitude of velocity Δ_v and the relative deviation in the direction of velocity Δ_Θ:

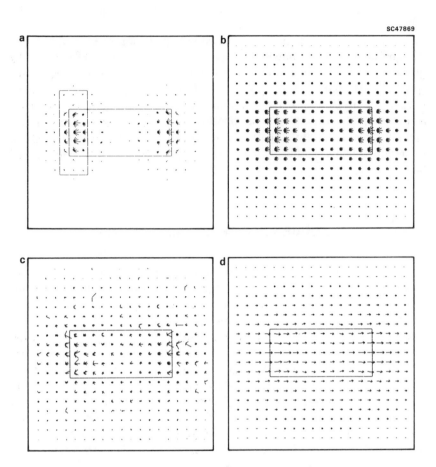

FIG. 6.9. Robustness of the neuronal network. A dark bar (outlined in all images) is moved parallel to its orientation towards the right. **(a)** Due to the aperture problem, those *U* neurons whose receptive field only "see" the straight elongated edges of the bar—and not a corner—will fail to respond to this moving stimulus, because it remains invisible on the basis of purely local information. The ON subfield of the receptive field of a vertically oriented *U* cell is superimposed for comparison purposes. **(b)** Only after information has been integrated, following the smoothing process inherent in the second stage of our algorithm, that the *V* neurons respond to this motion. We predict that the type 2 cells of Albright (1984) in MT will respond to this stimulus, whereas cells in V1 will not. **(c)** Subsequently, we randomly "lesion" 25% of all *V* neurons; that is, their output is set to 0. The resulting distribution of *V* cells is obviously perturbed. **(d)** However, given the redundancy built into the *V* cells (at each location $n=16$ neurons signal the direction of motion), the final population-coded velocity field differs only on average by 3% from the flow field computed with no damaged neurons.

$$\Delta_v = \frac{\sigma_x}{<v>},$$ (13)

and

$$\Delta_\Theta = \frac{\sigma_y}{<v>}.$$ (14)

Using some basic facts from probability theory (Papoulis, 1984), it can be shown that

$$\Delta_v = \frac{f_v(n)}{\sqrt{p}},$$ (15)

and

$$\Delta_\Theta = \frac{f_\Theta(n)}{\sqrt{p}},$$ (16)

with

$$f_v(n) = \frac{[\Sigma cos^3(\Theta_k)]^{1/2}}{[\Sigma cos^2(\Theta_k)]},$$ (17)

and

$$f_\Theta(n) = \frac{[\Sigma sin^2(\Theta_k)cos(\Theta_k)]^{1/2}}{[\Sigma cos^2(\Theta_k)]},$$ (18)

and $\Theta_k = 2\pi k/n$. The sum is taken in all four cases over all angles $|\Theta_k| < 90°$. Both functions behave as $n^{-1/2}$ for $n \to \infty$. In other words, the accuracy of the representation increases as the number of neurons at each location increases. Figure 6.10a,b plots these two functions. Note that, with the exception of $n = 4$, $f_v(n)$ is always less than 1.

Let us compare the performance of the population coded representation against the accuracy of a winner-take-all network, that is a coding scheme in which the neuron with the highest firing rate completely inhibits all other $n - 1$ neurons and therefore represents velocity. Under identical statistical assumptions, we have

$$\Delta_v = \frac{1}{\sqrt{p}},$$ (15′)

and

$$\Delta_\Theta = \delta\Theta.$$ (16′)

We thus arrive at the somewhat surprising result that the accuracy with which the magnitude of the velocity is represented in the population coding is always superior to that of the winner-take-all coding, as long as neurons

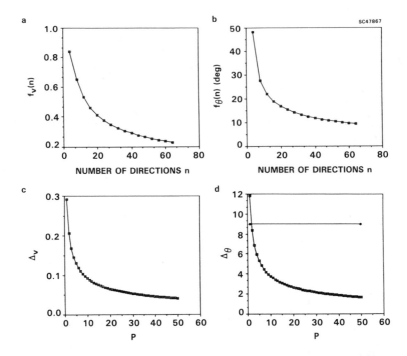

FIG. 6.10. Accuracy of the population or vector-sum coding scheme *versus* the winner-take-all representation. Neuronal firing rates are assumed to have Poisson statistics. **(a)** Plot of $f_v(n)$, where n is the number of neurons at each location representing the velocity (Eq. 17). $f_v(n)$ is also the ratio of the accuracy of the magnitude of velocity in the winner-take-all to the population coding scheme (i.e. Eqs. (15) and (15')). Thus, except for $n=4$, where both schemes are equally accurate, the population coding representation is always more accurate. **(b)** Plot of $f_\theta(n)$ in degree of angle (Eq. 18) as a function of n. **(c)** Mean deviation of the magnitude of velocity in the population coding scheme (Δ_v; Eq. (15)) as a function of the mean firing rate p for $n = 40$. **(d)** Mean deviation of the direction of velocity in the population-coding scheme (Δ_θ; Eq. (16)) as a function of the mean firing rate p for $n = 40$. In the winner-take-all scheme, the mean deviation $\Delta_\theta = 2\pi/40 = 9°$ (solid line). Thus, for all values of $p > 2$, the winner-take-all scheme is less accurate than the population-coding scheme we use.

in both representations have an identical mean rate of firing p (Fig.6.10a). Things are somewhat more complicated for the accuracy of the direction of velocity. While Δ_v is constant in the winner-take-all coding scheme, it decreases towards zero as both $n \to \infty$ and/or $p \to \infty$ (as the mean firing rate increases, numbers can be represented more accurately). For $n=40$, the cross-over point is for $p=2$ (Fig.6.10d).

Thus, under most circumstances, a winner-take-all representation such as the one used by Bülthoff and his colleagues (1989) will be **much** less accurate than a population coding scheme. Furthermore, devising such a network of many neurons, all of which are completely suppressed by the firing of the most active unit, is very difficult, given the known constraints of biophysics and cortical anatomy (Koch & Ullman, 1985).

DISCUSSION

The principal contribution of this chapter is to show how a well-known algorithm for computing optical flow, based on minimizing a quadratic functional via a relaxation scheme, can be mapped onto the early visual system of primates. While the details of our model are bound to be incorrect, it does explain qualitatively a number of perceptual phenomena and illusions as well as electrophysiological experiments on the basis of a single unifying principle: The final optical flow should be as smooth as possible.

Note that this "neuronal network" implementation has some properties very different from the resistive network implementation (of Fig. 6.1). Whereas two nodes per location suffice to represent the velocity in the resistive network, at least $n = 4$ half-wave rectifying neurons are required in our neuronal model. Note that the robustness of the latter representation to errors in the individual hardware components increases as n increases. If one of the resistances in the circuit shown in Fig.6.1 is grounded, the voltage at the associated node will be zero, whereas a missing synapse in the neuronal implementation will at worst lead to a small deviation in the represented velocity (as long as n is large). This distributed and coarse population coding scheme is similar to the coding believed to be used in the system controlling eye movements in the mammalian superior colliculus (Lee, Rohrer, & Sparks, 1988). Detecting the most active neuron at each location (winner-take-all scheme), as in the Bülthoff and colleagues (1989) model, is not required.

Recently, two studies have further refined our understanding of gradient-based optical flow methods (Uras et al., 1989; Yuille & Grzywacz, 1988). Behind the motion coherence theory of Yuille and Grzywacz is the principal idea that a higher degree of smoothness has a number of desirable properties, in particular that the interactions between point measurements fall off to zero at large distances. They are thus led to the use of higher derivatives in the second term of the variational functional (equation 1) imposing smoothness. Our network can be simply adapted to their form by increasing the range of the spatial interactions among our presumed MT neurons V (Fig.6.2). Uras and colleagues (1989) showed that the aperture problem can be avoided by exploiting a different definition of optical flow:

$d \nabla I/dt = 0$. This results in the use of second order spatial and temporal derivatives of the image brightness pattern to yield a dense optical flow field, in addition to the conventional smoothness term. Their algorithm can be mapped onto our representation by changing the definition of the local motion detecting cells U in equation 5. Specifically, even-symmetric receptive fields (e.g., a central ON field with adjacent OFF subfields on both sides) are required to implement the second spatial derivative. It is presently a topic of active research whether these schemes give rise to different psychophysical or electrophysiological predictions. However, we believe that neither their local estimate of motion nor the simpler one we are using in the form of eq. (15) are compatible with the known electrophysiological properties of directional-selective cortical simple and complex cells. We are presently investigating threshold type of directional-selective models which can give rise-under certain conditions — to second-order properties (Suarer & Koch, 1989). All of these schemes, however, can be implemented at the neuronal level using the type of representation we have already outlined.

REFERENCES

Adelson, E. H., & Bergen, J. R. (1985). Spatio-temporal energy models for the perception of motion. *J. Opt. Soc. Am. A, 2,* 284–299.

Adelson, E. H., & Movshon, J. A. (1982). Phenomenal coherence of moving visual patterns. *Nature, 200,* 523–525.

Albright, T. L. (1984). Direction and orientation selectivity of neurons in visual area MT of the macaque. *Journal of Neurophysiology, 52,* 1106–1130.

Allman, J. M., & Kass, J. H. (1971). Representation of the visual field in the caudal third of the middle temporal gyrus of the owl monkey (*Aotus trivirgatus*). *Brain Research, 31,* 85–105.

Allman, J., Miezin, F., & McGuinness, E. (1985). Direction- and velocity- specific responses from beyond the classical receptive field in the middle temporal area (MT). *Perception, 14,* 105–126.

Ballard, D. H., Hinton, G. E., & Sejnowski, T. J. (1983). Parallel visual computation. *Nature, 306,* 21–26.

Baker, C. L., & Braddick, O. J. (1982). Does segregation of differently moving areas depend on relative or absolute displacement. *Vision Research, 7,* 851–856.

Baker, J. F., Petersen, S. E., Newsome, W. T., & Allman, J. M. (1981). Visual response properties of neurons in four extrastriate visual areas of the owl monkey (*Aotus trivirgatus*): A quantitative comparison of medial, dorsomedial, dorsolateral and middle temporal areas. *Journal of Neurophysiology, 45,* 397–416.

Blake, A., & Zisserman, A. (1987). *Visual Reconstruction.* Cambridge, MA: MIT Press.

Braddick, O. J. (1974). A short-range process in apparent motion. *Vision Research, 14,* 519–527.

Braddick, O. J. (1980). Low-level and high-level processes in apparent motion. *Philosophical Transactions of the Royal Society London B, 298,* 227 – 264.

Bülthoff, H. H., Little, J. J., & Poggio, T. (1989). Parallel computation of motion: Computation, psychophysics and physiology. *Nature.*

Bülthoff, H. H., & Götz, K. G. (1979). Analogous motion illusion in man and fly. *Nature, 278,* 636–638.

Cynader, M., & Regan, D. (1982). Neurons in cat visual cortex tuned to the direction of motion in depth: effect of positional disparity. *Vision Research, 22,* 967-982.

DeYoe, E. A., & van Essen, D. C. (1988). Concurrent processing streams in monkey visual cortex. *Trends in Neuroscience, 11,* 219-226.

Dow, B. M. (1974). Functional classes of cells and their laminar distribution in monkey visual cortex. *Journal of Neurophysiology, 37,* 927-946.

Enroth-Cugell, C., & Robson, J. G. (1966). The contrast sensitivity of retinal ganglion cells of the cat. *Journal of Physiology (London), 187,* 517-552.

Fennema, C. L., & Thompson, W. B. (1979). Velocity determination in scenes containing several moving objects. *Comput. Graph. Image Proc., 9,* 301-315.

Geman, S., & Geman, D. (1984). Stochastic relaxation, Gibbs distribution and the Bayesian restoration of images, *IEEE Trans. Pattern Anal. Machine Intell., 6,* 721-741.

Grimson, W. E. L. (1981). *From images to surfaces.* Cambridge, MA: MIT Press.

Harris, J., Koch, C., Luo, J., & Wyatt, J. (1989). Resistive fuses: Analog hardware for detecting discontinuities in early vision. In Mead, C. & Ismail, M. *Analog VLSI Implementations of Neural Systems.* (Eds.). Ulurver: Norwell, MA.

Hassenstein, B., & Reichardt, W. (1956). Systemtheoretische Analyse der Zeit-, Reihenfolge-nund Vorzeichenauswertung bei der Bewegungsperzeption des Rüsselkäfers *Chlorophanus. Z. Naturforschung, 11b,* 513-524.

Hildreth, E. C. (1984). *The measurement of visual motion,* Cambridge, MA: MIT Press.

Hildreth, E. C., & Koch, C. (1987). The analysis of visual motion. *Annual Review of Neuroscience, 10,* 477-533.

Horn, B. K. P. (1986). *Robotic Vision.* Cambridge, MA: MIT Press.

Horn, B. K. P., & Schunck, B. G. (1981). Determining optical flow. *Artificial Intelligence, 17,* 185-203.

Hubel, D. H., & Wiesel, T. N. (1962). Receptive fields, binocular interactions and functional architecture in the cat's visual cortex. *Journal of Physiology (London), 160,* 106-154.

Hutchinson, J., Koch, C., Luo, J., & Mead, C. (1988). Computing motion using analog and binary resistive networks. *IEEE Computer, 21,* 52-61.

Kearney, J. K., Thompson, W. B., & Boley, D. L. (1987). Optical flow estimation: An error analysis of gradient-based methods with local optimization. *IEEE Trans. Pattern Anal. Machine Intell., 9,* 229-244.

Koch, C. (1989). Seeing chips: Analog VLSI Circuits for Computer Vision. *Neural Computation 1:* 184-200.

Koch, C., Marroquin, J., & Yuille, A. L. (1986). Analog neuronal networks in early vision. *Proceedings of the National Academy of Sciences USA, 83,* 4263-4267.

Koch, C., Poggio, T., & Torre, V. (1982). Retinal ganglion cells: A functional interpretation of dendritic morphology. *Philosophical Transactions of the Royal Society London B, 298,* 227-264.

Koch, C., Wang, H. T., Mathur, B., Hsu, A., & Suarez, H. (1989). Computing Optical flow in resistive networks and in the primate visual system. In *Proc. IEEE Workshop on Visual Motion,* Irvine, CA, March 20-22.

Köhler, W. (1969). *The task of Gestalt psychology.* Princeton: Princeton University Press.

Kofka, K. (1931). Die Wahrnehmung von Bewegung, In *Handbuch der normalen und pathologischen Physiologie.* A Bethe et al., (Eds.), Vol. II (pp. 1166-1265). Berlin: Springer.

Kofka, K. (1935). *Principles of Gestalt Psychology,* New York: Harcourt, Brace & World.

Lee, C., Rohrer, W. H., & Sparks, D. L. (1988). Population coding of saccadic eye movements by neurons in the superior colliculus. *Nature, 332,* 357-360.

Limb, J. O., & Murphy, J. A. (1975). Estimating the velocity of moving images in television signals. *Comput. Graph. Image Proc., 4,* 311-327.

Lindemann, E. (1922). Experimentelle Untersuchungen über das Entstehen und Vergehen von Gestalten, *Psych. Forschung 2,* 5-60.

Livingstone, M., & Hubel, D. (1988). Segregation of form, color, movement, and depth: Anatomy, physiology and perception. *Science, 240,* 740–749.

Lund, J. S., Lund, R. D., Hendrickson, A. E., Bunt, A. H., & Fuchs, A. F. (1976). The origin of efferent pathways from the primary visual cortex, area 17, of the macaque monkey as shown by retrograde transport of horseradish peroxidase. *Journal of Comparative Neurology, 164,* 287–304.

Marr, D. (1982). *Vision.* San Francisco, CA: W. H. Freeman.

Marr, D., & Hildreth, E. C. (1980). Theory of edge detection. *Proceedings of the Royal Society London B, 297,* 181–217.

Marr, D., & Poggio, T. (1977). Cooperative computation of stereo disparity. *Science, 195,* 283–287.

Marr, D., & Ullman, S. (1981). Directional selectivity and its use in early visual processing. *Proceedings of the Royal Society London B, 211,* 151–180.

Maunsell, J. H. R., & van Essen, D. (1983a). Functional properties of neurons in middle temporal visual area of the macaque monkey. I. Selectivity for stimulus direction, speed and orientation. *Journal of Neurophysiology, 49,* 1127–1147.

Maunsell, J. H. R., & van Essen, D. (1983b). Functional properties of neurons in middle temporal visual area of the macaque monkey. II. Binocular interactions and sensitivity to binocular disparity. *Journal of Neurophysiology, 49,* 1148–1167.

Maunsell, J. H. R., & van Essen, D. (1983c). The connections of the middle temporal visual area (MT) and their relationship to a cortical hierarchy in the macaque monkey. *Journal of Neuroscience, 3,* 2563–2586.

Mead, C. (1989). *Analog VLSI and neural systems.* Reading, MA: Addison-Wesley.

Movshon, J. A., Adelson, E. H., Gizzi, M. S., & Newsome, W. T. (1985). The analysis of moving visual patterns. In C. Chagas, R. Gattass, & C. Gross (Eds.), Exp. Brain Res. Suppl. II: Pattern Recognition Mechanisms (pp. 117–151). Heidelberg: Springer.

Nakayama, K. (1985). Biological motion processing: A review. *Vision Research, 25,* 625–660.

Nakayama, K., & Silverman, G. H. (1988). The aperture problem – II. Spatial integration of velocity information along contours. *Vision Research, 28,* 747–753.

Newsome, W. T., & Pare, E. B. (1988). A selective impairment of motion perception following lesions of the middle temporal visual area (MT). *Journal of Neuroscience, 8,* 2201–2211.

Orban, G. A., & Gulyàs, B. (1988). Image segregation by motion: Cortical mechanisms and implementation in neural networks. In R. Eckmiller & Ch. v. d. Malsburg (Eds.), *Neural Computers,* NATO ASI Series, V. F41 (pp. 149–158). Springer Verlag: Heidelberg.

Poggio, T., Gamble, E. B., & Little, J. J. (1988). Parallel integration of visual modules. *Science, 242,* 337–340.

Poggio, T., & Koch, C. (1985). Ill-posed problems in early vision: From computational theory to analog networks. *Proceedings of the Royal Society London B, 226,* 303–32.

Poggio, T., & Reichardt, W. (1973). Considerations on models of movement detection. *Kybernetik, 13,* 223–227.

Poggio, T., Torre, V., & Koch, C. (1985). Computational vision and regularization theory. *Nature, 317,* 314–319.

Ramachandran, V. S., & Anstis, S. M. (1983). Displacement threshold for coherent apparent motion in random-dot patterns. *Vision Research, 12,* 1719–1724.

Ramachandran, V. S., & Inada, V. (1985). Spatial phase and frequency in motion capture of random-dot patterns. *Spatial Vision, 1,* 57–67.

Rodman, H., & Albright, T. (in press). Single-unit analysis of pattern-motion selective properties in the middle temporal area (MT). *Experimental Brain Research.*

Saito, H., Yukie, M., Tanaka, K., Hikosaka, K., Fukuda, Y., & Iwai, E. (1986). Integration of direction signals of image motion in the superior sulcus of the macaque monkey. *Journal of Neuroscience, 6,* 145–157.

Stone, L. S., Mulligan, J. B., & Watson, A. B. (1988). Neural determination of the direction of motion: contrast affects the perceived direction of motion. *Neuroscience Abstracts, 14,* 502.5.

Suarez, H., & Koch, C. (1989). Linking simple cells with quadratic models of motion perception. *Neuroscience Abstracts* in press.

Tanaka, K., Hikosaka, K., Saito, H., Yukie, M., Fukuda, Y., & Iwai, E. (1986). Analysis of local and wide-field movements in the superior temporal visual areas of the macaque monkey. *Journal of Neuroscience, 6,* 134–144.

Ullamn, S. (1979). *The interpretation of visual motion.* Cambridge, MA: MIT Press.

Ullman, S. (1981). Analysis of visual motion by biological and computer systems. *IEEE Computer, 14*(8), 57–69.

Uras, S., Girosi, F., Verri, A., & Torre, V. (1988). A computational approach to motion perception. *Biological Cybernetics, 60:* 79–87.

van Doorn, A. J., & Koenderink, J. J. (1983). Detectability of velocity gradients in moving random-dot patterns. *Vision Research, 23,* 799–804.

Verri, A., & Poggio, T. (1989). Motion Field and Optical Flow: Qualitative Properties. *IEEE Trans. Pattern Anal. Machine Intell. 11:* 490–498.

Wang, H. T., Mathur, B. & Koch, C. (1989). Computing optical flow in the primate visual system. *Neural Computation.1:* 92–103.

Watson, A. B., & Ahumada, A. J. (1985). Model of human visual-motion sensing. *J. Opt. Soc. Am. A, 2,* 322–341.

Williams, D., & Sekuler, R. (1984). Coherent global motion percepts from stochastic local motions. *Vision Research, 24,* 55–62.

Yuille, A. L., & Grzywacz, N. M. (1988). A computational theory for the perception of coherent visual motion. *Nature, 333,* 71–73.

7

Correlation-Based Models of Neural Development

Kenneth D. Miller
University of California, San Francisco
Stanford University

The task of constructing the vertebrate central nervous system is tremendously complex. Perhaps 10^{12} neurons must migrate to their proper locations, send axons to the proper targets, and make hundreds or thousands of precise synaptic connections onto other neurons. The genome does not contain sufficient information to prespecify each connection. General genetic prespecification must be supplemented by dynamical rules whose result is to construct the nervous system in a useful and precise way.

Early stages of this process, in which neurons find their proper locations and send axons to roughly the right region of the correct target structure, are known in many instances to occur properly even when all electrical activity of neurons is blocked (Harris, 1981; Schmidt & Edwards, 1983; Shatz & Stryker, 1988). Later stages of this process in many structures, however, depend on patterns of neuronal electrical activity to achieve the final precision of synaptic connections. What is known about these activity-dependent processes of synaptic modification is generally consistent with a hypothetical rule first proposed by Hebb (1949): Synapses are strengthened if there is temporal correlation between their pre- and postsynaptic patterns of activity, and weakened otherwise.

In this chapter, I review some of the evidence that correlation-based mechanisms of synaptic modification operate in biological development. I then review theoretical studies to determine the expected outcomes of development under such mechanisms. These studies have been conducted in the context of models of the visual system, the system in which the existence of such correlation-based mechanisms is best established, but many of the conclusions are more general.

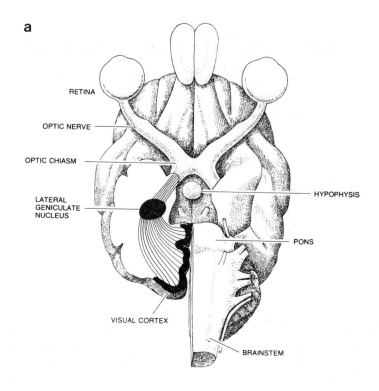

a

RETINA

OPTIC NERVE

OPTIC CHIASM

LATERAL
GENICULATE
NUCLEUS

VISUAL CORTEX

HYPOPHYSIS

PONS

BRAINSTEM

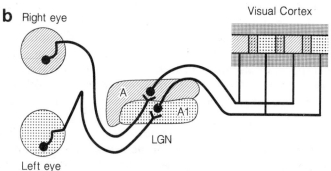

b Right eye

Visual Cortex

A

A1

LGN

Left eye

FIG. 7.1. Visual pathways in the cat. (a) The cat's brain, viewed from below. Portions of the right hemisphere (left in picture) have been dissected away to reveal the visual pathways, including the lateral geniculate nucleus (LGN) and visual cortex. Ganglion cells from each retina project axons to the LGN. LGN cells in turn project axons to the visual cortex. The right halves of each retina, which see the left half-field of vision, project axons to the LGN of the right hemisphere. That LGN in turn projects axons to the visual cortex of the same hemisphere. Thus the right LGN and

The mechanisms to be studied here are unsupervised: there is no teacher, error signal, or reinforcement signal. All the information for synaptic modification is found in the statistics of the input patterns of activity, and in the connectivity of the nervous system receiving the input. The line between supervised and unsupervised learning is sometimes unclear. For example, a teaching signal may be incorporated into the statistics of neural activity (Rumelhart & Zipser, 1986). Nonetheless, the mechanisms studied should be thought of as refining initially diffuse projections and developing a match between input signals and neural processing structure, rather than contributing to learning from reinforcement or error signals.

CORRELATION-BASED MECHANISMS OF SYNAPTIC MODIFICATION IN NEURAL DEVELOPMENT

Ocular Dominance Segregation in Mammalian Visual Cortex and Lateral Geniculate

The first neural evidence for correlation-based mechanisms of synaptic modification was provided by the pioneering studies of Hubel and Wiesel on the primary visual cortex of cats and monkeys, reviewed in Hubel and Wiesel (1977). More recent reviews of the field include Movshon and Van

---

right visual cortex receive inputs representing the left visual half-field in both eyes. The sorting of fibers, so that fibers from both right retinae go to the right LGN, and fibers from both left retinae go to the left LGN, occurs in the optic chiasm. Adapted from Guillery, 1974. Copyright © 1974 by SCIENTIFIC AMERICAN, Inc. All rights reserved. (b) Cartoon of the visual pathway, showing in more detail the fate of fibers representing each eye in the right hemisphere. Fibers from each eye project to separate laminae of the LGN. The two major such laminae in the cat, known as layers A and A1, are illustrated. Fibers from the eye contralateral to the LGN (the left eye, for the right LGN) project to layer A, while fibers from the ipsilateral eye (the right eye, for the right LGN) project to layer A1. Fibers representing similar receptive field points in each eye project to vertically aligned portions of layers A and A1. Retinotopically aligned geniculate cells, in turn, project axons to a retinotopically appropriate region of visual cortex, where they terminate in cortical layer 4. The axons representing each eye terminate in separate stripes or patches within this region. In the cat, as shown, there is some overlap at the borders of the two eyes' patches in layer 4; in the monkey, the two eyes' patches are cleanly separated. The cortex is depicted in cross-section, so that layers 1-3 are above and layers 5-6 below the layer 4 projection region. From Miller, Keller and Stryker, 1989. Copyright © 1989 by the AAAS.

Sluyters (1981); Sherman and Spear (1982); Stryker (1986); LeVay and Nelson (1989); and Rauschecker (1989). The visual cortex (area 17) is the first receiving area in cerebral cortex for visual sensory information. It receives signals from the lateral geniculate nucleus of the thalamus (LGN), which in turn receives signals directly from the two eyes (Fig. 7.1a).

The visual cortex extends many millimeters in each of the two dimensions along the cortical surface. These two dimensions contain a continuous map of the world as seen through the two eyes, so that neighboring areas of retina are represented by neighboring areas of cortex. The cortex thus contains a "retinotopic" map, a continuous map of the retinal surface. Visual cortical cells at any given point in the cortex respond to light stimulation from only a small "receptive field" area in the visual world, and this area shifts continuously across these two dimensions of cortex to yield a map of the visual world. In the third dimension, the cortex is about 2 mm in depth, consisting of six layers. The area of the visual world represented by visual cortical cells remains essentially constant through this depth. Such organization of cortical properties in a manner that is invariant through the depth of cortex is known as *vertical* or *columnar* organization. Columnar organization appears to be a general cortical feature (Mountcastle, 1978).

Cells from the two eyes project to separate laminae of the LGN (Fig. 7.1b), so that cells in the LGN are *monocular,* responding exclusively to stimulation of a single eye. Cells from the LGN project to layer 4 of the cortex, where they terminate in separate stripes or patches largely restricted to terminals representing a single eye. Many or, in some species, all visual cortical cells in layer 4 are monocular. Most visual cortical cells in other layers respond to stimulation through either eye, but respond preferentially to the eye that dominates layer 4 at that central location. Thus, visual cortical cells may be characterized by their *ocular dominance,* or eye preference, as first described by Hubel and Wiesel (1962). The stripes or patches of cortex that are dominated across the cortical depth by a single eye are known as *ocular dominance columns* (Fig. 7.2).

This patchy, segregated projection of LGN inputs to layer 4 of cortex develops from an initially diffuse, overlapping projection (Fig. 7.3a) (LeVay, Stryker, & Shatz, 1978). Initially, LGN inputs project to layer 4 in a single retinotopic map without apparent distinction by eye represented. Individual geniculate (LGN) cells project treelike arbors of terminal processes, the largest of which appear initially to extend uniformly over regions of cortex 2 mm in diameter (Levay & Stryker, 1979) (Fig. 7.3b). The geniculate cells are likely to be making synaptic contacts with cortical cells throughout the region of arborization. Subsequently, these arbors rearrange, so that inputs representing each eye become confined to alternating, approximately half-millimeter wide ocular dominance patches. This segre-

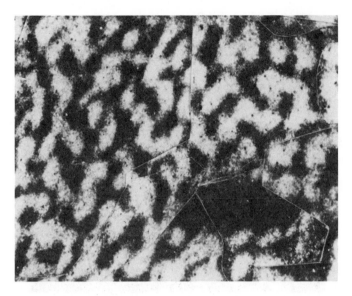

FIG. 7.2. Ocular dominance patches in layer 4 of cat visual cortex. Photomontage was constructed from sections taken through layer 4 of one hemisphere of flattened cortex. Geniculo-cortical afferent terminals serving the eye ipsilateral to the cortex (the right eye, if viewing the right visual cortex) were labelled and appear white. The large dark region is the representation in cortex of the portion of the visual field corresponding to the ipsilateral eye's blind spot (its optic disc). That region of cortex receives inputs only from the unlabeled eye. From Fig. 6D of Anderson et al., 1988. Reprinted by permission of the *Journal of Neuroscience.*

gation of inputs by eye represented begins at about 3 weeks of age in kittens (Shatz & Stryker, 1978), but prenatally in monkeys (Hubel, Wiesel, & Levay, 1977; Rakic, 1976, 1977).

The role of correlations among neuronal activities in this segregation process was first suggested by experiments demonstrating that abnormal visual experience leads to abnormal development of ocular dominance columns (Hubel & Wiesel, 1965; Wiesel & Hubel, 1965). When one eye is closed for even a few days in a young kitten (monocular deprivation), the LGN inputs representing the open eye take over far more than their normal share of visual cortex (Fig. 7.4) (Wiesel & Hubel, 1965; Shatz & Stryker, 1978). This effect occurs only during a critical period for developmental plasticity, and occurs most strongly from approximately $3\frac{1}{2}$ to 6 weeks of age in the kitten. The loss of cortical territory by the closed eye is due to competition with the open eye rather than to disuse, as can be seen in at least two ways. First, binocular deprivation (closing of both eyes) for a

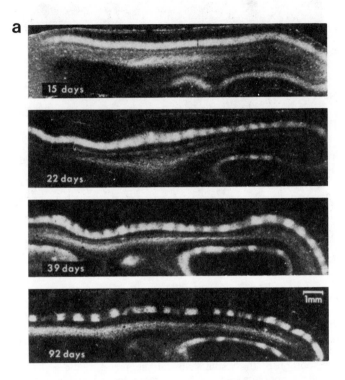

FIG. 7.3 Development of the geniculocortical projection in the cat. (a) Development of the input to layer 4 representing one eye. These are horizontal sections through one hemisphere of visual cortex, showing a cross-section of cortex as in Fig. 7.1b. Sections from cats of four different ages are shown. Geniculocortical afferent terminals serving the eye ipsilateral to the cortex were labelled and appear white. At 15 days of age, the innervation is uniform throughout layer 4. At later ages, inputs from that eye become progressively segregated into discrete patches of layer 4. Label is also present in axons in the white matter, visible as fainter, continuous label below layer 4. From LeVay and Stryker, 1979. Reprinted with permission from the Society for Neuroscience. (b) Development of the projections of individual geniculocortical afferent arbors. (1) At an early age, a putative geniculocortical afferent appears to project uniformly over an area of cortex about 2 mm in diameter. This afferent is believed to be of the type that projects the largest arbors. (2) At a later age, an afferent of the same type has its projection restricted to discrete patches of layer 4, presumably corresponding to the ocular dominance patches of its eye. (1), from LeVay and Stryker, 1979. Reprinted with permission from the Society for Neuroscience. (2), from Ferster and LeVay, 1978. Reprinted by permission of the *Journal of Comparative Neurology.*

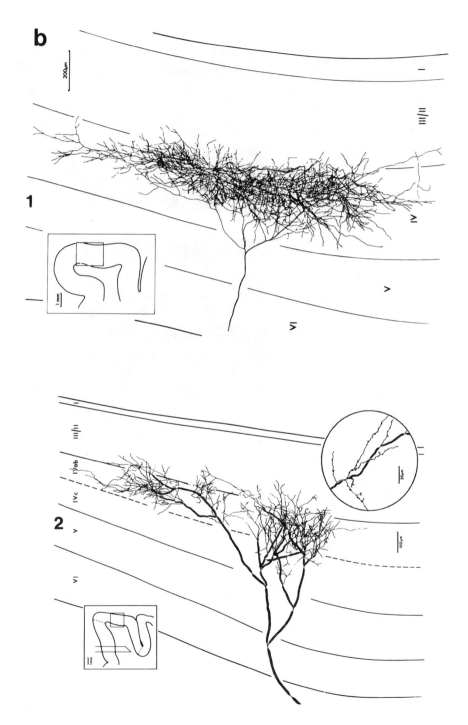

FIG 7.4. Effects of monocular deprivation in cats. Parasaggital sections (cut parallel to the midline) from visual cortex are shown. These sections intersect several portions of layer 4. Geniculocortical terminals serving the ipsilateral eye were labelled and appear white. (a): Hemisphere ipsilateral to the labelled eye in a normally reared cat, showing the normal pattern of geniculocortical termination restricted to discrete patches. (b): Hemisphere ipsilateral to the open eye in a cat which was monocularly deprived. Open eye terminals occupy most of layer 4. This animal had one eyelid sutured shut for many months, beginning prior to eye opening. Arrows indicate directions: A: anterior; P: posterior; D: dorsal; V: ventral. From Shatz and Stryker, 1978. Reprinted by permission of the Physiological Society.

Ipsilateral

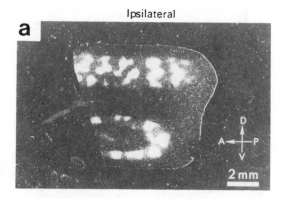

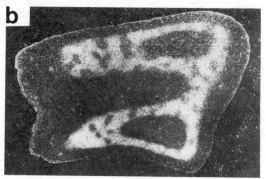

similar time during the critical period causes no abnormal effect to either eye's connections to cortex or ability to drive cortical cells. In addition, monocular deprivation causes no abnormal effects in regions of cortex that receive inputs from only one eye, where the closed-eye inputs face no competition from open-eye inputs (Guillery & Stelzner, 1970; Guillery, 1972). The changes due to monocular deprivation occur in cortex, rather than at a previous level of the visual system, as ocular dominance distribution in the LGN is completely normal after deprivation.

Treatments that preserve the equality of the two eyes' activities, but destroy the correlations or cause anticorrelations between them, also alter cortical ocular dominance organization during a critical period (Hubel & Wiesel, 1965). In artificial strabismus, the extraocular muscles are altered so that the two eyes point in different directions and thus never see the same scene at the same time. Alternating monocular deprivation, in which each eye is covered on alternate days, similarly disrupts correlations between the two eyes. After either treatment, the two eyes are unable to coactivate single cortical cells. Most cortical cells in all layers of cortex become monocular, driven exclusively by the eye that dominates the corresponding region of layer 4.

The role of neural activity in ocular dominance segregation was demonstrated most clearly in recent experiments by Stryker and Harris (1986) and Stryker and Strickland (1984) (Stryker, 1986). Pharmacological blockade was used to silence all neuronal activity in both eyes of kittens beginning before the normal onset of ocular dominance segregation. As a result of this treatment, the normal ocular dominance segregation of geniculate inputs did not occur. Subsequently, nearly all cortical cells responded well to stimulation of either eye. Other kittens received artificial electrical stimulation of the nerves from the two eyes while the eyes themselves were silenced. If inputs from both eyes were stimulated synchronously, the outcome was the same as in the absence of activity. When the same pattern of electrical stimulation was given to each eye, but in a manner that was binocularly asynchronous, the result was a cortex in which virtually all cells were monocularly driven, as in artificial strabismus or alternating monocular deprivation. Thus, neuronal activity is crucial to ocular dominance segregation, but the simple presence of activity does not determine that segregation will occur. Rather, the degree of synchrony or correlation of activity between the two eyes is key.

Recent experiments have proven that activity in the cortex, rather than simply in the eyes or the LGN, is crucial to cortical ocular dominance plasticity (Reiter, Waitzman, & Stryker, 1986). A blockade of all activity in cortex, both pre- and postsynaptic, without effects on activity in the eyes or the LGN, was sufficient to prevent monocular deprivation from causing any changes in cortical ocular dominance. Furthermore, the plasticity crucially depends on both postsynaptic and presynaptic cortical activity[1] (Reiter & Stryker, 1988; see also Bear & Cooper, chap. 2 in this volume[2]). This was shown by infusion of the drug muscimol into cortex. This drug mimics the inhibitory neurotransmitter GABA to hyperpolarize

---

[1]Previous evidence for a critical role of postsynaptic cells existed, based on the relation between orientation selectivity and ocular dominance in animals deprived of certain orientations in only one eye or of different orientations in each eye. (See reviews in Stryker, 1977, and Rauschecker, 1989).

[2]Reiter and Stryker infused muscimol into cortex. Muscimol hyperpolarizes postsynaptic cells, and thus both blocks their activity and prevents any currents through NMDA-receptor mediated channels. In the region in which all postsynaptic action potentials were blocked, the ocular dominance shift was to the closed eye; outside this region, the normal shift to the open eye was seen. Bear and colleagues infused APV, which blocks activation of NMDA receptors on postsynaptic cells (see discussion of NMDA receptors later in this chapter). No assessment was made of the region over which NMDA receptors were blocked. Close to the cannula, where the block should be most complete, the shift was to the closed eye. Further from the cannula, a population of cells with no shift was seen. We have shown that such APV infusion severely depresses or eliminates postsynaptic action potentials in response to visual stimulation, in a manner closely correlated to the degree of NMDA receptor blockade (Miller, Chapman, & Stryker, 1989). Hence, both treatments could be achieving their effects either by the depression or elimination of postsynaptic activity, or by the blockade of NMDA-receptor activated currents, or by some combination. In any case, the effect appears to result from alterations of postsynaptic rather than presynaptic responses.

and thus silence all postsynaptic cells, without apparent affect on presynaptic activity. After monocular deprivation in the presence of muscimol, there was an ocular dominance shift in favor of the closed, less-active eye. Hence the same pattern of geniculate input may lead to a strengthening or weakening of synaptic strengths, depending on the activation of the postsynaptic cell. In particular, inputs that are more active are strengthened relative to less active inputs when they can activate the postsynaptic cell, but weakened when the postsynaptic cell is hyperpolarized and silenced.

A reasonable interpretation of this evidence is that geniculate terminals serving the two eyes compete on the basis of their patterns of activity. Correlated inputs serving a single eye successfully coactivate cortical cells and are mutually strengthened. If one eye is slightly more successful in activating a cortical cell than the other, the synapses serving it are strengthened and those serving the less successful eye are correspondingly weakened. Inputs serving one eye thus may come to dominate a region of cortex, while inputs serving the opposite eye become weakened and are ultimately excluded. Such an interpretation requires that inputs from each eye be locally correlated in the absence of visual experience, because segregation begins prenatally in monkeys and is seen even in dark-reared kittens (Wiesel & Hubel, 1965). In adult cats, the maintained activity in darkness of neighboring retinal ganglion cells is correlated within each eye over tens of milliseconds (Mastronarde, 1983a, 1983b, 1989), and correlations may exist across all retinal ganglion cells within an eye over seconds or minutes (Rodieck & Smith, 1966; Levick & Williams, 1964). These correlations have not yet been studied in younger animals, but it is known that such maintained activity exists in the fetus in rats (Galli & Maffei, 1988; see also Shatz & Kirkwood, 1984).

Thus, correlations in maintained activity among neighboring neurons may serve to guide even fetal neural development. Indeed, recent work has shown that segregation of retinal ganglion cell axons into eye-specific layers in the LGN, a process that occurs entirely prenatally in some species such as cats, may also occur through activity-dependent competition between the two eyes. The fetal LGN, analogously to the visual cortex, initially receives an overlapping innervation by the retinal ganglion cells from the two eyes. These inputs subsequently segregate to form the eye-specific laminae (Shatz, 1983; Sretavan & Shatz, 1986; Rakic, 1976, 1977). Blockade of all neural activity in fetal cats, initiated before the normal onset of segregation, prevents segregation of these laminae in the fetal LGN (Shatz & Stryker, 1988). Studies of the development of retinal ganglion cell arbors in the fetal LGN under varying conditions of intraocular competition have also suggested a role for activity-dependent competition in development of laminar segregation (Garraghty, Shatz, Sretavan, & Sur, 1988; Garraghty, Shatz, & Sur, 1988; Sretavan & Shatz, 1987; Sretavan, Shatz, & Stryker, 1988; Sur, 1988; see reviews in Garraghty & Sur, 1988; Shatz, 1988).

Activity-Dependent Development in the Optic Tectum

Correlation-based mechanisms have been implicated in the development of the projection from the retina to the optic tectum of fish and amphibia (reviewed in Fawcett & O'Leary, 1985; Schmidt, 1985; Schmidt & Tieman, 1985; Udin & Fawcett, 1988). The optic tectum is the primary recipient of visual inputs in these species, which lack a cerebral cortex. The inputs to the optic tectum come directly from the contralateral eye; each tectum normally receives direct inputs from only a single eye. It is known that the activities of neighboring retinal ganglion cells are correlated in at least one such species (Arnett, 1978; Ginsburg, Johnsen, & Levine, 1984), so the substrate exists for a correlation-based mechanism.

During development, and after regeneration of a cut optic nerve, the tectum initially receives diffuse and only coarsely topographic projections from the retina. The axons of individual retinal cells arborize over regions of tectum many times larger than will their final arbors, and individual points in tectum receive input from visual areas much larger than in the mature tectum. Complete refinement of this diffuse map to its more precise adult state does not occur when all neural activity in the eye is pharmacologically blocked (Fig. 7.5) (Meyer, 1983; Schmidt & Edwards, 1983). Complete refinement also does not occur if all retinal ganglion cells are forced to fire synchronously by raising the animal with stroboscopic lighting in the absence of patterned visual images (Cook, 1987; Cook & Rankin, 1986; Eisele & Schmidt,1988; Schmidt & Eisele, 1985). Recent evidence indicates that interference with aspects of postsynaptic tectal cell responses is sufficient to suppress refinement of the map (Cline & Constantine-Paton, 1988; Schmidt, 1988).

Although the tectum is normally monocular, it is possible artificially to force two eyes to innervate a single tectum. When this occurs, the inputs from the two eyes in many cases segregate into eye-specific patches or stripes (Fig. 7.6) (Boss & Schmidt, 1984; Constantine-Paton & Law, 1978; Levine & Jacobson, 1975; Meyer, 1979). This provides intriguing evidence that ocular dominance patches can develop simply as a by-product of activity-dependent processes that exist for other purposes, as in this system the inputs from the two eyes never naturally interact. Although biochemical markers specific for retinotopic position, and potentially for eye of origin, appear to play an important role in normal retinotectal development, convincing evidence exists that such markers are not involved in patch formation (Fawcett & Willshaw, 1982; Ide, Fraser, & Meyer, 1983). Blockade of all activity in both eyes (Boss & Schmidt, 1984; Meyer, 1982; Reh & Constantine-Paton, 1985) prevents segregation of the stripes. Interference with elements of postsynaptic tectal responses alone appears sufficient to prevent stripe formation (Cline, Debski, & Constantine-Paton, 1987). Curiously, unlike in mammalian visual cortex, there is no monocular

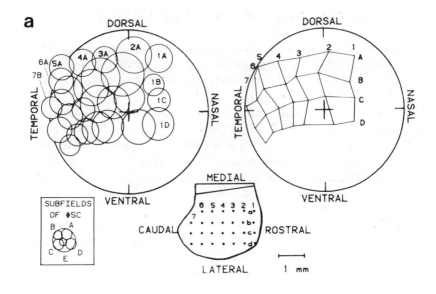

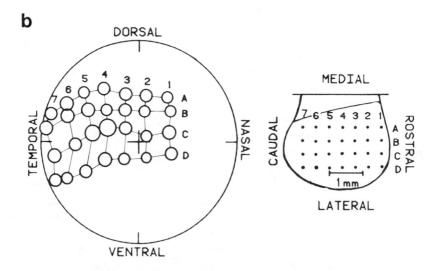

FIG. 7.5. Refinement of the visual map in fish optic tectum, and its prevention by blockade of neural activity. Optic nerves in adult animals were crushed, and a new projection from retina to tectum was then allowed to grow. (a) Retinotectal map in a fish in which all neural activity in the retina was pharmacologically blocked during regrowth. Multiunit recordings of retinal inputs were made from a regular grid of points in the tectum. Above, the two large

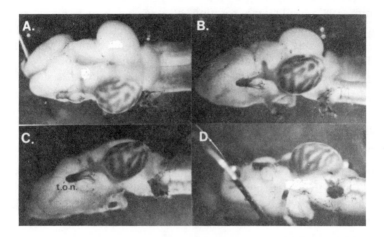

FIG. 7.6.   Ocular dominance stripes on the frog optic tectum. Such stripes form when two eyes are forced to innervate a single tectum, in this case by transplantion of a third eye. Figure shows four views of the same three-eyed tadpole brain after labeling the transplanted optic nerve (t.o.n.) and tract with HRP. Terminals from the transplanted eye appear dark. Total tectal length at this stage is approximately 2 mm. Photograph supplied by Dr. Martha Constantine-Paton.

deprivation effect (Meyer, 1982); complete blockade of activity in only one eye leads to apparently normal segregation.

The optic tectum in some species also receives an indirect innervation, via an intermediate nucleus, representing the ipsilateral eye. In at least one such species, but not in several other species tested, retinotopic matching of this

circles represent the visual field, and show the centers (right) and outer boundaries (left) of the receptive fields recorded at each point in tectum. Below is a drawing of the tectal surface, showing the grid of recording locations. Centers of receptive fields form a regular grid in the visual field, demonstrating that a coarse retinotopic map exists. However, receptive fields are large and extensively overlapping. The inset shows that a typical receptive field, number 5C, was composed of many, only partially overlapping retinal inputs. (b) Retinotectal map in a fish in which normal retinal activity existed during regrowth. The tectal surface is at right, with the grid of recording points again indicated. The visual field is at left, and the outer boundary of each receptive field is shown. Receptive fields are small, approximately the size of the receptive field of a single retinal input, and largely non-overlapping. From Schmidt and Edwards, 1983. Reprinted by permission of Elsevier Science Publishers BV.

indirect ipsilateral input with the direct contralateral input appears to occur via an activity-dependent mechanism (Keating, 1975; Udin, 1983; reviewed in Udin, 1985). Following rotation of one eye, which leaves neurons physically unchanged but alters their activity patterns, the ipsilateral input to the tectum adjusts to be in register with the input from the contralateral eye. The adjustment does not occur if the animal is reared in the dark. Again, interference with aspects of postsynaptic response is sufficient to prevent this adjustment (Scherer & Udin, 1988).

Activity-Dependent Development and Plasticity in Other Neural Systems

Many neural systems exhibit phenomena that may be explained by hypothesizing an activity-dependent, perhaps correlation-based mechanism of plasticity, but in which the location, activity-dependence, or correlation-dependence of the changes is not as well established as in the phenomena previously discussed.

Cells in mammalian visual cortex exhibit many properties besides ocular dominance. One of the most characteristic properties in many species is orientation selectivity: most cells respond best to an oriented bar or edge of light, rather than to a circular spot of light, and these cells each respond largely or only to a narrow range of orientations. Like ocular dominance, orientation selectivity is organized in columns: cells throughout the depth of cortex have the same preferred orientation, and this preferred orientation changes continuously as one moves across the cortex. It is clear that a mature orientation structure can develop without visual experience (Hubel & Wiesel, 1963; Wiesel & Hubel, 1974). Whether this development depends on prenatal maintained neuronal activity is not known. There is conflicting evidence as to whether preferred orientations of cells can be modified by visual experience. Some authors have concluded that such modification can occur during the critical period for ocular dominance plasticity in young kittens (reviewed in Fregnac & Imbert, 1984; Rauschecker, 1989). However, lack of exposure to certain orientations during the critical period leads to deterioration of responses of cortical cells that preferred those orientations. This effect would seem to reflect disuse rather than competition. Results that have been interpreted to demonstrate competitive modification of preferred orientations can be adequately explained by this disuse effect (Stryker, Sherk, Leventhal, & Hirsch, 1978). It remains of great interest to determine both theoretically and experimentally the possible role of activity-dependent competition in the development of orientation selectivity.

Mammalian retinal ganglion cells may be either on-center or off-center, and in adults maintained activity in darkness of these two types of cells is anticorrelated (Mastronarde, 1983a, 1983b, 1989). Individual cells in the

LGN normally receive only on-center or only off-center input. In the cat, action-potential blockade in one eye from birth leads most LGN cells responding to that eye to develop mixed on-center/off-center excitatory input (Dubin, Stark, & Archer, 1986). This treatment also leads to much greater than normal mixing onto LGN cells of two normally segregated types of retinal ganglion cells known as X-cells and Y-cells. In some species, on-center and off-center LGN cells are found in separate geniculate sublaminae (Conway & Schiller, 1983; LeVay & McConnell, 1982; Schiller & Malpeli, 1978; Stryker & Zahs, 1983). In two such species, inputs to cortex from on-center and off-center geniculate cells are segregated in cortex into separate patches much like ocular dominance patches (McConnell & LeVay, 1984; Zahs & Stryker, 1988). It is intriguing to think that one might be able to account for the various patterns of segregation observed simply with a correlation-based mechanism.

The left and right visual cortices are connected via axons passing through the corpus callosum. The left and right visual cortices represent the right and left visual hemifields, respectively. In the adult cat, these visual callosal connections come from and connect to the representation of the vertical midline, the only area represented in both hemispheres. Earlier in development these projections are more widespread. Alterations in visual experience during a critical period alter the final sources and/or terminations of these projections in a manner that could be explained by selection for a correlation in firing between callosal and geniculate inputs to cortical cells (Innocenti & Frost, 1979, 1980; Innocenti, Frost, & Illes, 1985).

In rat or mouse somatosensory cortex, individual whiskers are represented in discrete cylindrical columns known as "barrels." These barrels develop between postnatal days 2 and 5 or 6. Removal of whiskers during this time leads to rearrangements and shrinkage of the corresponding barrels and in some cases expansions of adjacent barrels (Belford & Killackey, 1980; Durham & Woolsey, 1984; Jeanmonod, Rice, & Van der Loos, 1981). This suggests that more active inputs may take over more cortical space during this critical period, but this interpretation is complicated by the potential presence of alterations, including cell death and degeneration, at intermediate stages of the somatosensory input from periphery to cortex (Jeanmonod et al., 1981).

Although this anatomical plasticity occurs only during a critical period, there is a great deal of physiological evidence that correlation-based mechanisms of plasticity may be active in somatosensory cortex of many species throughout adult life[3] (reviewed in Allard, 1989; Wall, 1988;

---

[3]Anatomy refers to structure, for example the physical locations and patterns of nerves and their connections. Physiology refers to function, in particular the patterns of electrical response of nerve cells. Thus, changes in synaptic strengths or weights, that is the effectiveness

Merzenich, Allard, Jenkins, & Recanzone, 1988). The body is mapped in a locally continuous way onto the cortex. This map can change throughout adult life with changing patterns of peripheral activity,[4] so that a more active peripheral area can come to activate a larger area of cortex while less active peripheral areas correspondingly lose cortical space (Merzenich, Kaas, Wall, Sur, Nelsen, & Felleman, 1983; Wall, Kaas, Sur, Nelson, Felleman, & Merzenich, 1986). Interpretation of many of these results is complicated by the fact that these changes, though assessed in cortex, may originate at any of several levels from the periphery to the cortex.

Some of the most striking results in adult somatosensory cortex are those in which only peripheral correlations, not amounts of activity, are altered. The monkey's fingers are represented in discrete, though adjacent, patches of somatosensory cortex. As a rule, individual cortical cells in these areas have receptive fields restricted to a single finger. Thus, the transition from the representation of one finger to that of the next is normally sudden and discontinuous. Patterns of correlation were altered by sewing together the skin surfaces of two adjacent fingers (Clark, Allard, Jenkins, & Merzenich, 1988). This leads the normally uncorrelated skin surfaces at the surgical boundary, which originate from separate fingers, to become correlated in their activity much as adjacent skin surfaces on any other continuous patch of skin. After several months, the cortical map was found to vary continuously from one finger to another. A large intermediate region of cortex was activated by both fingers.

Representations in adult somatosensory cortex generally can be moved in these experiments by no more than 600-700 μm across cortex (Allard, 1989; Merzenich et al., 1988). This distance limit has been interpreted to mean that the plasticity involves the strengthening or weakening of existing synapses rather than the movement of synapses to entirely new areas of cortex. That is, areas of the periphery might be represented by inputs that project effective synapses to the normal area of representation, and weak or relatively ineffective synapses to adjacent areas over 600-700μm; these relative strengths might be dynamically maintained by activity patterns, and alter when activity patterns alter.

In many regions in which two neural inputs innervate a single output region, a segregation of the two inputs into discrete columnar patches or stripes resembling ocular dominance columns is seen. In somatosensory cortex, neurons representing rapidly adapting and slowly adapting periph-

---

of synapses in activating the postsynaptic cell, without broad changes in the patterns of physical connectivity, would with current techniques only be detectable as a physiological change in the responses of the cells.

[4]Peripheral in this context refers essentially to the skin; more generally, to those areas that have receptors to detect somatosensory stimulation.

eral receptors are organized into patches, as are those representing glabrous and dorsal portions of skin (Merzenich, Nelson, Kaas, Stryker, Jenkins, Zook, Cynader, & Schoppmann, 1987; Sur, Wall, & Kaas, 1984). In primate prefrontal cortex (Goldman & Nauta, 1977; Goldman-Rakic & Schwartz, 1982; reviewed in Goldman-Rakic, 1984) and somatosensory cortex (Jones, Burton, & Porter, 1975; Jones, Coulter, & Wise, 1979), intra-hemispheric and inter-hemispheric (callosal) cortico-cortical connections terminate in alternating columns. Inputs from prefrontal and temporal cortices to caudate nucleus similarly are interdigitated (Selemon & Goldman-Rakic, 1985). In some cases the cells projecting to two different regions from one region are somewhat segregated and interdigitating (Arikuni, Sakai, & Kubota, 1983; Caminiti, Zeger, Johnson, Urbano, & Georgopoulos, 1985; Jones & Wise, 1977; Schwartz & Goldman-Rakic, 1984). There is no evidence at present as to whether these various patterns are established in an activity-dependent manner. However, these patterns are suggestive that the activity-dependent processes that lead to ocular dominance segregation may not be specific to the visual or sensory systems, but rather may occur more generally.

The optic tectum in mammals is known as the superior colliculus. In some higher mammals, it receives direct inputs from both eyes, which terminate in ocular dominance patches (reviewed in Fawcett & O'Leary, 1985; Schmidt & Tieman, 1985). These patches develop from an initially uniform, overlapping innervation by the two eyes. Activity dependence is indicated by the fact that monocular deprivation, if initiated sufficiently early in the segregation process, leads to a change in the size of the ipsilateral projection. The segregation process in this case involves death of some input cells rather than simply rearrangements and movement of terminal arbors.

The superior colliculus or optic tectum of mammals and birds contains a map of auditory space as well as a map of visual space (reviewed in Knudsen, Du Lac, & Esterly, 1987). The map of auditory space is synthesized from cues of inter-ear time and intensity differences that are changing rapidly during development as the animal's head and ears grow. Hence there is developmentally a need for plasticity to adjust the auditory space map to changing cues. In the barn owl, vision appears to calibrate the auditory map, as binocular visual deprivation from birth leads to a less precise and somewhat abnormal auditory spatial map (Knudsen, 1988). Developmental plasticity in the barn owl keeps the auditory map in register with the visual map. During a sensitive period in a young owl, plugging of one ear leads to an abnormal auditory map that is in register with the visual map only when the ear remains plugged (Knudsen, 1985). Once the head and ears reach adult size, this capacity to develop an abnormal map in response to abnormal auditory experience is lost. During a longer, critical period, exposure to normal auditory cues can reestablish a normal auditory map in a previously earplugged owl. This readjustment, as assessed behaviorally, occurs only if visual cues are present, and will match the auditory map to even a distorted visual map created by prisms (Knudsen & Knudsen, 1985). These phenomena may involve error-correcting mechanisms, in which visual assessment of errors in localization are used to correct the auditory map, rather than simple correlation-based mechanisms, in which visual and auditory inputs whose activities are correlated come to coinnervate tectal cells.

Other auditory maps may also show developmental dependence on patterns of neural activity. In the inferior colliculus of the mouse, an auditory area, cells normally sharpen their tuning for frequency of auditory inputs during the second and third postnatal weeks. Forcing all afferents to fire synchronously during this time by choice of an appropriate auditory stimulus prevents this sharpening (Sanes & Constantine-Paton, 1985), suggesting that sharpening may normally be caused by correlated firing among afferents tuned to similar frequencies. Circumstantial arguments based on contrasting the diffuse nature of anatomical projections with the precision and specificity of physiological responses suggest that many features of the auditory projection in mammals may require correlation-based mechanisms for their development and maintenance (Merzenich, Jenkins, & Middlebrooks, 1984).

In summary, in two well-studied systems, the mammalian visual cortex and optic tectum of fish and amphibia, strong evidence exists for correlation-based mechanisms of activity-dependent plasticity. Such mechanisms are strongly implicated in visual cortex in the development of ocular dominance columns, and in optic tectum in the development of ocular dominance stripes, receptive field refinement and, in one species, retinotopic matching of inputs. A wide variety of other systems display phenomena suggestive that similar mechanisms are active.

The selection of systems presented here should not blind one to the existence of many neural systems whose development may not depend on activity. A great variety of mechanisms underlie neural development and plasticity (Purves & Lichtman, 1985). For example, exchange of trophic (nutritive) factors between neurons and their targets allows nerve cells to dynamically adjust themselves to changing conditions presented by evolutionary development and individual growth (Purves, 1988; Purves, Snider, & Voyvodic, 1988). Similarly, biochemical markers of location, gradients of differential adhesion and fiber-fiber interactions can be used to organize topographic maps and to match innervation to target size and shape (Fraser, 1980; Willshaw & von der Malsburg, 1979). Activity-dependent mechanisms are of special interest because they make use of the functional activity of nerve cells to effect such dynamic adjustments. These mechanisms allow the nervous system to be altered and shaped by the animal's experience, and so provide a potential substrate for learning. Evolution has likely led to a precise selection of those times and locations in which the nervous system may be so altered by neural activity.

Having reviewed systems in which correlation-based mechanisms of synaptic plasticity may be active, I now turn briefly to consider the biological mechanisms that may underlie such plasticity.

BIOLOGICAL SUBSTRATES FOR CORRELATION-BASED MECHANISMS

At this writing, there is a single elegant and well-established mechanism known to embody a Hebbian mechanism of correlation-based synaptic plasticity. This is plasticity mediated by the N-methyl-D-aspartate (NMDA) receptor in certain areas of hippocampus (also discussed in McNaughton & Nadel, chap. 1 in this volume; Bear & Cooper, chap. 2 in this volume).

Synaptic currents triggered by activation of the NMDA receptor are both transmitter-activated and voltage-dependent (see reviews in Mayer & West-brook, 1987; Nicoll, Kauer, & Melenka, 1988). Thus, the currents are activated only if the presynaptic cell is active, releasing transmitter to bind to the receptor, and the postsynaptic cell is at least locally depolarized, alleviating a voltage-dependent block of the NMDA receptor-activated channels. This means that NMDA receptors provide precisely the trigger required by a Hebbian mechanism: a signal of correlated pre- and postsynaptic activation. When the NMDA-activated channels are opened they, unlike other related channels, allow calcium to enter the postsynaptic cell. Calcium in turn can trigger many events that may lead to strengthening of the synapse. Thus, in response to the signal of correlated activity, a calcium current passes that may be capable of enhancing synaptic strength. Because this calcium current can be local to a single synapse, the potentiation can be specific to active synapses.

This elegant mechanism has been implicated in a form of plasticity known as long term potentiation (LTP) in one region of hippocampus (McNaughton & Nadel, chap. 1 in this volume; reviewed in Brown, Chapman, Kairiss, & Keenan, 1988; Nicoll et al., 1988). It has clearly been shown that the conjunction of presynaptic activity and postsynaptic depolarization leads to a long-term strengthening of synaptic inputs specific to those inputs that were active. This provides a basis for cooperation and association among inputs: if a sufficient number of inputs are activated to depolarize the cell, all will be potentiated, as will any other input active while the cell remains depolarized. This potentiation occurs only if NMDA receptors are activated and if calcium is able to enter the cell through the channels activated by NMDA receptors. However, postsynaptic depolarization, transmitter activation of NMDA receptors and calcium entry is not sufficient to cause long-lasting potentiation; presynaptic activation is also necessary, perhaps to supply an additional unidentified factor (Kauer, Malenka, & Nicoll, 1988). Persistent activation of a calcium-dependent protein kinase appears necessary to the maintenance of the potentiation: blocking such kinases reversibly blocks LTP after it has been initiated (Malinow, Madison, & Tsien, 1988).

In the visual cortex and optic tectum, there is provocative, but far less compelling, evidence that NMDA receptors may be involved in activity-dependent plasticity. Understanding of the mechanisms underlying plasticity proceeds much more slowly in these systems than in hippocampus, for technical reasons. In these systems blockade of postsynaptic NMDA receptors prevents or alters the normally seen plasticity. This has been shown for ocular dominance plasticity in visual cortex (Kleinschmidt, Bear, & Singer, 1987; Bear & Cooper, chap. 2 in this volume), refinement of receptive fields in optic tectum (Cline & Constantine-Paton, 1988; Schmidt, 1988), ocular dominance segregation in optic tectum (Cline et al., 1987), and matching of the direct contralateral and indirect ipsilateral retinotopic maps in optic tectum (Scherer & Udin, 1988).

However, many mechanisms may be responsible for plasticity. It is well established that interference with the patterns of activity will disrupt or alter plasticity. Therefore, to show that activation of NMDA receptors is serving as a specific signal for activity-dependent plasticity, it is critical to show that blockade of those receptors does not otherwise interfere with activity. NMDA receptors appear to be involved in sensory-driven neural activity in many systems. We have shown that in visual cortex, normal sensory responses of cortical cells depend upon activation of NMDA receptors (Miller, Chapman, & Stryker, 1989). A similar result has been shown in somatosensory thalamus (Salt, 1986, 1987), and preliminary evidence of this exists in the LGN (Moody & Sillito, 1988) and optic tectum (Fox & Fraser, 1987). Hence, the effects of NMDA-receptor blockade on plasticity in visual cortex and optic tectum may simply represent the effect of blocking postsynaptic activity. It therefore remains unclear whether the NMDA-receptor mechanism of Hebbian plasticity is operating either in visual cortex or in optic tectum.

Many mechanisms have been proposed to underly plasticity. The final mechanism maintaining LTP in hippocampus appears to involve activation of a protein kinase. At least two different kinases may be capable of causing such potentiation, protein kinase C and type II calcium/calmodulin-dependent protein kinase (CaM kinase II) (Brown et al., 1988; Nicoll et al., 1988). Protein kinase C can be activated either by calcium or by activation of phosphatidyl inositol metabolism, while CaM Kinase II is activated by calcium (reviewed in Schwartz & Greenberg, 1987). Activation of phosphatidyl inositol metabolism can itself trigger release of intracellular calcium (reviewed in Nahorski, 1988). Each kinase can constitute a biochemical "switch": brief activation can alter the kinase so that it remains activated for a long period independent of the activating agent (Schwartz & Greenberg, 1987). CaM kinase II is localized in large quantities at the postsynaptic density in mammalian brain. Theoretical study has suggested that the kinetic properties of CaM kinase II allow the many molecules in the postsynaptic density to collectively store graded information (Lisman & Goldring, 1988), which presumably could be translated into graded levels of synaptic strength.

There may be many routes to the same final mechanism of plasticity. Calcium can enter the cell through activation of NMDA receptors, but it may also enter through voltage-dependent calcium channels or be released from intracellular stores. Voltage-dependent calcium channels, if located on dendritic spines, might contribute to a Hebbian mechanism (Gamble & Koch, 1987; see also Coss & Perkel, 1985; Miller, Rall, & Rinzel, 1985). Both voltage-dependent calcium channels and phophatidyl inositol metabolism can be activated or modulated by a wide variety of neurotransmitters and receptors (reviewed in Nahorski, 1988; Tsien, Lipscombe, Madison, Bley, & Fox, 1988).

Similarly, there may be many final mechanisms by which plasticity can be achieved. Cortical cells might, when active, release diffusible modulatory or trophic factors that are taken up in an activity-dependent way by presynaptic terminals and alter their synaptic strength (Fawcett & O'Leary, 1985; Garthwaite, Charles, & Chess-Williams, 1988; Lichtman & Purves, 1981; Piomelli, Volterra, Dale, Siegelbaum, Kandel, Schwartz, & Belardetti, 1987; Purves, 1988).[5] Such factors may also act on glial cells, which in turn may cause synaptic modification (Garthwaite et al., 1988; Muller, Engel, & Singer, 1988). Lynch and Baudry (1984) suggested that activation of a postsynaptic calcium-activated protease may expose postsynaptic receptors and thus enhance synaptic response. This protease when activated may also cause long-term activation of the protein kinases discussed earlier (Schwartz & Greenberg, 1987). At the neuromuscular junction, plasticity may be mediated by activity-dependent release by postsynaptic cells of proteases that destroy synaptic terminals, combined with protection from the effects of these proteases by presynaptic activity (O'Brien, Ostberg, & Vrbova, 1980). Theoretical proposals had previously been made that Hebb-type rules could be achieved by degradation of nonstabilized synapses, and stabilization of synapses by correlated pre- and postsynaptic activity (Changeux & Danchin, 1976; Stent, 1973). Mechanisms by which

---

[5]This proposal also provides a possible alternative or additional mechanism by which activation of NMDA receptors may lead to synaptic plasticity. Two candidate diffusible modulatory factors are released by neurons in some systems specifically in response to NMDA receptor activation (Dumuis, Sebben, Haynes, Pin, & Bockaert, 1988; Garthwaite et al., 1988).

calcium and synaptic activity might stabilize synapses have been suggested (Kater, Mattson, Cohan, & Conner, 1988).

Thus, evolution has had many tools available to construct the correlation-dependent mechanisms that we have seen acting in development. Although we lack detailed biochemical knowledge of the mechanisms underlying plasticity in these systems, it is profitable to study theoretically the outcomes to be expected from the general correlation-based rules shared by such mechanisms. Aspects of development common to such rules may be determined in a manner largely independent of the underlying details. This can allow distinctions to be drawn between general classes of mechanisms, such that each class produces a distinct developmental outcome. These points will be illustrated through theoretical studies of the development of ocular dominance columns in visual cortex.

THEORETICAL STUDIES OF DEVELOPMENT WITH A CORRELATION-BASED MECHANISM

The system of ocular dominance columns in mammalian visual cortex, which we have studied (Miller, 1989a; Miller, Keller, & Stryker, 1986, 1988, 1989; Miller & Stryker, 1988, 1989; Miller, Stryker, & Keller, 1988), has a number of advantages as a model system for the study of correlation-based mechanisms. First, it is the system that is best explored phenomenologically. Second, the nature of the competition simplifies the analysis. The competition is binary, between left- and right-eye inputs, rather than between larger numbers of patterns. The two sets of inputs begin from nearly equal strengths, so that one can assume a symmetry between them. Third, a large-scale structure organized across many postsynaptic cells develops. This enables distinctions to be drawn between mechanisms that would be indistinguishable in their action on a single isolated postsynaptic cell. The second and third advantages apply equally to ocular dominance stripes in frog optic tectum. There is a fourth advantage of visual cortex. Geniculate and visual cortical cells have all been born, and the geniculo-cortical projection has grown into layer 4, before column development begins (Luskin & Shatz, 1985; Rakic, 1976, 1977; Shatz, 1983; Shatz & Luskin, 1986). In cats, where column development begins after birth, it is clear that this projection is retinotopically ordered before column development begins (Hubel & Wiesel, 1963; Sherk & Stryker, 1976). One can therefore regard the retinotopic map as largely fixed while columns are forming, and thus ignore movement of synapses as opposed to changes in their strengths.[6] In the frog, in contrast, new cells are continuously born in both the eyes and the tectum. Differential patterns of growth of the eyes and the tectum force the retinotopic map to continuously reorganize, and this involves a mixture of activity-dependent and activity-independent interactions (Easter & Stuermer, 1984; Fraser, 1985; Reh & Constantine-Paton, 1984).

Formulation of a Simple Model

We model the LGN as two two-dimensional layers, one responding to each eye, and the cortex as a single two-dimensional layer representing layer 4. This model could apply equally to any situation in which two input layers innervate a single output layer. We let roman letters $x,y,$ . . . represent two-dimensional positions in cortex, and greek letters $\alpha,\beta,$ . . . represent two-dimensional positions in the LGN (Fig. 7.7). These positions are taken to be *retinotopic* positions, so that the position α can refer to a position either in the left- or right-eye LGN layer, and so that $x - \alpha$ can be meaningfully defined as the distance across cortex between the position x and the retinotopic position in cortex corresponding to α. $S^L(x,\alpha,t)$, $S^R(x,\alpha,t)$ designate the total synaptic strength or weight between LGN position α in the left or right eye, respectively, and cortical position x, at time t.

A few elements are crucial to any correlation-based model of development (Fig. 7.7). These are the elements that determine how synapses can influence one another's development. One element is correlation in the activities of the inputs. This is described by a set of correlation functions, $C^{LL}(\alpha - \beta)$, $C^{LR}(\alpha - \beta)$, which tell the correlation in activity between the left-eye input from α and, respectively, the left- or right-eye input from β. C^{RL} and C^{RR} are defined similarly. A second element is the initial connectivity. This is described by an arbor function, so called because it characterizes the extent of the terminal arborizations of inputs, as well as the dendritic spread of cortical cells. This is also known in connectionist literature as a fan-in or fan-out function. The arbor function, $A(x - \alpha)$, tells the number of synapses made between position α and position x. A third element is interaction across cortex, by which activity at one cortical location

---

[6]Although the retinotopic map does not substantially change during the period of column formation, it remains possible that the synaptic plasticity associated with development of ocular dominance occurs through continual local sprouting and retraction of synapses, rather than through modification of the strengths of fixed synapses as we assume here. It is likely that a model involving local sprouting and retraction would require only small additions to the framework we develop here, but this remains an important issue for analysis.

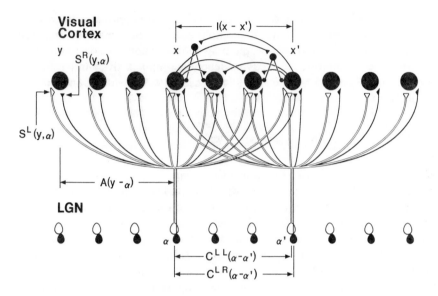

FIG. 7.7. Illustration of the major elements of the model and the notation. The LGN is modeled as consisting of two layers, one serving each eye. Each layer is two-dimensional, though only one dimension is illustrated. Greek letters α, α' label two-dimensional geniculate positions. The cortex is modeled as a single, two-dimensional layer with positions labeled by roman letters x, x', y. In the figure, x and x' are taken to be the cortical positions retinotopically corresponding to α and α', respectively. Geniculate cells project synapses to a range of cortical cells, centered about the retinotopically corresponding cortical position. The anatomical strength of the projection (the number of synapses) from the geniculate cell of either eye at α to the cortical cell at position y is proportional to the arbor function $A(y - \alpha)$. $A(y - \alpha)$ depends on the distance between y and the point x that corresponds retinotopically to α. The physiological strength of the projection (the effectiveness of the geniculate cell's activity in driving the cortical cell) is given by the total synaptic strength, $S^L(y,\alpha)$ for the left eye or $S^R(y,\alpha)$ for the right eye. S^L and S^R change during development in the model, while the arbor function A is held fixed; the assumption is made that anatomical changes occur late in development, after a pattern of synaptic strengths is established. Geniculate inputs are locally correlated in their firing. The correlation of a left-eye afferent at α with a left-eye afferent at α' is given by $C^{LL}(\alpha - \alpha')$, while its correlation with a right-eye afferent at α' is given by $C^{LR}(\alpha - \alpha')$. There is an influence across cortex, by which activation at the point x' influences growth of synapses at the point x. The sign and strength of this influence is given by the intracortical interaction function, $I(x - x')$.

From Miller, Keller, and Stryker, 1989. © 1989 by the AAAS.

influences the effectiveness of correlated synapses on different cortical cells at nearby locations. In the absence of such interactions, the competition occurring on each cortical cell would be independent, and hence one would not expect to see development of large-scale clustering of cortical properties such as ocular dominance. This intracortical influence is summarized by a cortical interaction function, $I(x - y)$, described further later. A fourth element is some means of stabilization to ensure that the strengths of individual synapses, and the total synaptic strength over any cell, stay within some bounded ranges. This framework can be used to study a variety of biological mechanisms. With knowledge of the three functions characterizing a neural system — the correlation functions, arbor function, and cortical interaction function — many aspects of development can be predicted, in ways that depend only very generally on the mode of stabilization.

The cortical interaction function is particularly dependent on the biological mechanism proposed to underlie plasticity. Therefore, understanding the dependence of developmental outcome on this function provides one of the key means of distinguishing between classes of mechanisms. In a Hebbian mechanism, the cortical interaction function is determined by intracortical synaptic connections. Two synapses firing in synchrony at distinct points in cortex will both tend to excite their postsynaptic cells. If the two postsynaptic cells excite one another, the two synapses will therefore increase the chance that the other's postsynaptic cell will be excited and hence will tend to enhance one another's growth via a Hebbian mechanism. Conversely if the two postsynaptic cells inhibit one another, the two synapses will tend to inhibit one another's growth. Thus, the cortical interaction function for a Hebbian mechanism is positive over distances at which cortical cells tend to excite one another, and negative over distances at which cortical cells tend to inhibit one another. For mechanisms that involve the release and uptake of a trophic or modification factor, the cortical interaction function must also describe spread of influence across cortex due to diffusion.

We ignore the detailed temporal structure of cortical activation, and regard interactions as instantaneous. We hypothesize that the tendency of two inputs to fire in a correlated way is the key feature to be abstracted, and the finer details of activity patterns can be ignored. We also assume that the time scale over which inputs must be correlated in order to influence one another's growth is much smaller than the time scale over which synapses are appreciably changing their strengths.

After averaging over input patterns, and ignoring the problem of stabilization for the moment, we arrive at an equation describing correlation-based mechanisms of development (derived in appendix 1). This equation expresses the changes in synaptic strengths with time, as a function of the

correlations among afferents, the spread of arbors, the intracortical interactions, and the synaptic strengths themselves:

$$\frac{d}{dt}S^L(x,\alpha,t) = \lambda A(x-\alpha)\sum_{y,\beta}I(x-y)[C^{LL}(\alpha - \beta)S^L(y,\beta,t)$$
$$+ C^{LR}(\alpha - \beta)S^R(y,\beta,t)] - \gamma S^L(x,\alpha,t) - \epsilon^L A(x - \alpha)$$

$$\frac{d}{dt}S^R(x,\alpha,t) = \lambda A(x-\alpha)\sum_{y,\beta}I(x-y)[C^{RR}(\alpha - \beta)S^R(y,\beta,t)$$
$$+ C^{RL}(\alpha - \beta)S^L(y,\beta,t)] - \gamma S^R(x,\alpha,t) - \epsilon^R A(x - \alpha)$$

(1)

λ, γ, ϵ^L and ϵ^R are constants. The last two terms of each equation express
decay or growth of synapses in the absense of interactions between them.
The first term expresses interactions between synapses, and can be summarized as follows. First, the influence exerted by any one synapse on another,
is a product of the correlation in activity between those two synapses (how
likely are they to be firing together?), the intracortical interaction (if they
are firing together, how do they influence one another?), and the strength
of the influencing synapse. For two synapses on the same postsynaptic cell,
this is just the product of their correlations and the influencing synaptic
strength, weighted by the constant $I(0)$. For synapses on different postsynaptic cells, this influence is weighted by the intracortical interaction
$I(x - y)$ between the respective postsynaptic locations. Second, interactions
are linear: The change in one synapse is a simple sum of the influences
exerted on it by each other synapse. Linearity is not necessary to the
analysis, but is used for simplicity at this stage. Third, to find the change in
total synaptic strength, sum over all influencing synapses, then multiply by
the arbor function, which represents the number of synapses being influenced. We have taken the three functions, correlations, connectivity, and
cortical interactions, to be fixed (time-invariant) as ocular dominance
columns develop.

Several types of stabilization are considered. We assume that individual
synapses cannot increase beyond some maximum strength, nor decrease
below some minimum. For synapses from LGN to cortex, the minimum
synaptic strength is zero: these synapses biologically are exclusively excitatory. We also consider the effects of conserving total synaptic strength over
a cortical cell or a geniculate cell, or of limiting these totals to remain within
a bounded range. Some justification for such limits is provided by
biological evidence for intrinsic limits to the total number of synapses

supported by a cell, though there is no direct evidence as to limits to total synaptic strength. In monkey visual cortex synapse number does not appear to be affected by visual experience during the time of ocular dominance column development (Bourgeois, Jastreboff, & Rakic, 1989). Similarly, in the goldfish optic tectum, total synapse number appears conserved in an activity-independent manner during post-regeneration map refinement (Hayes & Meyer, 1989a, 1989b). These findings suggest that activity is involved in determining the arrangements or strengths of synapses but not their number. When the full complement of retinal cells are forced to innervate only half a tectum, the number of synapses per tectal cell remains normal, indicating that on average each retinal cell makes only half the normal number of synapses (Hayes & Meyer, 1988b; Murray, Sharma, & Edwards, 1982). This suggests that there is a limited number of postsynaptic sites per tectal cell, for which incoming neurons must compete. Conversely, in several systems, if inputs are given a larger than normal target structure, they are unable to innervate the target cells with normal density, indicating intrinsic limits in the total innervation that can be supported by an input cell (Brown, Jansen, & Van Essen, 1976; Fladby & Jansen, 1987; Hayes & Meyer, 1988a; see also Schneider, 1973).

To understand how development proceeds under correlation-based mechanisms as modeled in these equations, we begin by considering development of a single, isolated cortical cell receiving inputs from the LGN. We then consider the reverse, the development of two isolated geniculate cells, one from each eye, projecting to the cortex. Finally, we consider how these two processes are knit together, and what new features are added, in development of the full system: two layers of geniculate cells projecting to a cortical layer.

How An Isolated Cortical Cell Develops

For an isolated cortical cell, the equations simplify. Suppressing the cortical index, x, letting $x = \alpha = 0$ be the cortical and LGN locations retinotopically corresponding to the position of the cortical cell, and taking $I(0) = 1$, the equations become

$$\frac{d}{dt}S^L(\alpha,t) = \lambda A(\alpha)\sum_\beta [C^{LL}(\alpha - \beta)S^L(\beta,t) + C^{LR}(\alpha - \beta)S^R(\beta,t)]$$
$$- \gamma S^L(\alpha,t) - \epsilon^L A(\alpha)$$

$$\frac{d}{dt}S^R(\alpha,t) = \lambda A(\alpha)\sum_\beta [C^{RR}(\alpha - \beta)S^R(\beta,t) + C^{RL}(\alpha - \beta)S^L(\beta,t)]$$
$$- \gamma S^R(\alpha,t) - \epsilon^R A(\alpha)$$

$$(2)$$

Figure 7.8 shows a typical developmental sequence for a cell under this equation. For this sequence, we have considered a 13 by 13 square of geniculate cells from each eye, with a connectivity $A(\alpha)$ to the cortical cell that tapered in strength gradually from the center of the square and was set to zero outside a circle of radius $6\frac{1}{2}$. Correlations between inputs from the

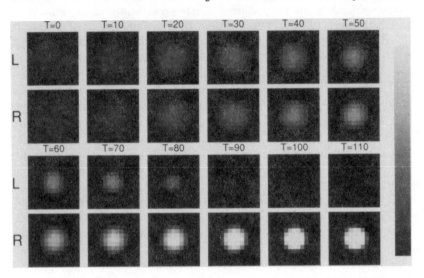

FIG.7.8. Development of an isolated cortical cell under equation 2. Vertically paired 13 by 13 squares show synaptic strengths of left- and right-eye inputs from each of 13 by 13 retinotopic positions at one time. The greyscale codes total synaptic strength from each input position, from strength 0 (black) to 11.2 (the maximum value of $8A(\alpha)$, white). Synaptic strengths at 12 successive times are shown. Time proceeds from left to right and top to bottom, beginning with the randomly assigned initial condition ($T = 0$) at top left and concluding with the 110th iteration ($T = 110$) at bottom right. Synaptic strength becomes concentrated in the center of the receptive field, and then becomes monocular as right-eye inputs grow at the expense of left-eye inputs. The cortical cell was constrained to keep a constant synaptic strength. This constraint was achieved by subtracting $\epsilon(t)A(\alpha)$ from each total synaptic strength after each iteration, where $\epsilon(t) = \dfrac{\Sigma_\alpha \left[\frac{d}{dt}S^L(\alpha,t) + \frac{d}{dt}S^R(\alpha,t)\right]}{\Sigma_\alpha[A^L(\alpha) + A^R(\alpha)]}$ and $A^L = A^R = A$.

Synaptic strengths were frozen if their value reached zero: they were no longer allowed to change, assigned derivatives of zero and omitted from the constraint. Parameters used were $\lambda = 0.0025$, $\gamma = \epsilon^L = \epsilon^R = 0$. The arbor function $A(\alpha)$ was that illustrated in Fig. 7.9. The correlation function was the same-eye correlation function with gaussian parameter 0.3 of Fig. 7.9.

same eye, C^{LL} and C^{RR}, were taken to fall gradually from one to zero as separation between the two inputs varied from zero to about six grid points; opposite eyes were neither correlated nor anticorrelated ($C^{LR} = C^{RL} = 0$). The arbor function and correlation function used are illustrated in Fig. 7.9. The cortical cell was constrained to keep a constant synaptic strength, so that one synapse's gain must be some other synapse's loss. Individual total synaptic strengths $S(\alpha)$ began with a randomly assigned synaptic strength near $A(\alpha)$. These synaptic strengths were then allowed to decrease until they reached zero, or increase until they reached $8A(\alpha)$.

Two features are immediately apparent from the simulation. First, central synapses in the receptive field grow more rapidly than do peripheral synapses, leading receptive fields to refine in size. Second, the synapses of one eye gradually come to grow faster than the synapses of the other, leading to a monocular cortical cell that receives inputs from only one eye. Development of monocularity occurs more slowly than refinement of the receptive field. These results are robust: they occur for all initial conditions tried, and are relatively insensitive to variations in the functions as will be discussed.

These features are easy to understand. Inputs in the center of the receptive field have more correlated neighbors than inputs in the periphery, provided that the correlations decrease with distance. Hence, the center of the receptive field will grow faster than the periphery. Similarly, one eye is likely initially to have slightly more total or central synaptic strength than the other due to the random initial conditions. This eye tends to gain slightly more strength than the other at each iteration, leading it to increase its advantage in a feedforward, accelerating process. This occurs more slowly than refinement, because the two eyes start out much more equal in numbers and strengths of correlated neighbors than do central versus peripheral synapses.

This understanding can be made more precise from consideration of the model equations. The equations are most illuminating if we transform them from right- and left-eye variables, S^R and S^L, to sum and difference variables: $S^S = S^R + S^L$, $S^D = S^R - S^L$. We assume the two eyes are equal in all respects as in the simulation, so that $C^{LL} = C^{RR} = C^{\text{SameEye}}$, $C^{LR} = C^{RL} = C^{\text{OppEye}}$, $\epsilon^L = \epsilon^R = \epsilon$. Define $C^S = C^{\text{SameEye}} + C^{\text{OppEye}}$, $C^D = C^{\text{SameEye}} - C^{\text{OppEye}}$. Then Eq. 2 becomes

$$\frac{d}{dt}S^S(\alpha,t) = \lambda A(\alpha)\sum_{\beta}C^S(\alpha - \beta)S^S(\beta,t) - \gamma S^S(\alpha,t) - 2\epsilon A(\alpha)$$

$$\frac{d}{dt}S^D(\alpha,t) = \lambda A(\alpha)\sum_{\beta}C^D(\alpha - \beta)S^D(\beta,t) - \gamma S^D(\alpha,t)$$

$$(3)$$

AFFERENT CORRELATION FUNCTIONS

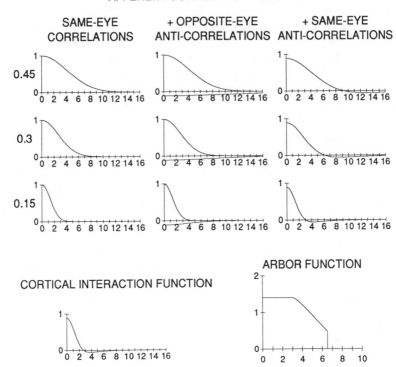

SAME-EYE CORRELATIONS   + OPPOSITE-EYE ANTI-CORRELATIONS   + SAME-EYE ANTI-CORRELATIONS

0.45

0.3

0.15

CORTICAL INTERACTION FUNCTION

ARBOR FUNCTION

FIG. 7.9. Functions used in simulations and numerical calculations for isolated cortical or geniculate cells. Value of function, vertical axis, versus distance in grid intervals, horizontal axis. All functions are circularly symmetric in two dimensions. A 13 by 13 square grid of inputs potentially connects to a single cortical cell, and conversely an input potentially connects to a 13 by 13 grid of cortical cells. Top: Correlation functions $C(\alpha)$. These summarize the correlation in activity between two afferents separated by a retinotopic distance α, either serving the same eye ($C^{LL}(\alpha)$ or $C^{RR}(\alpha)$, assumed equal), or serving opposite eyes ($C^{LR}(\alpha)$ or $C^{RL}(\alpha)$, assumed equal). The correlation functions in the left column (same-eye correlations) are positive within each eye, and zero between the two eyes: $C^{LL}(\alpha) = e^{-\alpha^2/(xD)^2}$, where $D = 13$ is the arbor diameter and $x = 0.45$, 0.3 or 0.15 for the top, middle, or bottom row respectively, and $C^{LR} = 0$. The positive correlations within each eye are shown. The correlation functions in the middle column (+ opposite-eye anticorrelations) are positive within each eye as in the left column, as shown by the curves above the horizontal axes; but in addition there are weaker, more broadly ranging negative correlations between the two eyes, shown by the curves below the horizontal axes. These negative correlations are given by $C^{LR}(\alpha) = \frac{1}{9}e^{-\alpha^2/(3xD)^2}$. The correlation functions in the right row (+ same-eye anticorrelations) have

Note that S^S and S^D have become decoupled, each developing independently of the other, which simplifies analysis.[7]

Individual total synaptic strengths $S(\alpha)$ begin with a randomly assigned synaptic strength $(1.0 + \eta(\alpha))A(\alpha)$ where $\eta(\alpha)$ is a number randomly drawn from a uniform distribution between -0.2 and 0.2. At the initial condition, then, $S^S(\alpha) = (2 + \eta^S(\alpha))A(\alpha)$, $S^D(\alpha) = \eta^D(\alpha)A(\alpha)$, where $\eta^S = \eta^L + \eta^R$, $\eta^D = \eta^L - \eta^R$, and η^S and η^D both range between -0.4 and 0.4. Since η^S is small, near the initial condition we can approximate $S^S(\alpha) \approx 2A(\alpha)$. Hence near the initial condition our equations become (ignoring the decay terms)

$$\frac{d}{dt}S^S(\alpha) = 2\lambda A(\alpha)(C^S * A)(\alpha)$$

$$\frac{d}{dt}S^D(\alpha) = \lambda A(\alpha)(C^D * (\eta A))(\alpha)$$

(4)

where the $*$ indicates convolution, $X * Y(\alpha) = \Sigma_\beta X(\alpha - \beta)Y(\beta)$.

Refinement of the receptive field is determined by the equation for S^S, the summed synaptic strength. Sites in the receptive field where $C^S * A$ is larger will initially grow faster. A is always positive or zero, and either flat or decreasing with increasing distance. Therefore if C^S is nonnegative and

---

[7]S^L and S^R appeared decoupled also, for our choice of correlation functions for which $C^{LR} = C^{RL} = 0$. However, they were coupled by the constraints, which fix $\Sigma_\alpha S^S(\alpha)$ to be a constant but do not modify the equation for S^D.

---

these same negative correlations added to the positive correlations within each eye, and have zero correlation between the two eyes. This creates a "Mexican hat" function within each eye, so that inputs are correlated at shorter distances and anticorrelated at longer distances, as illustrated. Bottom left: Cortical interaction function $I(x)$. This is a Mexican hat function, given by gaussians as for the correlation functions but with $x = 0.1333$. Bottom right: Arbor function $A(\alpha)$, representing the relative number of synapses made by an input to a cortical cell when the retinotopic position of the two differs by α. The arbor function tapers from the center of the 13 by 13 grid of inputs, so that more outlying inputs project less densely, and is set to zero for $\alpha > 6.5$. The function is constructed as follows: Inputs are modeled as projecting uniform circular arborizations of radius 6, and cortical cells as extending uniform circular dendritic fields of radius 3. The arbor function $A(\alpha)$ is taken proportional to the overlap of such an input arborization and cortical dendritic field when the two cells are separated by $\alpha < 6.5$. While these scales are arbitrary, they determine a scale in terms of which the other functions can be defined: One can characterize the correlation function by its variation over an arbor radius, in this case approximately ± 6 grid intervals.

decreases over the distance across a receptive field, central synapses will grow faster than peripheral ones. If C^S is perfectly flat, refinement will not occur. If C^S is "Mexican hat," positive at short distances and negative at longer distances, then, depending on the shapes of C^S and A, central synapses may grow more slowly than peripheral ones, by virtue of having more negatively correlated neighbors.

Development of monocularity is determined by the equation for S^D, the difference in strength between the two eyes. The initial condition for S^D is a small, random perturbation of $S^D = 0$, which may be positive or negative at each point α. This initial condition can be described as a mixture of very small amounts of a set of *characteristic patterns* of S^D, much as a curve can be decomposed by fourier analysis into a set of sine and cosine waves. Technically, these characteristic patterns of ocular dominance are the *eigenfunctions* of the operator that determines the time development of S^D. This is described more fully in appendix 2. The characteristic patterns are distinguished by the fact that each grows independently of the others, each at its own rate. The patterns grow exponentially, so that the fastest-growing pattern quickly dominates. A pattern is monocular if it is all positive or all negative, representing domination throughout the receptive field by a single eye.

The initial condition of S^D is a random mixture of small amounts of each characteristic pattern. Hence, the development of monocularity is determined by the answers to two questions. First, is the fastest-growing characteristic pattern of S^D monocular? If it is, there will be an intrinsic tendency for the cell to develop ocular dominance. Second, if it is monocular, what determines its relative advantage in growth rate over binocular patterns and over the tendency of S^S to refine and perhaps reach saturation? These will determine the speed and robustness with which ocular dominance will emerge.

The nature of the fastest-growing pattern is determined in large part by the fastest-growing eigenfunction of the correlation function C^D, though the arbor function also plays a role.[8]. The dependence on C^D is illustrated in Fig. 7.10. This shows the three fastest-growing characteristic patterns that result from each choice of correlation function illustrated in Fig. 7.9.

---

[8]To a reasonable approximation, one can think of the characteristic patterns as the eigenfunctions of the correlation function, restricted to the region over which $A(\alpha)$ is nonzero, but in truth they depend upon both the arbor function and the correlation function. Some authors, looking at similar equations, have described the solutions as the *principal components,* or eigenfunctions, of the correlation matrix (Baldi & Hornik, 1989; Linsker, 1988; Oja, 1982; Sanger, 1989). This is true if the correlation matrix tells the correlation between each pair of inputs, irrespective of their locations. If we wish the correlation function to describe the correlation between inputs just as a function of their locations, however, then the solutions must also take into account the arbor function, which describes the number of inputs from each location.

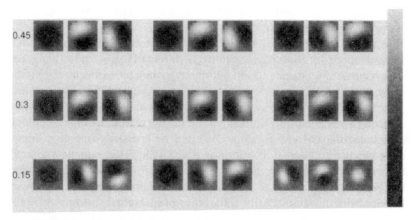

FIG. 7.10. The three fastest-growing characteristic patterns of ocular dominance, for each of the nine correlation functions of Fig. 7.9. The arbor function of Fig. 7.9 is used. These are the patterns of $S^D \equiv S^R - S^L$ which grow most quickly from an initial condition in which the two eyes' innervations are nearly equal. Each 13 by 13 square shows a pattern of S^D across a cortical cell's receptive field. The greyscale ranges from domination by one eye (white, S^D positive) to domination by the other (black, S^D negative). The sign of a pattern is arbitrary, because each pattern grows at the same rate if all its elements are multiplied by a constant such as -1. Hence, the important aspect of a pattern is not which eye dominates a region of the receptive field, but rather whether the receptive field is dominated everywhere by a single eye and hence is monocular, or is dominated by opposite eyes in different regions and hence is binocular. Each set of three patterns decreases in growth rate from left to right; the corresponding growth rates are shown in table 1.

The fastest-growing pattern of each set of three is at the set's left. This pattern is monocular provided C^D does not include significant anticorrelations within an arbor radius (about ±6 grid intervals). In the one case with such anticorrelations, the fastest-growing pattern is binocular (Fig. 7.10, lower right). The less rapidly C^D decreases with distance, the less rapidly the fastest-growing pattern decreases with distance and the more closely the pattern mimics the arbor function in shape. In the limit in which C^D is constant across an arbor diameter, the fastest-growing pattern is precisely given by the arbor function, meaning a pattern of dominance develops with equal strength at all synapses in the receptive field. This makes sense, because if C^D is constant, location in the receptive field loses all significance with respect to the synaptic modification rule for S^D. A less rapid decrease of C^D is achieved either by broadening of correlations within each eye (upward in Fig. 7.10), or by addition of broader anticorrelations between the two eyes (opposite-eye anticorrelations). A more rapidly decreasing C^D

is achieved by the reverse, or by addition of anticorrelations within each eye (same-eye anticorrelations).

A spatially broader correlation function C^D, in addition to leading to a spatially broader pattern of ocular dominance, also leads to a greater advantage in growth rate of the dominant monocular pattern relative to the other patterns (Table 7.1). In the limit of a constant C^D, the monocular pattern is the only one with a positive growth rate, all other patterns decaying away at the rate γ. This advantage in growth rate of the monocular over binocular paterns develops, because the broader correlation function increases the number of locations at which S^D's of like sign will contribute to one another's growth, and at which S^D's of opposite sign will detract from one another's growth. Opposite-eye anticorrelations also enhance the development of monocularity even if they only increase the amplitude of C^D without broadening it. This is so because they enhance the growth rates of the patterns of S^D relative to the growth rates of the patterns of S^S. A simple change in amplitude of both C^D and C^S would not enhance monocularity; it would be equivalent to a change in λ, changing the speed of development but, within a reasonable range, not altering the outcome. Opposite-eye anticorrelations, however, increase the amplitude of C^D while decreasing the amplitude of, and adding anticorrelations to, C^S. This enhances the growth of S^D relative to that of S^S. The speed of development of monocularity thus becomes proportionately faster relative to the speed of development of receptive field refinement, potentially allowing ocular dominance to develop further before saturation halts the development process.

Figure 7.11 displays the results of simulated time developments for the functions whose characteristic patterns were illustrated in Figure 7.10. As

TABLE 7.1
Growth Rates of Characteristic Patterns of Fig. 7.10.

Correlation Function	1st Pattern	2nd Pattern	3rd Pattern
Same-eye corr 0.45	67.6	23.0	23.0
+ Opp-eye anti-corr 0.45	81.0	23.8	23.8
+ Same-eye anti-corr 0.45	54.4	22.3	22.3
Same-eye corr 0.3	41.7	21.8	21.8
+ Opp-eye anti-corr 0.3	53.3	23.1	23.1
+ Same-eye anti-corr 0.3	30.7	20.5	20.5
Same-eye corr 0.15	14.0	10.9	10.9
+ Opp-eye anti-corr 0.15	21.1	13.1	13.1
+ Same-eye anti-corr 0.15	9.0	9.0	8.9

Growth rates are shown for $\lambda = 1$, $\gamma = 0$ in Eq. 3 for S^D. For other values, all growth rates would be multiplied by λ and decreased by subtraction of γ. Each pattern's growth rate is its eigenvalue, as explained in appendix 2.

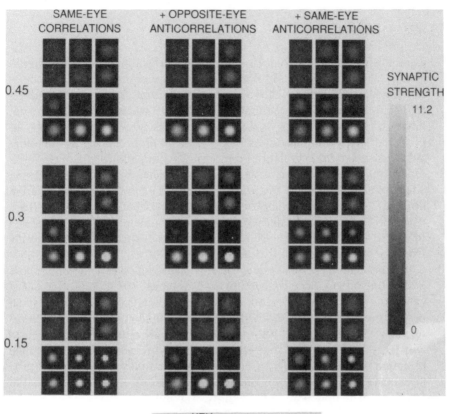

FIG. 7.11. Time development of an isolated cortical cell for each of the nine correlation functions of Fig. 7.9. As indicated in the key, for each correlation function the upper row of three left-right pairs shows inputs at times 0, 20, and 40, while the lower row of three left/right pairs shows inputs at times 60, 80, and 100. Synaptic strengths at each time are displayed as in Fig. 7.8. Broader correlations, or addition of opposite-eye anticorrelations, lead to more robust development of monocularity, while narrower correlations, or addition of same-eye anticorrelations, slow or prevent the development of monocularity. Each run used the same initial condition (time 0), arbor function, constraints, and parameters as used for Fig. 7.8, except that λ was adjusted to make initial changes in synaptic strengths more nearly equal with varying breadth of correlation function: $\lambda = 0.00075/x$, where $x = 0.45$, 0.3 or 0.15 is the parameter characterizing the breadth of the correlation functions.

expected from the analysis of the characteristic patterns, broader correlations within each eye, or addition of opposite-eye anticorrelations, enhance the development of monocularity, whereas addition of same-eye anticorrelations reduces ocular dominance. Note that when ocular dominance develops slowly, the less dominant, more slowly growing eye may, as predicted, grow to saturation before significant monocularity can develop. When same-eye anticorrelations are present within an arbor radius, development of monocularity is suppressed, as predicted by the fastest-growing characteristic pattern for that case. That pattern shows segregation of the synapses serving the two eyes into separate parts of the receptive field, whereas the time development leads to concentration of both eye's synapses in the receptive field center. This difference can be understood as resulting from the saturating nonlinearities.[9]

The basic features of our analysis of S^D remain accurate in the presence of nonlinearities. This is true for two reasons. First, near the initial condition nonlinearities can be ignored. The initial condition is a small perturbation of $S^D \equiv 0$, so that S^D is initially small everywhere. Nonlinear terms in S^D such as $(S^D)^2$ are therefore negligibly small in comparison to linear terms. Thus, although the true biological equation describing the time evolution of S^D is not likely to be linear, the equation will be linear near the initial condition. Second, the fastest-growing patterns of S^D near the initial condition will dominate the final, fully nonlinear results. This occurs because in the linear realm, the characteristic patterns grow exponentially. Therefore the fastest-growing patterns quickly become very dominant, even while the amplitudes of these patterns are still quite small and the equations still effectively linear. The final pattern will result from nonlinear interactions among these dominant patterns, and the more slowly growing patterns

---

[9]In the absence of opposite-eye anticorrelations, synapses serving the two eyes have no information as to the internal structure of one another's receptive field. Instead, interaction between the eyes, via the constraints, couples the synapses serving one eye only to the total synaptic strength serving the other eye. Hence it is not possible for the growth of the synapses serving the two eyes to be coordinated so as to occur in separate receptive field locations. The leading eigenfunction for S^D is nonetheless striped because, for synapses representing each eye, a striped pattern, positive in one part of the receptive field and negative in the other, grows faster than any other pattern in the absence of nonlinearities. This pattern is then the fastest-growing pattern of S^D, that is this pattern of initial differences between the two eyes grows faster than any other pattern of initial differences, because the two eyes grow independently except for constraints. In the presence of the saturating nonlinearities, which prevent synapses from having negative strengths, a circularly symmetric pattern representing each eye turns out to grow more rapidly than a pattern that has a positive stripe and a stripe of zero synaptic strength. Before the saturating nonlinearities are reached, a striped pattern of S^D grows, so that synapses representing each eye have a small advantage in opposite halves of the receptive field. After saturation, the pattern of S^D which emerges is approximately zero everywhere. Note that this final pattern of S^D, like that which develops early, sums to zero, so that no ocular dominance develops.

will not significantly contribute. Therefore, features common to all of the fastest-growing patterns, such as development of monocularity or, as discussed later, a wavelength of ocular dominance organization across cortex, will be robust to nonlinearities.[10] Our description of these aspects of cortical organization correctly describes the biology provided only that our postulated linear equation for S^D is a reasonable approximation to the true linear equation describing the development of S^D near the initial condition. We have shown elsewhere a specific example of the derivation of our equation for S^D as the linearization of a more complicated, nonlinear model of neural development (Miller & Stryker, 1989).

The precise developmental results will depend on the conditions that stabilize and limit synaptic growth. For example, if total synaptic strength over the cortical cell is conserved, the faster growth of the central synapses forces the peripheral synapses to lose strength and disappear. Alternative stabilization conditions might lead to retention of the peripheral synapses, but the receptive field would nonetheless become dominated, at least initially, by the faster-growing central synapses. Similarly, whether a cell becomes completely monocular or becomes dominated by one eye depends on the degree to which one eye's greater growth can force the other's to shrink before both reach saturation. Though the precise results of development or of simulation, and the absolute rates of growth, thus may depend greatly on the details, the tendencies to refinement and to ocular dominance, and the effects of features such as broader correlations or opposite-eye anticorrelations on relative rates of growth, are general.

The simple rules we have postulated are sufficient to understand the effects of experimental modifications of the normal patterns of activity. Alternating monocular deprivation or artificially induced strabismus lead to a virtual elimination of binocular cells. These treatments can be thought of as reducing opposite-eye correlations or inducing opposite-eye anticorrelations and thus enhancing the development of monocularity. Monocular deprivation, closing one eye in a young animal during a critical period, leads to dominance of most cortical cells by the open eye. We can model this in two ways. First, there will be a decrease in the amount of activity within the closed eye. This will decrease the size but not change the shape of the correlation function that describes correlations within that eye. In addition, there may be a disruption of correlated activity within the eye, which would

---

[10]It is possible for the initial pattern which develops out of linear interactions to be metastable. This means that it may eventually reorganize into a pattern with a different wavelength, determined by nonlinearities. This is unlikely in the ocular dominance system, as developmental studies (LeVay, Stryker & Shatz, 1978) show no obvious change in ocular dominance periodicity between its earliest detection and the final adult pattern. It may be possible to test this by following development of the columns within a single animal, using voltage sensitive dyes (Blasdel & Salama, 1986).

narrow the correlation function or otherwise change its shape. In either case, the closed eye would clearly be at a disadvantage, receiving less reinforcement through correlations at each timestep and hence growing more slowly than the open eye.[11]

The effects of brief monocular deprivation, modeled as a simple decrease in the amplitude of the correlation function within one eye, are illustrated in Fig. 7.12. Developmental sequences are shown with initial conditions and functions identical to those used for Fig. 7.8, except that during a period of 20 iterations the right eye is monocularly deprived. The figure shows the effects of depriving from times 0-20, 20-40, 40-60, 60-80, or 80-100, compared to the results without deprivation. Early deprivation leads to a complete shift in favor of the open eye, whereas later deprivation causes no distinguishable change from the nondeprived outcome. This is analogous to the biological result that monocular deprivation only leads to an ocular dominance shift during a critical period of development. Results in similations are virtually unchanged if deprivation remains in effect from the time of onset to time 100. Biologically, brief monocular deprivation during the critical period has nearly as strong a physiological effect as long-term deprivation (Hubel & Wiesel, 1970; reviewed in Movshon & Van Sluyters, 1981).[12]

The critical period in this simulation does not depend on stabilization of saturated synapses, or on other changes in the rules governing plasticity. Instead, the critical period in this simulation is a dynamical result. The influence of one synapse on another, as shown in the derivation of Eq. 2, is a product of two factors: the level of activity of the influencing synapse, and its synaptic strength. Hence, for any given disparity in activity level between the two eyes, there is a corresponding disparity in synaptic

---

[11]We have noted that in optic tectum, there is no effect of monocular deprivation. One possible explanation would arise if there are constraints in optic tectum conserving, or ensuring the equality of, the total synaptic strength over individual input cells from each eye. This might occur, for example if activity-dependent effects were much weaker than activity-independent effects that yield such conservation or symmetry. Ideas of a hierarchy of effects in the optic tectum have been developed by Fraser (1980, 1985).

[12]The physiological results of a few days of monocular deprivation may consist predominantly of a shift, to the open eye, of cells that were driven relatively equally by the two eyes (Hubel & Wiesel, 1970). Cells originally dominated by the closed eye may require slightly longer periods to undergo an ocular dominance shift. Deprivation for six days appears adequate to cause a physiological shift to the open eye about as strong as that resulting from long deprivation (Hubel & Wiesel, 1970). Anatomical results may show similar stages. After ten dys of deprivation, the anatomy shows only a greater clarity, as though deprived eye afferents were withdrawn from areas that had been innervated by both eyes (Shatz, Lindstrom, & Wiesel, 1977). Long deprivation leads the geniculocortical innervation to anatomically alter, so that the open eye's stripes become wider and the closed eye's become narrower or become islands in a sea of open-eye inputs (Shatz & Stryker, 1978).

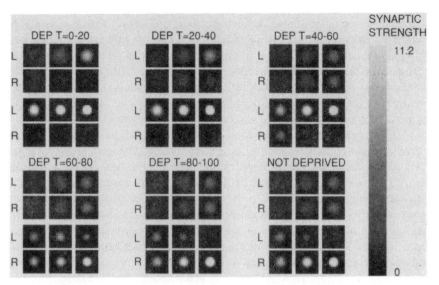

FIG. 7.12. The effects of monocular deprivation from times 0-20, 20-40, 40-60, 60-80, or 80-100, compared to the results without deprivation. Display is as in Fig. 7.11. Early deprivation leads to a complete shift in favor of the open (left) eye, while late deprivation causes no distinguishable change from the nondeprived outcome. All parameters, functions, and initial conditions are identical to those used in Fig. 7.8, except that the deprived eye's correlation function was multiplied by 0.7 during the 20 iterations of deprivation. Results are indistinguishable if deprivation remains in effect from the time of onset to time 100, except that deprivation from times 60-100 leads the two eyes' inputs to become more nearly equal in strength than does deprivation from times 60-80.

strengths that is sufficient to overcome the activity differential. Once an eye has a sufficient advantage in synaptic strength, it will continue to grow faster than the opposite eye even if deprived and rendered less active, and hence monocular deprivation will no longer cause an ocular dominance shift. Thus, brief deprivation initiated early in development, when the two eyes are nearly equal, leads the open eye to gain an advantage in synaptic strength sufficient for it to dominate the cell even if deprivation then ceases. Deprivation initiated late in development, in contrast, is no longer able to shift the final balance between the two eyes, even if deprivation persists and synapses are not stabilized.

This dynamical explanation of the critical period applies only to cells that are normally destined to become monocular. A binocular cell will always be subject to a monocular deprivation effect by this reasoning. In cats, many cells in the adult cortical layer 4 at the borders between ocular dominance stripes are binocular (Shatz & Stryker, 1978), an effect that occurs in the model when correlations within each eye are narrow compared to an arbor radius. Yet adult cats appear to show absolutely no effect of monocular deprivation (Hubel & Wiesel, 1970). Hence, to fully explain the biologically seen critical period, stabilization of saturated synapses or other biochemical changes in plasticity rules must be invoked. Nonetheless, it is possible that many aspects of the observed critical period are dynamical in origin.

An alternative experimental modification of normal development occurs when muscimol is infused into cortex to inhibit all cortical activity, as previously described. In this case, monocular deprivation causes a shift in favor of the *closed* eye. This is easily modeled if we assume a mechanism, such as a Hebbian mechanism, in which the correlation-based reward for coactivated synapses depends on postsynaptic activity. Synapses then will not be able to influence one another, because all cortical cells are always inhibited in the presence of muscimol. The influence between synapses is normally due to their excitatory or inhibitory influences on one another's postsynaptic cell, but now the synapses are without effect on the activity of the postsynaptic cell. Thus, as can be seen from the derivation of the equations from a Hebb synapse mechanism (appendix 1), the term involving synaptic interactions is eliminated from our equation. Instead, each synapse decays at a rate proportional to its mean activity. The more active, open-eye synapses decay more rapidly, leading the closed eye to dominate the cell, as observed experimentally.

In summary, under a correlation-based rule, if a set of inputs is correlated in a way that falls off with distance, without anticorrelations, two conclusions follow. First, central synapses in a receptive field will grow more rapidly than peripheral synapses. The more rapidly the correlations fall off with distance, the more pronounced this tendency. Second, if two different such sets of inputs, not mutually correlated, innervate a single cortical layer, there is a tendency for one set, selected randomly by the initial conditions, to grow more rapidly and come to dominate the cell. Greater amounts of correlation over a broader distance range within each input set enhance this tendency, by enhancing the rate of growth of monocular over binocular patterns of synaptic differences. Opposite-eye anticorrelations also enhance this tendency, both by broadening correlations and by enhancing the growth of ocular dominance over the development of receptive field refinement. The precise developmental results depend on the conditions that stabilize and limit synaptic growth, but the tendencies to refinement and to ocular dominance are general. The tendency to ocular dominance, in particular, is robust to nonlinearities. Results of development with more complicated correlation functions involving same-eye anticorrelations, or with experimental modifications of activity such as monocular deprivation or postsynaptic inhibition, can also be understood as we have described.

These results agree with the biological results attributed to correlation-based mechanisms: receptive fields sharpen, ocular dominance develops, and experimental modifications of activity during a critical period modify developmental outcomes in the manner predicted. Cases in which different sets of correlated inputs become matched based on their mutual correlations can be regarded as a particular case of the sharpening of receptive fields to a highly correlated group of inputs, in the case when correlations are not simply determined by distances between the inputs.

The development of large-scale patterns of receptive fields, such as ocular dominance stripes, requires consideration of a full layer of cortical cells. Before turning to this topic, we briefly reverse perspective and consider the development of the terminal arbors of an isolated pair of geniculate cells projecting to a layer of cortical cells.

How Isolated Geniculate Cells Develop

For the case of two geniculate cells, representing a single retinotopic position in each eye, innervating a cortical layer, the model equations simplify in a manner formally identical to Eq. 2 for a single cortical cell:

$$\frac{d}{dt}S^L(x,t) = \lambda A(x)\sum_y[C^{LL}(0)I(x-y)S^L(y,t) +$$
$$C^{LR}(0)I(x-y)S^R(y,t)] - \gamma S^L(x,t) - \epsilon^L(x)$$

$$\frac{d}{dt}S^R(x,t) = \lambda A(x)\sum_y[C^{RR}(0)I(x-y)S^R(y,t) +$$
$$C^{RL}(0)I(x-y)S^L(y,t)] - \gamma S^R(x,t) - \epsilon^R(x) \qquad (5)$$

Hence, letting $I^S(x - y) = I(x - y)[C^{\text{SameEye}}(0) + C^{\text{OppEye}}(0)]$, $I^D(x - y) = I(x - y)[C^{\text{SameEye}}(0) - C^{\text{OppEye}}(0)]$, the conclusions for development of the arbors of two isolated geniculate cells are identical, in terms of I^S, I^D and A, to the previous conclusions for the receptive field of an isolated cortical cell in terms of C^S, C^D, and A.

Assume $C^{\text{SameEye}}(0) > |C^{\text{OppEye}}(0)|$, so that the factors multiplying I in both I^S and I^D are positive and thus both I^S and I^D are simply scaled versions of I. Then if $I(x - y)$ is Mexican hat, with short-distance excitation and broader-ranging inhibition both found within an arbor radius, the arbors of the two inputs will tend to segregate from one another into separate patches of cortex, as in the case for receptive fields when same-eye anticorrelations are present and C^D is Mexican hat. Simulation of time development under this condition is shown in Fig. 7.13, for a case in which

$$C^{\text{OppEye}}(0) = -\frac{C^{\text{SameEye}}(0)}{4}.$$ [13] If $I(x)$ is purely excitatory, one geniculate

cell would be expected to grow faster than the other and to dominate the inputs to cortex from the given retinotopic position, as in the simulations of receptive field development for a purely excitatory correlation function.

There is an important difference in the case of isolated geniculate cells as opposed to an isolated cortical cell. The constraints used for stabilization now affect both S^S and S^D, whereas previously they affected only S^S. Previously, constraints on total synaptic strength over a cell were over a cortical cell, and the constraint drew no distinction between left- and right-eye synapses.[14] In the present case, the cells are two distinct geniculate cells, and any constraints on total synaptic strength over a cell must be placed separately on each cell. If total synaptic strength were strictly conserved over a cell, the arbors of each cell could rearrange and segregate from one another, but neither eye could gain or lose total synaptic strength. Then a pattern in which one eye's patches were wider than an arbor radius could not grow, because such a pattern would involve one eye's cell gaining more synaptic strength than the other's. A purely excitatory $I(x)$, or a Mexican hat $I(x)$ whose central excitatory part is sufficiently wide, would select such a pattern in the absence of constraints. With such functions, then, constraints can significantly alter ocular dominance segregation. In the presence of constraints, either each arbor would refine to its central part, or the two arbors would segregate from one another into separate patches of cortex, each about an arbor radius in width.

Development of the Geniculocortical Innervation

We are now prepared to understand many aspects of development when a left-eye and a right-eye geniculate layer innervate a cortical layer. In the

---

[13]In the absence of opposite-eye anticorrelations, the saturating nonlinearities defeat the tendency of S^D to develop a striped pattern, as discussed in footnote 9. The constraints of meshing the innervations of multiple cells when a complete geniculocortical innervation is considered, however, lead to patchy geniculate arbors even in the absence of opposite-eye anticorrelations. Hence the case with opposite-eye anticorrelations is illustrated here, for pedagogical purposes.

[14]Such a constraint could have drawn a distinction between left- and right-eye synapses. For example, if the constraint were multiplicative, achieved by multiplying each synaptic weight by a constant rather than by subtracting a constant from each synaptic weight, stronger synapses would be more heavily affected by the constraint. If total synaptic strength were growing in the absence of constraints, this constraint would penalize the dominant eye and tend to retard the development of ocular dominance segregation, as is briefly discussed later. The important point is that a constraint over a cortical cell can be formulated so as to have no effect on the equation for S^D and hence no effect on ocular dominance, whereas a constraint on geniculate cells must affect the equation for S^D.

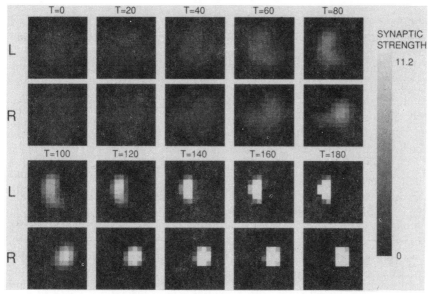

FIG. 7.13. Development of two geniculate cells, one serving each eye, innervating a cortical layer. The inputs segregate to innervate separate patches of cortex. The activities of the two geniculate cells are assumed to be negatively correlated with one another, as described in the text. Cortical interaction function was that shown in Fig. 7.9. Inputs serving each eye were constrained to keep a constant total synaptic strength, by subtraction of $\epsilon^L(t)A(\alpha)$ from each left-eye total synaptic strength after each iteration, where $\epsilon^L(t) = \dfrac{\Sigma_\alpha \frac{d}{dt} S^L(\alpha, t)}{\Sigma_\alpha A(\alpha)}$, and similarly for the right eye. Conventions, initial conditions, and parameters otherwise as in Fig. 7.8.

simplest case there are positive local correlations within each eye, and a Mexican hat cortical interaction function. Cortical cells will each tend toward monocularity. Greater breadth of local correlations or opposite-eye anticorrelations will yield an increased tendency toward monocularity. Arbors will tend to segregate into patches. The scale of the patches will be determined by the cortical interaction function, up to a limit imposed by the arbor function if synaptic strength over an input arbor is conserved. For the tendencies of cortical cells and geniculate arbors to mesh compatibly, cortical cells as a whole must segregate into alternating patches of cells dominated by a single eye, with the scale of the patches determined in the same manner as the scale of the patches of individual arbors.

Another way to understand the formation and scale of cortical patches is the following. Suppose each cortical cell becomes monocular. Their interactions via the cortical interaction function will then be most favorable, in terms of growth of their synapses, if cells with inputs from the left eye are surrounded by left-eye cells over distances at which the cortical interaction function is positive, and by right-eye cells over distances at which the cortical interaction function is negative. It is not possible for each cell to be at the center of its own such "bulls-eye"; but interactions will be most favorable over all cortical cells, if the segregation is into patches whose widths are given by the dominant oscillation in the cortical interaction function.

A simulation illustrating cortical development with positive same-eye correlations and a Mexican hat cortical interaction function is shown in Fig. 7.14. The functions used in this and other simulations of the geniculocortical innervation are shown in Fig. 7.15. For this simulation three 25 by 25 grids of cells were used to represent one cortical layer and two geniculate layers, one for each eye. Each geniculate cell was connected to a 7 by 7 square of cortical cells centered at the retinotopically corresponding point in the cortical grid, resulting in a total of $2 \times 25 \times 25 \times 7 \times 7 = 61,250$ connections. A simple "flat" arbor function was used, equal to 1 over the 7 by 7 arbor and zero outside.[15] Synapses were initially assigned a random strength near 1, and allowed to grow until they reached a strength of 8 or 0. Constraints were used to conserve total synaptic strength over each cortical cell, and to maintain total synaptic strength over each input cell within a range between 0.5 and 1.5 times the initial total. To eliminate boundary effects, periodic boundary conditions were used on the grids, so that left and right edges of the grids were taken to be adjacent, as were top and bottom edges.[16]

The cortex initially receives innervations of uniform strength from the two eyes, indicated by the intermediate grey color at time 0 (Fig. 7.14a). Gradually, the left-eye (black) and right-eye (white) inputs come to dominate alternating sets of cortical cells, yielding a pattern of ocular dominance stripes or patches. Individual cortical cells focus their input strength centrally, then become monocular as they continue to refine (Fig. 7.14b). As the inputs from the two eyes segregate and the full set of afferents from a single eye are restricted to innervate only half the cortical cells, individual

---

[15]A tapering arbor function effectively reduces the size of the arbor. Hence, because our arbor size was limited for computational reasons, we chose to use a flat arbor to maximize the chance to see significant internal structure in receptive fields. We have also studied the use of the tapering arbor function. Results for overall ocular dominance in that case are completely consistent with the results presented here; a smaller wavelength develops due to the effectively smaller arbor, and is correctly predicted by our analysis.

[16]The distance across visual cortex corresponds to 10 or 20 patch wavelengths, whereas interactions may be expected to be localized to at most a few wavelengths. Hence, the boundaries are likely to play little role in deciding whether patches will develop, or in determining their wavelength, though they may play a role in determining the detailed form or layout of the patches or stripes.

receptive fields become somewhat elongated. Individual geniculate cells from the two eyes focus their input and then sort into mutually exclusive, complementary right-and left-eye patches (Fig. 7.14c), much as appears to be the case in filled arbors in cats (Humphrey, Sur, Uhlrich, & Sherman, 1985a, 1985b; Levay & Stryker, 1979). The results are basically those predicted from consideration of the development of individual cortical and geniculate cells, though the meshing of the full cortical and geniculate grids leads to some alterations in details of receptive fields and afferent arborizations. These results are completely robust, being qualitatively identical for all sets of random initial conditions we have tried as well as for varying sizes of simulations (Miller, 1989a; Miller et al., 1989; Miller & Stryker, 1989).

A more complicated case to understand is one in which there are local correlations within each eye, and a purely excitatory cortical interaction function. Under these conditions, individual cortical cells will refine and become monocular, but so too will individual pairs of input cells. For these tendencies to mesh compatibly, large regions of cortex must become dominated by a single eye's inputs. There can be more than one such region, separated by fracture lines along which individual cortical cells or pairs of input cells are binocular. In simulations, one eye's inputs often take over the entire cortex. If a constraint is used conserving total synaptic strength over each input cell, isolated input cells will refine but a difference in strength between the two eyes cannot develop. For this to mesh with the tendency of isolated cortical cells to develop monocularity, each pair of input cell arbors must segregate into complementary patches of cortex, as in the case of a Mexican hat cortical interaction function. In this case, however, the purely excitatory cortical interaction provides no clue as to the size of the segregated patches. The size of the patches is selected by the arbor function: The cortex "tries" to assume its unconstrained form, in which one eye's domain spreads indefinitely over the cortex as a whole, but is limited by the need to accommodate both eyes within the breadth of a single initial arborization. Thus, a purely excitatory cortical interaction can support ocular dominance segregation, but maintenance of equality of the eyes depends on tight constraints on total synaptic strength of input cells. The results of simulations with an excitatory cortical interaction, with and without such constraints, are shown in Fig. 7.16. With tight constraints, development is essentially like that with a Mexican hat cortical interaction function, although there is a slight increase in the scale of the stripes. For comparison, results with a Mexican hat cortical interaction function with and without constraints are also shown. Constraints have essentially no effect in this case.

Dependence on the correlation function is as expected from the results for individual cells, as shown in Fig. 7.17. Broader correlations within each

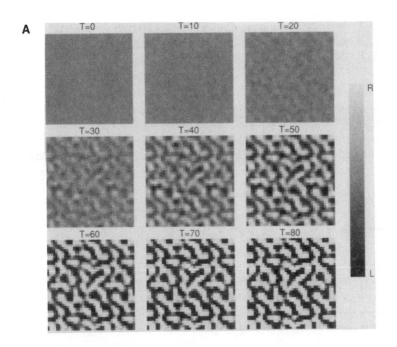

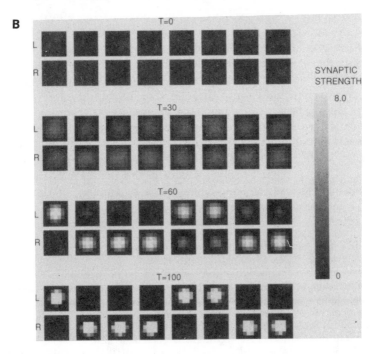

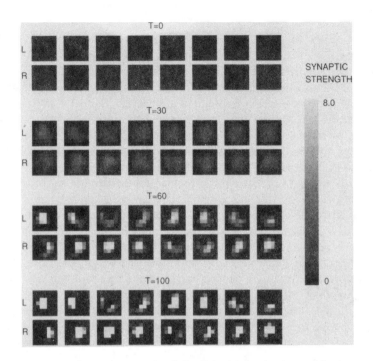

FIG. 7.14. Development of a full cortical layer innervated by two geniculate layers, one representing each eye. (a) The cortical grid, illustrated at each of nine times, from time 0 to the 80th iteration. The greyscale illustrates the ocular dominance, *OD,* of each cortical cell, $OD(x) \equiv \Sigma_{\alpha}[S^R(x,\alpha) - S^L(x,\alpha)]$, on a scale from monocular for the right eye (white) to monocular for the left eye (black). A pattern of ocular dominance segregation develops and then grows to monocularity. Each square shows 40 by 40 cortical cells, although the cortical grid was only 25 by 25, so that the pattern across the periodic boundary conditions can be seen; thus, the top 15 and bottom 15 rows within each square are identical, as are the left 15 and right 15 columns. (b) Development of receptive fields of eight cortical cells. Left- and right-eye inputs to each of eight adjacent cortical cells are illustrated at each of four times. The eight cells illustrated are the eight at the bottom left of the cortical pictures of (a). Each vertical L,R pair illustrates the left- and right-eye synaptic inputs to a single cortical cell at one time. Greyscale shows strength of synaptic input from each of the 7 by 7 geniculate positions which send input to the cortical cell. Receptive fields concentrate their strength centrally, refining in size, and become monocular. Adjacent groups of cells tend to become dominated by the same eye, providing the basis for ocular dominance segregation across the cortex as a whole. (c) Development of arbors of eight left-eye and eight right-eye geniculate cells, from eight adjacent geniculate grid positions. The eight grid positions are those in the geniculate corresponding retinotopically to the eight cortical cells illustrated in (b). Each

eye or addition of opposite-eye anticorrelations leads to a more completely monocular cortex. This agrees with experimental findings in which artificially induced strabismus or alternating monocular deprivation, which reduce correlations or induce anticorrelations between the eyes, lead to an increase in monocularity throughout the cortex (Hubel & Wiesel 1965). Narrower correlations within each eye lead to more binocular cells at the borders between eyestripes without otherwise altering the pattern of stripes. Same-eye anticorrelations also lead to more binocular cells at the borders between eye stripes and, if present within an arbor radius, tend to destroy monocularity and to destroy the regular cortical organization of ocular dominance.

Monocular deprivation within a critical period results in the open eye taking over many more cells and thus a much larger percentage of cortex, as seen experimentally and suggested by results on individual cells. The precise results of deprivation in the model depend on the time of onset, duration, and strength of deprivation, and the constraints which limit the degree to which afferent arbors can shrink in total synaptic strength. When deprivation is initiated early and maintained through development, the open eye takes over all cortical cells to the limits allowed by constraints. If constraints prevent the deprived eye from losing all cortical inputs, or if deprivation is initiated somewhat later in development, islands of cells dominated by the closed eye develop in the midst of a sea of open-eye cells,

---

vertical L,R pair illustrates the arbors of a left- and a right-eye geniculate cell from identical geniculate grid positions at one time. Greyscale shows synaptic strength of connection to each of the 7 by 7 cortical cells contacted by the arbor. Arbors focus their strength centrally, but then sort into complementary patches of cortex. The functions used for this simulation, illustrated in Fig. 7.15, were the "same-eye correlations" correlation function with parameter 0.3, and the Mexican hat cortical interaction function. The arbor function, as described in the text, was equal to one over a 7 by 7 square arbor and zero outside. $\epsilon^L \epsilon^R$, and γ were set to zero. $\lambda = 0.0069$. In cortical simulations in general, λ is set for each choice of functions so that average change in S^D per iteration should initially be about 0.003. This yields $0.003 < \lambda < 0.015$. Cortical cells were constrained to conserve total synaptic strength as described in legend to Fig. 7.8. Afferent arbors were then constrained as described in legend to Fig. 7.13, except that the factor subtracted from each synapse in an arbor was multiplied by minimum $\left\{ [(1 - \dfrac{S_{tot}}{49})/0.5]^2, 1.0 \right\}$ where S_{tot} is the total synaptic strength over the arbor. This has the effect of allowing total synaptic strength to vary between 0.5 and 1.5 of the average initial value of 49. Synaptic strengths were frozen if their value reached either zero or 8: they were no longer allowed to change, assigned derivatives of zero and omitted from the constraint.

AFFERENT CORRELATION FUNCTIONS

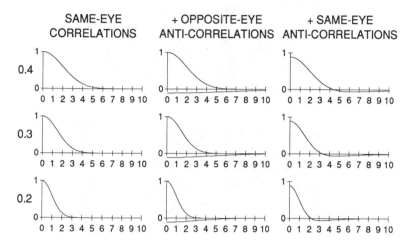

CORTICAL INTERACTION FUNCTIONS

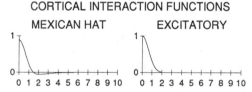

FIG. 7.15.   Functions used for simulations of full geniculocortical innervation. Function value, vertical axis, versus distance in grid intervals, horizontal axis. Top: Correlation functions. These are identical to those shown in Fig. 7.9, with two changes: $D = 7$ rather than 13; and $x = 0.4, 0.3, 0.2$ rather than 0.45, 0.3, 0.15. Bottom: Cortical interaction functions. Left, Mexican hat function, identical to the cortical interaction function of Fig. 7.9 but with $D = 7$. Right, a purely excitatory cortical interaction function, given by just the excitatory gaussian of the Mexican hat function.

as is seen in cats following monocular deprivation (Shatz & Stryker, 1978). These islands are spaced with a periodicity equal to that of the stripes that would form in the nondeprived cortex. With later onset or briefer duration of deprivation, or stronger limits to the degree to which individual afferents can shrink in total synaptic strength, the islands are linked into thin stripes, similar to the results seen in monkeys (Hubel et al., 1977). When the deprivation begins sufficiently late, the cortex develops normally, except that cells at the border of the two eyes' stripes that would become binocular without deprivation can become dominated by the open eye, as previously discussed. This is illustrated in Fig. 7.18, which shows the results of brief deprivation initiated at varying times in development. Early onset of brief

NO CONSTRAINTS   CONSTRAINTS

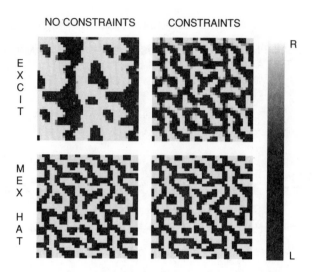

FIG. 7.16. Cortical patterns of ocular dominance resulting from development with the excitatory cortical interaction function of Fig. 7.15, with and without constraints fixing the total synaptic strength over each afferent arbor. For comparison, results using the Mexican hat cortical interaction function of Fig. 7.15, with identical constraints, are shown below. The final cortex (T=200) is shown in each case. Conventions, parameters, initial conditions, and arbor function as in Fig. 7.14. The correlation function used is "same-eye correlations" with parameter 0.4, rather than 0.3 as in Fig. 7.14. With 0.3, the excitatory cortical interaction function leads to patterns similar to those shown here, but many more cells in the final cortices are binocular.

deprivation leads deprived-eye stripes to become thin and broken. Later onset leads to progressively more equal widths of stripes, and sufficiently late onset is indistinguishable from normal development. The effects of longer durations of deprivation are illustrated in Miller et al. (1989).

To use these results to guide experiment, one would like to know how measurable features of the results, in particular the width of the stripes, depend on measurable biological parameters. We have suggested that the cortical interaction function determines the width if it is a Mexican hat function, and that if it is purely excitatory the width is determined by the arbor function. To achieve a more precise understanding, we again assume equality of the two eyes and, defining S^S, S^D, C^S, C^D as before, develop equations for S^S and S^D. Equation 1 becomes

$$\frac{d}{dt}S^S(x,\alpha,t) = \lambda A(x - \alpha)\sum_{y,\beta}I(x - y)C^S(\alpha - \beta)S^S(y,\beta,t)$$
$$- \gamma S^S(x,\alpha,t) - 2\epsilon(x,\alpha)$$

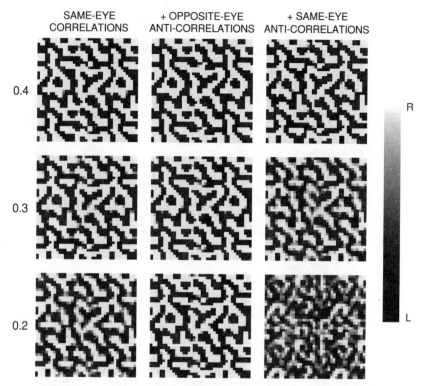

| SAME-EYE CORRELATIONS | + OPPOSITE-EYE ANTI-CORRELATIONS | + SAME-EYE ANTI-CORRELATIONS |

FIG. 7.17. Cortical patterns of ocular dominance resulting from development with each of the nine correlation functions of Fig. 7.15. Each development began with the same initial condition and used the same arbor and cortical interaction function, in all cases identical to those used in Fig. 7.14. The final cortex (T=200) is shown in each case. Conventions, parameters and constraints as in Fig. 7.14.

$$\frac{d}{dt}S^D(x,\alpha,t) = \lambda A(x - \alpha)\sum_{y,\beta}I(x - y)C^D(\alpha - \beta)S^D(y,\beta,t)$$

$$- \gamma S^D(x,\alpha,t) \tag{6}$$

The equation for S^D controls the development of a pattern of segregation between the two eyes. We again find the characteristic patterns of ocular dominance: the patterns of S^D that evolve independently, each at its own rate, from the random initial condition near $S^D = 0$. As before, any random initial condition can be expressed as a sum of such patterns, and the patterns each grow independently and exponentially so that the fastest-growing pattern will quickly dominate.

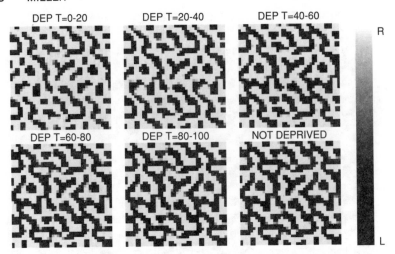

FIG. 7.18. Cortical patterns of ocular dominance resulting from brief monocular deprivation for 20 iterations during development. Results of initiating the 20 iterations of deprivation at iteration 0, 20, 40, 60, or 80 are shown, and compared to the results in the absence of deprivation. All parameters, functions, and initial conditions are identical to those used in Fig. 7.14, except that the deprived eye's correlation function was multiplied by 0.7 during the 20 iterations of deprivation. Final cortices (T = 200) are shown for each case. Synaptic strengths were frozen upon reaching the limiting values of 0 or 8, as described in Fig. 7.14 legend; without such stabilization, late onset of deprivation would convert the binocular cells at the patch borders into open-eye dominated cells.

For the full geniculocortical innervation, each characteristic pattern of ocular dominance consists of a receptive field of synaptic differences, and an oscillation of ocular dominance across cortex (Fig. 7.19; appendix 2). The receptive field specifies the pattern of ocular dominance within the receptive field of a single cortical cell, whereas the oscillation specifies the change of this pattern between cortical cells. The characteristic receptive field may be monocular (Fig. 7.19a) or binocular (Fig. 7.19b). If binocular, it may involve stripes of left- and right-eye input in different portions of the receptive field, or more complicated distributions of left- and right-eye input. The oscillation of the characteristic pattern means that, across cortical cells, there is a sinusoidal change as to which eye is dominant in each portion of the receptive field. If the characteristic receptive field is monocular, cortical cells will oscillate, across cortex, between domination by one eye and domination by the other. Thus, if a characteristic pattern has a monocular receptive field, cortical cells in the pattern will be grouped into ocular dominance patches or stripes. The width of a left-eye patch plus a right-eye patch is given by the wavelength of the pattern's oscillation.

Hence, to determine the width of ocular dominance stripes that should develop, we need to answer two questions. First, what determines whether the fastest-growing pattern has a monocular receptive field, and thus whether segregation of ocular dominance patches will occur? Second, if the fastest-growing pattern is monocular, what determines the wavelength of its oscillation?

The answer, for biologically reasonable choices of functions, is as suggested by our study of the development of isolated cells. The pattern of ocular dominance within a receptive field is largely determined by the correlation function C^D, so that the dominant oscillation in C^D (the wavelength of the peak of its fourier transform) shapes the fastest-growing receptive field. If that dominant oscillation is flat (infinite wavelength), or has a wavelength longer than the arbor diameter, the receptive field will be monocular. The oscillation in ocular dominance of geniculate arbors representing a single receptive field point is similarly largely determined by the dominant oscillation in the cortical interaction function I. The cortical oscillation is the sum of these two oscillations, that within receptive fields and that within arbors. The cortical oscillation determines the change between cortical cells of the ocular dominance of receptive fields, or the change between receptive field points of the ocular dominance of arbors. Thus, the cortical oscillation of the fastest-growing pattern is essentially determined by both C^D and the cortical interaction function I, as the sum of the dominant oscillation of each function. In the case of monocular receptive fields, for which the dominant oscillation in C^D is nearly flat, this is simply the dominant oscillation in I. Therefore, when monocular receptive fields form, they will be organized into ocular dominance patches with a width, of left- plus right-eye patch, corresponding to the peak of the fourier transform of the cortical interaction function I.

In the case of a purely excitatory cortical interaction function, the peak of the fourier transform of I corresponds to an infinite wavelength, that is dominance by a single eye everywhere. Addition of constraints on the total synaptic strength of input cells modifies the equation, forcing the left- and right-eye inputs from each retinotopic location to divide between them the cortical surface over which they initially arborize. The result is to suppress the growth of monocular patterns with wavelength longer than an arbor diameter, so that the fastest-growing monocular pattern has a wavelength of about an arbor diameter.

These results can be demonstrated by three methods. One method is to analyze the equation for S^D mathematically, and in particular to determine exact solutions in limiting cases or reasonable approximations. A second method is to numerically compute the characteristic patterns for varying

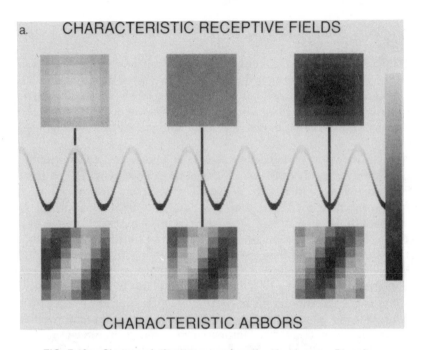

CHARACTERISTIC RECEPTIVE FIELDS

CHARACTERISTIC ARBORS

FIG. 7.19. Characteristic patterns of ocular dominance. The characteristic receptive field, and associated characteristic arbor, are illustrated at three positions for each of two characteristic patterns, one monocular (a) and one binocular (b). The sinusoids illustrate the oscillation of ocular dominance across cortex associated with each characteristic pattern, correctly scaled to the arbor and receptive field sizes. Greyscale codes S^D, the difference between the synaptic strengths of the two eyes, varying from dominance by one eye to dominance by the other. The characteristic receptive field shows the pattern of S^D within the receptive field of a cortical cell, illustrating the retinotopic positions from which the cell receives stronger left-eye or right-eye input. The characteristic arbor at the same point shows the pattern of S^D in the projections of the left- and right-eye geniculate arbors from the retinotopically corresponding point, illustrating the cortical positions to which the left eye or right eye projects more strongly from that retinotopic position. (a) A monocular characteristic pattern. At the cortical point corresponding to the leftmost receptive field, cortical cell inputs are dominated by the right eye. Afferents with the corresponding retinotopic position therefore project arbors such that the right eye afferents preferentially project to the central patch of the arbor (cortical right-eye stripe) and the left-eye afferents preferentially project to the peripheral patches (left-eye cortical stripe). Similarly, the central receptive field is at the border between left-eye and right-eye stripes, where the two eyes have equal innervation, and the rightmost receptive field is in the center of a left-eye stripe. The pattern shown here is one of the set (identical except for rotations of the direction of the oscillation) of fastest-

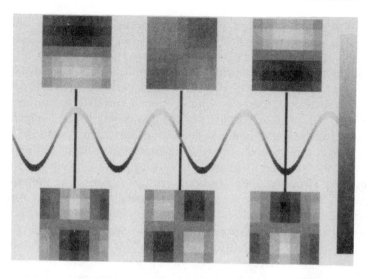

growing characteristic patterns for the correlation function "same-eye correlation 0.4," and the Mexican hat intracortical interaction, of Fig. 15. A flat 7 by 7 arbor function is used, = 1 within the 7 by 7 arbor, 0 outside. The oscillation projects in a direction perpendicular to the stripes across the arbors, rather than horizontally as depicted. (b) A binocular characteristic pattern. This is one of the set (identical except for rotations of the direction of the fastest-growing characteristic patterns for the correlation function "+ same-eye anticorrelations 0.2" of Fig. 7.15, with a Mexican hat cortical interaction and a flat 7 by 7 arbor as in (a). The oscillation projects horizontally as depicted. Receptive fields are dominated above by one eye and below by the other; the eye that dominates each region of a receptive field varies sinusoidally across cortical cells. The arbors show the corresponding pattern of geniculate projections necessary to sustain this cortical pattern of receptive fields. Note that the central receptive field is not strictly neutral, but itself has weak dominance by opposite eyes in different regions. The basis for this is briefly described in appendix 2.

forms of the cortical interaction, correlation, and arbor functions. A third method, which will not be further discussed here, is to analyze simulations of time development across varying functions, to see if monocular cells develop when predicted and, if so, if the period of ocular dominance segregation that develops is that predicted by the cortical interaction function. Such analysis shows that the patterns of ocular dominance develop as predicted (Miller, 1989a; Miller & Stryker, 1989).

One case in which the equations are easily soluble is the case of full connectivity. Then all geniculate cells are connected with equal numbers of synapses to all cortical cells, so that the arbor function is a constant: $A(x - \alpha) \equiv A$. In this case, the solutions are precisely as we have just suggested: a receptive field oscillation is determined by C^D, an oscillation across afferent arbors by I, and the cortical oscillation is the sum of these two oscillations. Constraints on input cell synaptic strengths in this case suppress the growth of monocular patterns with infinite wavelength, and leave all other patterns unaffected. Two other particularly simple cases in which the equations are exactly soluble occur if correlations are constant, $C^D(\alpha - \beta) \equiv C;$[17] or if correlations are sufficiently broad compared to arbors that one can approximate the correlation between $S^D(x,\alpha)$ and $S^D(y,\beta)$ by the *average* correlation of $S^D(x,\alpha)$ to all inputs synapsing onto the cortical cell at y. Both these limits allow reduction to a simple equation studied previously by Swindale (1980). In both cases, as suggested by the essential constancy of correlations over an arbor, monocular receptive fields develop. As expected, they are organized into ocular dominance patches with width of left- plus right-eye patches given by the wavelength of the peak of the fourier transform of I. If constraints on input cells are present, monocular organization with wavelength longer than an arbor diameter is suppressed.

Numerical computation of the characteristic patterns for a variety of choices of correlation function verify these predictions. Figure 7.20 shows results of computations for the functions used in Fig. 7.16. The growth rates of the characteristic patterns are shown as a function of inverse wavelength and degree of monocularity, and compared to the predictions of the broad correlations limit. As expected, constraints suppress the growth of longer-wavelength monocular patterns. This has no effect on the fastest-growing patterns for the Mexican hat cortical interaction function, but drastically alters the expected outcome for a purely excitatory cortical interaction function. We have shown elsewhere (Miller, 1989a; Miller et al., 1989; Miller & Stryker, 1989) that the broad correlations limit accurately predicts the growth rates of monocular patterns as a function of wavelength, even when the correlation function oscillates significantly so that the fastest-growing patterns are not monocular. The infinite arbor limit predicts, at least qualitatively, the maximum growth rate as a function of wavelength over all patterns, without concern for monocularity.

DISCUSSION

Biological Interpretation of the Results

The model we have developed predicts the development and width of periodic ocular dominance segregation in terms of functions describing input correlations, geniculocortical arbors and cortical interactions. We can compare the model results to experimental measurements.

---

[17]The correlations need only be constant over distances $\alpha - \beta$ less than the maximum diameter of an arbor plus the maximum distance over which the cortical interaction function $I(x)$ is nonzero; more widely separated inputs never interact.

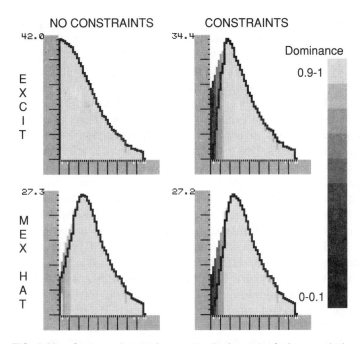

FIG. 7.20. Computed growth rate (vertical axes) of characteristic patterns of ocular dominance, as a function of inverse wavelength of the pattern (horizontal axes), for the two cortical interactions and the two choices of constraints on afferent arbors of Fig. 7.16. Black lines indicate predictions of the broad correlations limit, described in the text. Greyscale indicates maximum dominance of any characteristic pattern with the given wavelength and growth rate. Dominance is a measure of the degree of monocularity of the pattern's characteristic receptive field, on a scale from 0 for complete binocularity to 1 for complete monocularity. The constraints suppress the growth of monocular patterns with wavelength longer than an arbor diameter. This has a profound effect on the outcome when the excitatory cortical interaction function is used, selecting a wavelength of about an arbor diameter. There is little effect when the mixed excitatory/inhibitory interaction function is used, because that function normally selects a wavelength shorter than an arbor diameter. Maximum growth rates are at wavelengths of 7.3-8.3 grid intervals (excitatory function, with constraints) or 5.4-5.9 grid intervals (Mexican hat function). The number beside the vertical axis indicates the maximum growth rate of any pattern. The horizontal axis represents wavenumber; the wavelength in units of grid intervals is 25 divided by the wavenumber. The first bin on the horizontal axis represents wavenumbers 0-0.23; subsequent bins represent increments of 0.4 in wavenumber, so that the second bin represents wavenumbers 0.23-0.63, etc. The arbor and correlation functions are as in Fig. 7.16. From Miller, Keller, and Stryker, 1989. © 1989 by the AAAS.

In the visual cortex of adult cats, the final patches have a period (width of left- plus right-eye patch) of about 850 μm (Anderson, Olavarria, & Van Sluyters, 1988; Shatz, Lindstrom, & Wiesel, 1977; Swindale, 1988). Judging largely by the patchy extent of the final adult arbors, initial arbors in cats may fill a region with diameter 1-1.5 mm (X-cells) or larger than 2 mm (Y-cells) (Humphrey et al., 1985a, 1985b; LeVay & Stryker, 1979). To estimate the correlation function, we use measurements of correlations in maintained activities in darkness of retinal ganglion cells in adult cats (Mastronarde, 1983a, 1983b), and measurements of the retinotopic map onto the cortex (Tusa, Palmer, & Rosenquist, 1978). Together, these indicate that inputs representing a single eye are positively correlated at retinotopic separations corresponding to cortical distances of from $\frac{1}{2}$ (X-cells) to $\frac{3}{2}$ (Y-cells) of a geniculocortical arbor radius (Miller et al., 1989). Horizontal corticocortical synaptic interactions may be excitatory at short range, and appear to be inhibitory to distances of perhaps 400-500 μm (Hata, Tsumoto, Sato, Hagihara, & Tamura, 1988; Hess, Negishi, & Creutzfeldt, 1975; Toyama, Kimura, & Tanaka, 1981a, 1981b; Worgotter & Eysel, 1989). In addition, long-range synaptic interactions exist over distances of 1 mm or more (Gilbert & Wiesel, 1983). These interactions connect only discrete patches of cortex and so may quantitatively have less impact than the shorter-range interactions. In the adult, these long-range connections may connect cells of like orientation specificity by excitatory connections, and may also make inhibitory contributions to direction-selectivity (Tso, Gilbert, & Wiesel, 1986; Worgotter & Eysel, 1989). In the kitten, even before patch development but after the development of orientation selectivity, the long-range connections appear to connect many more patches than in the adult, with a periodicity consistent with the period of orientation columns as well as of the subsequent ocular dominance columns (Luhmann, Martinez Millan, & Singer, 1986).

The results of our analysis are consistent with the sizes suggested by these measurements. The observed patch period of about 850μm can be produced by a variety of short-range intracortical interactions including focal excitation with lateral inhibition over the range observed, ranging from excitation over a radius of 200μm or more surrounded by strong inhibition, to excitation over 50μm or less surrounded by weak inhibition. The longer-range intracortical interactions might be quantitatively negligible in comparison, but if not their periodicity (presumably due to the early periodicity of orientation columns) might also contribute to the period of ocular dominance patches. Similarly, a variety of arbor sizes, ranging from arbors uniform over a diameter of about 850μm to larger, tapering arbors, would yield 850μm patch periods by an arbor-driven mechanism. Such a mechanism seems consistent with X-cell, though not with Y-cell, initial arbor sizes. X-cells mature earlier and might therefore determine patch size (Garraghty, Sur, & Sherman, 1986).

In the model, correlations that are narrow relative to a geniculocortical arbor radius lead to increased binocularity at the borders between patches. In the cat, layer 4 does not consist entirely of monocular cells. Rather, there is a substantial overlap of left- and right-eye input at the borders between ocular dominance patches (Shatz & Stryker, 1978). If X-cells determine patch organization, this overlap is consistent with the fact that X-cells appear correlated over separations of only about $\frac{1}{2}$ of a geniculocortical arbor radius. The increase in monocularity seen with strabismus or alternating monocular deprivation is consistent with the increase in monocularity seen in the model when opposite eyes have decreased correlations or are anticorrelated.

Not all higher mammals develop ocular dominance segregation. Many New World monkeys show no segregation, although there are signs of periodicity in the innervation to cortex representing each eye (reviewed in LeVay & Nelson, 1989). The model suggests a possible explanation for this result. The development of a periodic difference in the synaptic strengths serving the two eyes follows robustly from the choice of correlation function and cortical interactions. However, whether this development of periodicity leads to monocularity and thus to segregation depends on the constraints. If the total synaptic strength over a cortical cell is limited, for example, then the synapses representing the weaker eye in a patch must decrease in strength as the synapses representing the stronger eye grow; this will lead to segregation. If synapses serving both eyes are increasing in strength everywhere, however, then the synapses representing the weaker eye will simply grow more slowly than those representing the dominant eye. In the absence of such constraints, then, one may see periodicity in each eye's innervation without seeing organization of monocular patches.

The model accounts simply for a number of other phenomena seen in development, including refinement of receptive fields, development of patchy geniculocortical arbors, and the effects of monocular deprivation including many elements of a critical period. In summary, a simple correlation-based plasticity rule, combined with a very simple model of geniculate correlations, geniculocortical connectivity, and cortical connectivity or interactions, is sufficient to account for a large part of the observed phenomenology of ocular dominance segregation. This lends plausibility to the notion that these phenomena depend largely on such simple elements, which many more detailed mechanisms would have in common.

Experiments Suggested by the Model

The most fundamental experiments suggested by the model are to characterize the correlations, arbors, and cortical interactions early in development when patch formation begins. Such measurements are quite difficult technically. These measurements, if made in differing brain regions or species, can be used to test a proposed developmental mechanism by determining whether the periodicity that emerges in each case is consistent with the measurements of the functions defined by the proposed mechanism. For example, area 18 of the cat has patches 1.5 to 2 times wider than those in area 17; arbors are also more widespread, as are correlations since area 18 is Y-cell dominated (Anderson et al., 1988; Humphrey et al., 1985a, 1985b; Swindale, 1988). If a Hebb mechanism is responsible, young kittens should show either a difference between the two regions in intracortical connectivities sufficient to account for the difference in patch width, or predominantly excitatory intracortical connections resulting in arbor-limited patch widths.

Perturbation of the three functions in an experimental preparation before the onset of segregation, and comparison of the resulting periodicity to the unperturbed case, can also test mechanisms. The model predicts that broader correlations within each eye will increase monocularity of layer 4 for mechanisms of the type we study. This could be tested by inducing broader correlations through pharmacological interventions in the retinas. One could also measure whether retinal correlations are broadened in animals deprived of pattern vision. Such animals have increased numbers of monocular cortical neurons (reviewed in Sherman & Spear, 1982). Measurement could also determine whether retinal correlations are broader relative to geniculocortical arbors in monkeys, which have almost completely segregated inputs to layer 4, than in cats, which have a more overlapping innervation.

If a Hebb mechanism underlies ocular dominance plasticity, periodic ocular dominance segregation depends on intracortical synaptic connections. Inhibition of all postsynaptic cells will eliminate activation of such connections. Such inhibition can be achieved by local infusion into cortex of muscimol, which mimics the inhibitory neurotransmitter GABA. If a Hebb mechanism is responsible for column development, one would not expect a periodic pattern of ocular dominance organization to occur in a muscimol-infused region, although individual cells might become monocular. Alternatively, one can attempt to modify rather than eliminate the intracortical interactions. Local infusion of bicuculline, which blocks the receptors for GABA, will selectively eliminate inhibitory intracortical connections. If the resulting purely excitatory intracortical synaptic connections yields patches with an increased period, this would be consistent with a Hebb mechanism whose period is determined by the intracortical interactions. If patch period were unchanged by bicuculline, one would conclude either that the period was normally arbor-limited (which could be tested by measuring whether intracortical interactions were predominantly excitatory during initial column development) or that a non-Hebb mechanism was involved.

Comparison to Other Models

Models of Ocular Dominance Segregation

A variety of related models of ocular dominance column formation have been developed. In a series of papers in the 1970s, Willshaw and von der Malsburg (1976, 1979; von der Malsburg & Willshaw, 1976, 1977; von der Malsburg, 1979) demonstrated that mechanisms like those described here, as well as mathematically similar mechanisms involving exchange of biochemical markers, could give rise to the development of ocular dominance stripes and to the development of topographic mappings. Fraser (1980, 1985) developed a model of development of the retinal projection to optic tectum incorporating a series of activity-independent interactions of varying strengths. When a weak activity-dependent competitive interaction is added and two eyes innervate a single tectum, ocular dominance stripes can form (Fraser, 1985). The model as implemented on a computer did not involve change of strength of individual synapses, but rather movements of whole terminal arbors of individual retinal cells; hence the width of stripes was determined by the arbor size, and was equal to either one or two terminal arbor widths.

Swindale (1980) assumed that synapses exert influences on one another's growth as a function of their eye of origin and the distance across cortex between them. He showed that if synapses facilitate synapses of the same eye at short distance and inhibit them at longer distances, and conversely inhibit synapses of the opposite eye at short distance and facilitate them at longer distances, many phenomena of ocular dominance stripes could be reproduced. The width of the stripes could be simply determined from these influences. Synapses were identified only by eye of origin without regard to retinotopic position of origin, and hence receptive field and arbor structures were not addressed. In the limit in which correlations within an eye extend very broadly compared to an arbor radius, our model yields an equation like Swindale's for cortical ocular dominance, but the influence between synapses becomes expressed in terms of measurable quantities, namely the correlation, arbor, and cortical interaction functions. Hence our model generalizes Swindale's to more complex correlation structures, while providing specific biological underpinnings to Swindale's postulated influence in the limit in which correlations extend broadly within each eye. Our model also allows understanding of receptive field and arbor as well as cortical structure, and demonstrates and analyzes much more generally the conditions under which columns may form.

Cooper and colleagues have studied development of monocularity in single cortical cells, using a Hebb rule whose postsynaptic threshold for synaptic modification depends nonlinearly on postsynaptic activity[18] (Bienenstock, Cooper, & Munro, 1982; Bear & Cooper, chap. 2 in this volume). The sliding threshold is an alternative method of stabilizing a Hebb synapse rule, that is of ensuring that total synaptic strengths stay within a reasonable range. The effect of this sliding threshold is to subtract a time-varying amount $\epsilon(t)$ from all synapses on a cortical cell at each timestep (see definition of ϵ^L in appendix 1), and thus to subtract $A(\delta)\epsilon(t)$ from the total synaptic strength $S(\delta)$.[19] When the mean output of the cortical cell is low compared to the desired level, less is subtracted from each synapse, raising the total synaptic strength over the cortical cell. This occurs when either the activity input to the cell, or the synaptic strength over the cell, or both, are low. When the mean output of the cortical cell is high, the cortical cell's total synaptic strength is lowered in a similar manner.

In contrast, we stabilized the Hebb synapse rule with constraints on total synaptic strength over a cortical cell. The effect of this constraint is also to subtract a time-varying amount $\epsilon(t)$ from all synapses on a cortical cell at each timestep. For a fixed level of mean input activity, the two rules are essentially identical. If mean input activity changes, the nonlinear sliding threshold causes an increase or decrease in total synaptic strength that returns mean cortical activity to the desired baseline, whereas constraints on total synaptic strength keep total synaptic strength fixed and allow the change in mean cortical activity to persist. The biological truth is likely not to be as simple as either of these rules. The changes in cortical cells in response to deprivation or saturation of input activity are likely to be complex. Nonetheless, it is of interest to contrast the behavior of the two rules in such situations (see also discussion in Bear & Cooper, chap. 2 in this volume):

1. The most obvious prediction of the nonlinear sliding threshold model is that, in response to a period of reduced activation, cortical cells should

---

[18]The idea of a linear sliding threshold for synaptic modification is virtually as old as the Hebb synapse itself (Rochester & Holland, 1956; see also Sejnowski, 1977). Previously the sliding threshold was often taken to be the mean activity of the postsynaptic cell, so that activity greater than the mean led to strengthening of correlated synapses, while activity less than the mean led to weakening of correlated synapses. Such a sliding threshold need not alter the mean activity itself. Bienenstock, Cooper, and Munro added the idea of a nonlinear dependence of the threshold on the mean postsynaptic activity, designed to return mean cortical activity to a fixed prespecified level despite lowering or raising of input activity.

[19]If different populations of inputs have different mean activity levels, as in monocular deprivation, the $\epsilon(t)$ subtracted from the less active inputs is proportionally smaller, as the definition of ϵ^L indicates. Less active inputs still lose strength relative to more active inputs, however, because more active inputs gain far more through synaptic interactions resulting from coactivation of the postsynaptic cell. If all inputs have the same mean activity level, $\epsilon(t)$ is identical for all synapses on the cortical cell.

develop increased total synaptic strength and thus become hyperreactive to normal stimulation.[20] In fact, binocular deprivation during the critical period never results in a subsequent increase in cortical responsiveness. Rather, such deprivation either leaves subsequent cortical responsiveness unchanged, as would be predicted by conservation of synaptic strength, or else decreases cortical responsiveness.[21]

2. When cortex is totally inhibited by infusion of muscimol, each synapse decays proportionally to its mean activity, without interaction between synapses. Using conservation of synaptic strength, monocular deprivation then leads to an ocular dominance shift to the closed eye, as observed experimentally. Using the nonlinear sliding threshold, one must assume that the threshold cannot slide sufficiently low to allow the more active eye's inputs to be rewarded. In this case, there is nothing to stabilize the synaptic strengths: All synaptic strengths will decrease to zero, although the open eye's strengths will decrease faster than the closed eye's.

3. After monocular deprivation, reverse suture (opening the previously deprived eye while simultaneously suturing closed the previously open eye) if initiated sufficiently early leads to an ocular dominance shift in favor of the newly opened eye. To model reverse suture, both models must assume some small ability of the newly opened eye to activate the postsynaptic cell in spite of the fact that it has just suffered from monocular deprivation. The newly opened eye then gains more than the closed eye from synaptic interactions, because the opened eye's activity is more effective in activating the postsynaptic cell. Yet the newly opened eye also loses more through decay, by virtue of having a greater quantity of activity while the cortical cell is often inactive. Both eyes are likely to have decreasing

---

[20]Bear and Cooper argue that binocular deprivation corresponds to an input of noise, and define this to mean that average input activity is 0. In this case, the cortical threshold has no effect, on the average, on synaptic strength (see definition of ϵ^L in appendix 1 for the case when $<f_1[a^L(\alpha,t)]> = 0$; Bear and Cooper use $f_1(a) = a$). However, the basis of this proposal is unclear, as ocular dominance segregation begins in utero in monkeys, and occurs in dark-reared animals. The proposal, even if accepted, does not provide a robust explanation of binocular deprivation. If average input activity were ϵ where $\epsilon > 0$, then hyperreactiveness would develop. Many forms of deprivation, yielding many different input activity levels, have been studied experimentally and none lead to subsequent hyperresponsiveness.

[21]Loss of responsiveness, as well as loss of selectivity of responses, occurs in a significant percentage of cortical cells after longer times of binocular deprivation in kittens. However, these effects do not appear to occur over short times of a few days to a week of binocular deprivation (Sherk & Stryker, 1976; see review in Movshon & Van Sluyters, 1981). In contrast, monocular deprivation over such short time causes strong shifts of ocular dominance. Therefore, these two effects of longer-term binocular deprivation may simply reflect atrophy due to disuse, which may occur through mechanisms different than the competitive mechanisms studied by the models. Alternatively, these effects might be explicable within the context of the models by postulating that inputs become uncorrelated, or that cortical cells fail to reach the threshold for synaptic reward.

input strength in the absense of conservation of synaptic strength, but it is not clear which eye will decrease faster. The nonlinear sliding threshold model assumes that the threshold slides faster than synaptic strengths decrease, so that eventually the average activation in response to the newly opened eye is suprathreshold and that eye can gain strength. Using conservation of total synaptic strength, one assumes that the input strength of the newly opened eye decreases relatively more slowly than that of the newly closed eye.[22]

4. Finally, when the cortex is disinhibited by application of bicuculline, there is significant reduction in the ocular dominance shift in response to subsequent monocular deprivation (Ramoa, Paradiso, & Freeman, 1988). Stimulus selectivity of cortical neurons was strongly reduced during bicuculline infusion: Cortical neurons responded to a much broader range of stimuli than normal, and to stimulation in a much larger portion of the visual field than normal. The investigators suggested that this may lead to an increase in the correlation between the spontaneous activity from the closed eye and the visually-driven responses of the open eye. They propose that such correlation accounts for the decreased effect of monocular deprivation. If this is the correct explanation of the reduced ocular dominance shift, the form of stabilization is irrelevant to the outcome.

To summarize, both methods are equivalent in normal circumstances. Neither method is perfect under conditions of deprivation or overstimulation of cortex. The robust features of a Hebb-type model, such as refinement of receptive fields and development of ocular dominance, depend on differentials in the relative rates of growth of different synaptic populations. These robust effects occur in most cases due to the synaptic interactions rather than to decay. The methods of stabilization of synaptic strengths determine the absolute values of the growth rates. These methods are motivated by mathematical convenience as much as or more than by biological knowledge. The important point in understanding a correlation-based model is to understand the reliable conclusions that can be drawn, and by and large this means understanding the results of the synaptic interactions that such models have in common.

---

[22]There is a critical period for reverse suture, as for monocular deprivation, experimentally as well as in both models. For a reverse shift to occur in the models, just as for ordinary monocular deprivation, the newly opened eye must more effectively activate the cell than the newly closed eye. This depends both on the differential in their activities, and on the differential in their synaptic strengths on the cell at the time of reversal. For any given differential in activity, there will be some "point of no return", a differential of synaptic strength which the activity difference can no longer reverse.

Some Related Correlation-Based Models

Linsker (1986, 1988) developed a model of plasticity that is formally nearly identical to ours. However, the implementation of the model is quite different. Linsker considered inputs from only a single eye. Arbors were assumed to be gaussian. Synapses were allowed to have either positive or negative strength, which was achieved in one of two ways. First, each individual synapse might be capable of being both positive and negative. In contrast, biological synapses are exclusively excitatory or exclusively inhibitory. Equivalently, there might be two populations, one exclusively positive, one exclusively negative, subject to conditions that render them the positive and negative halves of a single, statistically indivisible population. The two populations must have approximately identical distributions of locations and initial arborizations, and the correlation between the activities of two inputs must depend only on the distance between them, without regard for whether either is inhibitory or excitatory. This is biologically implausible, because an excitatory and an inhibitory population would be expected to have different inputs and different connectivities, and because inhibitory cells are often interneurons which, when active, inhibit nearby excitatory cells; but it is not impossible.

Linsker applied his model to study the development of orientation selectivity in a visual cortical layer from a non-oriented input layer. In cats, all cortical cells are oriented, so the non-oriented input layer must represent the LGN. Inputs from LGN to cortex are exclusively excitatory. This represents an additional problem for the use of negative synapses. In monkeys, the cortical layer 4 cells receiving geniculate input are not oriented. Hence orientation selectivity in monkeys might be regarded as emerging from projections from layer 4 of cortex to the upper layers, in which case both excitatory and inhibitory projections could be involved.

Because synapses from each location in Linsker's model can be either positive or negative, the initial condition is a random perturbation from all synapses having zero strength. Thus, formally, his model of a single eye's inputs with synapses of either sign, is equivalent to our model of S^D, the difference between the strength of two eyes.

His model involves four essential steps. First, with an input layer of random noise, all synapses are made to grow until saturation, without synaptic interactions (formally, the $-\epsilon$ decay term is made large and positive). Because arbors overlap, input cells at the next layer becomecorrelated in their activity by virtue of receiving common inputs. These correlations decrease with distance in proportion to the corresponding decrease in the overlap of arbors. Second, when a layer with such correlations projects to a cell in a third layer, the fastest-growing pattern is one that grows faster in the center than in the periphery of that cell's receptive field, as we have seen. The cell is stabilized by fixing the final summed synaptic strength over the cell (excitatory strength minus inhibitory strength).[23] This has the effect of fixing the final percentage of positive and negative synapses, because all synapses saturate at either the maximum positive or the maximum negative strength. When 30% of final synapses are forced to be negative, the result is a center of positive synapses surrounded by a ring of negative synapses. Hence, formation of these "center-surround" cells depends critically on the negative synapses and the stabilization condition. The robust feature is that central synapses grow faster than peripheral ones. In a layer of such "center-surround" cells, cells separated by short distances, whose centers overlap, have correlated activities, whereas cells separated by longer distances, such that one cell's center overlaps the other's surround, have anticorrelated activities. This yields a Mexican hat correlation function.

Third, suppose a layer with a Mexican hat correlation function, whether derived as just described or otherwise, projects to a cell in a further layer. We have seen that if such a correlation function is sufficiently narrow with respect to the arbor function, the fastest-growing receptive field pattern has a positive stripe adjacent to a negative stripe. Linsker used such a correlation function but with additional oscillations in sign with increasing distance, and found that oriented cells can result. I am told that oriented cells can also result from such a correlation function when synapses are required to remain positive (Linsker, private communication), though in my own experience special constraints seem necessary to avoid circularly symmetric results. Finally, Linsker showed that if these oriented cortical cells develop while connected by weak excitatory corticocortical synaptic connections, an interesting cortical organization of orientation modules can arise. Note that our eigenfunction analysis of S^D suggests that cortical organization should include an oscillation in phase, between positive and negative synapses, as one moves across cortex. Linsker's constraints, which force a majority of synapses on each cell to be positive, suppress the growth of oscillating modes in favor of modes with frequency zero. These points are discussed in greater detail elsewhere (Miller & Stryker, 1989).

In sum, Linsker developed a very similar model, and pointed out that Hebbian mechanisms can determine the structure of individual receptive

---

[23]Linsker's constraint consists of subtracting a term $-|k_2|(\bar{s} - \text{TARGET})$ from the expression for $\frac{d}{dt} s(\alpha)$, where $s(\alpha)$ is the strength of an individual synapse and $\bar{s}$ is the average value of s over the cortical cell. $|k_2|$ is large so that this term dominates $\frac{d}{dt} s(\alpha)$ for all α if the average synaptic strength is not approximately equal to TARGET, and thus drives s back toward TARGET. TARGET, in Linsker's notation, is $-k_1/k_2$.

fields and their cortical organization in very interesting ways. The value may be more as an important example of the capacities of Hebbian mechanisms than as a specific model of biological phenomena. Linsker's results can be simply understood on the basis of the eigenfunction analysis of the development of S^D.

A number of authors have recently explored similar models of Hebb-type development in a single postsynaptic cell, in which synapses may be positive or negative, in terms of an eigenfunction analysis and its relation to methods of statistical analysis or information theory (Baldi & Hornik, 1989; Linsker, 1988; Oja, 1982; Sanger, 1989). Our analysis contains two important features not seen in the other work. First, we have shown that as a model of S^D, that is of the development of ocular dominance, such models are biologically realistic and resilient against nonlinearities. In contrast, model outcomes that are dependent on the existence of both positive and negative synapses, on an initial condition which is a small random perturbation of synaptic strengths on both sides of zero, or on linearity cannot be regarded as applicable to biological systems. In addition, we have developed the eigenfunction analysis for a model with a layer of postsynaptic cells interconnected by synaptic interactions. In this context, two novel features arise. First, characteristic receptive fields (the eigenfunctions of the isolated cell) acquire a phase shift or characteristic oscillation between cortical cells to form the characteristic patterns or eigenfunctions of the system as a whole. Second, the characteristic receptive fields themselves are altered by the cortical interactions. In particular, monocular characteristic fields have both their growth rate and their degree of monocularity enhanced at the dominant frequency of the cortical interaction.

There is an interesting connection between the case of "identity mapping" in backpropagation networks, discussed by Zipser (chap. 8 in this volume), and simple Hebb-type models (Baldi & Hornik, 1989). Identity mapping is a form of unsupervised learning in which the input is also the desired output, and a layer of some number N of intermediate or hidden units are trained by backpropagation of error to produce this desired identity mapping. If the backpropagation network is linear, the hidden units extract the N fastest-growing eigenvectors of the input correlation matrix. An isolated Hebb-type cell is similarly predominantly shaped by the fastest-growing eigenvector of the input correlation matrix.

Outstanding Theoretical Questions

Many theoretical questions are raised by the problems we have addressed. We may roughly subdivide these as questions involving the application of simple correlation-based models to other problems, and questions about the effects of incorporating greater biological complexity into the models.

In the first category, one outstanding question involves application of simple models to a three-dimensional output structure. Under what conditions will two inputs segregate into stripes, that is a breakup of the retinotopic map into alternating patches, and under what conditions will they instead segregate into laminae, that is two complete retinotopic maps one above the other? The visual cortex in most species that show segregation, and the amphibia and fish optic tecta, form stripes, while the visual cortex in tree shrew (Kretz, Rager, & Norton, 1986), and the lateral geniculate nucleus, segregate into laminae. A simple proposal motivated by the model presented here is that inputs from a single eye extend in a plane with more excitatory connections, while the two eyes segregate from one another in a plane with more inhibitory connections. Alternatively, Schmidt (1985) suggested that inputs from a single eye may extend in a plan determined by a bias in the plane of extension of dendrites of receiving cells. A related, more specific, outstanding problem, is to study the conditions under which simple models will reproduce the variety of laminar segregation processes seen in the LGN. Both for studies of LGN and of cortex, one would like to understand the effects of having four statistical classes of inputs (ON- and OFF-cells from each eye), or even eight classes (X- and Y-cells of each of the four previous types). To pursue such models very far, one must have reasonable biological ideas of the correlations within and between the classes of inputs (Mastronarde, 1989).

Another problem is to understand the determinates of the form of ocular dominance stripes or patches. For example, in the monkey the stripes tend to be long and straight and to run perpendicular to the borders of primary visual cortex (LeVay, Connolly, Houde, & Van Essen, 1985). In the cat, the segregation is more patchy, irregular, and rarely straight, and does not run at any special angle with respect to the borders (Anderson et al., 1988). Our simple linear theory predicts the wavelength of periodicity, but the final form depends on a nonlinear interaction between all the characteristic patterns with that wavelength and hence cannot be predicted by the theory. Swindale (1980) showed that ocular dominance stripes resulting from the simple dynamics he proposed and a simple nonlinearity tend to run perpendicular to the borders. He also showed that a bias in the direction of cortical growth during column formation could lead to extension of the stripes in the direction of preferred cortical growth. Because his dynamics result as a simple limiting case from our model, similar results can be obtained with our model, but one would like to understand more generally when these results will or will not occur. A recent theory assumes the existence of patches or stripes of a fixed width, and proposes that their arrangement is determined by the need to optimize retinotopic match between inputs and cortex (Anderson et al., 1988; Jones, Van Sluyters, & Murphy, 1988). This theory can explain the variation of form across species by examining the diverging shapes of cortex or tectum and layouts of the overall retinotopic map in the various species considered. One would like to understand if correlation-based mechanisms would robustly tend to cause such optimization to occur.

Understanding the conditions under which simple correlation-based models will yield orientation selectivity with nonnegative synapses remains an important problem. Under such conditions, one would also like to understand the relationship of orientation to ocular dominance, both on individual cells and across the cortex as a whole. For example, if C^S is Mexican hat, like the function Linsker used to obtain oriented receptive fields, while C^D is purely positive, to produce monocularity, the eigenfunction analysis suggests that a monocular and oriented cell could develop even when all synapses remain positive. C^S and C^D can have the required form if $C^{SameEye}$ is Mexican hat and opposite eyes are anticorrelated. Monocular and at least somewhat oriented cells do develop in this case, provided that synapses are constrained by multiplication of all synapses by a constant after each timestep to preserve the sum of total synaptic strength, rather than by subtraction of a constant from all synapses. With subtractive constraints, monocularity may develop but the receptive field tends to refine to a circularly symmetric structure. However, multiplicative constraints will never allow monocularity to develop without opposite-eye anticorrelations, which seems overly restrictive.[24] One would like to understand more generally the classes of methods of stabilization and saturation that can yield the oriented result. More recently, I have proposed that interactions between ON-center and OFF-center inputs may yield oriented cells using positive synapses in a manner robust with respect to methods of stabilization (Miller, 1989b). ON- and OFF-center inputs are known to be anticorrelated with one another at retinotopic separations over which their centers overlap (Mastronarde, 1983a, 1983b). Orientation selectivity would

---

[24]Let the equations, before multiplicative constraints, be written $\frac{d}{dt}S^S = L^S S^S$, $\frac{d}{dt}S^D = L^D S^D$. Then, in the absence of the nonlinear cutoff of synaptic strengths at zero, it is easy to show that S^S will develop under multiplicative constraints into the principal eigenfunction of L^S (first noted in Oja, 1982; intuitively, S^S is really growing linearly because the multiplicative renormalization is only a change of scale, hence the principal eigenfunction will exponentially dominate). Given the nonlinear cutoff, it is plausible to think that the oriented structure would persist. The development of S^D, in the absence of the cutoff, involves the growth of all eigenfunctions of L^D but with growth rates equal to the corresponding eigenvalue minus the principle eigenvalue of L^S; that is, patterns of S^D must grow faster than the fastest pattern in S^S, or the multiplicative renormalization that keeps the sum constant will cause the difference to shrink. Hence, monocularity should develop if and only if the principal eigenfunction of L^D is monocular and has a larger eigenvalue than that of L^S. Note that this requires opposite-eye anticorrelations.

develop if these inputs were correlated with one another at greater distances of retinotopic separation; receptive fields like those of Fig. 7.19b would develop, where now black and white are to be interpreted as dominance by ON- versus OFF-center cells rather than by left- versus right-eye cells.

Many important problems are raised by the plasticity of somatotopic maps in adult somatosensory cortex. Monocular deprivation shifts are a crude form of the result that more active synapses gain more territory at the expense of less active synapses, but in that case a critical period arises due to the disconnection of one eye's inputs. One would like to understand the conditions under which a cortical map can be dynamically and reversibly maintained so that the amount of cortical territory controlled by a portion of the periphery is roughly porportional to the level of activity of that portion of the periphery, up to limits imposed by the finite extent of terminal arborizations. This might be achieved by the use of multiplicative constraints. An important feature of somatosensory plasticity appears to be the overlap rule: The degree of overlap of two receptive fields a fixed distance apart across cortex remains roughly constant (Allard, 1989; Merzenich et al., 1988; Sur, Merzenich, & Kaas, 1980). This is equivalent to the statement that receptive field size varies inversely with cortical magnification, or to the statement that point image size (the size of the cortical area activated by a given peripheral location) remains constant. Understanding the conditions under which a correlation-based rule will yield this result remains an outstanding problem.

The second type of question, as suggested, concerns the effects of incorporating greater biological complexity into the model. A more complex model might consider the possibility that intracortical connections, geniculocortical anatomical connectivity or input correlations are modifiable during development. Both excitatory and inhibitory intracortical synapses show modifications by early experience in cat visual cortex (Beaulieu & Colonnier, 1987), though it is not clear if such changes occur as early as patch formation. The final structure of ocular dominance patches develops through anatomical removal of geniculate input terminals from patches of opposite-eye input. Many postsynaptic cells in layer 4 of monkey visual cortex and in frog optic tectum similarly remove their dendrites from patches of inappropriate eye input (Katz & Constantine-Paton, 1988; Katz, Gilbert, & Wiesel, 1989). We have assumed that these anatomical changes in geniculocortical connectivity occur subsequent to the development of an initial physiological pattern of ocular dominance. Finally, both dendrites and retinogeniculate arbors of retinal ganglion cells are undergoing extensive modifications during the time of patch development (Ramoa, Campbell, & Shatz, 1988), and it is quite possible that geniculate circuitry is also developing at that time, so correlations among geniculate inputs may be changing during patch formation.

Many other factors might also contribute to the final developmental outcome under correlation-based models. For example, the details both of the arrangement of the grid of inputs, and of the retinotopic map of that grid onto cortex, might play important roles in the development of receptive field structure (Mallot, 1985; Soodak, 1987); so too may interactions among the many statistical subtypes of inputs serving each eye. Activity-independent interactions, among inputs and between inputs and postsynaptic cells, must be considered (Fraser, 1980, 1985). We have assumed that only pairwise correlations among inputs are significant to the activity-dependent interactions, but higher-order correlations may also play a role (see footnote 2, appendix 1). Details of the temporal structure of the plasticity mechanism, and in general greater biophysical detail, may contribute new features to development. In studying each potentially complicating factor, one would like to understand whether, and in what ways, they can lead to qualitatively new developmental outcomes or to significant quantitative alterations in development, in comparison to the outcomes already inherent in simple correlation-based interactions.

CONCLUSION

A variety of biophysical and biochemical mechanisms may underlie the plasticity associated with correlation-based mechanisms of neural development. In this chapter I have attempted to demonstrate that many features of development under such mechanisms can be studied and understood in terms of a few simple features that are largely independent of the underlying details. These features include the correlations in activity among input neurons; the connectivity between the input neurons and the receiving neurons; interactions by which coactive synapses influence one another's development; and the constraints or limits that stabilize synaptic strengths.

A simple model, in which correlations, connectivity, and interactions depend only on the distances between neurons and, in the case of correlations, on the eye represented, is sufficient to explain a wide variety of features of the development of ocular dominance patches in mammalian visual cortex. These features include the development of patches and the determination of their width; the refinement of individual cortical receptive fields; the refinement and confinement to patches of the terminal arbors of geniculate cells; the effects of the breadth of correlation or of opposite-eye anticorrelations on the degree of segregation that develops; and the effects on development of abnormal experience such as monocular deprivation, including elements of a critical period.

A critical feature characterizing a proposed mechanism of ocular dominance plasticity is the type of cortical interaction function it predicts. If a mechanism predicts a purely excitatory cortical interaction, it predicts ocular dominance periodicity determined by the arbor diameter and dependent on constraints that tightly conserve total synaptic strength over each geniculate terminal arbor. If a mechanism predicts a mixed excitatory and inhibitory cortical interaction, whose dominant oscillation is smaller than an arbor diameter, it predicts ocular dominance periodicity determined by the cortical interaction and not dependent on constraints on geniculate arbors. This provides a basis for experimental distinction between proposed mechanisms.

By understanding the features in a model that are responsible for the developmental outcome, one can gain insight into the elements of a proposed biological mechanism that may be critical to the observed biological outcomes. At the same time, one can learn which elements of the model's outcome are likely to be robust, and which are likely to depend on the probably unbiological details of implementation. In the model of visual development, the influences of synapses on one another through correlations lead to robust tendencies to development of receptive field refinement and monocularity. If individual cortical cells do tend to become monocular, the extension of influences across cortex by intracortical interactions leads robustly to an oscillation of ocular dominance with a period selected by the intracortical interactions. Other features of the model, such as the method of stabilization, may suppress or enhance the expression of these tendencies, but are not fundamentally responsible for them.

In conclusion, even a simple neural model can serve to unify a large group of phenomena in terms of measurable biological elements. At the same time, a model can point out new lines of distinction between mechanisms. In this way, neural modeling may play an important part in the effort to understand the mechanisms underlying neural development and function.

ACKNOWLEDGMENTS

I would like to acknowledge the advice, support, and collaboration of my graduate advisors, Michael P. Stryker and Joseph B. Keller, in the modeling work described in this chapter. I thank Barbara Chapman, Michael Stryker, and Kathleen Zahs for helpful comments on this chapter. I was supported while writing this chapter by National Science Foundation grant BNS-8820406, a Bioscience Grant for an International Joint Research Project from the NEDO, Japan, and a grant from the System Development Foundation, all awarded to Dr. Michael P. Stryker.

APPENDIX 1: FORMULATION OF THE MODEL
EQUATIONS

We use the following notation in addition to that defined in the text. $c(x,t)$ is the activity (membrane potential, or spike frequency) of the cortical cell at x at time t. $a^L(\alpha,t), a^R(\alpha,t)$ is the activity of the geniculate input representing the left or right eye, respectively, from position α at time t. We formulate equations for S^L. Equations for S^R are identical if L and R are exchanged throughout.

For a Hebb rule, the model equations may be formulated as follows. First, we formulate the equation for the Hebb plasticity rule itself. For an individual left-eye synapse from α to x, the change at a given time is proportional to a product of some function of postsynaptic activity times some function of presynaptic activity, that is to $[c(x,t) - c_{\text{thres}}(x)]f_1[a^L(\alpha,t)]$. For convenience, we have assumed the postsynaptic function is linear, but as discussed in the text and in appendix 2 this is not necessary to our analysis. $c_{\text{thres}}(x)$ is a fixed threshold; this could also be taken to be a function of mean cortical activity at x [Sejnowski, 1977; Bear and Cooper, chap. 2 in this volume]. f_1 is an arbitrary function, presumably monotonic and incorporating threshold and saturation effects. There are $A(x - \alpha)$ such synapses, all undergoing identical change, hence the total change must be multiplied by $A(x - \alpha)$. Finally we subtract terms representing possible activity-independent synaptic decays (or growths) to obtain the following equation for a Hebb rule:

$$\frac{d}{dt}S^L(X,\alpha,t) = \lambda A(x-\alpha)[c(x,t) - c_{\text{thres}}(x)]f_1[a^L(\alpha,t)] - \gamma S^L(x,\alpha,t)$$
$$- \epsilon'^L A(x-\alpha). \tag{A1}$$

Here λ, γ and ϵ' are constants.

Second, we formulate an equation for cortical activity as a function of input activity. We take the net LGN input to the cortical cell at x at time t to be

$$\text{net}_{\text{LGN}}(x,t) = \sum_\alpha \left\{ S^L(x,\alpha,t)f_2[a^L(\alpha,t)] + S^R(x,\alpha,t)f_2[a^R(\alpha,t)] \right\}.$$

f_2 incorporates threshold and saturation effects. We assume there is also cortical input given by $\Sigma_y B(x - y)c(y,t)$. $B(x - y)$ is a function describing intracortical synaptic connectivity, taken for simplicity to be fixed. We assume that cortical activity depends linearly on the net input, though again a nonlinear activation function can be accommodated. Finally, we assume there is some intrinsic cortical activity $c'(x)$. Thus,

$$c(x,t) = \text{net}_{\text{LGN}}(x,t) + \sum_y B(x - y)c(y,t) + c'(x).$$

In matrix notation, this is $(1 - \mathbf{B})\mathbf{c}(t) = \text{net}_{\text{LGN}}(t) + \mathbf{c}'$ where $\mathbf{1}$ is the identity matrix and $\mathbf{B}$ is the matrix with elements $\mathbf{B}_{xy} = B(x - y)$. Defining the intracortical interaction function $I(x - y)$ by the matrix equation[1] $\mathbf{I} = (1 - \mathbf{B})^{-1}$ yields

$$c(x,t) = \sum_y I(x - y)\text{net}_{\text{LGN}}(y,t) + c_{\text{int}}(x) \tag{A2}$$

where $\mathbf{c}_{\text{int}} = \mathbf{I}\mathbf{c}'$ is the intrinsic cortical activity in the absence of input activation.

Substituting equation $A2$ for $c(x)$ into equation $A1$ yields an equation for the change in synaptic strengths as a function of input activities. Averaging this equation over input patterns yields an equation in terms of the measurable statistical properties of the inputs.[2] Let correlation functions C^{LL}, C^{LR}, describing the correlation in firing between two left-eye inputs or between a left-eye and a right-eye input, respectively, be defined by[3]

$$C^{LL}(\alpha - \beta) = \langle f_1[a^L(\alpha,t)]f_2[a^L(\beta,t)]\rangle,$$

$$C^{LR}(\alpha - \beta) = \langle f_1[a^L(\alpha,t)]f_2[a^R(\beta,t)]\rangle,$$

---

[1]This inverse will exist if $\mathbf{B}$ is sufficiently small, mathematically, or biologically if we assume cortical activity is determined by input activity.

[2]The equation obtained is actually an infinite series. The lowest order term involves two-point correlations of the input activities, and is the term we present. The higher order terms include the three-point, four-point, . . . structure of the inputs, that is the tendency of three or more inputs to fluctuate together in their activities beyond what would be predicted from knowledge of their pairwise correlations. We discard these terms for simplicity, but note that they are small either if λ is small or if fluctuations are small. It is of interest to establish theoretically what nontrivial dynamics might arise from such higher order correlational structure. The averaging is done using the smoothing procedure which is described by Keller (1977).

[3]We assume here for simplicity that $\langle f_1[a^L(\alpha,t)]\rangle = 0$. If this is not the case, C^{LL} should be defined as $\langle f_1[a^L(\alpha,t)]f_2[a^L(\beta,t)]\rangle - \langle f_1[a^L(\alpha,t)]\rangle\langle f_2[a^L(\beta,t)]\rangle$ (and similarly for C^{LR}), so that $\lim_{\alpha\to\infty}C^{LL}(\alpha) = \lim_{\alpha\to\infty}C^{LR}(\alpha) = 0$. Then our equations are identical except that C^{LL}, C^{LR} are replaced everywhere by $C^{LL} + \theta$, $C^{LR} + \theta$ where $\theta = \langle f_1[a^L(\alpha,t)]\rangle\langle f_2[a^L(\beta,t)]\rangle$. Note that θ does not depend on L, R, α, or β if we assume that all inputs are statistically equivalent. This θ is the same as the parameter k_2 in Linsker (1986). θ would not appear in the equation obtained in the text for S^D, and hence its presence would not affect the analysis of the development of ocular dominance segregation.

where $< >$ signifies an average over input patterns. Then the equation obtained is

$$\frac{d}{dt} S^L(x,\alpha,t) = \lambda A(x-\alpha) \sum_{y,\beta} I(x-y)[C^{LL}(\alpha-\beta)S^L(y,\beta,t)$$
$$+ C^{LR}(\alpha-\beta)S^R(y,\beta,t)] - \gamma S^L(x,\alpha,t) - \epsilon^L A(x-\alpha)$$

(A3)

where $\epsilon^L = \epsilon' - \lambda[c_{int}(x) - c_{thres}(x)] <f_1[a^L(\alpha,t)]>$. This is Eq. 1 in the text.

This equation is not unique to a Hebb synapse mechanism, but can be derived from a variety of biological mechanisms. For example, in a mechanism relying on trophic factors, cortical cells release diffusible or actively transported substances, in proportion to their activity. The substances in turn are taken up by synaptic terminals in proportion to presynaptic activity, as would be expected if uptake occurs in conjunction with vesicle reuptake. If we assume synapses gain strength in proportion to the amount of substance they take up, then we can replace Eq. A1 by

$$\frac{d}{dt} S^L(x,\alpha,t) = \lambda A(x-\alpha) \sum_l E(x-l)[c(l,t) - c_{thres}(l)]f_1[a^L(\alpha,t)]$$
$$- \gamma S^L(x,\alpha,t) - \epsilon'^L A(x-\alpha).$$

(A4)

Here $\lambda E(x - l)$ expresses the influence of site l upon site x over the relevant times due to diffusion or transport. After substituting Eq. A2 for $c(l,t)$ into Eq. A4 and averaging, we again obtain Eq. A3, with $\Sigma_l E(x - l)I(l - y)$ in place of $I(x - y)$. If the diffusible or transported substances are released in an activity-dependent manner by the presynaptic terminals themselves, rather than by the cortical cells, Eq. A3 is obtained but now with $E(x - y)$ in place of $I(x - y)$. In this case the activity of the postsynaptic cell is of no importance to plasticity.

In addition to modifiable synapses represented by any of the mechanisms presented so far, we can consider chemospecific adhesion between input terminals and cortical cells. Such retinotopic adhesion is considered important in many models of retinotectal connections (Fraser, 1980, 1985; Whitelaw & Cowan, 1981). Suppose the degree of chemospecific adhesion between the input from α and the cortical cell at x depends only on $x - \alpha$. In this case, the retinotopic adhesion can be represented by a factor $R(x - \alpha)$ multiplying the terms in $\frac{d}{dt} S(x,\alpha,t)$. This is, formally, the role played by the arbor function. Hence, by letting $A(x - \alpha)$ represent the product of the chemospecific adhesion times the arbor strength, we can take account of retinotopic adhesion as well.

APPENDIX 2: THE CHARACTERISTIC PATTERNS OF OCULAR DOMINANCE

Eq. 3 or Eq. 6 for S^D in the text can be written

$$\frac{d}{dt}S^D + \gamma S^D = LS^D \tag{A5}$$

Here, S^D is the vector of synaptic weights, and L is a linear operator defined by the right side of Eq. 3 or 6. In Eq. 3, S^D is the vector with components $S^D_\alpha = S^D(\alpha)$, L is a matrix with entries $L_{\alpha\beta} = \lambda A(\alpha)C^D(\alpha - \beta)$, and $LS^D = \Sigma_\beta L_{\alpha\beta}S_\beta$. In Eq. 6, S^D has components $S^D_{(x,\alpha)} = S^D(x,\alpha)$, L has elements $L_{(x,\alpha);(y,\beta)} = A(x - \alpha)I(x - y)C^D(\alpha - \beta)$, and $LS^D = \Sigma_{(y,\beta)}L_{(x,\alpha);(y,\beta)}S^D(y,\beta)$.

The characteristic patterns of ocular dominance are the *eigenvectors* or *eigenfunctions* of the linear operator L in Eq. A5. The eigenvectors of any operator L are defined as those vectors S_i satisfying $LS_i = \omega_i S_i$ for some constant ω_i. ω_i is the *eigenvalue* of the eigenvector S_i, while i is an index enumerating the different eigenvectors.

For simplicity, it will be assumed that $C^D(\alpha) = C^D(-\alpha)$ and $I(x) = I(-x)$. Then the operator L of Eq. 3 or 6 has a complete basis of eigenvectors: That is, any vector L^D can be written as a weighted sum of eigenvectors $\Sigma_i c_i S_i$ for some unique set of coefficients c_i.[1] In addition, all eigenvalues are real numbers.

Let the synaptic strengths at time 0 be given by the vector $\Sigma_i c_i^0 S_i$. Then the unique solution to Eq. A5 at any time t is given by

$$S^D(t) = \sum_i c_i^0 S_i e^{(\omega_i - \gamma)t} \tag{A6}$$

This can be seen by applying $(\frac{d}{dt} + \gamma)$ to the right side of Eq. A6: the result is to multiply each S_i by ω^i. But applying L to the right side also results in multiplying each S_i by ω_i. Hence, the solution in Eq. A6 satisfies Eq. A5.

Eq. A6 shows that the eigenvectors of L each grow independently and exponentially. The eigenvector S_i grows with rate $\omega_i - \gamma$. The initial condition is a small perturbation of $S^D = 0$, and it can be assumed that every eigenvector is present in small amounts in that perturbation, so that no c_i^0 is equal to zero. Thus, if at least one growth rate $\omega_i - \gamma$ is positive, then the corresponding pattern of ocular dominance S_i will grow. In this

---

[1]We restrict ourselves to vectors S^D which are nonzero only within an arbor, that is such that $A(\alpha) = 0$ implies $S^D(\alpha) = 0$. Define $T(x,\alpha) = S^D(x,\alpha)/\sqrt{A(x - \alpha)}$ for $A(x - \alpha) \neq 0$, $T(x,\alpha) = 0$ otherwise. Then the matrix operation on T, L^T, has components $L^T_{(x,\alpha);(y,\beta)} = \sqrt{A(x - \alpha)}I(x - y)C(\alpha - \beta)\sqrt{A(y - \beta)}$. This matrix is symmetric, $L^T_{(x,\alpha);(y,\beta)} = L^T_{(y,\beta);(x,\alpha)}$, which implies it has a complete basis of eigenvectors, with real eigenvalues. This in turn implies that L does.

case, the condition $S^D = 0$ is unstable to small perturbations, and the fastest-growing eigenvector will quickly dominate. It was assumed in the discussion of characteristic patterns in the text that there is at least one such positive growth rate.

In considering Eq. 6 in the text, it is useful to transform variables from cortical and geniculate variables, (x, α), to cortical and receptive field variables, (x, r) where $r = x - \alpha$. Letting $r' = y - \beta$, the operator **L** becomes $L_{(x,r);(y,r')} = A(r)I(x - y)C^D(x - y - (r - r'))$. This operator is a convolution in the cortical variables, depending only on $x - y$ and not on x or y separately. Ignoring the cortical boundaries, this means, by fourier transform of the cortical variables, that the eigenfunctions of L must be of the form $e^{ik \cdot x} R(r)$, where k is a two-vector of real numbers defining a wavelength and direction of oscillation of ocular dominance across cortex. R is a function defining a characteristic receptive field of synaptic differences S^D. Assuming as before that $C^D(\alpha) = C^D(-\alpha)$ and $I(x) = I(-x)$, the real part and imaginary part of each such complex eigenfunction are both real eigenfunctions, with the same eigenvalue. These real eigenfunctions can be chosen of the form $\cos k \cdot x \, R^+(r) + \sin k \cdot x \, R^0(r)$, where R^0 has zero net ocular dominance $(\Sigma_r R^0(r) = 0)$ and R^+ may have net ocular dominance. R^+ is the leftmost receptive field of the patterns of Fig. 7.19, while R^0 is the central receptive field. If, as for the eigenfunction of Fig. 7.19a, $R^0 = 0$, then the eigenfunction is simply $\cos k \cdot x \, R^+(r)$, the product of a cortical oscillation and a receptive field function R^+.

More information on analysis of these equations can be found in Miller (1989a) and in Miller and Stryker (1989). For an introduction to the mathematics, see Hirsch and Smale (1974).

REFERENCES

Allard, T. (1989). Biological constraints on a dynamical network: The somatosensory nervous system. In S. J. Hanson & C. R. Olson (Eds.), *Connectionist modeling and brain function: The developing interface*. Cambridge, MA: MIT Press/Bradford.

Anderson, P. A., Olavarria, J., & Van Sluyters, R. C. (1988). The overall pattern of ocular dominance bands in cat visual cortex. *Journal of Neuroscience, 8*, 2183-2200.

Arikuni, T., Sakai, M., & Kubota, K. (1983). Columnar aggregation of prefrontal and anterior cingulate cortical cells projecting to the thalamic mediodorsal nucleus in the monkey. *Journal of Comparative Neurology, 220*, 116-125.

Arnett, D. W. (1978). Statistical dependence between neighboring retinal ganglion cells in goldfish. *Experimental Brain Research, 32*, 49-53.

Baldi, P., & Hornik, K. (1989). Neural networks and principal component analysis: Learning from examples without local minima. *Neural Networks, 2*, 53-58.

Beaulieu, C., & Colonnier, M. (1987). Effect of the richness of the environment on the cat visual cortex. *Journal of Comparative Neurology, 266*, 478-494.

Belford, G. R., & Killackey, H. P. (1980). The sensitive period in the development of the trigeminal system of the neonatal rat. *Journal of Comparative Neurology, 193,* 335–350.

Bienenstock, E. L., Cooper, L. N., & Munro, P. W. (1982). Theory for the development of neuron selectivity: Orientation specificity and binocular interaction in visual cortex. *Journal of Neuroscience, 2,* 32–48.

Boss, V. C., & Schmidt, J. T. (1984). Activity and the formation of ocular dominance patches in dually innervated tectum of goldfish. *Journal of Neuroscience, 4,* 2891–2905.

Bourgeois, J. P., Jastreboff, P. J., & Rakic, P. (1989). Synaptogenesis in visual cortex of normal and preterm monkeys: Evidence for intrinsic regulation of synaptic overproduction. *Proceedings of the National Academy of Sciences, 86,* 4297–4301.

Brown, M. C., Jansen, J. K. S., & Van Essen, D. (1976). Polyneuronal innervation of skeletal muscle in new-born rats and its elimination during maturation. *Journal of Physiology, 261,* 387–422.

Brown, T. H., Chapman, P. F., Kairiss, E. W., & Keenan, C. L. (1988). Long-term synaptic potentiation. *Science, 242,* 724–728.

Caminiti, R., Zeger, S., Johnson, P. B., Urbano, A., & Georgopoulos, A. P. (1985). Corticocortical efferent systems in the monkey: A quantitative spatial analysis of the tangential distribution of cells of origin. *Journal of Comparative Neurology, 241,* 405–419.

Changeux, J. P., & Danchin, A. (1976). Selective stabilization of developing synapses as a mechanism for the specification of neuronal networks. *Nature, 264,* 705–712.

Clark, S. A., Allard, T., Jenkins, W. M., & Merzenich, M. M. (1988). Receptive fields in the body-surface map in adult cortex defined by temporally correlated inputs. *Nature, 332,* 444–445.

Cline, H. T., & Constantine-Paton, M. (1988). NMDA receptor antagonist, APV, disorganizes the retinotectal map. *Society for Neuroscience Abstracts, 14,* 674.

Cline, H. T., Debski, E. A., & Constantine-Paton, M. (1987). N-methyl-d-asparate receptor antagonist desegregates eye-specific stripes. *Proceedings of the National Academy of Sciences USA, 84,* 4342–4345.

Constantine-Paton, M., & Law, M. I. (1978). Eye-specific termination bands in tecta of three-eyed frogs. *Science, 202,* 639–641.

Conway, J. L., & Schiller, P. H. (1983). Laminar organization of tree shrew dorsal lateral geniculate nucleus. *Journal of Neurophysiology, 50,* 1330–1342.

Cook, J. E. (1987). A sharp retinal image increases the topographic precision of the goldfish retinotectal projection during optic nerve regeneration in stroboscopic light. *Experimental Brain Research, 68,* 319–328.

Cook, J. E., & Rankin, E. C. (1986). Impaired refinement of the regenerated retinotectal projection of the goldfish in stroboscopic light: A quantitative WGA-HRP study. *Experimental Brain Research, 63,* 421–430.

Coss, R. G., & Perkel, D. H. (1985). The function of dendritic spines: A review of theoretical issues. *Behavioral and Neural Biology, 44,* 151–185.

Debski, E. A., & Constantine-Paton, M. (1988). The effects of glutamate receptor agonists and antagonists on the evoked tectal potential in *rana pipiens. Society for Neuroscience Abstracts, 14,* 674.

Dubin, M. W., Stark, L. A., & Archer, S. M. (1986). A role for action-potential activity in the development of neuronal connections in the kitten retinogeniculate pathway. *Journal of Neuroscience, 6,* 1021–1036.

Dumuis, A., Sebben, M., Haynes, L., Pin, J. P., & Bockaert, J. (1988). NMDA receptors activate the arachidonic acid cascade system in striatal neurons. *Nature, 336,* 68–70.

Durham, D., & Woolsey, T. A. (1984). Effects of neonatal whisker lesion on mouse central trigeminal pathways. *Journal of Comparative Neurology, 223,* 424–447.

Easter, S. S., Jr., & Stuermer, C.A.O. (1984). An evaluation of the hypothesis of shifting terminals in goldfish optic tectum. *Journal of Neuroscience, 4,* 1052–1063.

Eisele, L. E., & Schmidt, J. T. (1988). Activity sharpens the regenerating retinotectal projection in goldfish: Sensitive period for strobe illumination and lack of effect on synaptogenesis and on ganglion cell receptive field properties. *Journal of Neurobiology, 19,* 395–411.

Fawcett, J. W., & O'Leary, D. D. M. (1985). The role of electrical activity in the formation of topographic maps in the nervous system. *Trends in Neurosciences, 8,* 201–206.

Fawcett, J. W., & Willshaw, D. J. (1982). Compound eyes project stripes on the optic tectum in *xenopus. Nature, 296,* 350–352.

Ferster, D. & LeVay, S. (1978). The axonal arborizations of lateral geniculate neurons in the striate cortex of the cat. *Journal of Comparative Neurology, 182,* 923–944.

Fladby, T., & Jansen, J. K. S. (1987). Postnatal loss of synaptic terminals in the partially denervated mouse soleus muscle. *Acta Physiologica Scandinavia, 129,* 239–246.

Fox, B. E. S., & Fraser, S. E. (1987). Excitatory amino acids in the retino-tectal system of xenopus laevis. *Society for Neuroscience Abstracts, 13,* 766.

Fraser, S. E. (1980). Differential adhesion approach to the patterning of nerve connections. *Developmental Biology, 79,* 453–464.

Fraser, S. E. (1985). Cell interactions involved in neuronal patterning: An experimental and theoretical approach. In G. M. Edelman, W. E. Gall, & W. M. Cowan (Eds.), *Molecular bases of neural development* (pp. 481–508). New York: Wiley.

Fregnac, Y., & Imbert, M. (1984). Development of neuronal selectivity in the primary visual cortex of the cat. *Physiological Review, 64,* 325–434.

Galli, L., & Maffei, L. (1988). Spontaneous impulse activity of rat retinal ganglion cells in prenatal life. *Science, 242,* 90–91.

Gamble, E., & Koch, C. (1987). The dynamics of free calcium in dendritic spines in response to repetitive synaptic input. *Science, 236,* 1311–1315.

Garraghty, P. E., Shatz, C. J., Sretavan, D. W., & Sur, M. (1988). Axon arbors of X and Y retinal ganglion cells are differentially affected by prenatal disruption of binocular inputs. *Proceedings of the National Academy of Science USA, 85,* 7361–7365.

Garraghty, P. E., Shatz, C. J., & Sur, M. (1988). Prenatal disruption of binocular interactions creates novel lamination in the cat's lateral geniculate nucleus. *Visual Neuroscience, 1,* 93–102.

Garraghty, P. E., & Sur, M. (1988). Interactions between retinal axons during development of their terminal arbors in the cat's lateral geniculate nucleus. In M. Bentivoglio & R. Spreafico (Eds.), *Cellular thalamic mechanisms* (pp. 465–477). Amsterdam: Elsevier Science BV.

Garraghty, P. E., Sur, M., & Sherman, S. M. (1986). Role of competitive interactions in the postnatal development of X and Y retinogeniculate axons. *Journal of Comparative Neurology, 251,* 216–239.

Garthwaite, J., Charles, S. L., & Chess-Williams, R. (1988). Endothelium-derived relaxing factor release on activation of NMDA receptors suggests role as intercellular messenger in the brain. *Nature, 336,* 385–387.

Gilbert, C. D., & Wiesel, T. N. (1983). Clustered intrinsic connections in cat visual cortex. *Journal of Neuroscience, 3,* 1116–1133.

Ginsburg, K. S., Johnsen, J. A., & Levine, M. W. (1984). Common noise in the firing of neighboring ganglion cells in gold fish retina. *Journal of Physiology, 351,* 433–451.

Goldman, P. S., & Nauta, W. J. H. (1977). Columnar distribution of cortico-cortical fibers in the frontal association, limbic, and motor cortex of the developing rhesus monkey. *Brain Research, 122,* 393–413.

Goldman-Rakic, P. S. (1984). Modular organization of prefrontal cortex. *Trends in Neurosciences, 7,* 419–424.

Goldman-Rakic, P. S., & Schwartz, M. L. (1982). Interdigitation of contralateral and ipsilateral columnar projections to frontal association cortex in primates. *Science, 216,* 755–757.

Guillery, R. W. (1972). Binocular competition in the control of geniculate cell growth. *Journal of Comparative Neurology, 144,* 117–130.

Guillery, R. W. (1974). Visual pathways in albinos. *Scientific American, 230,* (5), 44–54.

Guillery, R. W., & Stelzner, D. J. (1970). The differential effects of unilateral lid closure upon the monocular and binocular segments of the dorsal lateral geniculate nucleus in the cat. *Journal of Comparative Neurology, 139,* 413–422.

Harris, W. A. (1981). Neural activity and development. *Annual Reviews of Physiology, 43,* 689–710.

Hata, Y., Tsumoto, T., Sato, H., Hagihara, K., & Tamura, H. (1988). Inhibition contributes to orientation selectivity in visual cortex of cat. *Nature, 335,* 815–817.

Hayes, W. P., & Meyer, R. L. (1988a). Retinotopically inappropriate synapses of subnormal density formed by misdirected optic fibers in goldfish tectum. *Developmental Brain Research, 38,* 304–312.

Hayes, W. P., & Meyer, R. L. (1988b). Optic synapse number but not density is constrained during regeneration onto surgically halved tectum in goldfish: HRP-EM evidence that optic fibers compete for fixed numbers of postsynaptic sites on the tectum. *Journal of Comparative Neurology, 274,* 539–559.

Hayes, W. P., & Meyer, R. L. (1989a). Normal numbers of retinotectal synapses during the activity-sensitive period of optic regeneration in goldfish: HRP-EM evidence implicating synapse rearrangement and collateral elimination during map refinement. *Journal of Neuroscience, 9,* 1400–1413.

Hayes, W. P., & Meyer, R. L. (1989b). Impulse blockade by intraocular tetrodoxin during optic regeneration in goldfish: HRP-EM evidence that the formation of normal numbers of optic synapses and the elimination of exuberant optic fibers is activity independent. *Journal of Neuroscience, 9,* 1414–1423.

Hebb, D. O. (1949). *The organization of behavior.* New York: Wiley.

Hess, R., Negishi, K., & Creutzfeldt, O. (1975). The horizontal spread of intracortical inhibition in the visual cortex. *Experimental Brain Research, 22,* 415–419.

Hirsch, M. W. & Smale, S. (1974). *Differential equations, dynamical systems and linear algebra.* New York: Academic Press.

Hubel, D. H., & Wiesel, T. N. (1962). Receptive fields, binocular interaction and functional architecture in the cat's visual cortex. *Journal of Physiology, 160,* 106–154.

Hubel, D. H., & Wiesel, T. N. (1963). Receptive fields of cells in striate cortex of very young, visually inexperienced kittens. *Journal of Neurophysiology, 26,* 994–1002.

Hubel, D. H., & Wiesel, T. N. (1965). Binocular interaction in striate cortex of kittens reared with artificial squint. *Journal of Neurophysiology, 28,* 1041–1059.

Hubel, D. H., & Wiesel, T. N. (1970). The period of susceptibility to the physiological effects of unilateral eye closure in kittens. *Journal of Physiology, 206,* 419–436.

Hubel, D. H., & Wiesel, T. N. (1977). Functional architecture of macaque monkey visual cortex. *Proceedings of the Royal Society of London Series B, 198,* 1–59.

Hubel, D. H., Wiesel, T. N., & LeVay, S. (1977). Plasticity of ocular dominance columns in monkey striate cortex. *Philosophical Transactions of the Royal Society of London Series B, 278,* 377–409.

Humphrey, A. L., Sur, M., Uhlrich, D. J., & Sherman, S. M. (1985a). Projection patterns of individual X- and Y-cell axons from the lateral geniculate nucleus to cortical area 17 in the cat. *Journal of Comparative Neurology, 233,* 159–189.

Humphrey, A. L., Sur, M., Uhlrich, D. J., & Sherman, S. M. (1985b). Termination patterns of individual X- and Y-cell axons in the visual cortex of the cat: Projections to area 18, to the 17/18 border region, and to both areas 17 and 18. *Journal of Comparative Neurology, 233,* 190–212.

Ide, C. F., Fraser, S. E., & Meyer, R. L. (1983). Eye dominance columns from an isogenic double-nasal frog eye. *Science, 221,* 293–295.

Innocenti, G. M., & Frost, D. O. (1979). Effects of visual experience on the maturation of the efferent system to the corpus callosum. *Nature, 280,* 231–234.

Innocenti, G. M., & Frost, D. O. (1980). The postnatal development of visual callosal connections in the absence of visual experience or of the eyes. *Experimental Brain Research, 39,* 365–375.

Innocenti, G. M., Frost, D. O., & Illes, J. (1985). Maturation of visual callosal connections in visually deprived kittens: A challenging critical period. *Journal of Neuroscience, 5,* 255–267.

Jeanmonod, D., Rice, F. L., & Van der Loos, H. (1981). Mouse somatosensory cortex: Alterations in the barrelfield following receptor injury at different early postnatal ages. *Neuroscience, 6,* 1503–1535.

Jones, D. G., Van Sluyters, R. C., & Murphy, K. M. (1988). A computational model for the overall pattern of ocular dominance bands in striate cortex of cat and monkey. *Society for Neuroscience Abstracts, 14,* 1122.

Jones, E. G., Burton, H., & Porter, R. (1975). Commissural and cortico-cortical 'columns' in the somatic sensory cortex of primates. *Science, 190,* 572–574.

Jones, E. G., Coulter, J. D., & Wise, S. P. (1979). Commissural columns in the sensory-motor cortex of monkeys. *Journal of Comparative Neurology, 188,* 113–136.

Jones, E. G., & Wise, S. P. (1977). Size, laminar and columnar distribution of efferent cells in the sensory-motor cortex of monkeys. *Journal of Comparative Neurology, 175,* 391–438.

Kater, S. B., Mattson, M. P., Cohan, C., & Conner, J. (1988). Calcium regulation of the neuronal growth cone. *Trends in Neurosciences, 11,* 315–321.

Katz, L. C., & Constantine-Paton, M. (1988). Relationships between segregated afferents and postsynaptic neurons in the optic tectum of three-eyed frogs. *Journal of Neuroscience, 8,* 3160–3180.

Katz, L. C., Gilbert, C. D., & Wiesel, T. N. (1989). Local circuits and ocular dominance columns in monkey striate cortex. *Journal of Neuroscience, 9,* 1389–1399.

Kauer, J. A., Malenka, R. C., & Nicoll, R. A. (1988). NMDA application potentiates synaptic transmission in the hippocampus. *Nature, 334,* 250–252.

Keating, M. J. (1975). The time course of experience-dependent synaptic switching of visual connections in *Xenopus laevis. Proceedings of the Royal Society of London Series B, 189,* 603–610.

Keller, J. B. (1977). Effective behavior of heterogeneous media. In U. Landman (Ed.), *Statistical mechanics and statistical methods in theory and application* (pp. 631–644). New York: Plenum.

Kleinschmidt, A., Bear, M. F., & Singer, W. (1987). Blockade of 'NMDA' receptors disrupts experience-dependent plasticity of kitten striate cortex. *Science, 238,* 355–358.

Knudsen, E. I. (1985). Experience alters the spatial tuning of auditory units in the optic tectum during a sensitive period in the barn owl. *Journal of Neuroscience, 5,* 3094–3109.

Knudsen, E. I. (1988). Early blindness results in a degraded auditory map of space in the optic tectum of the barn owl. *Proceedings of the National Academy of Sciences USA, 85,* 6211–6214.

Knudsen, E. I., Du Lac, S., & Esterly, S. D. (1987). Computational maps in the brain. *Annual Reviews of Neuroscience, 10,* 41–65.

Knudsen, E. I., & Knudsen, P. F. (1985). Vision guides the adjustment of auditory localization in young barn owls. *Science, 230,* 545–548.

Kretz, G., Rager, G., & Norton, T. T. (1986). Laminar organization of on and off regions and ocular dominance in the striate cortex of the tree shrew (*Tupaia belangeri*). *Journal of Comparative Neurology, 251,* 135–145.

LeVay, S., Connolly, M., Houde, J., & Van Essen, D. C. (1985). The complete pattern of ocular dominance stripes in the striate cortex and visual field of the macaque monkey. *Journal of Neuroscience, 5,* 486–501.

LeVay, S., & McConnell, S. K. (1982). On and off layers in the lateral geniculate nucleus of the mink. *Nature, 300,* 350–351.

LeVay, S., & Nelson, S. B. (1989). The columnar organization of visual cortex. In A. Leventhal (Ed.), *The electrophysiology of vision.* London: Macmillan Press.

LeVay, S., & Stryker, M. P. (1979). The development of ocular dominance columns in the cat. In J. A. Ferrendelli (Ed.), *Aspects of developmental neurobiology* (pp. 83–98). Bethesda: Society for Neuroscience.

LeVay, S., Stryker, M. P., & Shatz, C. J. (1978). Ocular dominance columns and their development in layer IV of the cat's visual cortex: A quantitative study. *Journal of Comparative Neurology, 179,* 223–244.

Levick, W. R., & Williams, W. O. (1964). Maintained activity of lateral geniculate neurones in darkness. *Journal of Physiology, 170,* 582–597.

Levine, R., & Jacobson, M. (1975). Discontinuous mapping of retina into tectum innervated by both eyes. *Brain Research, 98,* 172–176.

Lichtman, J. W., & Purves, D. (1981). Regulation of the number of axons that innervate target cells. In D. R. Garrod & J. D. Feldman (Eds.), *Development in the nervous system* (pp. 233–243). Cambridge: Cambridge University Press.

Linsker, R. (1986). From basic network principles to neural architecture. *Proceedings of the National Academy of Sciences, 83,* 7508–7512, 8390–8394, 8779–8783.

Linsker, R. (1988). Self-organization in a perceptual network. *Computer, 21,* 105–117.

Lisman, J. E., & Goldring, M. A. (1988). Feasibility of long-term storage of graded information by the calcium/calmodulin-dependent protein kinase molecules of the postsynaptic density. *Proceedings of the National Academy of Sciences USA, 85,* 5320–5324.

Luhmann, H. J., Martinez Millan, L., & Singer, W. (1986). Development of horizontal intrinsic connections in cat striate cortex. *Experimental Brain Research, 63,* 443–448.

Lynch, G., & Baudry, M. (1984). The biochemistry of memory: A new and specific hypothesis. *Science, 224,* 1057–1063.

Malinow, R., Madison, D. V., & Tsien, R. W. (1988). Persistent protein kinase activity underlying long-term potentiation. *Nature, 335,* 820–824.

Mallot, H. A. (1985). An overall description of retinotopic mapping in the cat's visual cortex areas 17, 18, and 19. *Biological Cybernetics, 52,* 45–51.

Malsburg, C. von der. (1979). Development of ocularity domains and growth behavior of axon terminals. *Biological Cybernetics, 32,* 49–62.

Malsburg, C. von der, & Willshaw, D. J. (1976). A mechanism for producing continuous neural mappings: Ocularity dominance stripes and ordered retino-tectal projections. *Experimental Brain Research, Supplement 1,* 463–469.

Malsburg, C. von der, & Willshaw, D. J. (1977). How to label nerve cells so that they can interconnect in an ordered fashion. *Proceedings of the National Academy of Sciences USA, 74,* 5176–5178.

Mastronarde, D. N. (1983a). Correlated firing of cat retinal ganglion cells. I. Spontaneously active inputs to X and Y cells. *Journal of Neurophysiology, 49,* 303–324.

Mastronarde, D. N. (1983b). Correlated firing of cat retinal ganglion cells. II. Responses of X- and Y-cells to single quantal events. *Journal of Neurophysiology, 49,* 325–349.

Mastronarde, D. N. (1989). Correlated firing of retinal ganglion cells. *Trends in Neurosciences, 12,* 75–80.

Mayer, M. L., & Westbrook, G. L. (1987). The physiology of excitatory amino acids in the vertebrate central nervous system. *Progress in Neurobiology, 28,* 197–276.

McConnell, S. K., & LeVay, S. (1984). Segregation of ON- and OFF-center afferents in mink visual cortex. *Proceedings of the National Academy of Sciences USA, 81,* 1590–1593.

Merzenich, M. M., Allard, T., Jenkins, W. M., & Recanzone, G. (1988). Self-organizing processes in adult neo-cortex. In W. von Seelen, U. M. Leimhos, & G. Shaw (Eds.), *Organization of neural networks: Structures and models.* New York: VCH Publishers.

Merzenich, M. M., Jenkins, W. M., & Middlebrooks, J. C. (1984). Observations and hypotheses on special organizational features of the central auditory nervous system. In G. M. Edelman, W. E. Gall, & W. M. Cowan (Eds.), *Dynamic aspects of neocortical function* (pp. 397–424). New York: Wiley.

Merzenich, M. M., Kaas, J.H., Wall, J. T., Sur, M., Nelson, R. J., & Felleman, D. J. (1983). Progression of change following median nerve section in the cortical representation of the hand in areas 3b and 1 in adult owl and squirrel monkeys. *Neuroscience, 10,* 639–665.

Merzenich, M. M., Nelson, R. J., Kaas, J. H., Stryker, M. P., Jenkins, W. M., Zook, J. M., Cynader, M. S., & Schoppmann, A. (1987). Variability in hand surface representations in areas 3b and 1 in adult owl and squirrel monkeys. *Journal of Comparative Neurology, 258,* 281–296.

Meyer, R. L. (1979). "Extra" optic fibers exclude normal fibers from tectal regions in goldfish. *Journal of Comparative Neurology, 183,* 883–902.

Meyer, R. L. (1982). Tetrodotoxin blocks the formation of ocular dominance columns in goldfish. *Science, 218,* 589–591.

Meyer, R. L. (1983). Tetrodotoxin inhibits the formation of refined retinotopography in goldfish. *Developmental Brain Research, 6,* 293–298.

Miller, J. P., Rall, W., & Rinzel, J. (1985). Synaptic amplification by active membrane in dendritic spines. *Brain Research, 325,* 325–330.

Miller, K. D. (1989b). Orientation-selective cells can emerge from a Hebbian mechanism through interactions between ON- and OFF-center inputs. *Society for Neuroscience Abstracts, 15.*

Miller, K. D. (1989a). *Ph. D. Thesis, Stanford University Medical School.* University Microfilms, Ann Arbor.

Miller, K. D., Chapman, B., & Stryker, M. P. (1989). Responses of cells in cat visual cortex depend on NMDA receptors. *Proceedings of the National Academy of Sciences, 86,* 5183–5187.

Miller, K. D., Keller, J. B., & Stryker, M. P. (1986). Models for the formation of ocular dominance columns solved by linear stability analysis. *Society for Neuroscience Abstracts, 12,* 1373.

Miller, K. D., Keller, J. B., & Stryker, M. P. (1988). Network model of ocular dominance column formation: Analytical results. *Neural Networks, 1,* S266.

Miller, K. D., Keller, J. B., & Stryker, M. P. (1989). Ocular dominance column development: Analysis and simulation. *Science, 245,* 605–615.

Miller, K. D., & Stryker, M. P. (1988). Models for the formation of ocular dominance columns: Computational results. *Society for Neuroscience Abstracts, 14,* 1122.

Miller, K. D., & Stryker, M. P. (1989). The development of ocular dominance columns: Mechanisms and models. In S. J. Hanson & C. R. Olson (Eds.), *Connectionist modeling and brain function: The developing interface.* Cambridge, MA: MIT Press/Bradford.

Miller, K. D., Stryker, M. P., & Keller, J. B. (1988). Network model of ocular dominance column formation: Computational results. *Neural Networks, 1,* S267.

Moody, C. I., & Sillito, A. M. (1988). The role of the n-methyl-d-aspartate (NMDA) receptor in the transmission of visual information in the feline dorsal lateral geniculate nucleus (dlgn). *Journal of Physiology, 396,* 62P.

Mountcastle, V. B. (1978). An organizing principle for cerebral function: The unit module and the distributed system. In G. M. Edelman & V. B. Mountcastle (Eds.), *The mindful brain* (pp. 7-50). Cambridge, MA: MIT Press.

Movshon, J. A., & Van Sluyters, R. C. (1981). Visual neural development. *Annual Reviews of Psychology, 32,* 477-522.

Muller, C. M., Engel, A. K., & Singer, W. (1988). Development of astrocytes in the cat visual cortex. *Society for Neuroscience Abstracts, 14,* 745.

Murray, M., Sharma, S., & Edwards, M. A. (1982). Target regulation of synaptic number in the compressed retinotectal projection of goldfish. *Journal of Comparative Neurology, 209,* 374-385.

Nahorski, S. R. (1988). Inositol polyphosphates and neuronal calcium homeostasis. *Trends in Neurosciences, 11,* 444-448.

Nicoll, R. A., Kauer, J. A., & Malenka, R. C. (1988). The current excitement in long-term potentiation. *Neuron, 1,* 97-103.

O'Brien, R. A. D., Ostberg, A. J., & Vrbova, G. (1980). The effect of acetylcholine on the function and structure of the developing mammalian neuromuscular junction. *Neuroscience, 5,* 1367-1379.

Oja, E. (1982). A simplified neuron model as a principal component analyzer. *Journal of Mathematical Biology, 15,* 267-273.

Piomelli, D., Volterra, A., Dale, N., Siegelbaum, S. A., Kandel, E. R., Schwartz, J. H., & Belardetti, F. (1987). Lipoxygenase metabolites of arachidonic acid as second messengers for presynaptic inhibition of *Aplysia* sensory cells. *Nature, 328,* 38-43.

Purves, D. (1988). *Body and brain: A trophic theory of neural connections.* Cambridge, MA: Harvard University Press.

Purves, D., & Lichtman, J. W. (1985). *Principles of neural development.* Sunderland, MA: Sinauer Associates, Inc.

Purves, D., Snider, W. D., & Voyvodic, J. T. (1988). Trophic regulation of nerve cell morphology and innervation in the autonomic nervous system. *Nature, 336,* 123-128.

Rakic, P. (1976). Prenatal genesis of connections subserving ocular dominance in the rhesus monkey. *Nature, 261,* 467-471.

Rakic, P. (1977). Prenatal development of the visual system in the rhesus monkey. *Philosophical Transactions of the Royal Society of London Series B, 278,* 245-260.

Ramoa, A. S., Campbell, G., & Shatz, C. J. (1988). Dendritic growth and remodeling of cat retinal ganglion cells during fetal and postnatal development. *Journal of Neuroscience, 8,* 4239-4261.

Ramoa, A. S., Paradiso, M. A., & Freeman, R. D. (1988). Blockade of intracortical inhibition in kitten striate cortex: effects on receptive field properties and associated loss of ocular dominance plasticity. *Experimental Brain Research, 73,* 285-296.

Rauschecker, J. P. (1989). Mechanisms of visual plasticity as a model for the formation of long-term memory. *Physiological Reviews.*

Reh, T. A., & Constantine-Paton, M. (1984). Retinal ganglion cell terminals change their projection sites during larval development of *rana pipiens. Journal of Neuroscience, 4,* 442-457.

Reh, T. A., & Constantine-Paton, M. (1985). Eye-specific segregation requires neural activity in three-eyed *rana pipiens. Journal of Neuroscience, 5,* 1132-1143.

Reiter, H. O., & Stryker, M. P. (1988). Neural plasticity without postsynaptic action potentials: Less-active inputs become dominant when kitten visual cortical cells are pharmacologically inhibited. *Proceedings of the National Academy of Sciences USA, 85,* 3623-3627.

Reiter, H. O., Waitzman, D. M., & Stryker, M. P. (1986). Cortical activity blockade prevents ocular dominance plasticity in the kitten visual cortex. *Experimental Brain Research, 65,* 182-188.

Rochester, N., Holland, J. H., Haibt, L. H., & Duda, W. L. (1956). Tests on a cell assembly theory of the action of the brain, using a large digital computer. *IRE Transactions on Information Theory, IT-2,* 80–93. Reprinted in J. A. Anderson & E. Rosenfeld (Eds.), *Neurocomputing: Foundations of research* (pp. 68–79). Cambridge, MA: MIT Press/ Bradford, 1988.

Rodieck, R. W., & Smith, P. S. (1966). Slow dark discharge rhythms of cat retinal ganglion cells. *Journal of Neurophysiology, 29,* 942–953.

Rumelhart, D. E., & Zipser, D. (1986). Feature discovery by competitive learning. In D. E. Rumelhart & J. L. McClelland (Eds.), *Parallel distributed processing: Explorations in the microstructure of cognition* (Vol. 1, pp. 151–193). Cambridge, MA: MIT Press/Bradford.

Salt, T. E. (1986). Mediation of thalamic sensory input by both NMDA receptors and non-NMDA receptors. *Nature, 322,* 263–265.

Salt, T. E. (1987). Excitatory amino acid receptors and synaptic transmission in the rat ventrobasal thalamus. *Journal of Physiology, 391,* 499–510.

Sanes, D. H., & Constantine-Paton, M. (1985). The sharpening of frequency tuning curves requires patterned activity during development in the mouse, *Mus musculus. Journal of Neuroscience, 5,* 1152–1166.

Sanger, T. D. (1989). An optimality principle for unsupervised learning. In D. Touretzky (Ed.), *Advances in neural information processing systems* (pp. 11–19). San Mateo, CA: Morgan Kaufmann.

Scherer, W. S., & Udin, S. B. (1988). The role of NMDA receptors in the development of binocular maps in *xenopus* tectum. *Society for Neuroscience Abstracts, 14,* 675.

Schiller, P. H., & Malpeli, J. G. (1978). Functional specificity of lateral geniculate nucleus laminae of the rhesus monkey. *Journal of Neurophysiology, 41,* 788–797.

Schmidt, J. T. (1985). Formation of retinotopic connections: Selective stabilization by an activity-dependent mechanism. *Cellular and Molecular Neurobiology, 5,* 65–84.

Schmidt, J. T. (1988). NMDA blockers prevent both retinotopic sharpening and LTP in regenerating optic pathway of goldfish. *Society for Neuroscience Abstracts, 14,* 675.

Schmidt, J. T., & Edwards, D. L. (1983). Activity sharpens the map during the regeneration of the retinotectal projection in goldfish. *Brain Research, 269,* 29–39.

Schmidt, J. T., & Eisele, L. E. (1985). Stroboscopic illumination and dark rearing block the sharpening of the retinotectal map in goldfish. *Neuroscience, 14,* 535–546.

Schmidt, J. T., & Tieman, S. B. (1985). Eye-specific segregation of optic afferents in mammals, fish and frogs: The role of activity. *Cellular and Molecular Neurobiology, 5,* 5–34.

Schneider, G. E. (1973). Early lesions of superior colliculus: Factors affecting the formation of abnormal retinal projections. *Brain, Behavior and Evolution, 8,* 73–109.

Schwartz, M. L., & Goldman-Rakic, P. S. (1984). Callosal and intrahemispheric connectivity of the prefrontal association cortex in rhesus monkey: Relations between intraparietal and principal sulcal cortex. *Journal of Comparative Neurology, 226,* 403–420.

Schwartz, J. H., & Greenberg, S. M. (1987). Molecular mechanisms for memory: Second-messenger induced modifications of protein kinases in nerve cells. *Annual Review of Neuroscience, 10,* 459–476.

Sejnowski, T. J. (1977). Storing covariance with nonlinearly interacting neurons. *Journal of Mathematical Biology, 4,* 303–321.

Selemon, L. D., & Goldman-Rakic, P. S. (1985). Longitudinal topography and interdigitation of corticostriatal projections in the rhesus monkey. *Journal of Neuroscience, 5,* 776–794.

Shatz, C. J. (1983). The prenatal development of the cat's retinogeniculate pathway. *Journal of Neuroscience, 3,* 482–499.

Shatz, C. J. (1988). The role of function in the prenatal development of retinogeniculate connections. In M. Bentivoglio & R. Spreafico (Eds.), *Cellular thalamic mechanisms* (pp. 435–446). Amsterdam: Elsevier Science Publishers BV.

Shatz, C. J., & Kirkwood, P. (1984). Prenatal development of functional connections in the cat's retinogeniculate pathway. *Journal of Neuroscience, 4,* 1378–1397.

Shatz, C. J., Lindstrom, S., & Wiesel, T. N. (1977). The distribution of afferents representing the right and left eyes in the cat's visual cortex. *Brain Research, 131,* 103–116.

Shatz, C. J., & Stryker, M. P. (1978). Ocular dominance in layer IV of the cat's visual cortex and the effects of monocular deprivation. *Journal of Physiology, 281,* 267–283.

Shatz, C. J., & Stryker, M. P. (1988). Tetrodotoxin infusion prevents the formation of eye-specific layers during prenatal development of the cat's retinogeniculate projection. *Science, 242,* 87–89.

Sherk, H., & Stryker, M. P. (1976). Quantitative study of cortical oreintation selectivity in visually inexperienced kitten. *Journal of Neurophysiology, 39,* 63–70.

Sherman, S. M., & Spear, P. D. (1982). Organisation of visual pathways in normal and visually deprived cats. *Physiological Review, 62,* 738–855.

Soodak, R. E. (1987). The retinal ganglion cell mosaic defines orientation columns in striate cortex. *Proceedings of the National Academy of Sciences USA, 84,* 3936–3940.

Sretavan, D. W., & Shatz, C. J. (1986). Prenatal development of retinal ganglion cell axons: Segregation into eye-specific layers within the cat's lateral geniculate nucleus. *Journal of Neuroscience, 6,* 234–251.

Sretavan, D. W., & Shatz, C. J. (1987). Axon trajectories and pattern of terminal arborization during the prenatal development of the cat's retinogeniculate pathway. *Journal of Comparative Neurology, 255,* 386–400.

Sretavan, D. W., Shatz, C. J., & Stryker, M. P. (1988). Modification of retinal ganglion cell morphology by prenatal infusion of tetrodotoxin. *Nature, 336,* 468–471.

Stent, G. S. (1973). A physiological mechanism of Hebb's postulate of learning. *Proceedings of the National Academy of Sciences USA, 70,* 997–1001.

Stryker, M. P. (1977). The role of early experience in the development and maintenance of orientation selectivity in the cat's visual cortex. In E. Poppel, R. Held, & J. E. Dowling (Eds.), *Neurosciences research program bulletin* (Vol. 15, N. 3, pp. 454–462). Cambridge, MA: MIT Press.

Stryker, M. P. (1986). The role of neural activity in rearranging connections in the central visual system. In R. J. Ruben, T. R. Van De Water, & E. W. Rubel (Eds.), *The biology of change in otolaryngology* (pp. 211–224). Amsterdam: Elsevier Science B. V.

Stryker, M. P., & Harris, W. (1986). Binocular impulse blockade prevents the formation of ocular dominance columns in cat visual cortex. *Journal of Neuroscience, 6,* 2117–2133.

Stryker, M. P., Sherk, H., Leventhal, A. G., & Hirsch, H. V. (1978). Physiological consequences for the cat's visual cortex of effectively restricting early visual experience with oriented contours. *Journal of Neurophysiology, 41,* 896–909.

Stryker, M. P., & Strickland, S. L. (1984). Physiological segregation of ocular dominance columns depends on the pattern of afferent electrical activity. *Investigative Opthalmology Supplements, 25,* 278.

Stryker, M. P., & Zahs, K. R. (1983). On and off sublaminae in the lateral geniculate nucleus of the ferret. *Journal of Neuroscience, 3,* 1943–1951.

Sur, M. (1988). Development and plasticity of retinal X and Y axon terminations in the cat's lateral geniculate nucleus. *Brain, Behavior and Evolution, 31,* 243–251.

Sur, M., Merzenich, M. M., & Kaas, J. H. (1980). Magnification, receptive-field area, and 'hypercolumn' size in areas 3b and 1 of somatosensory cortex in owl monkeys. *Journal of Neurophysiology, 44,* 295–311.

Sur, M., Wall, J. T., & Kaas, J. H. (1984). Modular distribution of neurons with slowly adapting and rapidly adapting responses in area 3b of somatosensory cortex in monkeys. *Journal of Neurophysiology, 51,* 724–744.

Swindale, N. V. (1980). A model for the formation of ocular dominance stripes. *Proceedings of the Royal Society of London Series B., 208,* 243–264.

Swindale, N. V. (1988). Role of visual experience in promoting segregation of eye dominance patches in the visual cortex of the cat. *Journal of Comparative Neurology, 267,* 472–488.

Toyama, K., Kimura, M., & Tanaka, K. (1981a). Cross-correlation analysis of interneuronal connectivity in cat visual cortex. *Journal of Neurophysiology, 46,* 191–201.

Toyama, K., Kimura, M., & Tanaka, K. (1981b). Organization of cat visual cortex as investigated by cross-correlation technique. *Journal of Neurophysiology, 46,* 202–214.

Tsien, R. W., Lipscombe, D., Madison, D. V., Bley, K. R., & Fox, A. P. (1988). Multiple types of neuronal calcium channels and their selective modulation. *Trends in Neurosciences, 11,* 431–438.

Tso, D. Y., Gilbert, C. D., & Wiesel, T. N. (1986). Relationships between horizontal interactions and functional architecture in cat striate cortex as revealed by cross correlation analysis. *Journal of Neuroscience, 6,* 1160–1170.

Tusa, R. J., Palmer, L. A., & Rosenquist, A. C. (1978). The retinotopic organization of area 17 (striate cortex) in the cat. *Journal of Comparative Neurology, 177,* 213–235.

Udin, S. B. (1983). Abnormal visual input leads to development of abnormal axon trajectories in frogs. *Nature, 301,* 336–338.

Udin, S. B. (1985). The role of visual experience in the formation of binocular projections in frogs. *Cellular and Molecular Neurobiology, 5,* 85–102.

Udin, S. B., & Fawcett, J. W. (1988). Formation of topographic maps. *Annual Reviews of Neuroscience, 11,* 289–327.

Wall, J. T. (1988). Variable organization in cortical maps of the skin as an indication of the lifelong adaptive capacities of circuits in the mammalian brain. *Trends in Neurosciences, 11,* 549–557.

Wall, J. T., Kaas, J. H., Sur, M., Nelson, R. J., Felleman, D. J., & Merzenich, M. M. (1986). Functional reorganization in somatosensory cortical areas 3b and 1 of adult monkeys after median nerve repair: Possible relationships to sensory recovery in humans. *Journal of Neuroscience, 6,* 218–233.

Whitelaw, V. A., & Cowan, J. D. (1981). Specificity and plasticity of retinotectal connections: A computational model. *Journal of Neuroscience, 1,* 1369–1387.

Wiesel, T. N., & Hubel, D. H. (1965). Comparison of the effects of unilateral and bilateral eye closure on cortical unit responses in kittens. *Journal of Neurophysiology, 28,* 1029–1040.

Wiesel, T. N., & Hubel, D. H. (1974). Ordered arrangement of orientation columns in monkeys lacking visual experience. *Journal of Comparative Neurology, 158,* 307–318.

Willshaw, D. J., & Malsburg, C. von der. (1976). How patterned neural connections can be set up by self-organization. *Proceedings of the Royal Society of London Series B, 194,* 431–445.

Willshaw, D. J., & Malsburg, C. von der. (1979). A marker induction mechanism for the establishment of ordered neural mappings: Its application to the retinotectal problem. *Philosophical Transactions of the Royal Society of London Series B, 287,* 203–243.

Worgotter, F., & Eysel, U. Th. (1989). On the influence and topography of excitation and inhibition at orientation-specific visual cortical neurons in the cat. Manuscript submitted for publication.

Zahs, K. R., & Stryker, M. P. (1988). Segregation of on and off afferents to ferret visual cortex. *Journal of Neurophysiology, 59,* 1410–1429.

8

Modeling Cortical Computation With Backpropagation

David Zipser
Institute for Cognitive Science,
University of California, San Diego

Sometimes an unexpected observation leads to a new way to approach an old problem. In January 1987, as part of a study of the backpropagation learning procedure, I was trying to train an artificial neural network to add a pair of vectors. This is the kind of computation that must be done in the brain to get the true spatial location of a viewed object using information about retinal location and eye position. Vector addition is linear, and, even with the nonlinear retinal representation of one of the input vectors I was using, it can be accurately approximated by a single layer of linear units. However, I used a more elaborate network than the task required; a network with an extra, or hidden, layer. This network easily learned the task; what was unexpected were the properties developed by the hidden units. The simulated retinal receptive fields and eye position responses of these units closely resembled those found in a cortical area that computes spatial location. In fact, using Richard Andersen's extensive experimental data on the response patterns of parietal neurons, it was found that the hidden units could account in considerable detail for the properties of about half the neurons in this area (Zipser & Andersen, 1987, 1988a, 1988b). This was unexpected because parietal neurons have complex response patterns that had previously been assumed to be producible only by networks that closely resembled the physiology of real cortex. These observations seem to imply that we can discover the internal representations used in the brain by using a technique that does not depend on a detailed analysis of the underlying physiology.

These observations about the monkey parietal lobe were not isolated results. Later in this chapter I describe some additional models using the same paradigm that have been developed both by our group and other groups. Examination of these models suggests that for hidden units to emulate cortical neurons it is necessary for the artificial network to be taught to do a computation that is to some degree homologous to one done by the brain area being modeled. The precise degree of homology required is not yet known, but it is sufficiently flexible to allow good models to be built without too much difficulty. This property of backpropagation is still only an empirical result, not a theoretical deduction. Why should it be so? Why backpropagation? Will other learning algorithms work also? Does backpropagation learning actually take place in the brain, and, if so, where might the teacher signals come from, and could it be implemented physiologically? How can we tell if the similarity between the hidden units and real neurons is significant? These questions and others that will arise can best be addressed in the context of a detailed understanding of the actual learning paradigm used and the results observed.

LEARNING AND NEURAL COMPUTATION

Learning is to neural networks what programming is to digital computers: a way to specify what is to be computed. There is, however, a fundamental difference between learning and programming in the way the function to be computed is specified. Computers need an algorithmic description of functions—the familiar program. On the other hand, learning requires an explicit description of functions consisting of a list of pairs of inputs and corresponding function values, that is, outputs. The activity of programming is replaced with the activity of training. During training, examples of input and output from the function description list are presented to a network, which changes its synaptic weights, as prescribed by a learning procedure, until the function can be computed with the desired accuracy. Learning procedures of sufficient power to approximate virtually any function are now available. Of course, there are limits on what can be achieved in practice, but recent experience shows that many functions of great importance to computational neurobiology can be learned with currently available procedures. In particular, it is possible to train artificial neural networks to do many computations also done in the brain. Although there is no compelling a priori reason why the brain and a modeled network should compute in similar ways, considerable similarity is observed empirically. The meaning of this similarity is not yet known, but it is reasonable to propose that it comes from an underlying analogy between the computations in real and model networks. This analogy, in turn, must be a consequence of some constraint on the way computations are done that is similar in the brain and learning procedure.

The observed analogy between brain and learned computations provides the basis for a new paradigm for analyzing brain computational mechanisms. What might be called the standard paradigm, explained most clearly by David Marr (1982), involves, first, finding an analytical description of the function, or more generally the mapping, to be computed, and then generating representations and algorithms that can be used by neural networks to compute it. Then, hopefully, the analysis of these representations and algorithms will give insight into real neural mechanisms. The new paradigm, based on learning, dispenses with the need to find an analytical function definition or to create internal representations and algorithms to implement it. The learning paradigm requires only that a sufficiently large sample of relevant input and output data be available. It is seldom harder and sometimes much easier to get these input-output lists than it is to obtain algorithms. Of course, if a function definition is known, it can be used to generate the input-output list. The training process itself generates the internal representation and algorithm required to do the computation. The justification for the learning paradigm rests on the empirical observation that the internal representation generated by training actually resembles that found in the brain. A separate, and much more speculative, question is whether the brain also learns to do computation and, if so, by what mechanism? Although of immense importance, this question is not central to the use or significance of the learning paradigm for neural modeling. However, the general success of the learning paradigm can hardly fail to shed some light on this problem.

The learning paradigm can be used in several ways. In cases where analysis of a cognitive task suggests that a particular function is computed in the brain, this function can be used to generate the input-output lists required to train the response properties of units in an artificial neural network. In cases where no function is known but where empirical input-output data is available, the data can be used to train the network. The response properties of real and modeled neurons can then be compared. If they are similar, we can conclude that the brain region involved is at least capable of carrying out the hypothesized computation.

Many different training algorithms ranging from simple single-unit, unsupervised learning to multilayer error-correcting procedures can be used to simulate neural response properties (Hinton, in press). Here, I focus on the use of multilayer, supervised learning procedures, particularly on the backpropagation algorithm (Parker, 1982; Rumelhart, Hinton, & Williams, 1986; Werbos, 1974). Only the simplest form of backpropagation-trained networks have so far been used for neural network modeling. These are the strictly layered feedforward networks with one layer of hidden units. In these networks, every hidden unit is connected to all inputs and every output unit is connected to all the hidden units. There are no direct connections between input and output and no recurrent connections of any kind. This is certainly a much simpler connection pattern than occurs in any cortical area. Particularly striking in this regard is the complete lack of recurrent lateral connections. The units in the hidden and output layers are very simple models of neurons that use average firing rates, not individual spikes, to represent their input and output values. The output of a neuron is computed as the synaptic strength weighted sum of the input activities passed through an S-shaped function that limits the outputs to the range 0 to 1.

Backpropagation, as described so far, is considered a supervised learning procedure because some external source, or teacher, must provide the correct output to pair with each input. There are learning paradigms in which no teacher is used. These unsupervised procedures cannot learn arbitrary functions but rather are limited to learning something about the statistical properties of the inputs. The statistical analysis of the inputs carried out by unsupervised learning procedures often leads to neural units that act like feature detectors. A particularly interesting example is the development of quite realistic orientation-selective neurons in model networks trained with a simple Hebbian learning procedure (Linsker, 1987). Backpropagation is basically a supervised learning procedure, but it can also be used in an essentially unsupervised mode, called identity mapping, in which the input is also the teacher. This form of backpropagation is of interest to neurobiology because it can account for some of the feature detector properties of neurons (Cottrell, Munro, & Zipser, 1989; Elman & Zipser, 1988; Zipser, 1989). An example from the primary visual system will be given later.

BACKPROPAGATION TRAINED MODEL
OF MONKEY PARIETAL AREA 7A

The more that is known about a particular brain area and what it computes, the easier it is to make a learning-based model of it. In particular, it is necessary to know, or be able to guess, either the function computed or the input-output list. Knowledge of the function itself is not really enough, because the format in which the input and output information is represented must also known. In practice there is often incomplete information about some of these formats. In this case, several formats can be tested to see how they affect the response properties of the relevant units. In this way, the modeling effort can give insight into the inputs to an area and to its possible projection patterns. Monkey parietal area 7a is particularly well suited to this kind of modeling because extensive experimental study has provided much of the prerequisite information. Figure 8.1 shows the location of area 7a in the parietal lobe and its relation to some other visual areas such as MT, which is involved in analyzing motion.

Many lines of experimental work strongly point to a function likely to be computed by area 7a. Lesions to the posterior parietal cortex in monkeys

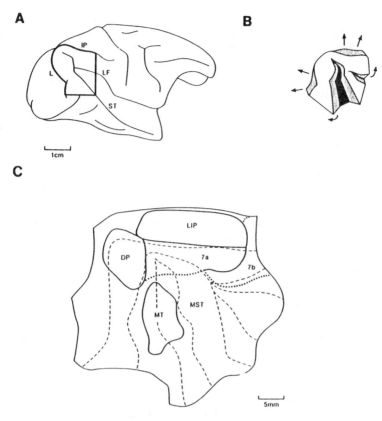

FIG. 8.1. Area 7a shown in a parcellation of inferior parietal lobual and adjoining dorsal aspect of prelunate gyrus based on physiological, connectional, myeloarchitectural, and cytoarchitectural criteria. A: lateral view of monkey hemisphere. B: outlined cortex isolated from rest of brain. C: location of several cortical areas. ST, superior temporal sulcus; L, lunate sulcus; LF, lateral fissure; IP, intraparietal sulcus; DP, dorsal prelunate area; LIP, lateral intraparietal area; MT, middle temporal area; MST, medial superior temporal area. From "The Role of the Inferior Parietal Lobule in Spatial Perception and Visual-Motor Integration." In *The Handbook of Physiology, Vol. 5,* by R. A. Andersen, 1987, Bethesda, MD: American Physiological Association. Copyright 1988 by the American Physiological Association. Reprinted by permission.

and humans produce profound spatial deficits in both motor behavior and perception (Andersen, in press; Bock, Eckmiller, & Andersen, in press; Critchley, 1953; Lynch, 1980). Single-unit recording studies showed that units in this area responded to changes in eye position and retinal location when a monkey viewed a fixed target. Based on these studies, Andersen and colleagues (Andersen, Essick, & Siegel, 1985; Andersen & Mountcastle,

1983; Andersen, Siegel, & Essick, 1987) proposed that parietal area 7a takes part in a spatial transformation from observation-based to head-centered coordinates by combining retinal-based and eye-position information. Only a two-dimensional version of the problem was actually considered, because all the single-unit studies were carried out using visual stimuli on a frontal screen. The problem was further simplified by keeping the head and body positions rigidly fixed. This simplified version of the problem requires the addition of two vectors, one representing eye position and the other representing the retinal location of the viewed stimulus.

The sum of the eye position and retinal location vectors for a stationary visual stimulus is invariant with eye position. This is true because as the eyes move the location of the projection of the stimulus on the retina, it also moves in a compensatory way. If the addition of these two vectors was carried out by a single layer of neurons with cell bodies in area 7a, the output responses of these neurons would be invariant with eye position because it would represent the location of the fixed external stimulus. No units were found in area 7a with responses invariant with eye position. Instead, units were found with output responses that depended on both eye position and retinal location, but in a way that changed with eye position. These units that combine both eye and retinal position constitute about half the neurons in area 7a. This was a perplexing result because by combining eye position and retinal location these neurons seem to have started to compute an eye position independent, stable location of an external stimulus but not to have completed it. It turns out that when a network with a layer of hidden units is used to model this computation, these observations can be accounted for quite nicely by equating the neurons in area 7a with the hidden units in the network.

The process of training the network consists of repeatedly giving it inputs representing the retinal location of a stimulus and the current eye position and training it to produce the associated head-centered location of the stimulus on its output units. The teacher provides the correct values of the output unit representation of head-centered location. Learning requires a large number of training cycles. The longer the training goes on, the more accurate the output becomes. Training typically continued until the error with which the output indicated stimulus location was about equal to the distance between screen points that projected to neighboring retinal units. That is, training was stopped before hyperacuity set in. This required about 1,000 training cycles. Further training produced more accurate outputs but does not qualitatively change the response properties of the hidden units.

Although no attempt was made to model the physical structure of area 7a, we did try to model the format of its input using experimental data. The area 7a neurons relevant to the model's input are the eye-position neurons, responding to eye position only, and the visual neurons, responding to visual stimulation only. These neurons presumably represent the eye-position and retinal location information used by area 7a as input, so we modeled the network's input on their properties. The properties of the visual and eye-position neurons and how they were used to represent the input to the model network are shown in Fig. 8.2. Most of the eye-position neurons in area 7a respond monotonically to either the horizontal or vertical position of the eyes in the orbit. This was modeled by using 32 units with eye-position response parameters selected from the experimentally observed range. The visual neurons in area 7a have large, peaked retinal receptive fields with the peaks distributed over the whole retina. The retinal location input was modeled using 64 units with receptive fields shaped like the simplest, most symmetrical fields found experimentally. The peaks of these receptive fields were distributed evenly over the modeled retinal space. Every unit in the input layer is connected to each of the hidden units, which are connected to all of the output units. The synaptic weights are initially set to small random values. The whole model network is diagrammed in Fig. 8.3.

A cycle of training consists of picking an eye position and retinal location at random and converting them to the format used for input to the network. This input activity pattern is then propagated throughout the network, first to the hidden units and then to the output units. The resulting output unit activity pattern is subtracted from the correct pattern in the teacher pattern. The resulting difference, or error, is used to modify the synaptic weights of the output and hidden units as prescribed by the backpropagation proce-dure. Note that the teacher pattern and the output units have matching formats. At the beginning of training, the values of the output units and the teacher pattern do not match closely, whereas after the network has been successfully trained to do a computation, they are nearly equal.

According to the hypothesis of the model, the information to be used as a teacher is the true spatial location of the stimulus. However, there is no direct experimental basis for determining the output or teacher format. As is pointed out later, the results are not very sensitive to the teacher format. The formats used initially were derived from the input format on the rationale that this would be biologically plausible. Two different teacher formats were used, each representing spatial location in a head-centered frame. One format represented spatial location as the eye position at which the stimulus would be foveated. In this case, the output layer and corresponding teacher pattern consisted of 32 eye-position units with properties like those of the eye-position inputs to the model. The other format represented head-centered spatial location as the retinal location of the stimulus when looking straight ahead. In this case, the output layer and teacher pattern consisted of 64 units arranged in the same way as the retinal input to the network. Note that although the format of the output layer corresponded to part of the input layer in each of these cases, the actual

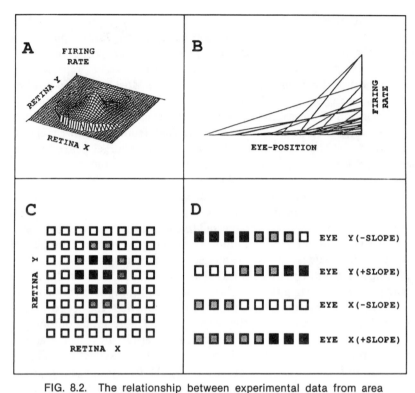

FIG. 8.2. The relationship between experimental data from area 7a and input to the model network. (a) The receptive field of a neuron in area 7a that responds only to visual stimulation and not to changes in eye position. The receptive field was measured and plotted as detailed in the caption to Fig. 8.4. The receptive field shown is 80° in diameter with a single, almost Gaussian peak at the center of the retina. Fields like this were assumed to reflect the retinal stimulation input to area 7a, and were used as a basis for designing the input to the model network, as described in (c) below. (b) The response of 30 eye-position neurons in area 7a. These neurons changed their activity as a nearly linear function of eye position, but showed no effect of visual stimulation. The majority of such neurons fall into one of four classes: those that increase their activity with eye movement either to the right, to the left, up, or down. Neurons from all four classes are plotted in (b) as if they were all of the class that increases activity with eye movement to the right. Note that the slopes and intercepts of the responses differ greatly between neurons. (c) The visual stimulus to the model was formatted using 64 units. Each of these units has a Gaussian receptive field of the type seen in (a). The centers of these fields are uniformly distributed on a grid as shown. The response of this array to a point visual stimulus of the kind used is indicated by the relative darkening of the units. (d) The eye-position input to the model consists of 32 units

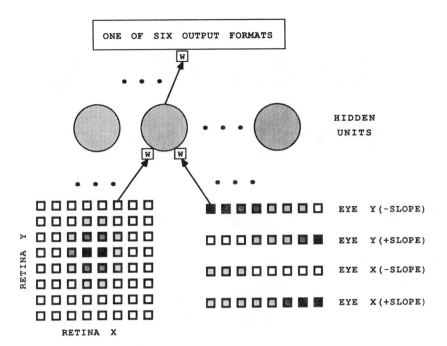

FIG. 8.3. Back propagation network used to model area 7a. The input, hidden, and output layers are described in the text and in Fig. 8.2. The input to the network consists of retinal position and eye-position information. The output activation of the hidden and output layer units is given by the logistic: *output activation* $= 1/(1 + e^{-net})$, where *net = weighted sum of inputs + bias.* The arrows indicate the direction of activity propagation. The *w*s are the weights changed by learning. The network was simulated on a Symbolics 3600 LISP machine using the P3 parallel system simulator (Zipser & Rabin, 1986). Adapted from "A Back Propagation Programmed Network that Simulates Response Properties of a Subset of Posterior Parietal Neurons" by D. Zipser and R. A. Andersen, 1988, *Nature, 331,* p. 3. Copyright 1988 by Macmillan Magazines Ltd. Reprinted by permission.

divided into four groups of 8. Each group represents neurons in one of the observed classes. The slopes and intercepts for each unit's response was chosen at random, but in the figure the units have been drawn in order of increasing response for their respective direction specificities. Adapted from "A Back Propagation Programmed Network that Simulates Response Properties of a Subset of Posterior Parietal Neurons" by D. Zipser and R. A. Andersen, 1988, *Nature, 331,* p. 3. Copyright 1988 by Macmillan Magazines Ltd. Reprinted by permission.

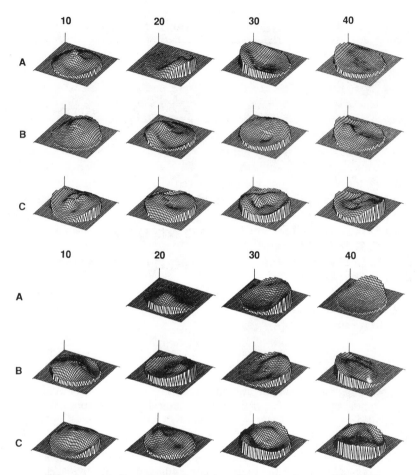

FIG. 8.4. (a) Experimentally determined retinal receptive fields (Andersen, Essick, & Siegel, 1985; Zipser & Andersen, 1988). The data for drawing each of these receptive field plots comes from measurements of the firing rate of a single area 7a neuron at 17 different retinal locations. These locations were at the center and at 10°, 20°, 30°, and 40° out. A neighborhood smoothing procedure was used to create the plots shown here. The receptive fields are arranged in rows with the eccentricity of the field maxima increasing to the right, and in columns with the complexity of the fields increasing downward. All the fields in row A have single peaks; those in B a major peak and a few distinguishable minor peaks. The fields in C are the most complex. The data has been normalized so the highest peak in each field is the same height. (b) Hidden unit retinal receptive fields generated by the back-propagation model. These plots were generated in same way as those of Fig. 8.4a except that the

364

values appearing on the input and output layers are completely different. In particular, the input layer values represent location in an observation-based reference frame, whereas the output layer values represent location in a head-centered frame.

These two different teacher formats were used to train the model in separate training sessions. With both of the teacher formats, the network learned to compute the transformation from observation-based to head-centered coordinates postulated to occur in area 7a. What is really interesting about these training simulations is how the network learned to do this computation in a way analogous to area 7a. This can be seen by comparing the hidden units' response patterns to the firing rates of the neurons in area 7a that respond to both visual stimulus and eye position. The experimental data available for comparison with the model consist of measurements of retinal receptive fields at fixed eye positions and of the effects of different eye positions with fixed stimulus retinal location. Both of these measurements have been compared to the model to determine the degree of similarity.

The comparison of experimental and model receptive fields is shown in Fig. 8.4. The experimental data on which this comparison is based was collected several years before the model was developed, and no new data has been obtained since that time. In these comparisons, normalized firing rates are compared to normalized hidden unit activity. The comparison is difficult because there is such a wide variety of large, complex fields. The only feature of the receptive fields that could be quantitatively compared between model and experiment was the eccentricity of the location of the peak of activity. However, using a smoothing algorithm to visualize the overall shape of the receptive fields allows a more revealing semiquantitative comparison to be made. In Fig. 8.4, the fields are arranged in columns of the same eccentricity of the highest peak and in rows with fields of about the same complexity of peak structure. Complexity of peak structure is based on an estimate of the number of major and minor peaks. At the present time this is the best method of comparison available. The small number of available experimental fields hinders the development of meaningful statistical comparisons. The top row in Figs. 8.4a and 8.4b has the

data came from computer simulations of the model network. All the fields, except for the three on the left in row C, are from units that have received 1,000 learning trials. The remaining three are from untrained units and represent fields that result from the initial random assignment of synaptic weights. Adapted from "A Back Propagation Programmed Network that Simulates Response Properties of a Subset of Posterior Parietal Neurons" by D. Zipser and R. A. Andersen, 1988, *Nature, 331,* pp. 2, 4. Copyright 1988 by Macmillan Magazines Ltd. Reprinted by permission.

fields with one major peak and no significant minor ones. The center row has fields with a clear major peak and at most a few minor peaks. The bottom row has all the rest. Although this measure of peak complexity is only semiquantitative, it does simplify the comparison of model and experimental fields. Although only 12 fields from model and experiment are compared, they represent all the complexity-eccentricity types observed. All field types observed in the model were also found in area 7a. The reverse is not true. Fields with an eccentricity of 10° and a single peak are observed in area 7a but are very rarely seen in the model. Note also that three of the fields in the bottom row of Fig. 8.4b come from the model before it has been trained. The data in Fig. 8.4 make it quite clear that there is considerable similarity between the shapes of the retinal receptive fields of model and experiment.

The pattern of variation in visual response as a function of eye position, when the retinal location of the visual stimulus is kept fixed, is called the *spatial gain field*. Spatial gain fields were measured by having the monkey fixate nine different positions on a frontal screen. At each of these fixation points the response was first measured in the absence of visual stimulation. Then the response was measured with a visual stimulus flashed at a screen position chosen to keep its retinal location fixed. Measurements at these nine points constitute the spatial gain field data for each area 7a neuron tested (Zipser & Andersen, 1988a). The firing rate of most area 7a neurons changes in a systematic way as a function of eye position in both the presence and the absence of visual stimulation. Because the intensity and retinal location of the visual stimulus is the same at each eye position, it might be expected that the effect of visual stimulation could be computed by just adding a constant representing the effect of the visual stimulus to the eye position response in the absence of visual stimulation. This is not what is observed. Rather, the contribution of visual stimulation to the total response changes as a function of eye position. This nonlinear interaction between eye position and visual response is also seen in the model hidden units.

To facilitate the comparison of experiment and model, we have visual ized these nonlinear interactions by using the concentric circle pattern described in Fig. 8.5. The outer diameter of each circle is proportional to the normalized activity of a unit in the presence of visual stimulation. The width of the annulus is proportional to the activity in the absence of a visual stimulus. The dark inner disk is the difference between these and represents the apparent effect of visual stimulation. Fig. 8.5 shows 12 spatial gain fields from area 7a compared to 12 fields from model hidden units. Each field consists of an array of nine circle patterns with each circle placed at a position corresponding to the location of the fixation at which it was measured. As can be seen by examination of Fig. 8.5, the spatial gain fields of both model and experiment show a wide variety of complex patterns.

Many of the spatial gain fields could be fitted to planes appropriately tilted in the horizontal and vertical directions. All the total gain fields (outer circles) of the model hidden units were approximately planar. This compares with 80% for the area 7a neurons. About 55% of the visually evoked gain fields observed experimentally (inner dark disks) were also planar. The fraction of planar visually evoked hidden unit gain fields depends on which teacher format is used. With the monotonic, eye-position teacher format, 78% of the visual response gain fields were planar or at least monotonic. With the Gaussian, retinal teacher format, only 36% fall in this class. For both model and experiment there was also a class of visually evoked gain fields (inner dark disks) that were radically nonmonotonic (see Fig. 8.5, fields g, h, and i).

Comparison of the gain fields of model and experiment using both the shape of the total and visually evoked fields and the details of the circular patterns that make up each field reveal the high degree of similarity. In particular, the general form of the nonlinear combination of eye-position and visual stimulation responses are similar in the model and area 7a. In the model, this nonlinear interaction is a consequence of the S-shaped input-output function used to model the neural units. The source of this nonlinearity in the brain is unknown. As in the case of retinal receptive fields, a more quantitative comparison is frustrated by the wide variety of experimentally observed fields. However, the fact that every kind of hidden unit retinal receptive field and spatial gain field can be matched quite closely to one found experimentally supports the conjecture that area 7a and the model network are computing the same function in analogous ways.

We are now faced with the interesting problem of determining the significance of the observed similarities. Of course, a better measure of the degree of similarity would be useful. This is partly a technical problem involving the paucity of experimental examples. It is also a conceptual problem, because we do not have clear criteria that can be used to measure these similarities. The fact that all the observed neurons are not accounted for by the model is not too troubling because the model is not designed to account for all the computation going on in area 7a. Consider, for example, head movements and three-dimensional spatial representation, both of which are known to be reflected in the responses of area 7a neurons. Leaving aside these considerations and assuming that the similarities observed are significant, nonchance observations, what do they mean?

The complexity of the response properties accounted for is one indication that the observed similarities are nontrivial. The neurons in area 7a have a very wide spectrum of complex, uneven retinal receptive fields and spatial

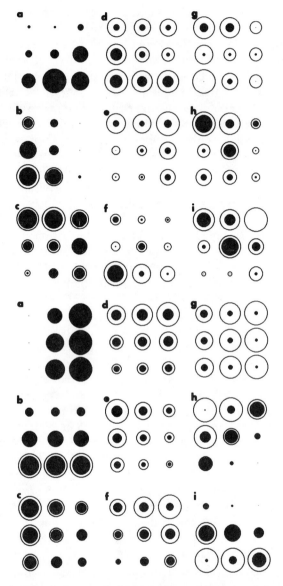

FIG. 8.5. The spatial gain fields of nine neurons from area 7a (Zipser & Andersen, 1988). The diameter of the darkened inner circle, representing the visually evoked gain fields, is calculated by subtracting the background activity recorded for 500 ms before the stimulus onset from the total activity during the stimulus. The outer circle diameter, representing the total response gain fields, corresponds to the total activity during the stimulus. The annulus

gain fields. The fact that a very similar spectrum is generated by the model is in part due to the properties of the backpropagation procedure. Recall that the least square minimizing algorithm does not have a unique solution. Each time the learning procedure is run with a new set of random starting weights, the hidden units differ from those generated in other runs. The overall distribution of types is the same, but exact repeats of detailed individual responses are virtually impossible. The complexity of the solutions found by the learning paradigm are inherent properties of the algorithm itself, not a feature introduced by the investigator. All this suggests that the model network and the brain are so similar because they are both subject to the same constraints in programming their computations.

How these constraints are imposed on the brain is not clear, but the simplest hypothesis proposes that the brain also learns the computations using a learning procedure with about the same overall constraints as backpropagation. We know that other procedures such as Boltzmann machine learning (Ackley, Hinton, & Sejnowski, 1985) tend to give the same hidden unit response spectrums when trained on the same problems. The Boltzmann machine is also a gradient descent algorithm, but uses a different measure of error and a different algorithm for minimizing it. In fact, there is likely to be a whole family of learning procedures that produce essentially the same results as backpropagation because they share some essential underlying computational constraints.

An important property of any model of the type described here is its sensitivity to free parameters. If the performance of a model is determined by the value of parameters adjusted to make it fit the data, little confidence can be put in the ultimate relevance of the model. The backpropagation model of area 7a is quite insensitive to the values of its few free parameters. Such factors as the number of hidden units, the learning rate, and the number of training cycles can be varied over wide ranges with little effect on the results. The model has a great number of adjustable parameters, that is, the connection weights, but these are determined in a constrained way by

---

diameter corresponds to the background activity that is due to an eye position signal alone, recorded during the 500 ms prior to the stimulus presentation. (b) Hidden unit spatial gain fields generated by the model network. Fields a—f were generated using the monotonic format output; the rest used the Gaussian format output. Adapted from "A Back Propagation Programmed Network that Simulates Response Properties of a Subset of Posterior Parietal Neurons" by D. Zipser and R. A. Andersen, 1988, *Nature, 331*, pp. 2,4. Copyright 1988 by Macmillan Magazines Ltd. Reprinted by permission.

the learning algorithm, not set in an arbitrary way by the investigator. One of these weightlike parameters is the bias. It can be learned, but when this is done one subtle feature of the resulting model differs from experimental observation. The residual gain fields (the inner circles in Fig. 8.5), have the opposite slope from the total gain fields (the outer circles). Although this is sometimes observed experimentally, it is fairly rare. The model does this because the learned bias values tend to be near zero. This means that the resting output of the modeled neurons is near half maximum, and due to the nonlinearity of the logistic function, an inverted residual gain field results. The resting—that is, without visual input—level of the real neurons in area 7a is generally quite low. To simulate this low resting level, the bias of the hidden units in the model is clamped at a negative value rather than learned. This leads to the model learning a very realistic set of spatial gain fields. The retinal receptive fields are not qualitatively affected by this modification. Of course, it would be nice to eliminate even this small amount of parameter changing.

Another kind of parameterlike variable under the control of the investigator is the teacher format. The model is quite robust to changes in teacher format as shown by the studies described later.

THE ROLE OF THE TEACHER

When using the backpropagation modeling paradigm, the nature of the teacher is a critical factor in determining which computation is learned. Recall that the teacher provides the correct output values for each input. The teacher must therefore provide the same number of values as there are output units—in the case of our area 7a model, the teacher-provided information that represented the location of a visual stimulus in head-centered coordinates. There are many possible formats for this representation. Perhaps the simplest is to use just two values, one representing the horizontal and the other representing the vertical position of the stimulus on the frontal screen. Because we are concerned with monkeys with fixed head positions, this is a way to represent head-centered location. In the model previously described, two different teacher formats were used, an eye-position and a retinal format, to represent head-centered location. Recall the distinction between teacher format and the information represented by the teacher. Although several different teacher formats have been mentioned, they have all represented the same information.

NEW TEACHER FORMATS

When the effects of different teacher formats and different information on the area 7a model were investigated, it was possible to show that when the teacher contains head-centered location information in a variety of different formats, the networks resemble 7a quite closely. On the other hand, when a teacher is used that does not contain explicit head-centered location information, the networks generated differ significantly from what is observed in area 7a. This is so even though the information provided by this teacher is consistent with the required hidden unit response pattern and a format is used that works when given head-centered information.

In the previous models two different formats were used to represent head-centered stimulus location (Zipser & Andersen, 1987). Whereas all the gain fields produced by both formats were of types found in 7a, neither format produced the exact quantitative distribution of types found in 7a. To further analyze the effect of teacher format on the kinds of hidden units generated, four additional teacher formats that represent stimulus location in a head-centered frame were used. The simplest of these formats taught a small number of output units to vary their activity linearly with the x- or y-position of the stimulus on the frontal screen. The activity of these units was 0.0 at one extreme of possible stimulus locations and 1.0 at the other extreme. Two additional simple output formats consisted of units that vary monotonically but nonlinearly with stimulus position. One varies as the square of position, whereas the other varies as an S-shaped function of position. A logistic function of the same type used to compute the output of the units in the backpropagation network was used. The most complex new output format was a combination of the retinal and eye position formats used in the original model. In this case, the network was trained to produce both of these complex output representations of stimulus location simultaneously.

All these new versions of the teacher format could train the transformation carried out by area 7a. Examination of the retinal receptive fields of the hidden units generated showed that all the expected receptive field types were present for all versions of the model. The frequency distribution of the various receptive field eccentricities varies in magnitude but not in shape between the different versions (see Table 8.1). Although all are similar to the experimentally observed distribution in area 7a, they have somewhat fewer of the lower eccentricity fields. An examination of the lower eccentricity experimental receptive fields shows them to be mostly of the most complex type, row C in Fig. 8.4. This complex type is rare among trained model receptive fields, but is common in the model receptive fields before training, presumably because the initial weights for the model are chosen at random.

All six versions of the teacher also produced eye-position gain fields of types found in area 7a (see Table 8.1), but there was a considerable spread in the ratio of types. The most realistic ratio was generated by the mixed format. This was to be expected because the gain field-type distribution is

TABLE 8.1
Data From Different Teacher Formats

Teacher Format	% at Each Eccentricity					Mono./Irreg.[b]
	0	10	20	30	40	
7a[a]	0	19	25	16	40	1.22
Linear	0	8	8	8	46	11.5
Squashed	0	6	12	36	46	15.7
Squared	2	6	8	30	54	11.5
Eye	0	6	20	20	54	3.55
Retina	8	2	12	12	42	0.56
Mixed	4	6	16	28	46	1.27
Untrained	2	20	18	12	36	N/A

[a]Refers to the distribution found in monkey cortex.
[b]Monotonic/irregular is the ratio of monotonic to irregular visually evoked eye-position gain fields, that is, the inner circles of Fig. 8.5.

skewed too far one way for the monotonic format and too far the other way for the Gaussian format that make up this complex type. From these simulation studies we may conclude that as long as the network is explicitly taught the location of the stimulus, the hidden units generated are all of types actually found in area 7a. Differences in the teacher format affect mainly the distribution of the various types.

A TEACHER OF A DIFFERENT KIND

A reasonable question to ask is whether a teacher is really needed to model area 7a or will some form of unsupervised learning suffice? Simple Hebbian learning, competitive learning, and a form of backpropagation learning called identity mapping are in this category (Ackley, Hinton, & Sejnowski, 1985; Linsker, 1987; Rumelhart & Zipser, 1985). All of these procedures exploit some aspect of correlations between inputs to generate feature detector units. It seems unlikely that any of these procedures could give rise to the kind of neurons found in area 7a because these neurons respond to combinations of uncorrelated inputs, that is, to eye-position and retinal stimulus location. However, examination of the hidden units in the trained network indicates that, in addition to serving as an intermediate step in a coordinate transformation, they also encode sufficient information to allow the original eye position and retinal location to be reconstructed. That is, if we first train a network to do the area 7a transformation, and then fix the hidden unit weights, it would be possible to train an output layer to regenerate the input patterns. This would give us a network that could reproduce input patterns on its output units after passing all information through a small number of hidden units.

Networks of this kind are called identity mapping networks and have been extensively studied. It is important to note that the hidden units in identity mapping networks learn an efficient feature encoding of the input patterns when the number of hidden units is smaller than the number of input lines. Backpropagation identity mapping is fairly well understood computationally (Baldi & Hornik, in press). The hidden units can be thought of as representing the basis vectors of some vector space. The pattern of activity induced on the hidden units by an input pattern is then the projection of that pattern onto the hidden unit space. It can be shown that backpropagation identity mapping forces the hidden unit vectors to be some linear transformation of the eigenvectors of the input correlation matrix. This result is exact for linear hidden units and a good approximation for the typical logistic hidden unit. When the number of hidden units is less than the number of inputs, not all the eigenvectors can be represented, so not all the information in the input is represented in the hidden units. However, backpropagation guarantees that the available hidden units will account for the maximum possible amount of input variance. Backpropagation identity mapping is one of the most powerful of the unsupervised learning procedures. If backpropagation identity mapping fails to generate hidden units of the kind found in area 7a, it seems unlikely that any other completely unsupervised approach will succeed.

Networks trained by backpropagation identity mapping were found to produce hidden units that are significantly different from those observed in area 7a or by using teachers that represent head-centered location. The units found with identity mapping did not combine visual and eye-position inputs. Rather they separated these out so that the vast majority of hidden units were either eye position only or retinal position only. This was particularly striking because the random weight distribution used at the start of training gave rise to hidden units that combine eye and retinal position, although not in the coordinated way found in most area 7a spatially tuned units. These units had to be actively destroyed by the identity mapping process. Perhaps if the teacher signal had been included with the input, the identity mapping network would have learned the required correlation between eye and retinal position. This is not strictly unsupervised learning.

These results demonstrate that the backpropagation model of area 7a is robust with respect to teacher format so long as the teacher explicitly represents the location of the stimulus in space. All formats with this property gave rise to hidden units of types actually seen in area 7a, whereas the details of teacher format and other parameters only affected the quantatitive distribution of unit types. This result is consistent with the hypothesis that the backpropagation network is actually simulating the computational algorithm used by area 7a.

OTHER MODELS

The significance of the learning paradigm for the analysis of cortical computation depends on how widely it is applicable. At about the same time the area 7a model was being developed, Lehky and Sejnowski (1987) used the backpropagation learning paradigm to model a different computation in another cortical area. They trained a network model of the primary visual cortex to determine the principle curvatures and their orientations of viewed surfaces. The input format was based on existing knowledge of the input to primary visual cortex. The output was trained to compute the transformation from the retinotopic image to curvature coordinates. The hidden units in this network developed the response properties of classical simple cells, whereas the output units resembled complex cells in some ways. This result is instructive because it demonstrates that neurons that had previously been identified as edge or bar detectors could also be viewed as taking part in computing three-dimensional curvature from shading.

These results highlight an important question raised by the learning paradigm: If the brain learns these computations, where do the teachers come from? Although this question does not have to be answered to use learning techniques to analyze cortical computation, it must be addressed if the hypothesis that the brain actually uses learning to program networks is to be tenable. In the area 7a model, teachers that could be obtained locally from signals present in the cortical area being modeled were used. This demonstrates that, at least in principle, local teachers are available. One way to guarantee the presence of a local teacher is to have the teacher be the same as the input. In this case the network learns to do an identity map. Experience gained using identity mapping in speech recognition and image compression (Cottrell, Munro, & Zipser, 1989; Elman & Zipser, 1988) shows that this often leads to the representation of important stimulus features in a very efficient way. It has been demonstrated that even weaker unsupervised procedures such as simple Hebbian learning can generate some of the properties of visual neurons (Linsker, 1987). When identity mapping was applied to simplified models of the visual system, hidden units were found that encoded stimulus location, depth, and orientation (Zipser, 1989). The results on depth representation provide a good example of the ability of the identity mapping technique to account for observed neuron response properties.

HIDDEN UNIT IDENTITY MAP ENCODING
OF STEREO DEPTH

The visual cortex contains many binocular neurons, some of which are involved in extracting depth information from stereo images on the two retinas. To see if hidden units would encode depth information using only identity mapping and, if so, what internal representation was used, a simplified binocular model of the visual system was used. To avoid the complexities of three dimensions, linear retinas with depth as the second dimension were used. The method for determining disparity and the identity mapping network are shown in Figs. 8.6 and 8.7. On each training cycle, a location is picked at random, within a circle around the fixation point. This location is then projected to the retinas through the focal point of each eye. The activity for each unit of the retinal array is computed as a Gaussian function of its distance from the location of this projection point. The depth of the chosen location, relative to the fixation point, is encoded in the disparity between its location on the two retinas. The flat, linear retinas used here are an approximation to a horizontal slice through the curved retinas of the eye.

The relationship between hidden unit activity and spatial location is studied using a graphic display. To generate this display the input spot is systematically scanned over the disk of possible spatial locations after

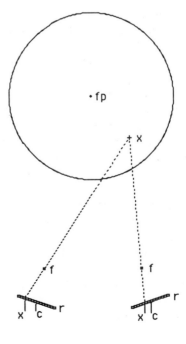

FIG. 8.6. Method for computing disparities during training of two retina identity mapping network. The fixation point is indicated by *fp, c* is the center of the retinas, *x* is the location of the stimulus in space and its projection on the retinas, and *f* is the focal point for each eye. From "Programming Neural Nets to Do Spatial Computations" by D. Zipser. In *Models of Cognition*, N. Sharkey (Ed.), 1989, Norwood, NJ: Ablex. Copyright 1989 by Ablex Publishing. Reprinted by permission.

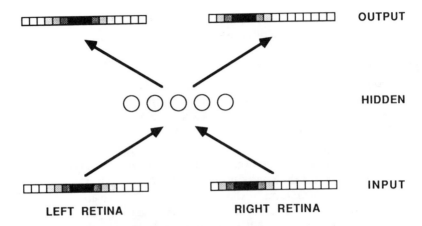

FIG. 8.7. The two retina identity mapping network. All input units are connected to all hidden units, which are connected to all output units. From "Programming Neural Nets to Do Spatial Computations" by D. Zipser. In *Models of Cognition*, N. Sharkey (Ed.), 1989, Norwood, NJ: Ablex. Copyright 1989 by Ablex Publishing. Reprinted by permission.

training is completed. At every position of the spot, the activity of each hidden unit is plotted at a corresponding position on the computer display. In this way, a separate disk-shaped pattern is generated for each hidden unit. The pixels in the display used can only be set to black or white, so to get a graded effect, each pixel is set to black with a probability approximately proportional to hidden unit activity. To clearly define the disk, the probability of setting a pixel to black is slightly greater than zero even when activity is zero. This produces a display in which the degree of darkening over an area is roughly proportional to unit activity. To more clearly show the activity pattern, a set of contour lines is superimposed on the display by plotting white pixels whenever the activity of a unit falls within certain evenly spaced narrow bands.

The results obtained from computer runs with two, three, four, and nine hidden units are shown in Fig. 8.8. The network with only two hidden units could not solve the problem. In this network the input stimuli were mapped to identically corresponding positions on the two output arrays; that is, there was no disparity. For three or more hidden units, the disparity present in the input was recreated to some degree on the output. The accuracy with which disparity was reproduced was quite good with four units and virtually perfect with nine units. Close examination of the data in Fig. 8.8 reveals several interesting points. In the case of two hidden units, the contour lines in the two eyes are completely parallel to each other. This means that no depth information can be derived from the activity of the hidden units because their activity values remain proportional for all depths at any given

FIG. 8.8.   Hidden unit activities plotted as a function of stimulus location in space for the two retina identity mapping network. Runs using two three, four, and nine hidden units are shown. From "Programming Neural Nets to Do Spatial Computations" by D. Zipser. In *Models of Cognition*, N. Sharkey (Ed.), 1989, Norwood, NJ: Ablex. Copyright 1989 by Ablex Publishing. Reprinted by permission.

lateral displacement. The contour lines are angled in depth to compensate for the additional lateral movement required to produce a fixed displacement on the retina as a point gets further from the observer. For more than two hidden units, the contour lines are no longer exactly parallel. This provides a complex coordinate system in depth that the output units can use in recreating the required disparity. In the case of nine hidden units, sections of the contour lines run nearly perpendicular to each other, providing detailed depth information. In no case did the network solve the problem by treating the two eyes separately. For example, in the case of four hidden units, a simple solution would be to dedicate two of the hidden units of each eye. What is actually observed is a distributed, binocular representation for each hidden unit. Monocular units did not occur because backpropagation identity mapping works by generating hidden units that capture the correlations in the input patterns. When, instead of the relatively small amount of disparity that results from depth, a large amount of random uncorrelated disparity is used in the training, the hidden units do become monocular. This is analogous to the loss of binocular neurons in animals with defects preventing eye convergence.

These results show that the hidden unit representation that develops in the identity-mapped network can encode depth information. Is this representation of depth also used in the cortex? To find out, the disparity response of the hidden units was compared to that found experimentally in primary visual cortex. Disparity has been extensively studied in areas 17 and 18 of the cat (Ferster, 1981; LeVay & Voigt, 1988), where a wide spectrum of disparity response patterns is found. The response patterns can be roughly divided into two major classes: the tuned excitatory neurons and the near and far neurons. The tuned excitatory neurons have narrow excitatory response functions tuned to very small disparity. In contrast, the near and far neurons are broadly tuned to respond to stimuli either in front of or beyond the fixation point, respectively.

The corresponding disparity responses of hidden units in the identity mapping network are shown in Fig. 8.9. On the left of each column are examples of disparity tuned neurons found in the cat visual areas by LeVay and Voigt (1988). On the right are disparity tuning curves of hidden units from stereo identity mapping networks. Whereas all the types of hidden unit response patterns found in the backpropagation trained networks were also found in the brain, the reverse was not true. In particular, no hidden units that matched the sharply tuned neurons of the type in Fig. 8.9a, b, and f were found.

There is clearly something incomplete about the identity mapping model of binocularity because of its inability to generate the sharply tuned excitatory units. On the other hand, its ability to account for the complex, irregular spectrum of real near and far cells indicates that the representation it generates is actually used in the cortex.

SIGNIFICANCE OF THE LEARNING PARADIGM FOR NEUROBIOLOGY

From the point of view of neurophysiology, one of the most significant aspects of the learning paradigm is its ability to account for the complex, even ragged, spectrum of real neuron response patterns typically observed. The actual computational mechanisms used by the brain may often involve complicated neural response patterns that are not understandable intuitively, but that can be understood by using a network learning technique. Perhaps in the future, neurobiologists will publish a wider spectrum of their response data, even when these cannot be correlated in an obvious way with the process being studied. This will provide the data needed to resolve the question of how general the learning paradigm is and will also facilitate objectively matching model and experiment.

It is generally the hidden units that correspond to the neurons found in the cortex. No units corresponding to the output units of the trained network were found in the cortex in the case of the area 7a model. The majority of cortical cells recorded from are likely to be pyramidal neurons

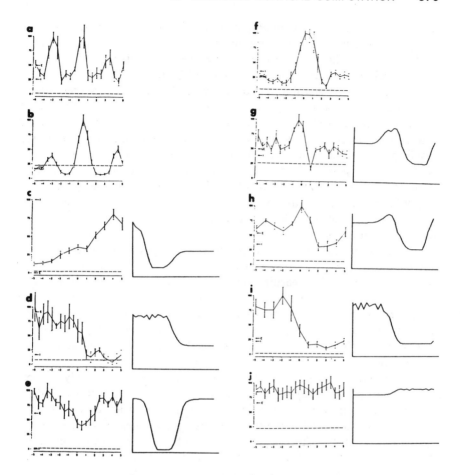

FIG. 8.9. Comparison between disparity tuned neurons in cat visual cortex and hidden unit responses from networks that identity map stereo images. The horizontal axis is disparity and the vertical axis is percent maximum unit response. The experimental data are on the left of each set and the hidden unit responses are on the right. No hidden unit responses that closely matched a, b, and f were found. In case c, the shapes of the curves are similar but the experimental neuron is a far unit while the hidden unit is a near unit. From "Ocular Dominance and Disparity Coding in Cat Visual Cortex" by S. LeVay and T. Voigt, 1988, *Visual Neuroscience, 1.* Copyright 1988 by Cambridge University Press. Reprinted by permission.

that project out of their immediate cortical region. This suggests that the hierarchy of cortical computations may involve using only the partial results of the hidden representation as inputs to the next stage. Some preliminary analysis suggests that any computation that can be performed using the outputs from one stage as the inputs to the higher stage can also be done using the hidden unit representation from the lower stage as input to the higher stage. If this turns out to be a theme used in the cortex, neurons corresponding to output units will often not be found.

A feature of the learning paradigm, which I think was unexpected and has led to some controversy, is its ability to account for the behavior of whole sets of real neurons without detailed reference to the physiological mechanisms underlying their behavior. This is certainly an unexpected result and goes against conventional thinking in biology, which has traditionally benefited from a close adherence to experiment. There is an important example in biology of a theory getting ahead of detailed physiology—that is, the discoveries of Mendel. It took nearly a century to get a handle on the physiological mechanisms involved, but when this was done the original theory remained valid within its domain of relevance. This unexplained theory with its hypothetical genes also served as a strong stimulus to experimental investigation. I think the current observations using backpropagation learning have somewhat of the same flavor. The theory can account for observed behavior but says nothing about the physiological mechanisms involved. These will have to be found by the usual experimental paradigms of neurobiology. But the theory can play an important role by clarifying just what must be explained and by explaining the significance of otherwise uninterpretable results.

The learning paradigm can also be improved to more narrowly bracket the range of possible physiologies. Most important in this vein would be a deeper understanding of just what characteristics of a learning procedure are necessary to model real neural response properties. It already seems unlikely that only backpropagation will work. As the results from using other learning procedures become available it will be possible to generalize experience and produce a better and more useful theory. Also as more experimental information on synaptic modification rules and network architectures becomes available, the range of plausible learning procedures will be narrowed.

The absence of unique solutions to the squared error minimization problem characteristic of backpropagation may have considerable significance for the way adaptation is used to configure the brain. Neurobiologists have long sought to determine the degree to which adaptation is used to mold the properties of the brain. The common wisdom is that the basic properties of neurons and the overall connectivity pattern is genetically determined, while at some level of detail adaptive processes take over. The nonuniqueness property makes it impossible for the genome to know beforehand just which unit will have which response property. This means that if learning is used in some brain area to determine the response properties of neurons, it must also be used in any other area that gets inputs from this trained region because the genes could not have the information required to make detailed connections. On the other hand, if adaptation is limited to sharpening but not changing the response properties of neurons, then the genes would have to supply much more of the connection information, because adaptation cannot fully program the computation. Unfortunately this is going to be difficult, but not impossible, to sort out experimentally. The reason for the difficulty is interesting, because it gives insight into a possible role for genetic influence. The initial random starting values of the weights in the backpropagation learning networks influence the final outcomes strongly. When the same starting weights are used to retrain for the same function, most of the time very similar patterns of hidden unit response properties develop, independent of the order of presentation of the training patterns. Of course, if the details of the inputs are changed or a different function is learned, the hidden unit response properties will be completely modified. It is the particular initial weight values that most influence the final result, all else being equal. It is as if the final microstructure of the brain is fixed at birth to a much greater degree than it is actually programmed by the genes. Sometimes the response properties of hidden units are very different on different runs starting from the same initial weight values. This observation suggests that it will be tricky to disentangle the relative roles of genes and learning at the neuron level because the initial conditions, even when random, can dominate the future course of events. This result also strengthens the long-held belief that genes can determine much of the course adaptation will take by providing only a statistical structure to the distribution of initial connections.

A small number of hidden units, typically 10 to 30, is sufficient to provide accurate output values for the area 7a model. The actual brain area, however, has millions of neurons. Even considering the need to use many real neurons to get high dynamic range and accuracy, there are far more neurons than required by the hypothesized computation. This probably means that area 7a is doing something more than just the simple computation we have assigned to it. The spatial locations of many objects can be simultaneously represented in area 7a, which is one of the most obvious and intriguing possibilities. This should be experimentally testable.

Another important issue raised by this work is the question of whether the computation accomplished by area 7a is learned. Our results do not imply that it is; it could be genetically programmed to use computational procedures analogous to those found by backpropagation learning. If, however, cortical computations are learned by an error-correcting procedure, they will require teacher signals to be present in the brain. The failure of identity mapping to simulate the type of neurons present in 7a is significant in this regard because it suggests that no completely unsupervised learning procedure will work. This is an important issue, because backpropagation is quite difficult to implement given our current understanding of neuron function. It is not, however, impossible to implement backpropagation using plausible neurophysiological concepts as has been described elsewhere (Zipser & Rumelhart, in press).

REFERENCES

Ackley, D., Hinton, G. E., & Sejnowski, T. (1985). A learning algorithm for Boltzmann machines. *Cognitive Science, 9,* 147–169.

Andersen, R. A. (1987). The role of the inferior parietal lobule in spatial perception and visual-motor integration. In F. Plum, V. B. Mountbastle, & S. R. Geiger (Eds.), *The handbook of physiology* (Vol. V, pp. 483–518). Bethesda, MD: American Physiological Association.

Andersen, R. A. (in press). The neurobiological basis of spatial cognition: Role of the parietal lobe. In J. Stiles-Davis, M. Kritchevsky, & U. Bellugi (Eds.), *Spatial cognition: Brain bases and development.* Chicago: University of Chicago Press.

Andersen, R. A., Essick, G. K., & Siegel, R. M. (1985). Encoding of spatial location by posterior parietal neurons. *Science, 230,* 546–548.

Andersen, R. A., & Mountcastle, V. B. (1983). The influence of the angle of gaze upon the excitability of the light-sensitive neurons of the posterior parietal cortex. *Journal of Neurosciences, 3,* 532–548.

Andersen, R. A., Siegel, R. M., & Essick, G. K. (1987). Neurons of area 7 activated by both visual stimuli and oculomotor behavior. *Experimental Brain Research, 67,* 316–322.

Baldi, P. & Hornik, K. (in press). Neural networks and principal component analysis: Learning from examples without local minima. *Neural Computation.*

Bock, O., Eckmiller, R., & Andersen, R. A. (in press). Goal-directed arm movements in trained monkeys following ibotenic acid lesions in the posterior parietal cortex. *Brain Research.*

Cottrell, G. W., Munro, P. W., & Zipser, D. (1989). Image compression by back propagation: A demonstration of extensional programming. In N. E. Sharkey (Ed.), *Models of cognition.* Norwood, NJ: Ablex.

Critchley, M. (1953). *The parietal lobes.* New York: Hafner.

Elman, J., & Zipser, D. (1988). Learning the hidden structure of speech. *Journal of the Acoustical Society of America, 83,* 1615–1626.

Ferster, D. (1981). A comparison of binocular depth mechanisms in areas 17 and 18 of the cat visual cortex. *Journal of Physiology, 311,* 623–655.

Hinton, G. E. (in press). Connectionist learning procedures. *Artificial Intelligence.*

Lehky, S. R., & Sejnowski, T. J. (1987). Extracting 3-D curvatures from images of surfaces using a neural model. *Society of Neuroscience Abstracts, 13,* 1451.

LeVay, S., & Voigt, T. (1988). Ocular dominance and disparity coding in cat visual cortex. *Visual Neuroscience, 1,* 395–414.

Linsker, R. (1987). From basic network principles to neural architecture: Emergence of orientation selective cells. *PNAS, 83,* 8390–8394.

Lynch, J. C. (1980). The functional organization of posterior parietal association cortex. *Behavioral Brain Sciences, 3,* 485–534.

Marr, D. (1982). *Vision.* San Francisco, CA: W. H. Freeman.

Parker, D. B. (1982, October). *Learning logic.* Invention Report, S81–64, File 1. Office of Technology Licensing, Stanford University.

Rumelhart, D. E., Hinton, G. E., & Williams, R. J. (1986). Learning internal representations by error propagation. In D. E. Rumelhart & J. L. McClelland (Eds.), *Parallel distributed processing: Explorations in the microstructure of cognition* Vol. 1, (pp. 318-362). Cambridge, MA: MIT Press/Bradford Books.

Rumelhart, D. E., & Zipser, D. (1985). Feature discovery by competitive learning. *Cognitive Science, 9,* 75-112.

Werbos P. (1974). *Beyond regression: New tools for prediction and analysis in the behavioral sciences.* Unpublished doctoral dissertation (Economics), Harvard University, Cambridge, MA.

Zipser, D. (1989). Programming neural nets to do spatial computations. In N. E. Sharkey (Ed.), *Models of cognition.* Norwood, NJ: Ablex.

Zipser, D., & Andersen, R. A. (1987). A network model using back propagation learning simulates the spatial tuning properties of posterior parietal neuron. *Society for Neuroscience Abstracts, 13,* 1452.

Zipser, D., & Andersen, R. A. (1988a). A back propagation programmed network that simulates response properties of a subset of posterior parietal neurons. *Nature, 331,* 679-684.

Zipser, D., & Andersen, R. A. (1988b). The role of the teacher in learning-based models of parietal area 7a. *Brain Research Bulletin,* 21, 505-512.

Zipser, D., & Rabin, D. (1986). P3: A parallel network simulating system. In D. Rumelhart & J. McClelland (Eds.), *Parallel distributed processing: Explorations in the microstructure of cognition* (Vol. 1) Cambridge, MA: MIT Press/Bradford Press.

Zipser, D., & Rumelhart, D. E. (in press). Neurobiological significance of new learning models. In E. Schwartz (Ed.), *Computational neuroscience.* Cambridge, MA: MIT Press.

Author Index

Subject Index